INTERNATIONAL PERSPECTIVES ON END-OF-LIFE LAW REFORM

Much has been written about whether end-of-life law should change and what that law should be. However, the barriers and facilitators of such changes – law reform perspectives – have been virtually ignored. Why do so many attempts to change the law fail but others are successful? *International Perspectives on End-of-Life Law Reform* aims to address this question by drawing on ten case studies of end-of-life law reform from the United Kingdom, the United States, Canada, the Netherlands, Belgium and Australia. Written by leading end-of-life scholars, the book's chapters blend perspectives from law, medicine, bioethics and sociology to examine sustained reform efforts to permit assisted dying and change the law about withholding and withdrawing life-sustaining treatment. Findings from this book not only shed light on changing end-of-life law but also provide insight more generally into how and why law reform succeeds in complex and controversial social policy areas.

BEN P. WHITE is Professor of End-of-Life Law and Regulation in the Australian Centre for Health Law Research in the Faculty of Business and Law, Queensland University of Technology. His research expertise focuses on end-of-life decision-making, and as a former law reform commissioner, he has had a long-standing involvement in law reform.

LINDY WILLMOTT is Professor of Law in the Australian Centre for Health Law Research (of which she was a foundation Director) in the Faculty of Business and Law, Queensland University of Technology. She has extensively researched in the end-of-life field, and has had broad practical experience as a law reform commissioner.

CAMBRIDGE BIOETHICS AND LAW

This series of books – formerly called Cambridge Law, Medicine and Ethics – was founded by Cambridge University Press with Alexander McCall Smith as its first editor in 2003. It focuses on the law's complex and troubled relationship with medicine across both the developed and the developing world. In the past twenty years, we have seen in many countries increasing resort to the courts by dissatisfied patients and a growing use of the courts to attempt to resolve intractable ethical dilemmas. At the same time, legislatures across the world have struggled to address the questions posed by both the successes and the failures of modern medicine, while international organisations such as the WHO and UNESCO now regularly address issues of medical law. It follows that we would expect ethical and policy questions to be integral to the analysis of the legal issues discussed in this series. The series responds to the high profile of medical law in universities, in legal and medical practice, as well as in public and political affairs. We seek to reflect the evidence that many major health-related policy and bioethics debates in the UK, Europe and the international community over the past two decades have involved a strong medical law dimension. With that in mind, we seek to address how legal analysis might have a trans-jurisdictional and international relevance. Organ retention, embryonic stem cell research, physician-assisted suicide and the allocation of resources to fund health care are but a few examples among many. The emphasis of this series is thus on matters of public concern and/or practical significance. We look for books that could make a difference to the development of medical law and enhance the role of medico-legal debate in policy circles. That is not to say that we lack interest in the important theoretical dimensions of the subject, but we aim to ensure that theoretical debate is grounded in the realities of how the law does and should interact with medicine and health care.

Series Editors

Professor Graeme Laurie, *University of Edinburgh*
Professor Richard Ashcroft, *City, University of London*

Books in the Series

Marcus Radetzki, Marian Radetzki and Niklas Juth *Genes and Insurance: Ethical, Legal and Economic Issues*

Ruth Macklin *Double Standards in Medical Research in Developing Countries*

Donna Dickenson *Property in the Body: Feminist Perspectives*

Matti Häyry, Ruth Chadwick, Vilhjálmur Árnason and Gardar Árnason *The Ethics and Governance of Human Genetic Databases: European Perspectives*

J. K. Mason *The Troubled Pregnancy: Legal Wrongs and Rights in Reproduction*

Daniel Sperling *Posthumous Interests: Legal and Ethical Perspectives*

Keith Syrett *Law, Legitimacy and the Rationing of Health Care: A Contextual and Comparative Perspective*

Alasdair Maclean *Autonomy, Informed Consent and Medical Law: A Relational Change*

Heather Widdows and Caroline Mullen *The Governance of Genetic Information: Who Decides?*

David Price *Human Tissue in Transplantation and Research: A Model Legal and Ethical Donation Framework*

Matti Häyry *Rationality and the Genetic Challenge: Making People Better?*

Mary Donnelly *Healthcare Decision-Making and the Law: Autonomy, Capacity and the Limits of Liberalism*

Anne-Maree Farrell, David Price and Muireann Quigley *Organ Shortage: Ethics, Law and Pragmatism*

Sara Fovargue *Xenotransplantation and Risk: Regulating a Developing Biotechnology*

John Coggon *What Makes Health Public? A Critical Evaluation of Moral, Legal, and Political Claims in Public Health*

Mark Taylor *Genetic Data and the Law: A Critical Perspective on Privacy Protection*

Anne-Maree Farrell *The Politics of Blood: Ethics, Innovation and the Regulation of Risk*

Stephen W. Smith *End-of-Life Decisions in Medical Care: Principles and Policies for Regulating the Dying Process*

Michael Parker *Ethical Problems and Genetics Practice*

William W. Lowrance *Privacy, Confidentiality, and Health Research*

Kerry Lynn Macintosh *Human Cloning: Four Fallacies and Their Legal Consequence*

Heather Widdows *The Connected Self: The Ethics and Governance of the Genetic Individual*

Amel Alghrani, Rebecca Bennett and Suzanne Ost *Bioethics, Medicine and the Criminal Law Volume I: The Criminal Law and Bioethical Conflict: Walking the Tightrope*

Danielle Griffiths and Andrew Sanders *Bioethics, Medicine and the Criminal Law Volume II: Medicine, Crime and Society*

Margaret Brazier and Suzanne Ost *Bioethics, Medicine and the Criminal Law Volume III: Medicine and Bioethics in the Theatre of the Criminal Process*

Sigrid Sterckx, Kasper Raus and Freddy Mortier *Continuous Sedation at the End of Life: Ethical, Clinical and Legal Perspectives*

A. M. Viens, John Coggon and Anthony S. Kessel *Criminal Law, Philosophy and Public Health Practice*

Ruth Chadwick, Mairi Levitt and Darren Shickle *The Right to Know and the Right Not to Know: Genetic Privacy and Responsibility*

Eleanor D. Kinney *The Affordable Care Act and Medicare in Comparative Context*

Katri Lõhmus *Caring Autonomy: European Human Rights Law and the Challenge of Individualism*

Catherine Stanton and Hannah Quirk *Criminalising Contagion: Legal and Ethical Challenges of Disease Transmission and the Criminal Law*

Sharona Hoffman *Electronic Health Records and Medical Big Data: Law and Policy*

Barbara Prainsack and Alena Buyx *Solidarity in Biomedicine and Beyond*

Camillia Kong *Mental Capacity in Relationship: Decision-Making, Dialogue, and Autonomy*

Oliver Quick *Regulating Patient Safety: The End of Professional Dominance?*

Thana Cristina de Campos *The Global Health Crisis: Ethical Responsibilities*

Jonathan Ives, Michael Dunn and Alan Cribb *Empirical Bioethics: Theoretical and Practical Perspectives*

Alan Merry and Warren Brookbanks *Merry and McCall Smith's Errors, Medicine and the Law* (second edition)

Donna Dickenson *Property in the Body: Feminist Perspectives* (second edition)

Rosie Harding *Duties to Care: Dementia, Relationality and Law*

Ruud ter Meulen *Solidarity and Justice in Health and Social Care*

David Albert Jones, Chris Gastmans and Calum MacKellar *Euthanasia and Assisted Suicide: Lessons from Belgium*

Muireann Quigley *Self-Ownership, Property Rights, and the Human Body: A Legal Perspective*

Françoise Baylis and Alice Dreger *Bioethics in Action*

John Keown *Euthanasia, Ethics and Public Policy: An Argument against Legislation* (second edition)

Amel Alghrani *Regulating Assisted Reproductive Technologies: New Horizons*

Britta van Beers, Sigrid Sterckx and Donna Dickenson *Personalised Medicine, Individual Choice and the Common Good*

David G. Kirchhoffer and Bernadette J. Richards *Beyond Autonomy: Limits and Alternatives to Informed Consent in Research Ethics and Law*

Markus Wolfensberger and Anthony Wrigley *Trust in Medicine: Its Nature, Justification, Significance, and Decline*

Catriona A. W. McMillan *The Human Embryo in vitro: Breaking the Legal Stalemate*

Ben P. White and Lindy Willmott *International Perspectives on End-of-Life Law Reform: Politics, Persuasion and Persistence*

International Perspectives on End-of-Life Law Reform

POLITICS, PERSUASION AND PERSISTENCE

Edited by

BEN P. WHITE

Queensland University of Technology

LINDY WILLMOTT

Queensland University of Technology

CAMBRIDGE
UNIVERSITY PRESS

CAMBRIDGE
UNIVERSITY PRESS

University Printing House, Cambridge CB2 8BS, United Kingdom

One Liberty Plaza, 20th Floor, New York, NY 10006, USA

477 Williamstown Road, Port Melbourne, VIC 3207, Australia

314–321, 3rd Floor, Plot 3, Splendor Forum, Jasola District Centre, New Delhi – 110025, India

103 Penang Road, #05–06/07, Visioncrest Commercial, Singapore 238467

Cambridge University Press is part of the University of Cambridge.

It furthers the University's mission by disseminating knowledge in the pursuit of
education, learning, and research at the highest international levels of excellence.

www.cambridge.org
Information on this title: www.cambridge.org/9781108489775
DOI: 10.1017/9781108779364

A catalogue record for this publication is available from the British Library.

Library of Congress Cataloging-in-Publication Data
NAMES: White, Ben, 1975 May 10– editor. | Willmott, Lindy, editor.
TITLE: International perspectives on end-of-life law reform : politics, persuasion, and persistence / edited
by Benjamin Peter White, Queensland University of Technology; Lindy Willmott, Queensland
University of Technology.
DESCRIPTION: Cambridge, United Kingdom ; New york, NY : Cambridge University Press, 2021. |
Series: Cambridge bioethics and law | Includes index.
IDENTIFIERS: LCCN 2021025353 (print) | LCCN 2021025354 (ebook) | ISBN 9781108489775 (hardback) |
ISBN 9781108747516 (paperback) | ISBN 9781108779364 (epub)
SUBJECTS: LCSH: Right to die–Law and legislation. | Euthanasia–Law and legislation. |
Assisted suicide–Law and legislation. | Bioethics. | Law reform. | BISAC: LAW / Medical Law &
Legislation | LAW / Medical Law & Legislation
CLASSIFICATION: LCC K3611.E95 I58 2021 (print) | LCC K3611.E95 (ebook) | DDC 344.04/197–dc23
LC record available at https://lccn.loc.gov/2021025353
LC ebook record available at https://lccn.loc.gov/2021025354

ISBN 978-1-108-48977-5 Hardback

Contents

Preface   *page* ix
About the Editors   xi
List of Contributors   xiii
Table of Cases   xix
Table of Statutes, Bills and Regulations   xxv

1   End-of-Life Law Reform: Context and Challenges   1
    Ben P. White and Lindy Willmott

2   The Path from *Rodriguez* to Bill C-14 and Beyond: Lessons
    about MAiD Law Reform from Canada   17
    Jocelyn Downie and Kate Scallion

3   The Extension of the Belgian Euthanasia Law to Minors in 2014   40
    Kasper Raus, Luc Deliens and Kenneth Chambaere

4   The Role of Scientific Evaluations of the Dutch Termination
    of Life on Request and Assisted Suicide (Review Procedure)
    Act: Old Law, New Boundaries   63
    Agnes van der Heide, Johan Legemaate, Johannes (Hans)
    J. M. van Delden and Bregje Onwuteaka-Philipsen

5   The Challenging Path to Voluntary Assisted Dying Law
    Reform in Australia: Victoria as a Successful Case Study   84
    Lindy Willmott and Ben P. White

6   Should Assisted Dying Require the Consent of a High
    Court Judge?   113
    Penney Lewis

7   Aid in Dying in the United States: Past, Present and Future   145
     David Orentlicher

8   The Medical Regulator as Law Reformer: Québec's Act
     Respecting End-of-Life Care   165
     Mona Gupta

9   Extrajudicial Resolution of Medical Futility Disputes:
     Key Factors in Establishing and Dismantling the Texas
     Advance Directives Act   180
     Thaddeus Mason Pope

10   Challenging Mandatory Court Hearings for People
     in Vegetative and Minimally Conscious States: How to Change
     the Law   202
     Celia Kitzinger and Jenny Kitzinger

11   Withholding and Withdrawing Life-Prolonging Treatment
     and the Relevance of Patients' Wishes: Reforming the Mental
     Capacity Act 2005   232
     Emily Jackson

12   International Perspectives on Reforming End-of-Life Law   250
     Ben P. White, Lindy Willmott, Jocelyn Downie, Penney Lewis,
     Celia Kitzinger, Jenny Kitzinger, Kenneth Chambaere,
     Thaddeus Mason Pope, Luc Deliens, Mona Gupta, Emily Jackson,
     Agnes van der Heide, Eliana Close, Katrine Del Villar
     and Jodhi Rutherford

Index   277

Preface

The law that regulates end-of-life decision-making is constantly evolving. Public discussion, interest group advocacy, media engagement and inquiries by law reform bodies ensure ongoing public debate about existing law as well as proposals for reform. While much has been written describing the current state of end-of-life law, advocating for what the law should be, and analysing how this law operates in practice, very little has been written about how and why law reform occurs in this area. Yet this issue is critical: some reforms of end-of-life law involve fundamental changes to how society regulates very significant decisions. Further, reform in this area, particularly in relation to assisted dying, has historically been very challenging to achieve.

This collection aims to shed light on why some law reform efforts to change end-of-life law succeed and others fail. The genesis of this collection was informal discussions with colleagues about how to bring about end-of-life law reform. It soon became clear from these discussions that the same question was being asked across the globe and there were lessons to be learnt from international experience.

This prompted a workshop, 'Law Reform in the End-of-Life Field', at the 2nd International Conference on End of Life Care: Law, Ethics, Policy and Practice held at Dalhousie University, Canada in September 2017. Members of the authorial teams from all but one of the chapters in this collection attended and presented a paper at that workshop (circulated prior to all workshop participants). Each paper had a nominated commentator and was critically and constructively discussed by the group. Those papers, which evolved into the ten case studies in this collection, provide insights into end-of-life law reform efforts in the United Kingdom, the United States, Canada, Australia, Belgium and the Netherlands.

We are grateful for the collegiality and collaborative spirit of the contributing authors over the course of writing this collection. In addition to the workshop review, a later draft of each chapter was sent to two other authorial groups for critical feedback. This not only strengthened the individual chapters but also elicited new connections and intersections between chapters, enhancing the overall continuity and focus of the collection.

Further collaboration also occurred in writing the concluding chapter which draws together global themes from the ten reform case studies. The collection's contributing authors were invited to participate in writing this chapter, and the outcome was a thought-provoking collaboration enriched by international and interdisciplinary perspectives. The opportunity to consider collectively with this group the implications of the ten case studies for law reform more generally was the most enjoyable part of editing this collection. We acknowledge the important contribution that all of the authors made, not just through writing their own chapters but to the collection as a whole.

We hope that this book is of interest to those considering how society regulates end-of-life decision-making. Our primary goal in bringing together these international case studies is to inform those involved in, or contemplating, end-of-life reform, whether from an academic, professional or policy perspective. We also hope that the case studies may be of value to those grappling with reform in other complex social policy areas.

We thank Emily Bartels (Queensland University of Technology), who provided extensive assistance with the preparation of the manuscript including providing research assistance, formatting and referencing chapters, co-ordinating the many versions of chapters with authors, and compiling the index and tables. We also thank Rebecca Meehan (Queensland University of Technology) for her assistance with the book proposal, research assistance for early chapters and initial administrative co-ordination. Our thanks also go to Chrystal Gray (Dalhousie University), who assisted with the organisation and logistics of the initial workshop. We are grateful too for the support of Cambridge University Press in the preparation and completion of the book, particularly that of Finola O'Sullivan and Marianne Nield.

We acknowledge the Australian Centre for Health Law Research in the Faculty of Business and Law, Queensland University of Technology. The Centre provided some support with administrative tasks to prepare the manuscript, but more importantly, we are grateful to work and research with tremendous colleagues in the Centre, particularly in the End-of-Life Research Program. A number of the authors in this collection are either based at the Centre or are adjunct professors with the Centre, and we are fortunate to be part of that generous health law community.

We thank our families for their tireless support through this and other projects. Ben thanks Kylie, Madeleine, Ella, Matilda, Adelaide and Amelia. Lindy acknowledges Jim, Kaley, Robbie, Jessie, Matt, Phoebe, Lachlan, Kelly, Ben, Henry and Oscar.

We conclude this preface as we began: noting that end-of-life law is constantly evolving. As a result, by the time this book is published, there will be new legislation (or existing legislation will be amended) and new cases that change the landscape of end-of-life law in various parts of the world. We have endeavoured to present the law and reform developments as at 30 June 2020, but have taken the opportunity (where possible during the publishing process) to mention some later developments.

About the Editors

Ben P. White is Professor of End-of-Life Law and Regulation in the Australian Centre for Health Law Research in the Faculty of Business and Law, Queensland University of Technology. He was a Foundation Director of the Centre and his research area is end-of-life decision-making with a particular focus on voluntary assisted dying. His programme of research has been funded by a series of Australian Research Council and National Health and Medical Research Council grants examining the law, policy and practice of end-of-life decision-making. He is currently undertaking a four-year Australian Research Council Future Fellowship: *Optimal Regulation of Voluntary Assisted Dying*. White has also had a long-standing interest in law reform, beginning with his doctoral thesis which examined the role of consultation in law reform processes. He has served as both a full-time and part-time commissioner at the Queensland Law Reform Commission, and his academic research and submissions have been extensively used by law reform bodies investigating end-of-life issues.

Lindy Willmott is Professor of Law and member of the Australian Centre for Health Law Research in the Faculty of Business and Law at the Queensland University of Technology. She researches extensively in the end-of-life field, particularly in relation to voluntary assisted dying. She has co-authored multiple texts, as well as the website *End of Life Law in Australia* (https://end-of-life.qut.edu.au/), and is involved in empirical research projects funded by the Australian Research Council and the National Health and Medical Research Council. Willmott co-leads a project funded by the Commonwealth Department of Health to provide legal training to health professionals, and projects funded by the Victorian Department of Health and Human Services and the Western

Australian Department of Health to provide legal training to medical practitioners (Victoria) and medical and nurse practitioners (Western Australia) on voluntary assisted dying. She has been a board member of Palliative Care Australia, and a former commissioner with the Queensland Law Reform Commission.

List of Contributors

Kenneth Chambaere is Interdisciplinary Professor of Public Health, Sociology and Ethics of the End of Life at the Alliance End-of-Life Care Research Group of Ghent University and Vrije Universiteit Brussel, Belgium. He obtained an MSc in Sociology in 2004 and a postgraduate degree in Logic, History and Philosophy of Science in 2005, before obtaining a PhD in Medical-Social Sciences in 2010. Kenneth's research focuses on three main themes: (1) end-of-life practices; (2) palliative care in and by the community; and (3) end-of-life care for people in vulnerable positions. Assisted dying (euthanasia and assisted suicide) has been a topic of specific interest throughout his academic career to date.

Eliana Close is Lecturer in the Faculty of Business and Law and a member of the Australian Centre for Health Law Research at the Queensland University of Technology. She is a postdoctoral research fellow on the *Optimal Regulation of Voluntary Assisted Dying* research project, as part of Professor Ben White's Australian Research Council Future Fellowship. Close has a BSc (First Class Honours) in Psychology from the University of Calgary, Canada, and an MA from Oxford University, where she studied law as a Rhodes Scholar. She has published nationally and internationally on various aspects of end-of-life law, policy and practice, with a focus on decision-making about potentially life-sustaining treatment, voluntary assisted dying, and healthcare rationing. Her PhD explored the extent to which law and policy on 'futile' or 'non-beneficial' treatment at the end of life addresses resource allocation.

Johannes (Hans) J. M. van Delden is Full Professor of Medical Ethics at the University Medical Center of Utrecht University (UMC Utrecht), the Netherlands. He leads the project on patient and public participation for the hospital and for the medical school in UMC Utrecht. He has worked for many years as a practising nursing home physician. He has published nearly 300 international and more than a 100 national articles on the practice and ethics of end-of-life decisions, research ethics and ethical issues in the care for the elderly. At his department, he has built a research team which has created a strong track record in the ethics of end-of-life decisions, research ethics and ethics of biomedical innovation. He served as the chair of the International Bioethics Committee of UNESCO. He has also served as the president of the Council of International Organisations of Medical Sciences (CIOMS), and as the chair of the workgroup for the revision of the CIOMS ethical guidelines for biomedical research.

Katrine Del Villar is a postdoctoral research fellow and member of the Australian Centre for Health Law Research in the Faculty of Business and Law at the Queensland University of Technology. She researches in the area of voluntary assisted dying and other legal issues arising at the end of life. She completed her PhD in mental health law, focusing on advance decision-making, and has enduring research interests in medical law and ethics, including consent and capacity. She teaches health law and ethics and constitutional law. Prior to her academic appointments, Del Villar worked as an associate to Justice Gaudron of the Australian High Court, as a solicitor in private practice for a national firm and as a research officer for the Commonwealth Parliamentary Library.

Luc Deliens trained in medical sociology and is Professor of Palliative Care Research and Director of the End-of-Life Care Research Group of the Vrije Universiteit Brussel and Ghent University in Belgium (www.endoflifecare.be). His team includes more than sixty people, the country's largest research group in palliative care and end-of-life studies, including a research programme on euthanasia and other end-of-life decisions. Internationally, he chairs the European Association for Palliative Care (EAPC) Reference Group on Public Health and Palliative Care and co-chairs the EAPC Research Network. He is involved in different ongoing national and international research projects. He has successfully supervised forty-seven PhDs and is currently supervising about twenty PhD students. He has published more than 500 papers and more than 50 book chapters and received several scientific awards for his research. He is also an elected member of the Royal Academy of Medicine of Belgium.

Jocelyn Downie is the James S. Palmer Chair in Public Policy and Law at the Schulich School of Law and University Research Professor at Dalhousie University. She is an adjunct professor at the Australian Centre for Health Law Research at the Queensland University of Technology. Her work on end-of-life law and policy includes: Special Advisor to the Canadian Senate Committee on Euthanasia and Assisted Suicide; author of *Dying Justice: A Case for Decriminalizing Euthanasia and Assisted Suicide in Canada*; and member of the Royal Society of Canada Expert Panel on End-of-Life Decision-Making, the plaintiffs' legal team in *Carter v. Canada (Attorney General)*, the Provincial-Territorial Expert Advisory Group on

Physician-Assisted Dying, and the Canadian Council of Academies Expert Panel on Medical Assistance in Dying.

Mona Gupta is a psychiatrist at the Centre Hospitalier de l'Université de Montréal (CHUM) and Clinician-Investigator at the Centre de Recherche du CHUM. She is also Associate Clinical Professor in the Department of Psychiatry and Addictions of the Université de Montréal. The broad theme of her area of inquiry is the interface of ethics and epistemology in psychiatry. Her specific research interests include standards of evidence and conceptions of error in psychiatry, intersubjectivity and assisted dying for persons with mental disorders.

Agnes van der Heide is Professor of End-of-Life Care and Decision-Making in the Department of Public Health at Erasmus MC, University Medical Center Rotterdam, the Netherlands. She was trained as a physician and epidemiologist and has been working in empirical end-of-life care research since 1995. Her research is focused on epidemiological, clinical, ethical and legal issues in end-of-life care and end-of-life decision-making. She has been the principal investigator of many end-of-life care research projects at the local, national and international level. She has co-led the five-yearly nationwide survey studies on developments in end-of-life decision-making practices in the Netherlands since 1995 and was one of the main investigators in the studies to evaluate the Dutch Termination of Life on Request and Assisted Suicide (Review Procedure) Act. Currently, she is coordinating a twelve-country research project on the experience of dying and preferences in end-of-life care.

Emily Jackson is Professor of Law at the London School of Economics and Political Science, where she teaches Medical Law. Her research interests have principally been in relation to end-of-life care, assisted reproduction and the regulation of the pharmaceutical industry. She is a Fellow of the British Academy, and a member of the British Medical Association's Medical Ethics Committee. She has previously been a member and then Deputy Chair of the Human Fertilisation and Embryology Authority, and a Judicial Appointments Commissioner.

Celia Kitzinger is Honorary Professor in the School of Law and Politics at Cardiff University. She has a background in academic psychology, is a Chartered Psychologist and Fellow of the British Psychological Society, an accredited mediator and has published widely on gender and sexuality, same-sex marriage rights, communication and conversation analysis, and end-of-life decision-making. With Jenny Kitzinger, she co-directs the Coma and Disorders of Consciousness Research Centre. Celia is currently working on 'remote justice' (court hearings conducted via video-conferencing platforms) in the context of the COVID-19 pandemic and co-directs the award-winning Open Justice Court of Protection Project. She tweets as @KitzingerCelia.

Jenny Kitzinger is Professor in the School of Journalism, Media and Culture at Cardiff University. She has a background in social anthropology and has published widely on media influence, sexual violence, the AIDS crisis, science and health reporting, focus group research and end-of-life decision-making. With Celia Kitzinger, she co-directs the Coma and Disorders of Consciousness Research Centre. Jenny is currently working with Dr Julie Latchem-Hastings to develop e-learning to roll out changes in law and guidelines to inform everyday practices in hospitals, rehabilitation centres and care homes. She tweets as @JennyKitzinger.

Johan Legemaate is Professor of Health Law at the University of Amsterdam (Faculties of Law and Medicine) and a judge in the Central Medical Disciplinary Board. Since the beginning of the 1990s he has written extensively on legal issues in end-of-life care. He was involved in the second (2012) and third (2017) evaluation of the Dutch Termination of Life on Request and Assisted Suicide (Review Procedure) Act. In 2015, he co-authored the first Code of Practice of the regional review committees on euthanasia.

Penney Lewis studied mathematics, law and philosophy in the United States, Canada and the United Kingdom, where she is Professor of Law and Co-Director of the Centre of Medical Law and Ethics, King's College London. In the area of medical law, her research focuses on end-of-life issues including advance decision-making, and refusal and withdrawal of treatment. She has published widely on assisted dying, including her 2007 Oxford University Press monograph, *Assisted Dying and Legal Change*. She is a member of the Human Tissue Authority and the Clinical Ethics Committee of St. Christopher's Hospice, and was a member of the UK Donation Ethics Committee. From 2020 she is on secondment to the Law Commission as the Commissioner for Criminal Law, helping to modernise and simplify the criminal law, medical and bio-law, and the interface between law and science.

Bregje Onwuteaka-Philipsen, health scientist, is Professor of End-of-Life Research at the Department of Public and Occupational Health at Amsterdam UMC in the Netherlands. In this department she chairs the research section, Quality and Organisation of Care, and leads the research group Public Health at the End of Life. She also chairs the Expertise Center for Palliative Care of Amsterdam UMC. Her research focuses on advance care planning, palliative care and medical end-of-life decision-making. Since 1995 she has been involved in the Dutch nation-wide evaluation studies on regulation and legalisation of euthanasia and physician-assisted suicide, and since 2001 has led these studies (together with Agnes van der Heide).

David Orentlicher is the Judge Jack and Lulu Lehman Professor of Law at the University of Nevada, Las Vegas (UNLV) William S. Boyd School of Law, and Director of the UNLV Health Law Program, a partnership of the School of Law and the School of Public Health. He is author of *Matters of Life and Death* and co-author of *Health Care Law and Ethics*, now in its ninth edition, and he has written widely in medical and legal journals on end-of-life decisions. David has testified before the US Congress, had his scholarship cited by the US Supreme Court and has served on many national, state and local commissions. Before entering teaching, he directed the medical ethics program at the American Medical Association, where he helped write the AMA's policies on end-of-life decisions.

Thaddeus Mason Pope is Professor of Law at Mitchell Hamline School of Law in Saint Paul, Minnesota. He has published more than 200 articles and papers in leading medical journals, law reviews, bar journals, nursing journals, bioethics journals and also book chapters. He co-authored the 1,500-page *The Right to Die: The Law of End-of-Life Decision Making* and runs the popular Medical Futility Blog. Thaddeus co-authored both clinical practice guidelines for medical aid in dying and policy guidance on ethics in critical care for major professional medical societies. Apart from his scholarship, Thaddeus has served as a legal consultant and expert witness in court cases involving end-of-life treatment.

Kasper Raus is a philosopher and medical ethicist by training, who obtained his PhD at Ghent University on ethical issues relating to palliative sedation and euthanasia. He is currently teaching general and medical ethics at Ghent University as Visiting Professor and is working at Ghent University Hospital as a medical ethicist, where he combines research with policy work. His current research focuses on a range of topics such as end-of-life ethics, interhospital collaboration and new medical technologies. He is also a member of various research groups as well as the ethics committee of the Forensic Psychiatric Centre of Ghent and Antwerp.

Jodhi Rutherford is a sessional lecturer at the Faculty of Business and Law, Queensland University of Technology and a member of the Australian Centre for Health Law Research. Rutherford is a socio-legal researcher with a background in law and political science. Her doctoral research is focused on voluntary assisted dying and the role of interest groups in the process of law reform.

Kate Scallion is a lawyer. She completed both her JD and her LLM at Dalhousie University in 2018 and 2019, respectively. In addition to end-of-life law and policy, her research interests include anti-doping and sports law. Her LLM thesis looked at whether or not the Canadian Charter of Rights and Freedoms applies to the Canadian Anti-Doping Program.

Table of Cases

AUSTRALIA

Wake and Gondarra v. Northern Territory and Asche (1996) 5 NTLR 170 268

BELGIUM

Judgment 153/2015, Constitutional Court of Belgium (29 October 2015) 40, 44–5, 47, 50, 56–8, 116, 268

CANADA

AA (Re) [2016] BCSC 570 119, 138
AB v. Canada (Attorney General) [2016] ONSC 1912 119, 138
AB v. Canada (Attorney General) [2017] ONSC 3759 24, 138
AB v. Ontario (Attorney General) [2016] ONSC 2188 119, 138
BC v. Canada (Attorney General) [2016] ONSC 3231 120, 138
Bedford v. Canada (Attorney General) [2013] SCC 72 19
Canada (Attorney General) v. EF [2016] ABCA 155 119, 139
Carter v. Canada (Attorney General) [2012] BCSC 886 19, 20–1, 38, 135, 178, 258, 262
Carter v. Canada (Attorney General) [2013] BCCA 435 38, 135, 178
Carter v. Canada (Attorney General) [2015] 1 SCR 331 4, 6, 12, 17–19, 22, 31, 38, 120, 135, 137–9, 142, 165, 167, 178, 252–4, 258, 261–2, 264–5
Carter v. Canada (Attorney General) [2016] 1 SCR 13 38, 120, 178
CD v. Canada (Attorney General) [2016] ONSC 2431 119, 138
EF v. Canada (Attorney General) [2016] ONSC 2790 119, 138
FG v. Canada (Attorney General) [2016] ONSC 3099 120, 138
GH v. Canada (Attorney General) [2016] ONSC 2873 119, 138
HH (Re) [2016] BCSC 971 119, 138
HS (Re) [2016] ABQB 121 119, 138
IJ v. Canada (Attorney General) [2016] ONSC 3380 119, 138

Lamb and British Columbia Civil Liberties Association v. Canada (Attorney General) [2016] Supreme Court of British Columbia, No. S-165851
  25, 29, 38
MN v. Canada (Attorney General) [2016] ONSC 3346 119, 138
OP v. Canada (Attorney General) [2016] ONSC 3956 120
Patient 0518 v. RHA 0518 [2016] SKQB 176 119, 138
Patient v. Canada (Attorney General) [2016] MBQB 63 119, 138
R v. Heywood [1994] 3 SCR 761 18–19
R v. Malmo-Levine [2003] 3 SCR 571 18–19
R v. Morgentaler [1988] 1 SCR 30 122
R v. Oakes [1986] 1 SCR 103 25
Rodriguez v. British Columbia (Attorney General) [1993] 3 SCR 519 4, 17–20, 37–8,
  135, 137, 264
Truchon v. Canada (Attorney General) [2019] QCCS 3792 1, 17–18, 25–6, 30–1, 36,
  38, 123, 142, 167, 168, 176, 178, 200, 259, 261–2, 269
Truchon v. Canada (Attorney General) [2020] QCCS 772 37–8, 179
Truchon v. Canada (Attorney General) [2020] QCCS 2019 37–8, 179
Truchon v. Canada (Attorney General) [2020] QCCS 4388 37–8, 179
Truchon v. Canada (Attorney General) [2021] QCCS 590 37–8, 179
Tuckwell (Re) [2016] ABQB 302 119, 138
WV v. Canada (Attorney General) [2016] ONSC 2302 119, 138
XY v. Canada (Attorney General) [2016] ONSC 2585 119, 138

COLOMBIA

Sentence C-239 (1997), Ref. Expedient D-1490 (Constitutional Court of the
  Republic of Colombia, 20 May 1997) 6, 41, 115, 142, 253
Sentence T-970 (2014), Ref. Expedient T-4.067.849 (Constitutional Court of the
  Republic of Colombia, 15 December 2014) 142

EUROPEAN COURT OF HUMAN RIGHTS

Evans v. United Kingdom – 14238/18 *(inadmissible)* [2018] ECHR 297 11
Evans v. United Kingdom – 18770/18 [2018] ECHR 357 11
Gard and Another v. United Kingdom [2017] ECHR 605 11
Gross v. Switzerland (2014) 58 EHRR 7 (ECHR) 138
Haas v. Switzerland (2011) 53 EHRR 33 (ECHR) 138
Koch v. Germany (2013) 56 EHRR 6 (ECHR) 138
Nicklinson and Lamb v. United Kingdom (2015) 61 EHRR SE7 (ECHR) 138
Pretty v. United Kingdom (2002) 25 EHRR 1 (ECHR) 137
Sanles Sanles v. Spain [2001] EHRLR 348 (ECHR) 138

GERMANY

Second Senate of the Federal Constitutional Court, Zum Urteil des Zweiten Senats
  vom. 26 February 2020, Bundesverfassungsgericht 2, 6

INDIA

Common Cause (A Regd. Society) v. Union of India and Another (Unreported, Supreme Court of India, Civil Original Jurisdiction, Writ Petition (Civil) No. 215 of 2005, 9 March 2018) 2

THE NETHERLANDS

Court of Appeal Arnhem-Leeuwarden, 13 May 2015, ECLI:NL:GHARL:2015:3444 75
Court of Appeal of s-Hertogenbosch, 31 January 2018, ECLI:NL:GHSHE:2018:345 76
District Court of The Hague, 11 September 2019, ECLI:NL:RBDHA:2019:9506 75
Gelderland District Court, 22 October 2013, ECLI:NL:RBGEL:2013:397 75
Netherlands Jurisprudence [Nederlandse Jurisprudentie] (1973) District Court of Leeuwarden, 21 February 1973, No. 183 64
Netherlands Jurisprudence [Nederlandse Jurisprudentie] (1985) Supreme Court, 27 November 1984, No. 106 65
Netherlands Jurisprudence [Nederlandse Jurisprudentie] (2003) Supreme Court, 24 December 2002, No. 167 66
Office of Public Prosecutions v. Chabot, Netherlands Jurisprudence [Nederlandse Jurisprudentie] (1994) Supreme Court, 21 June 1994, No. 656 66
Regional Disciplinary Tribunal for Healthcare Amsterdam, 12 November 2013, ECLI:NL:TGZRAMS:2013:55 74
Regional Disciplinary Tribunal for Healthcare Amsterdam, 20 August 2013, ECLI:NL:TGZRAMS:2013:26 74
Regional Disciplinary Tribunal for Healthcare The Hague, 24 July 2018, ECLI:NL:TGZRSGR:2018:165 75
Supreme Court, 14 March 2017, ECLI:NL:HR:2017:418 75
Supreme Court, 21 April 2020, ECLI:NL:HR:2020:712 75

NEW ZEALAND

Seales v. Attorney-General [2015] 3 NZLR 556 135, 138

SOUTH AFRICA

Stransham-Ford v. Minister of Justice and Correctional Services [2015] ZAGPPHC 230 138

UNITED KINGDOM

A Clinical Commissioning Group v. P [2019] EWCOP 18 248
A Local Authority v. E [2012] EWHC 1639 235
A London Local Authority v. JH [2011] EWCOP 2420 234
Abertawe Bro Morgannwg University Local Health Board v. RY [2017] EWCOP 2 247

Aintree University Hospitals NHS Foundation Trust (Respondent) v. James (Appellant) [2013] UKSC 67 215, 232, 234–5, 245

Airedale NHS Trust v. Bland [1993] AC 789 121, 211, 213, 215, 218, 224, 234

Alder Hey Children's NHS Foundation Trust v. Evans and Another [2018] EWHC 308 11

Alder Hey Children's NHS Foundation Trust v. Evans and Another [2018] EWHC 953 11

Alder Hey Children's NHS Foundation Trust v. Evans and Others [2018] EWHC 818 11

An NHS Trust v. DE [2013] EWHC 2562 (Fam) 234

An NHS Trust v. Y (Re Y) [2018] UKSC 46 3, 131, 202, 207–8, 210, 226, 228, 232, 247, 254–5, 263

Bolam v. Friern Hospital Management Committee [1957] 1 WLR 582 233–4

Briggs v. Briggs and Others [2016] EWCOP 48 215

Briggs v. Briggs and Others [2016] EWCOP 53 206, 235

Brunner v. Greenslade [1971] Ch 993 216

Cambridge University Hospitals NHS Foundation Trust v. BF [2016] EWCOP 26 238

Director of Legal Aid Casework and Others v. Briggs [2017] EWCA Civ 1169 216

E (A Child) (Rev 1) [2018] EWCA Civ 550 11

Evans and Another v. Alder Hey Children's NHS Foundation Trust and Another (Rev 1) [2018] EWCA Civ 984 11

Evans and Another v. Alder Hey Children's NHS Foundation Trust and Others [2018] EWCA Civ 805 11

Great Ormond Street Hospital v. Yates and Another [2017] EWHC 1909 11

Great Ormond Street Hospital v. Yates and Others [2017] EWHC 972 10

In Re Z (Local Authority: Duty) [2004] EWHC 2817 137

In the Case of Charlie Gard (Unreported decision of Supreme Court of the United Kingdom 19 June 2017, Lady Hale, Lord Kerr and Lord Wilson) 10

King's College Hospital NHS Foundation Trust v. C [2015] EWCOP 80 125

M v. A Hospital [2017] EWCOP 19 215–16, 225

M v. N [2015] EWCOP 76 237, 240–1

NHS Cumbria CCG v. Rushton [2018] EWCOP 41 246–7

NHS Trust v. Y and Anor [2017] EWHC 2866 209

Portsmouth NHS Trust v. Wyatt [2004] EWHC 2247 (Fam) 240

R (Burke) v. General Medical Council [2005] EWCA Civ 1003 137, 215, 225, 239

R (Conway) v. Secretary of State for Justice [2020] QB 1 2, 249

R (Lamb) v. Secretary of State for Justice [2019] EWHC 3606 2

R (Newby) v. Secretary of State for Justice [2019] EWHC 3118 2

R (Nicklinson) v. Ministry of Justice [2015] AC 657 113, 124, 126–7, 135, 138, 143, 249

R (Purdy) v. Director of Public Proceedings [2010] 1 AC 345 12, 135, 137, 254

R (T) v. Secretary of State for Justice [2018] EWHC 2615 2

RAO v. ROO [2018] EWCOP 33 236

RB v. Brighton and Hove City Council [2014] EWCA Civ 561 239

Re A (Children) (Conjoined Twins: Surgical Separation) [2001] Fam 147 121

Re B (Adult: Refusal of Medical Treatment) [2002] EWHC 429 121, 125, 135, 138

Re F (Mental Patient: Sterilisation) [1990] 2 AC 1 233–4

Re M (Adult Patient) (Minimally Conscious State: Withdrawal of Treatment) [2011] EWHC 2443 234–5

Re M (Statutory Will) [2009] EWHC 2525 (Fam) 234, 240
Re T (Adult: Refusal of Medical Treatment) [1993] Fam 95 125–6
Ross v. Lord Advocate [2016] CSIH 12 135, 137
Royal Bournemouth and Christchurch Hospitals NHS Foundation Trust v. TG [2019] EWCOP 21 236, 246
Salford Royal NHS Foundation Trust v. P [2017] EWCOP 23 246
Sheffield Teaching Hospitals v. TH [2014] EWCOP 4 237
St George's NHS Foundation Trust v. P [2015] EWCOP 42 237
St George's Healthcare NHS Trust v. S [1998] 3 WLR 936 131
U v. Centre for Reproductive Medicine [2002] EWCA Civ 565 126
United Lincolnshire Hospitals NHS Trust v. N [2014] EWCOP 16 237
University Hospitals Birmingham NHS Foundation Trust v. HB [2018] EWCOP 39 236
Wye Valley NHS Trust v. B [2015] EWCOP 60 235, 237, 241
Yates and Another v. Great Ormond Street Hospital For Children NHS Foundation Trust and Another (Rev 1) [2017] EWCA Civ 410 10

UNITED STATES

Aguocha-Ohakweh v. Harris County Hospital District, No. 4:16-CV-903 (SD Tex. 11 April 2017) 195
Ahn v. Hestrin, No. RIC 1607135 (Riverside County Sup. Ct, Cal. 2016) 193, 198
Baxter v. State, 224 P 3d 1211 (Mont. 2009) 6, 114, 145, 193, 243
Baxter v. State, No. ADV-2007-787, 2008 WL 6627324 (Mont. Dist. Ct., 5 December 2008) 135
Bouvia v. Superior Court, 225 Cal. Rptr. 297 (Ct App. 1986) 151
California Advocates for Nursing Home Reform v. Smith, No. A147987 (Cal. App. 22 July 2019) 193
City of Philadelphia v. Commonwealth, 838 A 2d 566 (Pa. 2003) 189
Commonwealth v. Twitchell, 617 NE 2d 609 (Mass. 1993) 152
Compassion in Dying v. Washington 79 F 3d 790 (9th Cir. 1996) 135
Cruzan v. Director, Missouri Department of Health, 497 US 261 (1990) 157, 160
Davis v. Memorial Hermann, No. 2009-07079 (Harris County District Court, Tex. 4 February 2009) 195
De Paz Gonzalez v. Duane, No. 4:20-CV-00072-A (ND Tex. 2020); No. 20-10615 (5th Cir. 31 March 2021) (oral argument) 190
Dunn v. Methodist Hospital, No. 2015-69681 (Harris County District Court, Tex. 20 November 2015) (temporary restraining order) 195
Gonzales v. Oregon, 546 US 243 (2006) 159, 193
Gonzales v. Seton Family Hospitals, No. 1:07-CV-00267 (WD Tex. 4 April 2007) 195
In re Conroy, 486 A 2d 1209 at 1221–3 (NJ 1985) 150–1, 156
In re L.S., 87 P 3d 521 (Nev. 2004) 152
In re Quinlan, 355 A 2d 647 (NJ 1976) 149–51, 157
John F. Kennedy Hospital v. Heston, 279 A 2d 670 at 672–3 (NJ 1971) 149
Kelly v. Houston Methodist Hospital, No. 01-17-00866-CV (Tex. App. 26 March 2019) 196
Kelly v. Houston Methodist Hospital, No. 19-0390 (Tex. 4 October 2019) 196

Kelly v. Houston Methodist, No. 2015-69681 (Harris County, 189th District Court, Tex. 24 October 2016) 198

Kelly v. Methodist Hospital, No. 2015-69681 (Harris County, 189th Judicial District, Tex. 13 October 2017) 196

Lee v. State, 869 F. Supp. 1491 (D. Or. 1994) 193

Obergefell v. Hodges, 135 S. Ct 2584 (2015) 147

Ohakweh v. Harris Health System, No. 4:20-cv-01651 (SD Tex. 12 May 2020) 195

Petro v. Grewal, No. MER-C-53-19 (NJ Sup. Ct, 1 April 2020) 193, 198

Planned Parenthood of Southeastern Pennsylvania v. Casey, 505 US 833 (1992) 150

Rains v. Belshe, 32 Cal. App. 4th 157 (1995) 192

State v. Stanko, 974 P 2d 1132 (Mont. 1998) 152

Superintendent of Belchertown State School v. Saikewicz, 370 NE 2d 417, 425–6 (Mass. 1977) 148

T.B.L. v. Cook Children's Medical Center, No. 323-112330-19 (Tarrant County, 323rd District Court, Tex. 20 November 2019) 197–8

T.L. v. Cook Children's Medical Center, 607 S.W.3d 9 (Tex. App. 24 July 2020), rev. denied, No. 20-0644 (Tex. 16 October 2020), cert. denied, 141 S. Ct. 1069 (11 January 2021), on remand, No. 048-112330-19 (Tarrant County Dist. Ct. Tex.) 181, 196–7

Vacco v. Quill, 527 US 793 (1997) 156

Walker v. Superior Court, 763 P 2d 852 (Cal. 1988) 152

Washington v. Glucksberg, 521 US 702 (1997) 138, 156, 159, 160

Washington v. Harper, 494 US 210 (1990) 192

Table of Statutes, Bills and Regulations

AUSTRALIA

Death with Dignity Bill 2016 (SA) 4, 87
End-of-Life Choices (Voluntary Assisted Dying) Act 2021 (Tas) 1, 4, 6, 87–8, 112
Euthanasia Laws Act 1997 (Cth) 4, 85, 193
Guardianship and Administration Act 2019 (Vic) 2
Human Rights Act 2019 (Qld) 97
Medical Treatment Planning and Decisions Act 2016 (Vic) 2
Restoring Territory Rights (Assisted Suicide Legislation) Bill 2015 (Cth) 87
Rights of the Terminally Ill Act 1995 (NT) 4, 69, 85, 142, 193
Voluntary Assisted Dying Act 2017 (Vic) 4, 6, 27, 84, 92, 96–7, 99–100, 115, 261, 267, 270–1
Voluntary Assisted Dying Act 2019 (WA) 1, 4, 6, 27, 85, 111, 115
Voluntary Assisted Dying Bill 2013 (Tas) 116
Voluntary Assisted Dying Bill 2016 (Tas) 4, 116
Voluntary Assisted Dying Bill 2017 (NSW) 4, 87, 116, 131
Voluntary Assisted Dying Bill 2019 (WA) 87

BELGIUM

Amendment to Law Proposal Concerning Euthanasia, 2000, S 2-244/3 52
Belgian Constitution 56
Bill Amending art. 3 of the Law of 28 May 2002 on Euthanasia, Concerning Euthanasia on Minors, 16 September 2008, S 4-920 52
Bill Amending art. 3 of the Law of 28 May 2002 on Euthanasia, Concerning Euthanasia on Minors, 16 August 2010, S 5-21 52
Bill Amending the Law of 28 May 2002 on Euthanasia as Concerns Minors, 7 July 2004, S 3-804/1 54
Bill Amending the Law of 28 May 2002 on Euthanasia as Concerns Minors, 19 December 2007, K. 52-611 52
Bill Amending the Law of 28 May 2002 on Euthanasia as Concerns Minors of 15 Years and Older, 23 September 2010, S 5-179 52, 54

Bill Amending the Law of 28 May 2002 on Euthanasia, Concerning Euthanasia on Minors, 7 February 2013, K 53-2633 52

Bill Amending the Law of 28 May 2002 on Euthanasia, to Enable Euthanasia on Minors, S 5-2170 59

Bill Amending the Law of 28 May 2002 on Euthanasia, to Enable Euthanasia on Minors, S 5-2170/1 40, 52, 54, 59

Bill on the Extension of the Law of 28 May 2002 on Euthanasia to Minors, the Medical Assistance to the Patient Who Performs the Life-Terminating Action Himself or Herself and the Punishment of Assisted Suicide, 25 January 2013, S 5-1947 52

Bill Supplementing the Law of 28 May 2002 on Euthanasia as Concerns Minors, 15 June 2006, K. 51-2553/1 52

Bill Supplementing the Law of 28 May 2002 on Euthanasia as Concerns Minors, 12 December 2006, S 3-1993 52, 54

Bill Supplementing the Law of 28 May 2002 on Euthanasia, Concerning Minors, 28 November 2007, S 4-431 52

Bill Supplementing the Law of 28 May 2002 on Euthanasia, Concerning Minors, 26 May 2008, S 4-785 52

Bill Supplementing the Law of 28 May 2002 on Euthanasia, Concerning Minors, 28 October 2010, K 53-496 52

Bill Supplementing the Law of 28 May 2002 on Euthanasia, Concerning Minors, 9 May 2012, S 5-1610 52, 54

Bill Supplementing the Law of 28 May 2002 on Euthanasia as Concerns Minors, 4 December 2013, S 5-2170/8 54, 59–61

Law of 14 June 2002 Concerning Palliative Care, Belgian Official Gazette (26 October 2002) 2002/022868, 49160 44

Law of 22 August 2002 Concerning the Rights of the Patient, Belgian Official Gazette (26 September 2002) 2002/22737, 43719 47, 59

Law of 28 February 2014 Amending the Law of 28 May 2002 on Euthanasia to Extend Euthanasia to Minors, Belgian Official Gazette (12 March 2014) 2014/009093, 21053 41

Law of 28 May 2002 on Euthanasia, Belgian Official Gazette (22 June 2002) 2002/09590, 28515 5, 41

CANADA

An Act Respecting End-of-Life Care, RSQ 2014, c. S-32.0001 (Québec) 2, 6, 16, 38–9, 115, 142, 166–7, 174–5, 179

Bill 52, An Act Respecting End-of-Life Care, 1st Sess., 41st Leg., Québec, 2013 (assented to 10 June 2014), RSQ c. S-32.0001 21

Bill C-14, An Act to Amend the Criminal Code and to Make Related Amendments to Other Acts (Medical Assistance in Dying), SC 2016, c. 3 1, 17–18, 23, 25–31, 35–7, 167, 175, 178

Bill C-7, An Act to Amend the Criminal Code (Medical Assistance in Dying), SC 2021, c. 2 2, 17–18, 28–31, 34–7, 39, 123, 168, 178–9

Canadian Charter of Rights and Freedoms, Canada Act 1982 (UK) c. 11, sch. B, pt. 1 10, 18–19, 20, 25–6, 36, 120, 167, 178, 253, 261, 264–5, 269

Criminal Code RSC 1985, c. C-46 1, 6, 17, 19, 24, 31, 116, 122–3, 166–9, 178–9

Regulations for the Monitoring of Medical Assistance in Dying: Ginette Petitpas
  Taylor, Minister for Health, 'Registration: SOR/2018-166: Criminal Code',
  Canada Gazette, pt. 2, vol. 152, no. 16, 27 July 2018, at 3077 31, 38–9

COLOMBIA

República de Colombia Ministerio de Salud y Protección Social, Protocolo para la
  aplicación del procedimiento de eutanasia en Colombia (2015) 119
República de Colombia Ministerio de Salud y Protección Social, Resolución 1216
  de 2015 por medio de la cual se da cumplimiento a la orden cuarta de la sentencia
  T-970 de 2014 de la Honorable Corte Constitucional en relación con las
  directrices para la organización y funcionamiento de los Comités para hacer
  efectivo el derecho a morir con dignidad (2015) 115, 119

EUROPEAN INSTRUMENTS

Convention for the Protection of Human Rights and Fundamental Freedoms
  (European Convention on Human Rights), agreed at Rome, 4 November 1950 2,
  12, 56, 124–6, 216, 240

FRANCE

Loi 2016-87 du 2 février 2016 créant de nouveaux droits en faveur des malades et des
  personnes en fin de vie. Journal Officiel 2016. 0028 [Law No. 2016-87 of 2
  February 2016 on Creating New Rights for the Sick and People at the End of Life]
  (France) JO, 2 February 2016 3

INTERNATIONAL INSTRUMENTS

United Nations Convention on the Rights of Persons with Disabilities, General
  Assembly Resolution 61/106, 24 January 2007 243
United Nations Convention on the Rights of the Child, General Assembly
  Resolution 44/25, 20 November 1989 56

ITALY

Rules on Informed Consent and Advance Treatment Provisions 2017 (Law N. 219) 2

KOREA

Act on Hospice and Palliative Care and Decisions on Life-Sustaining Treatment for
  Patients at the End of Life, Act No. 14013 3

LUXEMBOURG

Law of 16 March 2009 on Euthanasia and Assisted Suicide 6, 115–16

THE NETHERLANDS

Dutch Penal Code 63, 68, 71–2
Termination of Life on Request and Assisted Suicide (Review Procedures) Act of 1
  April 2002 5, 63–4, 67–8, 82, 148

NEW ZEALAND

End of Life Choice Act 2019 (NZ) 1, 82, 106, 253

SWITZERLAND

Criminal Code 1937 6

TAIWAN

Patient Right to Autonomy Act 2019 2

UNITED KINGDOM

Assisted Dying (No. 2) HC Bill (2015–16) [7] 123, 127
Assisted Dying HL Bill (2014–15) 6 123, 125–6
Assisted Dying HL Bill (2015–16) 25 123, 127
Assisted Suicide (Scotland) Bill, Bill 40, Scottish Parliament, Sess. 4 (2013) 116, 121
Constitutional Reform Act 2005 (England and Wales) 211
Court of Protection Rules 2017 (England and Wales) 211
Court of Protection, Practice Direction 13B: Court Bundles (1 July 2015) 214
Court of Protection, Practice Direction 14C: Fees for Examiners of the Court (1
  December 2017) 214
Court of Protection, Practice Direction 9E: Applications Relating to Serious
  Medical Treatment (1 July 2015) 211, 213–15, 222–4, 230
End of Life Assistance (Scotland) Bill (2010) [38] 116, 133
Mental Capacity (Amendment) Act 2019 (England and Wales) 244
Mental Capacity Act 2005 (England and Wales) 16, 125, 131, 209–10, 214–16, 227,
  232–4, 239–40, 242–5, 248, 254

UNITED STATES

Affordable Health Choices Act of 2009 (HR 3200) 13
An Act to Enact the Maine Death with Dignity Act, 22 Me Rev Stat Ann § 2140
  (2019) (Maine) 1, 6, 115, 158, 199

Constitution of the United States 196
Controlled Substances Act, 21 USC §§ 801–904 (2001) 159
Death with Dignity Act of 2016, DC Code §§ 7–661 (2017) (District of Columbia) 6,
115, 199
Death with Dignity Act, Or Rev Stat §§ 127.800–127.995 (1994) (Oregon) 6, 27, 69,
118, 146–7, 163, 199
Death with Dignity Act, Wash Rev Code §§ 70.245.010–70.245.903 (2008)
(Washington) 6, 115, 119, 261
Dept. of State Health Services, Hospital Licensing, 43(37) Tex. Reg. 5952–56 (14
September 2018) 195
Elizabeth Whitefield End-of-Life Options Act, H.B. 47, 55th Legis. (2021) (New
Mexico) 164, 199
Emergency Medical Treatment and Labor Act, 42 USC § 1395dd (1986) 185
End of Life Option Act, Cal Health and Safety Code §§ 443–443.22 (2015)
(California) 6, 115, 146, 199
End-of-Life Options Act, Colo Rev Stat §§ 25-48-101–25-48-123 (2017) (Colorado) 6,
115, 158, 199
H.B. 3074, 2015 Leg., 84th Sess. (Tex. 2015) 194
H.B. 284, 2019 Leg., 66th Sess. (Mont. 2019) 193, 200
H.B. 3158, 2019 Leg., 86th Sess. (Tex. 2019) 194
H.B. 3369, 2019 Leg., 86th Sess. (Tex. 2019) 194
H.B. 3597, 2019 Leg., 86th Sess. (Tex. 2019) 194
H.B. 3743, 2019 Leg., 86th Sess. (Tex. 2019) 194
H.B. 995, 2019 Leg., 85th Sess. (Tex. 2019) 194
H.B. 2419, 2020 Leg., 66th Sess. (Wash. 2020) 261
H.B. 2609, 2021 Leg., 87th Sess. (Tex. 2021) 201
H.B. 3099, 2021 Leg., 87th Sess. (Tex. 2021) 201
Health Care Decisions Act, Va Code § 54.1-2990 (2018) (Virginia) 185
Ky Rev Stat Ann, § 211.296 (2019) (Kentucky) 3
Medical Aid in Dying for the Terminally Ill Act, NJ Stat Ann §§ 26:16-1–26:16-20
(2019) (New Jersey) 1, 6, 115, 199
Ohio Rev Code Ann, § 3701.36 (2019) (Ohio) 3
Our Care, Our Choice Act 2018, Haw Rev Stat §§ 327-1–327-25 (2018) (Hawaii) 6,
115, 118, 133, 158, 199
Patient Choice and Control at End of Life Act, Vt Stat Ann §§ 5281–93 (2013)
(Vermont) 6, 115, 143, 158, 199
Reporting and Collecting Medical Aid-in-Dying Medication Information, 6 CCR
1009-4 (2017) (Colorado, Department of Public Health and Environment) 115
S.B. 303, 2013 Leg., 83rd Sess. (Tex. 2013) 199
S.B. 11, 2017 Leg., 85th Sess. (Tex. 2017) 195
S.B. 2089, 2019 Leg., 86th Sess. (Tex. 2019) 194
S.B. 2129, 2019 Leg., 86th Sess. (Tex. 2019) 194
S.B. 2355, 2019 Leg., 86th Sess. (Tex. 2019) 194
S.B. 290, 2021 Leg., 67th Sess. (Mont. 2021) 193
S.B. 917, 2021 Leg., 87th Sess. (Tex. 2021) 201
S.B. 1381, 2021 Leg., 87th Sess. (Tex. 2021) 201
S.B. 1944, 2021 Leg., 87th Sess. (Tex. 2021) 201
Texas Advance Directives Act, Tex Health and Safety Code § 166.046 (1999) (Texas)
15, 180–201, 251, 260, 263, 268, 272

Texas Constitution 196
Uniform Determination of Death Act, Nev Rev Stat § 451.008 (2017) (Nevada) 200
Uniform Health Care Decisions Act, Cal Probate Code §§ 4735, 4740 (2000)
  (California) 185

End-of-Life Law Reform

Context and Challenges

Ben P. White and Lindy Willmott*

INTRODUCTION

The law that regulates end-of-life decision-making is the subject of ongoing scrutiny and is constantly changing internationally. Although trajectories and timelines may be different in different parts of the world, there is constant pressure to reform in this area. Even if there are not current proposals for change or review of the law initiated by the State (or individual members of parliament), there is persistent agitation for reform from key stakeholders, and the state of end-of-life law is the subject of ongoing public debate.

The most obvious example is whether law should change to allow assisted dying (or to change or repeal current assisted dying laws where they exist). Recent developments around the time of writing include new laws being passed to permit assisted dying in the Australian states of Western Australia[1] and Tasmania;[2] New Jersey[3] and Maine[4] in the United States; and New Zealand.[5] There have also been significant judicial decisions that have recently changed the law on assisted dying. One example is the *Truchon* case,[6] which successfully challenged limits on access to assisted dying under both the Canadian federal law[7] and the

---

* The authors would like to acknowledge the helpful research assistance of Emily Bartels.

[1] Voluntary Assisted Dying Act 2019 (WA).

[2] End-of-Life Choices (Voluntary Assisted Dying) Act 2021 (Tas).

[3] Medical Aid in Dying for the Terminally Ill Act, NJ Stat Ann §§ 26:16-1–26:16-20 (2019) (New Jersey).

[4] An Act to Enact the Maine Death with Dignity Act, 22 Me Rev Stat Ann § 2140 (2019) (Maine).

[5] End of Life Choice Act 2019 (NZ).

[6] *Truchon v. Canada (Attorney General)* [2019] QCCS 3792. This case is discussed further in Chapter 2. See also the discussion in Ben P. White et al., 'Comparative and Critical Analysis of Key Eligibility Criteria for Voluntary Assisted Dying under Five Legal Frameworks' (2021) *University of New South Wales Law Journal* (in press).

[7] The eligibility requirement in Criminal Code RSC 1985, c. C-46, s. 241.2(2)(d) (introduced by Bill C-14, An Act to Amend the Criminal Code and to Make Related Amendments to Other

Québec law.[8] This decision prompted the federal government to pass amendments to that law via Bill C-7.[9] Other examples are the German constitutional ruling[10] which struck down laws prohibiting assisted suicide services, and the English case of *Newby*,[11] the most recent in a series of such cases arguing that the existing prohibition on assisted dying breaches the European Convention on Human Rights.[12]

But end-of-life law, as we outline below, is not just about – or even mostly about – assisted dying. There has also been ongoing reform or debates in relation to other areas of law that deal with death and dying. One of the other main legal issues in this field is the law that governs the provision, withholding or withdrawing of potentially life-sustaining treatment. Although perhaps less topical than assisted dying, these laws continue to evolve with ongoing change to the relevant adult guardianship, mental capacity or medical treatment legislation. Hong Kong is consulting on new legislative proposals to recognise advance directives in statute,[13] and there were recent sweeping changes to adult guardianship and medical treatment legislation in the Australian state of Victoria.[14] In addition, there were new or updated laws dealing with withholding and withdrawing life-sustaining treatment in Italy[15] and Taiwan.[16] There have also been important judicial developments. The Indian Supreme Court declared that withholding and withdrawing life-sustaining treatment may be permissible in certain circumstances.[17] In the United Kingdom, the Supreme Court recently settled ongoing debate concluding that court approval is

---

Acts (Medical Assistance in Dying) SC 2016, c. 3) that the person's 'natural death has become reasonably foreseeable' was held to be invalid.

[8] The eligibility requirement in An Act Respecting End-of-Life Care, RSQ 2014, c. S-32.0001 (Québec), s. 26(3) that the person be at the 'end of life' was held to be invalid.

[9] Bill C-7, An Act to Amend the Criminal Code (Medical Assistance in Dying), SC 2021, c. 2.

[10] Second Senate of the Federal Constitutional Court, Zum Urteil des Zweiten Senats vom. 26 February 2020, Bundesverfassungsgericht.

[11] *R (Newby)* v. *Secretary of State for Justice* [2019] EWHC 3118.

[12] Convention for the Protection of Human Rights and Fundamental Freedoms, agreed at Rome, 4 November 1950, in force 3 September 1953, 213 UNTS 221. Other recent cases are: *R (Conway)* v. *Secretary of State for Justice* [2020] QB 1; *R (T)* v. *Secretary of State for Justice* [2018] EWHC 2615; *R (Lamb)* v. *Secretary of State for Justice* [2019] EWHC 3606.

[13] 'End-of-Life Care: Legislative Proposals on Advance Directives and Dying in Place', Consultation Document from the Food and Health Bureau (2019 Government of the Hong Kong Special Administrative Region), www.gov.hk/en/residents/government/publication/consultation.

[14] Guardianship and Administration Act 2019 (Vic) (in force in 2020); Medical Treatment Planning and Decisions Act 2016 (Vic) (in force in 2018).

[15] Rules on Informed Consent and Advance Treatment Provisions 2017 (Law N. 219) (Italy).

[16] Patient Right to Autonomy Act 2019 (Taiwan).

[17] *Common Cause (A Regd. Society)* v. *Union of India and Another* (Unreported, Supreme Court of India, Civil Original Jurisdiction, Writ Petition (Civil) No. 215 of 2005, 9 March 2018).

not required to withdraw or withhold clinically assisted nutrition and hydration from a patient with a 'prolonged disorder of consciousness'.[18]

Another area of end-of-life law – that governing palliative care – is also changing albeit less rapidly than the preceding two areas. In 2016, France introduced a law that allowed terminally ill patients to access continuous deep sedation.[19] A new Korean law, in addition to dealing with decisions about life-sustaining treatment, specifically established a framework to improve the provision of palliative care in that country.[20] Other examples are the recently passed laws in New Jersey,[21] Kentucky[22] and Ohio[23] in the United States which establish advisory councils with the mission of enhancing awareness of and access to palliative care.

Unsurprisingly, much has been written about whether these different areas of end-of-life law should be reformed and, if so, what should be the optimal legal position.[24] However, the barriers and facilitators of such changes – law reform perspectives – have been neglected in the literature.[25] Yet this topic is vitally important. Many of these changes to the law represent seismic shifts in how society regulates end-of-life decision-making. But we know very little about why some attempts to change the law fail and others succeed. A classic example of this is assisted dying in Australia. There have been four laws in Australia permitting assisted

---

[18] *An NHS Trust* v. *Y* [2018] UKSC 46. This case, and the reform efforts that preceded it, are examined in Chapter 10. See also the discussion of this case in Chapter 11.

[19] Loi 2016-87 du 2 février 2016 créant de nouveaux droits en faveur des malades et des personnes en fin de vie. Journal Officiel 2016. 0028 [Law No. 2016-87 of 2 February 2016 on Creating New Rights for the Sick and People at the End of Life] (France) JO, 2 February 2016. This law is an amendment to the French Public Health Code. See also Ruth Horn, 'The "French Exception": The Right to Continuous Deep Sedation at End of Life' (2018) 44 *Journal of Medical Ethics* 204–5.

[20] Act on Hospice and Palliative Care and Decisions on Life-Sustaining Treatment for Patients at the End of Life, Act No. 14013 (Korea).

[21] NJ Rev Stat Ann, § 26.2H-5r (2019) (New Jersey).

[22] Ky Rev Stat Ann, § 211.296 (2019) (Kentucky).

[23] Ohio Rev Code Ann, § 3701.36 (2019) (Ohio).

[24] See, for example, those arguing in favour of assisted dying: Sheila McLean, *Assisted Dying: Reflections on the Need for Law Reform* (New York: Routledge-Cavendish, 2007); Hazel Biggs, *Euthanasia, Death with Dignity and the Law* (Oxford: Hart Publishing, 2001); Jocelyn Downie, *Dying Justice: A Case for Decriminalizing Euthanasia and Assisted Suicide in Canada* (Toronto: University of Toronto Press, 2004). In relation to those arguing against changing the law, see, for example, Margaret Somerville, *Death Talk: The Case against Euthanasia and Physician Assisted Suicide*, 2nd ed. (Montreal: McGill University Press, 2014); John Keown, *Euthanasia, Ethics and Public Policy: An Argument against Legalisation*, 2nd ed. (Cambridge: Cambridge University Press, 2018). There are also books that present both sides of the debate including Emily Jackson and John Keown, *Debating Euthanasia* (Oxford: Hart Publishing, 2011).

[25] There are a few notable exceptions, although these books tend to focus on assisted dying and only in the United States: see, for example, Daniel Hillyard and John Dombrink, *Dying Right: The Death with Dignity Movement* (New York: Routledge, 2001); Nina Clark, *The Politics of Physician Assisted Suicide* (New York: Routledge, 1997); Howard Ball, *At Liberty to Die: The Battle for Death with Dignity in America* (New York: New York University Press, 2012).

dying. The first was the Rights of the Terminally Ill Act 1995 (NT) in the Northern Territory, which was promptly overturned by the federal government nine months later.[26] The other three laws – the Voluntary Assisted Dying Act 2017 (Vic) in Victoria, the Voluntary Assisted Dying Act 2019 (WA) in Western Australia and the End-of-Life Choices (Voluntary Assisted Dying) Act 2021 (Tas) in Tasmania – were passed some twenty years later. Why did these four laws pass, but more than forty other attempts to change the law in Australian Parliaments in the intervening two decades fail?[27] Similar questions arise in Canada. Why did the Canadian Supreme Court decision of *Carter*[28] permit medical assistance in dying despite a contrary decision of the same court twenty years earlier in *Rodriguez*?[29] There are other examples across the globe. The question of why end-of-life law changes sometimes but not others is critically important. This is particularly so given the historical trend of changing law in this sensitive area being very difficult to achieve.

WHAT IS END-OF-LIFE LAW?

This book is about reform of end-of-life law so some attempt to define the boundaries of this field is needed. For our purposes, we consider end-of-life law as that which deals with decision-making leading up to death but does not include the law that operates after that time. This latter exclusion means that the law governing organ and tissue donation by a deceased person and the law governing the determination of death fall outside this book. Although important legal issues in their own right, they principally deal with decisions made *after* a person's death (or as part of certifying their death), rather than as part of end-of-life decision-making, and so won't be considered further.

On this approach, end-of-life law is comprised of three main areas alluded to earlier: the law that governs assisted dying, withholding or withdrawing life-sustaining treatment and palliative care. However, as we will see, there are some

---

[26] Euthanasia Laws Act 1997 (Cth).
[27] As at the end of 2015, fifty-one bills dealing with assisted dying had been introduced into various Australian Parliaments since 1993. Seven of these bills sought to remove the prohibition imposed by the Commonwealth Government on territories (as opposed to states) legislating in this area and five sought to hold a referendum on law reform. The remaining thirty-nine bills proposed a model for law reform permitting some form of assisted dying: Lindy Willmott, Ben White, Christopher Stackpoole, Kelly Purser and Andrew McGee, '(Failed) Voluntary Euthanasia Law Reform in Australia: Two Decades of Trends, Models and Politics' (2016) 39 *University of New South Wales Law Journal* 1–46 at 10. Since that paper was published, there have been a number of other assisted dying bills considered by Australian Parliaments including the Death with Dignity Bill 2016 (SA), the Voluntary Assisted Dying Bill 2017 (NSW) and the Voluntary Assisted Dying Bill 2016 (Tas), bringing the total number of Australian Bills seeking to legalise assisted dying to over forty: Ben White and Lindy Willmott, 'Future of Assisted Dying Reform in Australia' (2018) 42 *Australian Health Review* 616–20.
[28] *Carter v. Canada (Attorney General)* [2015] 1 SCR 331.
[29] *Rodriguez v. British Columbia (Attorney General)* [1993] 3 SCR 519.

types of end-of-life decisions that challenge this categorisation and test boundaries. Below we consider briefly these three areas and provide some commentary about terminology so as to guide consistent discussion of these topics in the chapters that follow. Terminology is important in this area to avoid the disputes that are sometimes caused by the use of different language. We also note that it is, of course, not possible to outline the law internationally on these topics comprehensively, so the discussion that follows is necessarily general.

Assisted Dying

Assisted dying is a term increasingly used to describe collectively the practices of both voluntary euthanasia and assisted suicide. We use the terminology of assisted dying as a global concept but, for reasons of clarity, will briefly define other terms commonly used in this debate.[30] We consider euthanasia to be when, for the purpose of relieving suffering, a person performs an action with the intention of ending the life of another person. It is voluntary euthanasia when this act is done in response to a request for it to happen from a competent person. An example is when a patient receives an injection that will end their life, at their competent request, from a doctor. Assisted suicide is when a competent person dies after another provides them with the means or knowledge to kill themselves. If it is a doctor or physician providing that assistance, this is often called physician-assisted suicide. An illustration of this is when a doctor provides a person with a prescription to obtain medication that, if taken, will end their life.

A note about terminology for assisted dying also requires an acknowledgement that there are a variety of terms used in different parts of the world. Examples include voluntary assisted dying (often used in Australia), medical assistance in dying (the Canadian term), aid in dying or medical aid in dying (increasingly used in the United States) and euthanasia (the terminology generally adopted in Belgium and the Netherlands). While contributing authors have tended to use local terminology in their chapters, we generally adopt the more generic 'assisted dying' in this chapter.

At present, assisted dying is lawful in very few parts of the world. In most places, depending on the circumstances, local law may regard it as the crime of murder, manslaughter or assisting suicide. However, there has been an international trend to reform the law and permit assisted dying. In Europe, assisted dying is lawful under certain circumstances in the Netherlands,[31] Belgium,[32]

---

[30] In defining these terms, we draw on Ben White and Lindy Willmott, 'How Should Australia Regulate Voluntary Euthanasia and Assisted Suicide?' (2012) 20 *Journal of Law and Medicine* 410–38.

[31] Termination of Life on Request and Assisted Suicide (Review Procedures) Act of 1 April 2002 (Netherlands).

[32] Law of 28 May 2002 on Euthanasia, *Belgian Official Gazette* (22 June 2002) 2002/ 09590, 28515.

Luxembourg,[33] Switzerland[34] and Germany.[35] In the United States, there are now ten jurisdictions where physician-assisted suicide is legal: Oregon,[36] Washington,[37] Vermont,[38] California,[39] Colorado,[40] the District of Columbia,[41] Hawaii,[42] New Jersey[43] and Maine[44] through legislation, and in Montana by way of court decision.[45] In Canada, in response to *Carter*,[46] the Canadian Parliament amended its Criminal Code to permit medical assistance in dying in 2016.[47] Assisted dying is also lawful in the Australian state of Victoria[48] (and will be lawful in Western Australia and Tasmania too[49]) and in the South American country of Colombia.[50]

Withholding or Withdrawing Potentially Life-Sustaining Treatment

Withholding or withdrawing potentially life-sustaining treatment occurs where treatment that may be necessary to keep a person alive is not provided or is stopped after initially being provided. An example of withdrawing such treatment is

[33] Law of 16 March 2009 on Euthanasia and Assisted Suicide (Luxembourg).

[34] Criminal Code 1937 (Switzerland). This Act does not establish a regime facilitating assisted dying but rather makes assisting a suicide an offence only if it is done for 'selfish' motives.

[35] Second Senate of the Federal Constitutional Court, Zum Urteil des Zweiten Senats vom. 26 February 2020, Bundesverfassungsgericht. This case did not establish a regime facilitating assisted dying but rather struck down laws prohibiting assisted suicide services on constitutional grounds, concluding that such a prohibition in practice precluded a person's ability to seek assisted suicide.

[36] Death with Dignity Act, Or Rev Stat §§ 127.800–127.995 (1994) (Oregon).

[37] Death with Dignity Act, Wash Rev Code §§ 70.245.010–70.245.903 (2008) (Washington).

[38] Patient Choice and Control at End of Life Act, Vt Stat Ann §§ 5281–93 (2013) (Vermont).

[39] End of Life Option Act, Cal Health and Safety Code §§ 443–443.22 (2015) (California).

[40] End-of-Life Options Act, Colo Rev Stat §§ 25-48-101–25-48-123 (2017) (Colorado).

[41] Death with Dignity Act of 2016, DC Code §§ 7–661 (2017) (District of Columbia).

[42] Our Care, Our Choice Act 2018, Haw Rev Stat §§ 327-1–327-25 (2018) (Hawaii).

[43] Medical Aid in Dying for the Terminally Ill Act, NJ Stat Ann §§ 26:16-1–26:16-20 (2019) (New Jersey).

[44] An Act to Enact the Maine Death with Dignity Act, 22 Me Rev Stat Ann § 2140 (2019) (Maine).

[45] *Baxter* v. *State*, 224 P 3d 1211 (Mont. 2009).

[46] *Carter* v. *Canada (Attorney General)* [2015] 1 SCR 331.

[47] An Act to Amend the Criminal Code and to Make Related Amendments to Other Acts (Medical Assistance in Dying) SC 2016 (Canada). This federal legislation was preceded by Québec law permitting assisted dying: An Act Respecting End-of-Life Care, RSQ 2014, c. S-32.0001 (Québec).

[48] Voluntary Assisted Dying Act 2017 (Vic).

[49] Voluntary Assisted Dying Act 2019 (WA); End-of-Life Choices (Voluntary Assisted Dying) Act 2021 (Tas). The Tasmanian Act has passed but has not yet commenced to allow time for implementation planning.

[50] A court decision in Colombia permitted assisted dying in 1997 (Sentence C-239 (1997), Ref. Expedient D-1490 (Constitutional Court of the Republic of Colombia, 20 May 1997)), which was followed by government regulations to facilitate the practice in 2015: Protocolo Para La Aplicación Del Procedimiento De Eutanasia En Colombia 2015 [Government of Colombia, Report 2015, Protocol for the Application of the Procedure of Euthanasia in Colombia] (Colombia), www.minsalud.gov.co/sites/rid/Lists/BibliotecaDigital/RIDE/DE/CA/Protocolo-aplicacion-procedimiento-eutanasia-colombia.pdf.

removing a ventilator from a person who has a prolonged disorder of consciousness or is in a state of post-coma unresponsiveness. Withholding treatment could happen when a decision is made not to provide clinically assisted nutrition and hydration (such as through a tube inserted into the stomach) to a person with advanced dementia who is no longer able to take food or hydration orally.

These decisions can be lawful in most Western countries although the law does vary internationally. There are broadly three situations when this is permitted. The first is when a competent person decides to refuse potentially life-sustaining treatment. Legal systems generally respect this right to refuse medical treatment absent any other authorisation to provide it. A person's decision to not receive treatment must be respected even if that treatment is necessary to stay alive and even if the refusal of treatment is contrary to medical advice.[51] Most jurisdictions also recognise advance directives which allow a person to make these decisions when competent, which take effect later after that ability to decide has been lost.[52]

The second situation is when a person lacks decision-making capacity, and their substitute or surrogate decision-maker refuses treatment. Although not as widely recognised as the first situation, many Western countries facilitate this decision-making through adult guardianship, medical treatment or mental capacity laws.[53] In the case of children who lack capacity to decide for themselves, parents are generally recognised as having this power.[54]

Finally, a doctor can also make the decision to withhold or withdraw potentially life-sustaining treatment. Again, this varies between countries, but the law generally does not require doctors to provide treatment that will not benefit a patient. This is commonly framed as allowing a doctor to not provide potentially life-sustaining treatment if they determine that treatment is not in a patient's best interests or is 'futile' or 'non-beneficial'.[55]

---

[51] Lindy Willmott, Ben White and Shih-Ning Then, 'Withholding and Withdrawing Life-Sustaining Medical Treatment', in Ben White, Fiona McDonald and Lindy Willmott (eds.), *Health Law in Australia*, 3rd ed. (Rozelle: Thomson Reuters, 2018) 571–623 at [14.40]; Alan Meisel, Kathy Ceminara and Thaddeus Pope, *The Right to Die: The Law of End-of-Life Decision Making*, 3rd ed. (Online: Aspen Publishers, 2004 (updated annually)) at ch. 12; Jonathan Herring, *Medical Law and Ethics*, 7th ed. (Oxford: Oxford University Press, 2018) 571–2; Jocelyn Downie, 'End of Life Law and Policy', in Joanna Erdman, Vanessa Gruben and Erin Nelson (eds.), *Canadian Health Law and Policy*, 5th ed. (Toronto: LexisNexis, 2017).

[52] Willmott, White and Then, 'Withholding and Withdrawing Life-Sustaining Medical Treatment', [14.100], [14.150]; Meisel, Ceminara and Pope, *The Right to Die*, ch. 7; Herring, *Medical Law and Ethics*, 216–18, 512–13, 526; Downie, 'End of Life Law and Policy'.

[53] Willmott, White and Then, 'Withholding and Withdrawing Life-Sustaining Medical Treatment', [14.110]–[14.260]; Meisel, Ceminara and Pope, *The Right to Die*, ch. 8.

[54] Willmott, White and Then, 'Withholding and Withdrawing Life-Sustaining Medical Treatment', [14.280]–[14.290]; Meisel, Ceminara and Pope, *The Right to Die*, ch. 9; Herring, *Medical Law and Ethics*, 187–93, 530–4; Downie, 'End of Life Law and Policy'.

[55] Willmott, White and Then, 'Withholding and Withdrawing Life-Sustaining Medical Treatment', [14.50], [14.70]–[14.90]; Meisel, Ceminara and Pope, *The Right to Die*, ch. 13; Herring, *Medical Law and Ethics*, 526–34, 569–71; Lindy Willmott, Ben White and Jocelyn

Most Western legal systems distinguish between assisted dying (generally unlawful, subject to the above discussion) and withholding and withdrawing life-sustaining treatment (can be lawful). Not providing treatment can be lawful because it involves a *failure to treat* when there is no duty to provide that treatment. There is no duty because one of the three situations outlined above (refusal by a competent person, substitute or surrogate decision-maker refusal or doctor considers treatment is not beneficial) has arisen. By contrast, assisted dying involves taking *active steps* to end another's life (or assisting the person to do that themselves) and so breaches the criminal law.

Palliative Care

Law's role in this area arose because of concerns that otherwise appropriate palliative care could accelerate death. Although contested,[56] some considered that medication such as opioids, when given in sufficient doses needed to manage pain and symptoms, could suppress respiration and cause or hasten a person's death.[57] This could be seen as 'active steps' to end a patient's life and therefore unlawful.

The law's response was to draw on the ethical principle of the doctrine of double effect. This reasoning sanctions actions done with a good intention even if they may result in a foreseen bad outcome. Accordingly, the law in most Western countries protects doctors (and potentially others involved in providing the palliative care) when they provide appropriate palliative medication with the intention of relieving pain or symptoms, even if it might hasten death.[58] We note though that some argue that a doctor's intention is difficult to ascertain or may be mixed in terms of motivations, and so the operation of this law in practice may be unclear.[59]

Downie, 'Withholding and Withdrawal of "Futile" Life-Sustaining Treatment: Unilateral Medical Decision-Making in Australia and New Zealand' (2013) 20 *Journal of Law and Medicine* 907–24; Downie, 'End of Life Law and Policy'.

[56] For example, Fohr argues that properly administered palliative care does not hasten death and the respiratory depressant effect of some opioids can be counteracted and managed: S. A. Fohr, 'The Double Effect of Pain Medication: Separating Myth from Reality' (1998) 1 *Journal of Palliative Medicine* 315–28 at 316. See also Elaine M. Beller, Mieke L. van Driel, Leanne McGregor, Shani Truong and Geoffrey Mitchell, 'Palliative Pharmacological Sedation for Terminally Ill Adults (Review)' (2015) 1 *Cochrane Database of Systematic Reviews* CD010206.

[57] Ben White, Lindy Willmott and Michael Ashby, 'Palliative Care, Double Effect and the Law in Australia' (2011) 41 *Internal Medicine Journal* 485–92; Sotirios Santatzoglou, Alison Kate Lillie, Anthony Wrigley, Sue Ashby, Andrew Moore and Sue Read, 'Law, Ethics and End-of-Life Care: The Policy and Practice Interface in England' (2017) 23 *International Journal of Palliative Medicine* 213–18 at 216.

[58] See generally, Ben White and Lindy Willmott, 'Double Effect and Palliative Care Excuses', in Ben White, Fiona McDonald and Lindy Willmott (eds.), *Health Law in Australia*, 3rd ed. (Rozelle: Thomson Reuters, 2018) 625–46; Meisel, Ceminara and Pope, *The Right to Die*, 529–30, 536–7.

[59] Charles Douglas, Ian Kerridge and Rachel Ankeny, 'Managing Intentions: The End-of-Life Administration of Analgesics and Sedatives, and the Possibility of Slow Euthanasia' (2008) 22 *Bioethics* 388–96.

Other End-of-Life Practices

There are also 'new' end-of-life practices which challenge the categorisation of end-of-life law into these three areas. Sometimes this is because it may be unclear as to which category a practice belongs. An example of this is voluntary stopping eating and drinking ('VSED') by a competent adult with the intention of bringing about their death. For some, this is potentially lawful as it is akin to (if not equal to) withholding and withdrawing life-sustaining treatment.[60] Others regard this as a form of suicide, and those involved risk the charge of assisted suicide.[61] In addition, this practice may also cross over into the palliative care arena if palliative medication is provided to manage pain and symptoms while the person dies.[62]

Another end-of-life practice, controversial in some jurisdictions, is what is variously called deep continuous sedation, terminal sedation or palliative sedation. This is sometimes used when existing palliative care cannot manage pain or symptoms effectively and so medication is provided to sedate the person towards the end of their life.[63] This may not only involve palliative care but can also include the withholding or withdrawal of medical treatment including artificial nutrition and hydration.[64] Some consider it a form of 'slow euthanasia' when these two steps are combined.[65]

It is not necessary to resolve the issue of how to characterise these and other end-of-life practices in legal terms nor is it necessary to resolve the boundaries of their lawfulness. However, we note them here to acknowledge that the contours and categories of end-of-life law are evolving and intersecting.

---

[60] Ben White, Lindy Willmott and Julian Savulescu, 'Voluntary Palliated Starvation: A Lawful and Ethical Way to Die?' (2014) 22 *Journal of Law and Medicine* 376–86; Jocelyn Downie, 'An Alternative to Medical Assistance in Dying? The Legal Status of Voluntary Stopping Eating and Drinking (VSED)' (2018) 1 *Canadian Journal of Bioethics* 48–58; Thaddeus Mason Pope and Lindsey E. Anderson, 'Voluntarily Stopping Eating and Drinking: A Legal Treatment Option at the End of Life' (2011) 17 *Widener Law Review* 363–427.

[61] Ralf Jox, Isra Black, Gian Domenico Borasio and Johanna Anneser, 'Voluntary Stopping of Eating and Drinking: Is Medical Support Ethically Justified?' (2017) 15 *BMC Medicine* 186. Note, however, that McGee and Franklin argue that even if voluntary stopping of eating and drinking may be a form of suicide, those participating are not guilty of *assisting* a suicide: Andrew McGee and Franklin Miller, 'Advice and Care for Patients Who Die by Voluntary Stopping Eating and Drinking Is Not Assisted Suicide' (2017) 15 *BMC Medicine* 1–4.

[62] White, Willmott and Savulescu, 'Voluntary Palliated Starvation'.

[63] Nathan Cherny, Lukas Radbruch and the Board of the European Association for Palliative Care, 'European Association for Palliative Care (EAPC) Recommended Framework for the Use of Sedation in Palliative Care' (2009) 23 *Palliative Medicine* 581–93; Beller et al., 'Palliative Pharmacological Sedation for Terminally Ill Adults'.

[64] For a recent legal analysis of when palliative sedation also involves not providing artificial nutrition and hydration, see Jocelyn Downie and Richard Liu, 'The Legal Status of Deep and Continuous Palliative Sedation without Artificial Nutrition and Hydration' (2018) 12 *McGill Journal of Law and Health* 29–66.

[65] J. Andrew Billings and Susan D. Block, 'Slow Euthanasia' (1996) 12 *Journal of Palliative Care* 21.

Concluding Thoughts on End-of-Life Law

What emerges from even a superficial review of end-of-life law internationally is that there are significant similarities, at least at a macro level, in how Western nations regulate this field of care. This is not surprising as modern medicine and the organisation of health care in these countries, as well as societal trends, for example towards patient consumerism, pose the same sorts of questions for lawmakers. If medical treatment can continue to prolong life for extended periods, when should that stop and who should decide? If pain or other symptoms cannot be treated, should a person have an opportunity to end their life and, if so, in what circumstances?[66]

While these global issues and policy responses in different countries have many similarities, there is also a divergence of approaches. Each country has its own legal, political and societal culture that inevitably shapes local laws. For example, in his chapter, Orentlicher argues that a US preference for legal certainty by drawing 'bright lines' for decision-making can be contrasted with a European approach, at least in some countries, where there appears to be greater tolerance for laws that permit more discretion in decision-making.[67] The presence or absence of human rights instruments, and their relative robustness, has also shaped end-of-life law locally.[68]

We conclude this section by noting that ongoing change in end-of-life law, or at least efforts to change that law, lies ahead. This is one reason why we consider that this book about law reform in this area is important. For example, there is a slow but steady trend internationally to legalise assisted dying. There may also be a trend towards greater regulation of end-of-life care, reflecting a wider trend for more regulation of health matters and human activity generally. Illustrations of this include ongoing changes in adult guardianship, mental capacity and medical treatment legislation, but this trend is also evident in the increased use of the courts as arbiters in end-of-life matters.[69]

---

[66] These legal similarities identified in Western nations do not persist when compared with some other parts of the world where more pressing health law issues, such as basic access to health care, arise. In other words, dealing with laws about the end of life presupposes a certain standard of medical care, that is, that advanced life-sustaining treatment is available to prolong life and so issues of when to stop or not start it arise. Likewise, analysing laws about palliative care assumes that such care is available to patients.

[67] See Chapter 7.

[68] For example, see Chapter 2, and the role of the Canadian Charter of Rights and Freedoms in prompting assisted dying reform: Canadian Charter of Rights and Freedoms, Canada Act 1982 (UK) c. 11, sch. B, pt. 1, ss. 7, 15.

[69] See, for example, the high-profile cases of Charlie Gard and Alfie Evans. In relation to Charlie Gard, see: *Great Ormond Street Hospital v. Yates and Others* [2017] EWHC 972; *Yates and Another v. Great Ormond Street Hospital for Children NHS Foundation Trust and Another (Rev 1)* [2017] EWCA Civ 410; *In the Case of Charlie Gard (Unreported decision of Supreme Court of the United Kingdom*, 19 June 2017, Lady Hale, Lord Kerr and Lord Wilson); *Gard and Another*

THE CHALLENGES OF END-OF-LIFE LAW REFORM

Law reform means changing the law. As the chapters in this book illustrate, this can occur through legislation or judicial decisions, and sometimes even through changes to policy, especially if 'law' is broadly construed. However, much of the law reform literature is framed in terms of it being not simply a change to the law, but rather one that *improves* it.[70] The concept of law reform, therefore, is not a value-neutral one and carries with it some positive endorsement that the change to the law that has occurred represents progress. There will always be subjectivity in judgements as to whether or not legal change is positive and this is no doubt particularly apparent in controversial areas such as end-of-life decision-making. Some authors in this collection make clear their views on the merits of the law reform they are analysing but it is not necessary for this book overall to take a stance on this issue.

The challenge of achieving law reform, regardless of the field being considered, is well-known and a long-standing issue.[71] In England and Wales, and in other common law jurisdictions, the failure of existing mechanisms (primarily government departments and ad hoc review committees) to ensure law kept pace with society and its values led to calls for, and then the establishment of, permanent law reform commissions.[72] Beginning in the 1960s but continuing on for some decades, there was a movement to establish these commissions, initially with the very lofty goal of keeping *all* the law under review. This ambition has not been realised in practice with the tendency instead being to focus on discrete areas of law.[73]

---

v. *United Kingdom* [2017] ECHR 605; *Great Ormond Street Hospital v. Yates and Another* [2017] EWHC 1909. In relation to Alfie Evans, see: *Alder Hey Children's NHS Foundation Trust v. Evans and Another* [2018] EWHC 308; *E (A Child) (Rev 1)* [2018] EWCA Civ 550; *Evans v. United Kingdom – 14238/18 (inadmissible)* [2018] ECHR 297; *Alder Hey Children's NHS Foundation Trust v. Evans and Others* [2018] EWHC 818; *Evans and Another v. Alder Hey Children's NHS Foundation Trust and Others* [2018] EWCA Civ 805; *Evans v. United Kingdom – 18770/18* [2018] ECHR 357; *Alder Hey Children's NHS Foundation Trust v. Evans and Another* [2018] EWHC 953; *Evans and Another v. Alder Hey Children's NHS Foundation Trust and Another (Rev 1)* [2018] EWCA Civ 984.

[70] See, for example, the discussion of what law reform means in Hurlburt's foundational work: William H. Hurlburt, *Law Reform Commissions in the United Kingdom, Australia and Canada* (Edmonton: Juriliber, 1986), ch. 1.

[71] See, for example, the various discussions in Matthew Dyson, James Lee and Shona Wilson Stark (eds.), *Fifty Years of the Law Commissions: The Dynamics of Law Reform* (Oxford: Hart Publishing, 2016); Brian Opeskin and David Weisbrot (eds.), *The Promise of Law Reform* (Leichhardt: The Federation Press, 2005); Hurlburt, *Law Reform Commissions in the United Kingdom, Australia and Canada*.

[72] Hurlburt, *Law Reform Commissions in the United Kingdom, Australia and Canada*, 15–50. The classic call for a permanent full-time body devoted to keeping all of the law under review is Gerald Gardiner and Andrew Martin, 'The Machinery of Law Reform', in Gerald Gardiner and Andrew Martin (eds.), *Law Reform Now* (London: V. Gollancz, 1963).

[73] This more limited focus has been the case from the early days of law reform commissions: see, for example, Gordon J. Borrie, 'Law Reform: A Damp Squib?' (Inaugural Lecture, University

However, law reform commissions have made significant gains in improving many areas of law, including some of those which have been regarded as politically difficult.[74] The modern era has seen increasing use of other additional vehicles for reform such as ad hoc commissions of inquiry, parliamentary inquiries or single-topic commissions or committees, leading one writer to describe law reform now as 'a crowded field'.[75] Changes in law, this time via the courts, have also been driven by the growing impact of human rights instruments such as the European Convention on Human Rights.[76] Nevertheless, despite the various machinery which can change the law, reform is often slow and difficult, and the process can be opaque.

The nature of end-of-life law makes these generic challenges of law reform even more significant. First, reforming end-of-life law requires engaging with issues of obvious gravity. This area of law literally regulates matters of life and death and so choices about legal frameworks have significant and wide-reaching implications for individuals and society. Secondly, end-of-life issues give rise to complex ethical questions. They include weighing rights to self-determination and autonomy (and what they mean) and how they compete with the sanctity or value of life (if they do).[77] These debates also give rise to vexed concepts such as dignity, which is routinely used by both sides of an argument as supporting their case.[78]

Thirdly, there is a large body of complex empirical evidence about how end-of-life decisions are made, particularly in relation to assisted dying. Digesting and understanding what this evidence means and how it should be interpreted when making decisions about law and policy is difficult. Fourthly, the existing law governing end-of-life care which is being considered for reform is often already very complex. An example here is adult guardianship or mental capacity laws dealing

---

of Birmingham, Birmingham, 1970), 2. See also R. Rice, 'Editorial: The Law Commission's First 20 Years' (1986) 136 *New Law Journal* 201–2.

[74] For example, a report by the Australian Law Reform Commission on human tissue transplantation in 1977 was adopted throughout Australia and subsequently translated into foreign languages and used in several countries of South America to develop laws on the same subject: Michael Kirby, 'Are We There Yet?', in Brian Opeskin and David Weisbrot (eds.), *The Promise of Law Reform* (Leichhardt: The Federation Press, 2005), at 433, 439.

[75] David Weisbrot, 'The Future for Institutional Law Reform', in Brian Opeskin and David Weisbrot (eds.), *The Promise of Law Reform* (Leichhardt: The Federation Press, 2005), at 20.

[76] For examples in the end-of-life area, see *Carter* v. *Canada (Attorney General)* [2015] 1 SCR 331 (discussed in Chapter 2) and *R (Purdy)* v. *Director of Public Prosecutions* [2010] 1 AC 345.

[77] See, for example, Ben White, Lindy Willmott, Eliana Close and Jocelyn Downie, 'Withholding and Withdrawing Potentially Life-Sustaining Treatment: Who Should Decide?', in Ian Freckelton and Kerry Petersen (eds.), *Tensions and Traumas in Health Law* (Annandale: The Federation Press, 2017) 454–78; Lindy Willmott and Ben White, 'Assisted Dying in Australia: A Values-Based Model for Reform', in Ian Freckelton and Kerry Petersen (eds.), *Tensions and Traumas in Health Law* (Annandale: Federation Press, 2017) 479–510; Udo Schüklenk, Johannes J. M. van Delden, Jocelyn Downie, Sheila McLean, Ross Upshur and Daniel Weinstock, 'End-of-Life Decision-Making in Canada: The Report by the Royal Society of Canada Expert Panel on End-of-Life Decision-Making' (2011) 25 *Bioethics* 1–73 at 29–51.

[78] Schüklenk et al., 'End-of-Life Decision-Making in Canada', 38–45.

with substitute or surrogate decision-making (and increasingly supported decision-making). To illustrate, in some Australian states, these laws are or were spread across multiple statutes passed at different times which conflict and intersect in ways that legislators could not have anticipated.[79] Finally, end-of-life decision-making is often regarded as a politically dangerous area of policy-making and hence the political will to tackle reform in this area can be meagre.[80] These five features of end-of-life law make it difficult both to gain priority to be considered in a crowded reform agenda and for any proposed reform to be deliberated on in a rational way.

Contributing to the complexity of reform in this area are the powerful and often polarised interests that are an ever-present feature of these debates. Many of the issues in end-of-life law, and again, especially assisted dying, go to the core of some groups' mission and beliefs. One commonly cited example is the Catholic Church (although other churches and faith-based groups have been involved in these debates too in varying ways[81]). The Catholic Church has been outspoken in opposing assisted dying[82] and has also participated in reform debates about proposed changes in other areas of end-of-life law too.[83] Other important groups are health and medical organisations, particularly doctors' associations. The positions of these

[79] Examples are the previous guardianship and medical treatment legislation in South Australia (see Margaret Brown, 'The South Australian Advance Care Directive Act 2013: How Has the Decision Making Paradigm Changed?' (2018) 25 *Journal of Law and Medicine* 538–48) and in Victoria (see 'Inquiry into End of Life Choices', Final Report from the Legal and Social Issues Committee (2016 Parliament of Victoria, Legislative Council) 14).

[80] Law reform is often restricted to areas that the government perceives will have positive popularity in terms of votes: Hurlburt, *Law Reform Commissions in the United Kingdom, Australia and Canada*, 368. Plumb claims that in the Australian state of Tasmania, the strong (and vocal) opposition by the Australian Medical Association has influenced voting on bills. Members of Parliament, particularly members of the Liberal (conservative) party, are less likely to vote for end-of-life law reform due to the Australia Medical Association's opposition: Alison Plumb, 'The Future of Euthanasia Politics in the Australian State Parliaments' (2014) 29 *Australasian Parliamentary Review* 67–86 at 83. A different example from the United States is the significant controversy in 2009 when then President Obama attempted to introduce the Affordable Health Choices Act of 2009 (HR 3200) that would make voluntary end-of-life care discussions or 'advance planning' reimbursable for Medicare patients. The Act that was passed in 2010 left out the advance care planning reimbursement for fear of political backlash: Taylor E. Purvis, 'Debating Death: Religion, Politics, and the Oregon Death with Dignity Act' (2012) 85 *Yale Journal of Biology and Medicine* 271–84 at 280–1.

[81] See, for example, an analysis of the participation of religious actors in assisted dying debates in Scotland, England and Wales: Steven Kettell, 'How, When, and Why Do Religious Actors Use Public Reason? The Case of Assisted Dying in Britain' (2019) 12 *Politics and Religion* 385–408.

[82] Eli D. Stutsman, 'Political Strategy and Legal Change', in Timothy E. Quill and Margaret P. Battin (eds.), *Physician-Assisted Dying* (Baltimore: Johns Hopkins University Press, 2004), at 259; Ball, *At Liberty to Die*, 107; Purvis, 'Debating Death', 271, 276.

[83] See, for example, the involvement of the Catholic Church in debates surrounding the withholding and withdrawal of life-sustaining medical treatment: Kathy L. Cerminara, 'Theresa Marie Schiavo's Long Road to Peace' (2006) 30 *Death Studies* 101–12; Neville Warwick, 'They Shoot Horses Don't They? Or Only in Victoria: A Commentary on Re BWV: Ex Parte Gardner in the Light of the Papal Allocution "Persons in 'Vegetative State' Deserve Proper Care"' (2006) 83 *Australian Catholic Record* 62–81.

groups have varied depending on the issue. Often medical associations have opposed assisted dying law reform[84] but have generally been positive about reforms to laws supporting advance care planning or palliative care. Some disability groups have often, but not always, opposed assisted dying reform.[85] There are also issue-focused advocacy organisations in the end-of-life field, most notably dying with dignity or compassion in dying groups. They have been persistent in seeking to change the law on assisted dying and also generally participate in reform efforts in other areas of end-of-life law.

THE GOAL OF THIS BOOK

This book examines the complex domain of end-of-life law reform and aims to shed light on how and why reform might occur. In doing so, it seeks to reconcile two perspectives about legal change. On the one hand, 'all politics is local'[86] and this point is applicable to end-of-life reform. It is very local considerations such as the culture of a jurisdiction, shifts in public opinion, the identity and influence of proponents and opponents of change, key local events or crises, or shifts in political power over time that can determine whether and when end-of-life law can be changed.[87] On the other hand, John Griffiths and colleagues noted almost twenty years ago that the experiences of end-of-life law reform in various countries reflect changes happening internationally in the relationship between law, medicine and the state.[88] The questions that one country is grappling with are likely to be

---

[84] The American Medical Association has been identified by some as the strongest secular opponent to assisted dying reform: Ball, *At Liberty to Die*. The Australian Medical Association has also been significant in opposing changes to the law: see, for example, Chelsea Wallis, 'A Phronetic Inquiry into the Australian Euthanasia Experience: Challenging Paternalistic Medical Culture and Unrepresentative Health Policy' (2018) 25 *Journal of Law and Medicine* 837–58 at 849; Plumb, 'The Future of Euthanasia Politics', 67; Jodhi Rutherford, 'The Role of the Medical Profession in Victorian Assisted Dying Law Reform' (2018) 26 *Journal of Law and Medicine* 246–64. The British Medical Association is also opposed to assisted dying reform: The British Medical Association, 'The BMA's Position on Physician-Assisted Dying', British Medical Association, 28 February 2020, www.bma org.uk/ advice-and-support/ethics/end-of-life/the-bmas-position-on-physician-assisted-dying. Note, however, that some medical associations and bodies have taken a different approach: see Chapters 8 and 12.

[85] Some disability rights advocates maintain that assisted dying demeans the lives of individuals living with disabilities: Anna Gorman, 'Why Disability-Rights Activists Are Fighting Doctor-Assisted Suicide', *The Atlantic*, 30 June 2015, www.theatlantic.com/health/archive/2015/06/disability-rights-assisted-suicide-california/397235/. See also Alicia Ouellette, 'Barriers to Physician Aid in Dying for People with Disabilities' (2017) 6 *Laws* 23–31.

[86] This was a famous saying of the former Speaker of the United States House of Representatives, Tip O'Neill: Andrew Heywood, *Politics*, 2nd ed. (New York: Palgrave Macmillan, 2002), at 157.

[87] These factors are considered further in Chapter 12.

[88] John Griffiths, Alex Bood and Heleen Weyers, *Euthanasia and Law in the Netherlands* (Amsterdam: Amsterdam University Press, 1998), at 43, 157, 167–8.

very similar to those in other parts of the world. This means international perspectives have an important contribution to make in understanding global trends in end-of-life law reform. But these discussions must be calibrated and contextualised to understand their implications in a very particular local environment.

To address both global and local perspectives, the book adopts a case-study-based approach that draws on a range of international experiences in changing end-of-life law. There are ten case studies highlighting law reform insights from the United Kingdom, the United States, Canada, Australia, Belgium and the Netherlands. Each case study sheds light on the local contextual factors that were relevant to law reform, and collectively they provide an opportunity to reflect on wider global themes in this field. The chapters are written by leading authorial groups from the relevant country, many of whom have been directly involved in the law reform processes at the coalface. Although this is a predominantly legal book, the authorial group includes a range of disciplines including sociology, medicine and bioethics. This recognises that law reform is an undertaking that transcends disciplines,[89] and these interdisciplinary perspectives also helped shape the final collaborative chapter in the book which draws together global law reform themes.

The remainder of the book is in three parts. The first part examines assisted dying reform and is the subject of Chapters 2–8. Three chapters provide a 'roadmap' for reform and explain how and why the law changed in Canada (both federally and in Québec) and in Victoria, Australia. Other chapters examine the reform of an existing assisted dying law – the Belgian extension of assisted dying to minors – or a proposed reform under consideration – a proposal in England and Wales that the consent of a High Court judge be required to access assisted dying. The two remaining assisted dying case studies consider the principles underpinning the evolution of end-of-life law reform over time to recognise assisted dying in the United States, and the reform implications of the ongoing evaluation of the Dutch assisted dying laws and their operation in practice.

The second part, over the course of Chapters 9–11, considers reform of the law governing decisions about potentially life-sustaining treatment. One case study from the United Kingdom continues the 'roadmap to reform' model and describes how the requirement to obtain court approval before withdrawing artificial nutrition and hydration from certain patients was successfully challenged. Another examines how the Texas Advance Directives Act 1999, with its landmark 'futility' dispute resolution process, came to pass as well as subsequent efforts to dismantle it. The remaining life-sustaining treatment case study considers the judicial evolution of the best

---

[89] Weisbrot, 'The Future for Institutional Law Reform'.

interests test following the enactment of the Mental Capacity Act 2005 (England and Wales).

The third and final part of the book is the concluding analysis in Chapter 12 of the global law reform themes that emerged from an examination of the ten case studies. This was a collaborative exercise involving the book's contributing authors. Consistent with the point made earlier that all politics is local, some factors that promote reform are parochial. However, this chapter identifies other broader key features, such as a good law reform process and the emergence and use of social science evidence, which are significant for law reform success regardless of jurisdiction.

End-of-life law reform is a vexed area. Changes in this field are usually challenging and controversial. This book aims to shed light on how and when law reform in this field succeeds. It does so from an international perspective but with a clear understanding of the significance of local factors. In doing so, this book intends to support reform efforts to improve end-of-life law and thereby the quality of end-of-life care that people receive. It is hoped too that this book may make a contribution to understanding law reform more generally. It sits within a long-standing tradition of examining why law reform occurs and, as a case study of where legal change has been very difficult to achieve, may contribute to the broader field of law reform.

2

The Path from *Rodriguez* to Bill C-14 and Beyond

Lessons about MAiD Law Reform from Canada

Jocelyn Downie and Kate Scallion

INTRODUCTION

The path from Canada's first court challenge of the Criminal Code prohibition of euthanasia and assisted suicide in 1992 to the 2016 legislation permitting medical assistance in dying ('MAiD') and then to the court challenge and amendments to that legislation has been a long and arduous one.[1] From each milestone along the way, valuable lessons can be learned that help illuminate the path to assisted dying for other jurisdictions debating whether or not to lift their prohibitions on MAiD. These lessons can be drawn from a chronological narrative or a description of events organised thematically. While we have provided a chronology,[2] we have chosen the latter organising principle for the text in order to show the interconnections and avoid repetition (as oftentimes the same lesson can be drawn from multiple milestones). The themes discussed in this chapter are litigation strategy, consultation, legislative drafting, staged reform, and the legislative vs. judicial path.

A brief prefatory note is in order to explain the two potential paths to MAiD law reform in Canada. First, the legislative path. Criminal law falls within the jurisdiction of the federal Parliament. Prohibitions on MAiD are contained in federal legislation – that is, the Criminal Code of Canada.[3] Therefore, one approach to legislative reform is to seek to persuade the federal Parliament to amend the Criminal Code (as was tried unsuccessfully many times over the years[4]). The

---

[1]   *Rodriguez* v. *Canada (Attorney General)* [1993] 3 SCR 519 ('*Rodriguez*'); *Carter* v. *Canada (Attorney General)* [2015] 1 SCR 331 ('*Carter*'); Bill C-14, An Act to Amend the Criminal Code and to Make Related Amendments to Other Acts (Medical Assistance in Dying), SC 2016, c. 3 ('Bill C-14'); *Truchon* v. *Canada (Attorney General)* [2019] QCCS 3792 ('*Truchon*'); Bill C-7, An Act to Amend the Criminal Code (Medical Assistance in Dying), SC 2021, c. 2 ('Bill C-7').

[2]   See Appendix to this chapter.

[3]   Criminal Code, RSC 1985, c. C-46 ('Criminal Code').

[4]   Jocelyn Downie, 'Permitting Voluntary Euthanasia and Assisted Suicide: Law Reform Pathways for Common Law Jurisdictions' (2016) 16 *QUT Law Review* 84–112.

management and delivery of health services is a provincial/territorial matter so another approach to legislative reform is to seek to persuade a provincial/territorial government to pass MAiD legislation under its jurisdiction in respect of health (as was done in Québec[5]). Second, the judicial path. All laws in Canada must comply with the Charter of Rights and Freedoms, which guarantees protection for fundamental rights and freedoms, such as the right to life, liberty, and security of the person and the right to the equal protection and equal benefit of the law.[6] None of the rights or freedoms protected by the *Charter* may be infringed by a law or other state action unless the infringement can be demonstrably justified in a free and democratic society.[7] Therefore, the judicial path to reform is to persuade the courts that the statutory prohibitions violate the *Charter* and to have them strike down the prohibitions (as was successfully done in *Carter v. Canada (Attorney General)* ('*Carter*')[8] and *Truchon v. Canada (Attorney General)* ('*Truchon*')[9]).

In this chapter, we first explore the themes in relation to the path from *Rodriguez v Canada (Attorney General)*[10] to Bill C-14. We then reflect, in a more preliminary way as this path has only recently unfolded, on the path from Bill C-14 to Bill C-7.

FROM *RODRIGUEZ* TO BILL C-14

Litigation Strategy

One of the reasons why the plaintiffs in *Carter* succeeded in getting the Supreme Court of Canada (SCC) to strike down the complete prohibition of MAiD in 2015 was litigation strategy, specifically strategic decisions made about when to litigate and how to use social science and humanities evidence in litigation.

When to Litigate
Rodriguez, the first *Charter* challenge to the absolute prohibition on aiding suicide, failed in part because of a lack of relevant principles of fundamental justice.[11] Section 7 of the Charter of Rights and Freedoms establishes the right not to be deprived of the right to life, liberty, and security of the person except in accordance with the principles of fundamental justice.[12] In *Rodriguez*, the limits on the section 7 rights were found to have not violated any principles of fundamental justice and therefore the *Charter* challenge failed. But between *Rodriguez* and *Carter*, a few key

[5] See Chapter 8 for a discussion of the reform process in Québec.
[6] Canada Act 1982 (UK), c. 11, sch. B, pt. 1, ss. 7, 15 (the *Charter*).
[7] Ibid., s. 1.
[8] *Carter* [2015] 1 SCR 331.
[9] *Truchon* [2019] QCCS 3792.
[10] *Rodriguez* [1993] 3 SCR 519.
[11] *Rodriguez* [1993] 3 SCR 519.
[12] The *Charter*.

Charter cases occurred that introduced new principles of fundamental justice (e.g., *R v. Heywood* and *R v. Malmo-Levine*).[13] In *Carter*, at trial, the plaintiffs argued that the jurisprudence had changed the law with respect to the principles of fundamental justice, particularly in respect of those relating to overbreadth and gross disproportionality.[14] The SCC affirmed the trial decision that the Criminal Code prohibition on aiding suicide was indeed overbroad and grossly disproportionate.[15] It is important to note here that the developments in the principles of fundamental justice took place well outside the context of assisted dying. One leading case, *R v. Bedford*, for example, was a challenge to Canada's prostitution laws.[16] This highlights the fact that the anticipatory litigation strategy must involve keeping a watchful eye on a wide swathe of constitutional law.

Concerns about the risks of sliding down a slippery slope from voluntary MAiD to nonvoluntary or even involuntary MAiD were also influential in the SCC's decision in *Rodriguez*.[17] But between *Rodriguez*[18] and *Carter*,[19] a strong evidentiary base was established through research in permissive jurisdictions demonstrating that the slippery slopes do not manifest. Most significantly, the empirical evidence from Oregon in the United States, the Netherlands and Belgium clearly indicated that concerns about slippage from voluntary to nonvoluntary or involuntary and concerns about abuse of vulnerable individuals were not well-founded.[20]

Individuals in the field kept an eye on both of these factors for years after *Rodriguez* and the decision to litigate was only made when the conditions for these factors were favourable. The field-watchers identified these two critical developments and recognised and signalled when litigation had become viable.[21]

---

[13] *R v. Heywood* [1994] 3 SCR 761; *R v. Malmo-Levine* [2003] 3 SCR 571.
[14] *Carter v. Canada (Attorney General)* [2012] BCSC 886 at [974]–[1008] ('*Carter Trial*').
[15] *Carter* [2015] 1 SCR 331 at [85]–[90].
[16] *Bedford v. Canada (Attorney General)* [2013] SCC 72.
[17] *Rodriguez* [1993] 3 SCR 519.
[18] Ibid.
[19] *Carter* [2015] 1 SCR 331.
[20] There were many years of data from the Netherlands, Oregon and Belgium and academic literature that made this point. See, for example, Judith Rietjens, Paul J. van der Maas, Bregje D. Onwuteaka-Philipsen, Johannes J. M. van Delden and Agnes van der Heide, 'Two Decades of Research on Euthanasia from the Netherlands. What Have We Learnt and What Questions Remain?' (2009) 6 *Journal of Bioethical Inquiry* 271–83; Death with Dignity Act Annual Reports from the Oregon Health Authority (1998–2019 Public Health Division, Center for Health Statistics); Johan Bilsen, Joachim Cohen, Kenneth Chambaere, Geert Pousset, Bregje D. Onwuteaka-Philipsen, Freddy Mortier and Luc Deliens, 'Medical End-of-Life Practices under the Euthanasia Law in Belgium' (2009) 361 *New England Journal of Medicine* 1119–21; Margaret P. Battin, Agnes van der Heide, Linda Ganzini, Gerrit van der Wal and Bregje D. Onwuteaka-Philipsen, 'Legal Physician-Assisted Dying in Oregon and the Netherlands: Evidence Concerning the Impact on Patients in "Vulnerable" Groups' (2007) 33 *Journal of Medical Ethics* 591–7.
[21] See, for example, Jocelyn Downie and Simone Bern, 'Rodriguez Redux' (2008) 16 *Health Law Journal* 27–54 at 44–54.

How to Use Social Science and Humanities Research

In *Carter*, the trial judge was presented with thirty-six binders of documents, including 116 affidavits (of which eighteen witnesses were cross-examined).[22] In total, fifty-seven experts from eight different countries across North America, Europe, Australia and New Zealand participated, providing evidence from disciplines such as medicine, nursing, philosophy (particularly ethics), bioethics, law, sociology, disability studies and psychology. The entire *Rodriguez* record was submitted in *Carter* – and was dwarfed by all of the other evidence.[23]

The plaintiffs' legal team in *Carter* presented persuasive social science and humanities evidence, notably including ethics evidence. The evidence addressed such questions as: 'does current medical practice with respect to end-of-life care make distinctions that are ethically defensible (e.g., requiring respect for refusals of life-sustaining treatment, but prohibiting respect for requests for assisted dying) and is the distinction between suicide and assisted suicide ethically defensible?'; 'do the safeguards [in permissive jurisdictions] effectively prevent abuse of vulnerable individuals?'; 'has the legalisation of MAiD harmed or helped palliative care and physician–patient relationships?'[24] The plaintiffs' legal team was versed in the critical assessment of social science evidence and was able to demonstrate problems with much of the evidence submitted by the Attorney General. For example, the team argued, among other things, that an expert: made some factual statements without sources; made some statements with sources but the sources did not provide support for the statements; and made false statements about the law and practice in permissive jurisdictions.[25] Justice Smith was invited by the plaintiffs to, and did, identify deficiencies including the following: partiality; reliance on review of secondary sources rather than being the primary investigator; lack of relevant expertise in relation to specific evidence; publication in low-quality journals; and methodological flaws such as recall bias, response bias, and social desirability bias.[26]

As social science and humanities evidence takes on more and more of a critical role in constitutional litigation,[27] litigation strategy needs to incorporate finding, evaluating and effectively using such evidence.

---

[22] *Carter Trial* [2012] BCSC 886.

[23] Ibid.

[24] Jocelyn Downie, 'Social Science and Humanities Evidence in *Charter* Litigation: Lessons from *Carter v. Canada (Attorney General)*' (2018) 22 *International Journal of Evidence and Proof* 305–13 at 307.

[25] See, for example, Jose Pereira, 'Legalizing Euthanasia or Assisted Suicide: The Illusion of Safeguards and Controls' (2011) 18 *Current Oncology* e38–45; Jocelyn Downie, Kenneth Chambaere and Jan Bernheim, 'Pereira's Attack on Legalizing Euthanasia or Assisted Suicide: Smoke and Mirrors' (2012) 19 *Current Oncology* 133–8; *Carter Trial* [2012] BCSC 886 at [377], [504], [664], [796]–[797].

[26] Downie, 'Social Science and Humanities Evidence in *Charter* Litigation'.

[27] For critical reflections on the use of social science in *Charter* litigation, see the series of blog postings by Leonid Sirota on Double Aspect, https://doubleaspect.blog/author/enfantperdu/. See also Joseph Cheng, 'Fact or Friction: Social Science Evidence, the Courts and the

Consultation

Contrasting how the Québec government and the federal government developed permissive legislation for MAiD demonstrates how a thorough and robust consultative process can lead to better legislation and a more positive reception from stakeholders than a less comprehensive one.

When Québec started its process of exploring a legislative response to assisted dying, it invested considerable time and effort engaging with the public, stakeholder groups and experts. The first legislative seeds were sown in December 2009 when an all-party committee of Québec's National Assembly was formed to research assisted dying.[28] Throughout 2010, the committee consulted with thirty-two experts, received more than 300 submissions, and an online survey received more than 6,600 responses.[29] Eight public hearings were held in eight different cities between September 2010 and March 2011 and in June and July of 2012, committee members visited Belgium and Holland to observe assisted dying regimes.[30] The committee tabled its report in 2012 with twenty-four recommendations. In June of that year, Québec's Department of Justice convened a panel of seventeen experts to advise them. Québec did not begin drafting its end-of-life legislation until later in 2013. The bill was introduced in the National Assembly on 12 June 2013.[31] Following its introduction, further public consultations took place in September and October with the National Assembly approving the bill in principle on 29 October 2014. That approval was followed by a study by the health and social services committee, which formulated fifty-seven amendments to the legislation.[32] The bill was debated again in February 2014, before finally being passed on 5 June 2014. The legislation came into effect in December 2015.

The federal government, in contrast, did not undertake the same level of consultation. Indeed, there was no public consultation conducted by either Health Canada or Justice Canada. The federal government had time after the trial decision in *Carter*[33] and during the appeals to prepare for the possibility of a loss at the SCC (although it would have been surprising for the government to do that under any circumstances but especially as, in this instance, it was a right-wing conservative anti-MAiD government throughout that time period). Once the plaintiffs were successful at the SCC, the federal government, unlike Québec, did not

Charter', Research Paper No. 846 Canadian Institute for the Administration of Justice, https://ciaj-icaj.ca/en/?s=fact+or+friction.

[28] See Chapter 8 for a review of the steps taken by others prior to the legislative process.

[29] Jeff Heinrich, 'Bill C-52: A Timeline', *Montreal Gazette*, 6 June 2014, www.montrealgazette.com/health/bill+timeline/9510618/story.html.

[30] Ibid.

[31] Bill 52, An Act Respecting End-of-Life Care, 1st Sess., 41st Leg., Québec, 2013 (assented to 10 June 2014), RSQ c. S-32.0001.

[32] Heinrich, 'Bill C-52: A Timeline'.

[33] *Carter Trial* [2012] BCSC 886.

have the luxury of time. It was operating under the deadline imposed by the SCC decision in *Carter*.[34] In *Carter*, the SCC had declared the absolute prohibition on assisted dying to be unconstitutional and given the government of the day twelve months within which to respond (by suspending the coming into effect of the declaration for twelve months). During the period of the suspension, there was an election and the Conservative government was replaced by a Liberal one. The Liberal government was elected on 19 October 2015, and came into power on 4 November 2015. The new government went to the SCC and argued that, as there had been an election (during which many of the normal activities of government are suspended) and as they had just come into power, the twelve-month suspension should be extended. The SCC gave them an extra four months (the period of the election campaign).[35] Therefore it is certainly true that the federal Liberal government had far less time than the Québec government had for consultation. However, it is not true that they had no time. They could have started a consultation immediately upon coming into power. They did not do so. Indeed, between the time of coming into power and introducing the draft MAiD legislation on 14 April 2016, they did no public consultations. There is no evidence that they consulted with stakeholders and experts.

It is worth noting here that, referencing the tight deadline they inherited from the previous government, the new federal government could have decided to rely on consultations conducted by others. In particular, after waiting five months from the SCC decision in *Carter*, the previous Conservative government had commissioned a report from the External Panel on Options for a Legislative Response to *Carter v. Canada*.[36] The Expert Panel conducted an extensive public consultation and submitted a report on its findings. It did not make recommendations as the newly elected Liberal government removed making recommendations from the original mandate that had been given by the previous Conservative government. The provincial/territorial governments (all but Québec) had established a Provincial/Territorial Expert Advisory Group on Physician-Assisted Dying.[37] Their mandate was 'to provide non-binding advice to participating Provincial-Territorial Ministers of Health and Justice on issues related to physician-assisted dying. The advice is meant to assist provinces and territories in deciding what policies and procedures should be implemented within their jurisdictions in response to the Supreme

---

[34] *Carter* [2015] 1 SCR 331.

[35] Ibid.

[36] 'Consultation on Physician-Assisted Dying: Summary of Results and Key Findings', Final Report from the External Panel on Options for a Legislative Response to *Carter v. Canada* (15 December 2015 Government of Canada, Department of Justice).

[37] Final Report from the Provincial/Territorial Expert Advisory Group on Physician-Assisted Dying (30 November 2015 Government of Canada, Ministry of Health) (Co-chairs: Jennifer Gibson and Maureen Taylor). Eleven provinces and territories participated in this advisory group, representing all Canadian provinces and territories except Québec and British Columbia (the latter province, however, participated as an observer).

Court's decision in *Carter*.'[38] This group did not conduct a public consultation, but did consult with stakeholders and experts. It issued a report with findings and recommendations. Finally, a Special Joint Committee of the House and Senate also received submissions and heard testimony from stakeholders and experts. This Committee also issued a report on findings and made recommendations.[39] It is unclear what use the federal government made of the consultations conducted by these groups (beyond reading the reports). What is clear is that it went directly against key recommendations from the Provincial/Territorial Expert Advisory Group and the Special Joint Committee – both of which had made a deliberate attempt to engage with the stakeholders and experts (e.g., both recommended the inclusion of mature minors and advance requests and neither recommended narrowing the SCC eligibility criterion 'grievous and irremediable condition' while the government excluded both and narrowed the criterion by, for example, requiring that a person's natural death has become reasonably foreseeable and the person must be in an advanced state of irreversible decline in capability).

The impact of the lack of consultation was felt immediately. One would not expect unanimous approval of all aspects of the legislation. People will reasonably and not surprisingly disagree about policy positions taken in MAiD legislation (e.g., whether to require judicial pre-authorization in all cases of MAiD or to allow access to mature minors). However, there was confusion, controversy and litigation, which could perhaps have been avoided if the government had consulted with stakeholders and experts during the drafting process.[40] Each of these consequences is discussed further below.

Confusion

The legislation was greeted with much bewilderment over the meaning of some of the phrases used.[41] One example, as emerged from the House and Senate committee hearings on the legislation, is that the Federation of Medical Regulatory Authorities of Canada ('FMRAC') (all of the provincial/territorial Colleges of Physicians and Surgeons tasked with regulating physicians) was not consulted on the wording of the eligibility criteria. Had they been consulted, they would have

---

[38] Ibid. at 12.

[39] 'Medical Assistance in Dying: A Patient-Centered Approach', Report from the Special Joint Committee on Physician-Assisted Dying (February 2016 Parliament of Canada, House of Commons and Senate) (Joint Chairs: Hon. Kelvin Kenneth Ogilvie and Robert Oliphant).

[40] It must be acknowledged that there was also confusion, controversy and litigation in Québec even though there was extensive consultation. However, that doesn't mean that consultation could not have prevented some of the confusion, controversy and litigation over Bill C-14 and the claim is not that the lack of consultation was the only factor but rather was a factor (and could have been the or a deciding factor) in the confusion, controversy and litigation.

[41] For a full discussion of the confusing phrases and suggested interpretations, see Jocelyn Downie and Jennifer A. Chandler, 'Interpreting Canada's Medical Assistance in Dying Legislation', Institute for Research on Public Policy, 1 March 2018, irpp.org/research-studies/interpreting-canadas-medical-assistance-in-dying-maid-legislation/.

advised the government that the language of the requirement that a patient's 'natural death' has become 'reasonably foreseeable' was unworkable from the regulators' perspective and that, while it would be left to medical and nurse practitioners to determine whether the eligibility criteria are met in specific cases, the phrase 'reasonably foreseeable' is not one familiar to them; in fact, Dr. Douglas Grant, then president of FMRAC, said, '[t]his is legal, not medical, language, and I think we just heard that the lawyers don't even like it. The language is too vague to be understood or applied by the medical profession and too ambiguous to be regulated effectively.'[42] The predictable confusion caused implementation problems[43] and there was litigation seeking judicial clarification of the meaning of the phrase[44] and letters were sent by the British Columbia coroner to the BC College of Physicians and Surgeons raising questions about whether a particular case met the eligibility criteria.[45]

Controversy

The legislation was also greeted with a firestorm of controversy over some of the restrictive eligibility criteria[46] and procedural safeguards.[47] Undertaking a thorough

---

[42] Evidence to Standing Senate Committee on Legal and Constitutional Affairs, Senate, 42nd Parl., 1st Sess., issue no. 9, 10 May 2016 (Dr. Douglas Grant).

[43] See, for example, Shannon Proudfoot, 'Why Canada's Assisted Dying Law Is Confusing Doctors – and Patients', *Maclean's*, 18 November 2016, www.macleans.ca/news/canada/why-canadas-assisted-dying-law-is-confusing-doctors-and-patients/.

[44] *AB* v. *Canada (Attorney General)* [2017] ONSC 3759 ('AB').

[45] Jocelyn Downie, 'Has Stopping Eating and Drinking Become a Pathway to Assisted Dying?', Policy Options, Institute for Research on Public Policy, 23 March 2018, policyoptions.irpp.org/magazines/march-2018/has-stopping-eating-and-drinking-become-a-path-to-assisted-dying/;
Jocelyn Downie, 'It Can Happen Here: MAiD and Dementia in Canada', *Dalhousie Law Journal Blog*, 18 October 2019, blogs.dal.ca/dlj/2019/10/18/it-can-happen-here-maid-and-dementia-in-canada/.

[46] Criminal Code, s. 241.2(2):
(2) A person has a grievous and irremediable medical condition only if they meet all of the following criteria:
    (a) they have a serious and incurable illness, disease or disability;
    (b) they are in an advanced state of irreversible decline in capability;
    (c) that illness, disease or disability or that state of decline causes them enduring physical or psychological suffering that is intolerable to them and that cannot be relieved under conditions that they consider acceptable; and
    (d) their natural death has become reasonably foreseeable, taking into account all of their medical circumstances, without a prognosis necessarily having been made as to the specific length of time that they have remaining.

[47] Ibid., s. 241.2(3)(g):
'[E]nsure that there are at least 10 clear days between the day on which the request was signed by or on behalf of the person and the day on which the medical assistance in dying is provided or—if they and the other medical practitioner or nurse practitioner referred to in paragraph (e) are both of the opinion that the person's death, or the loss of their capacity to provide informed consent, is imminent—any shorter period that the first medical practitioner or nurse practitioner considers appropriate in the circumstances.'

and robust consultation might have avoided some of this controversy and increased the acceptance of the legislation. Even where one's own position on a particular policy matter is not reflected in the ultimate legislation, there is a greater likelihood of acceptance of that fact if the process of coming to a final position is transparent and everyone has had a chance to have their voices heard. Unlike the Québec legislation, with the federal legislation, there was a sense that some stakeholders had access to the critical governmental decision-makers behind closed doors. There was then no equal chance to attempt to change the minds of these decision-makers through counterarguments and evidence. In addition, the only opportunity to voice concerns and opposition to the legislation was in the highly politicised and temporally abridged process of the legislation making its way through Parliament.

Litigation
The legislation was also the subject of two court challenges[48] on the grounds that the restrictive eligibility criteria breached the right to life, liberty and security of the person and the right to equality under the *Charter*.[49] The plaintiffs in *Truchon* argued that the reasonably foreseeable criterion breached the *Charter*. The plaintiffs in *Lamb* argued that the incurable, advanced state of irreversible decline and the reasonably foreseeable criteria breached the *Charter*. The *Lamb* case was adjourned at the request of the plaintiffs and with the consent of the Attorney General after the Attorney General's expert evidence indicated that the lead plaintiff would meet the eligibility criteria for MAiD (under an unexpectedly expansive interpretation of 'reasonably foreseeable').[50] The judge in *Truchon* found that the reasonably foreseeable criterion breached the *Charter* and struck it down.[51]

Had the government consulted with key constitutional law experts[52] before introducing the legislation, they would have been told that these experts believed

Note—initially the waiting period was 15 days, but it was reduced to 10 days during the Parliamentary review process.

[48] *Truchon* [2019] QCCS 3792; *Lamb and British Columbia Civil Liberties Association v. Canada (Attorney General)* [2016] Supreme Court of British Columbia, No. S-165851 ('*Lamb*').
[49] The *Charter*: Section 1 of the *Charter* permits fundamental rights and freedoms to be infringed so long as the infringement can be demonstrably justifiable in a free and democratic society. Canadian case law has developed a section 1 test to determine whether or not *Charter* violations can be demonstrably justified: see *R v. Oakes* [1986] 1 SCR 103.
[50] Jocelyn Downie, 'A Watershed Month for Medical Assistance in Dying', Policy Options, Institute for Research on Public Policy, 20 September 2019, policyoptions.irpp.org/magazines/september-2019/a-watershed-month-for-medical-assistance-in-dying/.
[51] *Truchon* [2019] QCCS 3792.
[52] For example, Senator Serge Joyal, Peter Hogg and Joseph Arvay. It is clear from their submissions on Bill C-14 what they would have advised had they been consulted before the legislation was introduced: Senator Serge Joyal, 'Criminal Code: Bill to Amend – Second Reading – Debate Adjourned (Speech)', Senate of Canada, 2 June 2016, sencanada.ca/en/speeches/speech-by-senator-serge-joyal-during-the-second-reading-of-bill-c-14-medical-assistance-in-dying/; Peter Hogg, 'Brief to Standing Senate Committee on Legal and Constitutional Affairs', Senate of Canada, 6 June 2016, sencanada.ca/content/sen/committee/421/LCJC/Briefs/

the reasonably foreseeable criterion was unconstitutional as well as why the experts believed that and what would happen if Parliament passed the legislation with that criterion (i.e. immediate *Charter* challenges). If they had consulted and listened to the experts, they might then have avoided litigation, the delays on access for some and an insurmountable barrier for others (i.e. those who died without MAiD before the striking down of the provision), and the final rebuke from the court in *Truchon*[53] concluding that the experts had been right.

Now it might be argued that even if they had consulted with the experts, the government would not have followed their advice. It might be argued that the experts testified before the House and Senate committees and the government rejected their calls to remove 'reasonably foreseeable' as an eligibility criterion, therefore consultation would not have prevented the negative consequences listed above. It is indeed possible that the government would have ignored the experts even if they had consulted them. However, other results are also possible. In particular, perhaps hearing the results of a consultation *before* the legislation was introduced would have tipped the balance in the deliberations within the Prime Minister's Office or at the Cabinet table when deciding what to introduce. Perhaps it could have given those opposed to the 'reasonably foreseeable' criterion arguments to use against those supporting it. Changing the legislation before it is introduced (only possible with consultation before introduction) would have been easier than after. Consultation before introduction would have given Cabinet the opportunity and inclination to insist on changes to the legislation brought to them by the Minister of Justice – once it had been introduced, they might have feared looking like fools for having introduced it and then accepting an amendment to such a central component.

Legislative Drafting

Lawmakers obviously need to be very careful when drafting legislation. Ambiguity threatens the utility, legitimacy and validity of legislation. Furthermore, legislative drafting can result in unforeseen or unintended consequences. The federal

---

LCJC_June_6_2016_SN_Hogg_e.pdf; Evidence to Standing Senate Committee Legal and Constitutional Affairs, Senate, 42nd Parl., 1st Sess., issue no. 10, 6 June 2016 (Senator Serge Joyal); Joseph Arvay, Q. C. Lead Counsel in *Carter* v. *Canada*, Submission to the Standing Committee on Justice and Human Rights In view of its study on Bill C-14, An Act to Amend the Criminal Code and to make related amendments to other Acts (Medical Assistance in Dying) (5 May 2016); Evidence to Standing Senate Committee on Legal and Constitutional Affairs, Senate, 42nd Parl., 1st Sess., issue no. 8, 5 May 2016 (Joseph J. Arvay). Of course, not all of the constitutional law experts said the Bill was unconstitutional: see Evidence to Standing Committee on Justice and Human Rights, House of Commons, 42nd Parl., 1st sess., meeting no. 13, 4 May 2016 (Dianne Pothier).

[53] *Truchon* [2019] QCCS 3792.

legislation has been rightfully criticised for unclear language and unforeseen or unintended consequences. What follows are criticisms not directed at the policy positions taken in the legislation, but rather the drafting used to express them.

Ambiguity

The following phrases were found in Bill C-14: 'reasonably foreseeable'; and 'advanced state of irreversible decline in capability'. Providers and the public had many questions. Does 'reasonably foreseeable' include a temporal proximity require-ment or does it just require some level of predictability? If there is a temporal proximity requirement, what is it? Six months, twelve months, five years? How far along must a decline be to be 'advanced'? Is the assessment of irreversibility objective or subjective? The ambiguity led to variability in access due to struggles with the interpretation of key phrases.[54]

Fortunately, Bill C-14 did not use the term 'terminal'. 'Terminal' is a word that should be avoided for a number of reasons. The federal government rejected this term on the basis that 'terminal' would overly restrict access to MAiD.[55] The term has also been criticised as arbitrary (it must be defined in terms of a specific time frame and yet any time frame is arbitrary). It is also too vague – what length of time determines when a person is 'terminally ill'?

Also, fortunately, Bill C-14 did not use a time limit such as six or twelve months (unlike other jurisdictions such as Oregon in the United States[56] and Victoria and Western Australia in Australia[57]). Again, this was done so as not to limit access to MAiD and to give medical professionals more discretion to determine whether or not an individual qualifies for MAiD based on their unique medical circumstances.[58] Further, it is difficult to reliably estimate how much time a patient has left when diagnosed with an incurable disease, which Canada recognised in rejecting a time limit in MAiD criteria.[59]

---

[54] Downie and Chandler, 'Interpreting Canada's Medical Assistance in Dying Legislation'.

[55] Hansard, HC, 42nd Parl., 1st Sess., vol. 148, no. 45 (22 April 2016) at 1559 (Jody Wilson-Raybould): 'To be clear, the bill does not require that people be dying from a fatal illness or disease or be terminally ill. Rather, it uses more flexible wording … . This language was deliberately chosen to ensure that people who are on a trajectory toward death in a wide range of circumstances can choose a peaceful death instead of having to endure a long or painful one.'

[56] Death with Dignity Act, Or Rev Stat, c. 127 § 127.865 (1994) (Oregon).

[57] Voluntary Assisted Dying Act 2017 (Vic), s. 9(1)(d)(iii); Voluntary Assisted Dying Act 2019 (WA), s.16(1)(c)(ii).

[58] Evidence to Standing Committee on Justice and Human Rights, House of Commons, 42nd Parl., 1st Sess., issue no. 10, 2 May 2016 (Jane Philpott) at 1706.

[59] Debbie Selby, Anita Chakraborty, Tammy Lilien, Erica Stacey, Liying Zhang and Jeff Myers, 'Clinician Accuracy When Estimating Survival Duration: The Role of the Patient's Performance Status and Time-Based Prognostic Categories' (2011) 42 *Journal of Pain and Symptom Management* 578–588.

Unforeseen/Unintended Consequences

We now turn from ambiguity to unforeseen/unintended consequences. To illustrate, due to the way in which Bill C-14 was drafted with a requirement of reconfirmation of consent immediately before the provision of MAiD, the following could happen:[60]

- A patient could meet all of the eligibility criteria on a Friday. Her physician is not available to provide MAiD until the Monday and she unexpectedly lost capacity on Saturday. She would not be eligible for MAiD and would therefore continue to experience, by definition, intolerable suffering, until her natural death.[61]

- A patient might meet the eligibility criteria for MAiD but wishes to live a while longer, fear the loss of capacity, and so elect to die sooner than they otherwise would in order to not risk losing the opportunity for MAiD. This is what happened in the case of Audrey Parker.[62] Parker was assessed and found to be eligible for MAiD but wished to try to live through Christmas and New Years – her favourite holidays of the year. However, she was at risk of losing capacity and thus access to MAiD. Because Bill C-14 did not permit advance requests for MAiD, she chose to die by MAiD on 1 November 2018, that is, more than two months earlier than she would have preferred.[63]

- A patient might forego pain medication and other treatments in order to retain decision-making capacity during the assessments, through the mandatory ten-day waiting period and immediately prior to the procedure. This could mean ten days of intolerable suffering.[64]

- A patient who did not meet the eligibility criteria might stop eating and drinking in order to make their natural death become reasonably

---

[60] On 17 March 2021, the Canadian Parliament passed Bill C-7, An Act to Amend the Criminal Code (Medical Assistance in Dying), SC 2021, c. 2. Specific elements of Bill C-7 will be noted in footnotes associated with each of the unforeseen/unintended consequences to flag recent changes.

[61] Bill C-7, s 3.2 allows for a 'final consent waiver' for individuals who meet the eligibility criteria for MAiD and whose natural deaths have become reasonably foreseeable. Having set the date for Monday while competent, consent immediately prior to provision would not be required if the patient lost capacity over the weekend.

[62] Kayla Hounsell, 'N.S. Woman Choosing to Die Earlier than She Wants Due to "Extreme" Assisted-Dying Law', CBC News, 19 September 2018, www.cbc.ca/news/canada/medical-assistance-in-dying-legislation-1.4829100.

[63] This consequence is also avoided through the final consent waiver in Bill C-7.

[64] Bill C-7 removes the ten-day waiting period for those whose natural death has become reasonably foreseeable. So, this scenario is addressed for them. However, it introduces a ninety-day waiting period for those whose natural death has not become reasonably foreseeable so it remains a concern for them.

foreseeable such that they qualify for MAiD.[65] For example, a woman in British Columbia stopped eating and drinking in order to make her death reasonably foreseeable and, after fourteen days, was found to be eligible for MAiD under Bill C-14.[66] Individuals might also refuse preventive care in order to meet the reasonably foreseeable criterion. For example, a person with quadriplegia might refuse to be turned, which would lead to bedsores, which untreated would become infected, which untreated would cause death. Or a person with spinal muscular atrophy could indicate a clear intent to stop using a BiPap machine at night, which would lead to pneumonia, which untreated would cause death.[67]

It is not clear that the federal Parliament foresaw/intended such consequences of the ways in which Bill C-14 was drafted.

It is clear that extraordinary care should be exercised in drafting in an effort to try to avoid ambiguity and legislation should be stress-tested with experts to try to render visible potential consequences.

Staged Reform

The federal Parliament recognised that there were three issues of great significance about which they were not prepared to draw final conclusions within the tight timeline available for introducing Bill C-14. These were, specifically, access for mature minors, access through advance requests and access for individuals with mental illness as the sole underlying condition (who do not otherwise qualify). It took a conservative position on each of these issues (excluding mature minors and

[65] Bill C-7 removes 'reasonably foreseeable' as an eligibility criterion. Therefore, nobody needs to use voluntary stopping of eating and sdrinking ('VSED') or refusal of personal care to become eligible for MAiD. However, Bill C-7 retains 'reasonably foreseeable' as the determining factor as to which set of procedural safeguards must be followed – a minimal set for those whose natural death has become reasonably foreseeable and a significant set (including a ninety-day waiting period) for those whose natural death has not. People may therefore seek to use VSED or refusal of personal care to avoid the barriers created by the significant set of procedural safeguards.

[66] Downie, 'Has Stopping Eating and Drinking Become a Pathway'. There have also been cases in Québec. Jean Breault starved himself for fifty-three days and refused water for eight in order to satisfy the criteria for MAiD under Québec's legislation. Kate McKenna, 'Doctor-Assisted Death Obtained by Sherbrooke Man Who Starved Himself to Qualify', CBC News, 13 April 2016, www.cbc.ca/news/canada/montreal/sherbrooke-man-hunger-strike-death-1.3529392. A second Québecker, a woman suffering from multiple sclerosis, also starved herself to meet the eligibility criteria because she was otherwise ineligible under both the federal and provincial legislation: Pierre Viens, 'Hélène L. s'est laissée mourir de faim', *La Presse*, 29 August 2016, plus.lapresse.ca/screens/5f03380d-5fc6–4743-9187–787e12e26e65%7C_0.html.

[67] The Attorney General's uncontested expert in the *Lamb* case stated that this scenario would make Julia Lamb's natural death reasonably foreseeable: see Joseph Arvay, Letter to Sue Smolen (6 September 2010), British Columbia Civil Liberties Association, https://bccla.org/wp-content/uploads/2019/09/2019-09-06B-LT-Court_adjournment-of-triaL.pdf.

advance requests completely, and excluding most individuals with mental illness as a sole underlying condition *de facto* rather than *de jure*[68]), but the legislation also required the Ministers of Health and Justice to initiate independent reviews on these issues and to report back to Parliament on the results of the reviews.[69] The federal Parliament also mandated a review of Bill C-14 and of the state of palliative care in Canada to be conducted by a committee of the House or Senate or both jointly to commence at the beginning of the fifth year after Royal Assent.[70]

In December 2016, the federal government announced the Council of Canadian Academies ('CCA') would conduct the mandatory independent reviews on requests made by mature minors, advance requests, and requests where mental illness is the sole underlying condition. The CCA Expert Panel Reports were released in December 2018 and, while the Expert Panel was not mandated to make recommendations, it met its mandate to 'summarize the relevant evidence on the diverse perspectives and issues surrounding medical assistance in dying in these three circumstances' and 'facilitate an informed, evidence-based dialogue among Canadians and decision makers'.[71] The five-year review was due to start in June 2020 and the government had indicated that it intended that review to cover the three issues covered in the CCA reviews as well as the state of palliative care and any other issues arising from the implementation of the legal framework for medical assistance in dying in Canada.[72] However, this review did not happen and has been superseded by a review mandated by Bill C-7 (explained below).[73]

This staged reform process allowed a limited permissive regime to come into effect before all of the complex issues associated with MAiD could be finally resolved. It relieved some of the pressure at the time of the introduction of the legislation as individuals and groups with strong positions on these issues did not feel that this would

---

[68] The fact that mental illness as a sole underlying medical condition is not an exclusion criterion in Bill C-14 is recognised in *Truchon* [2019] QCCS 3792 at [421] and in the Council of Canadian Academies, 'The State of Knowledge on Medical Assistance in Dying Where a Mental Disorder is the Sole Underlying Medical Condition': Report from the Expert Panel Working Group on MAID Where a Mental Disorder is the Sole Underlying Medical Condition (2018 Council of Canadian Academies) at 35.

[69] Bill C-14, s. 9(1)-(2).

[70] Ibid., s. 10(1).

[71] Health Canada, 'Medical Assistance in Dying: Independent Reviews', Government of Canada, 25 February 2020, www.canada.ca/en/health-canada/services/medical-assistance-dying.html#a6. See also 'The State of Knowledge of Medical Assistance in Dying for Mature Minors', Report from the Expert Panel Working Group on MAID for Mature Minors (2018 Council of Canadian Academies); 'The State of Knowledge on Advance Requests for Medical Assistance in Dying', Report from the Expert Panel Working Group on Advance Requests for MAID (2018 Council of Canadian Academies); Council of Canadian Academies 'The State of Knowledge on Medical Assistance in Dying Where a Mental Disorder Is the Sole Underlying Medical Condition'.

[72] Charlie Pinkerton, 'MAiD Tweaks Portrayed as a Stopgap as Government Seeks "Consensus" on Complex Cases', *iPolitics*, 26 February 2020, https://ipolitics.ca/2020/02/26/maid-tweaks-portrayed-as-a-stopgap-as-government-seeks-consensus-on-complex-cases/.

[73] Bill C-7, s. 5.

be the only time they could hope to have their positions reflected in the legislation. It also ensured that the outstanding issues would be carefully addressed and Parliament given the opportunity to make evidence-informed public policy decisions about them. It also recognised that unforeseen issues might arise during implementation of the legislation and that it would be wise to have a statutorily mandated process which could surface and provide a prompt to reflect on and deal with them.

Legislative vs. Judicial Path

A significant difference between the federal and the Québec path to law reform lies in the fact that in Québec, the legislature decided to proactively address the issue of MAiD. In contrast, the federal government did nothing until confronted with the SCC striking down the Criminal Code's absolute prohibition on assisted dying.

Québec was proactive and was therefore able to engage in a thorough and robust consultative process and a thoughtful, careful and reflective process of legislative drafting. It set its own timeline, chose how to frame the issues and moved forward at a pace that allowed the public to be comfortable with it. Being proactive also enabled Québec to legislate the entire regulatory framework at once. As a result, the monitoring system was designed and implemented before the legislation came into force.

In contrast, the federal Conservative government was resistant to law reform and fought to keep the prohibition in the Criminal Code. Even once there was a Liberal government that was supportive of MAiD, it was reactive, responding to a deadline and parameters imposed by the SCC. As a result, there was no consultation process, the legislative drafting was rapid and the Parliamentary process was rushed. The monitoring and oversight system was not in place when MAiD became available (indeed, the legislation came into force on 17 June 2016, and the regulations establishing the monitoring and oversight system did not come into force until November 2018[74]).

Thus it can be seen that the legislative rather than judicial path may lead to better legislation. That said, in the face of inertia or active resistance, the judicial path may be the only way to get any legislative reform at all.

FROM BILL C-14 TO BILL C-7

Litigation Strategy

As it was in *Carter*,[75] the use of social science and humanities evidence in court was a critical component of the litigation strategy in *Truchon*.[76]

---

[74] Regulations for the Monitoring of Medical Assistance in Dying: Ginette Petitpas Taylor, Minister for Health, 'Registration: SOR/2018-166: Criminal Code', *Canada Gazette*, pt. 2, vol. 152, no. 16, 27 July 2018, at 3077.

[75] *Carter* [2015] 1 SCR 331.

[76] *Truchon* [2019] QCCS 3792.

Issues about which social sciences evidence was submitted included: 'the vulnerable persons that the requirements seek to protect' (specifically, 'patients who are
vulnerable due to physical or intellectual disability', 'patients who are vulnerable to
suicide and the phenomenon of suicide contagion', and 'patients whose psychiatric
illness is the only medical condition underlying their request for medical assistance
in dying'); and 'comparison with certain foreign regimes'.

Justice Christine Baudouin carefully reviewed all of the expert social science
evidence presented before her. Lessons for litigation strategy can be drawn from her
comments regarding why she found the plaintiffs' expert evidence more conclusive
than the Attorney General's. Specifically, she indicated that

Experts should:

- be knowledgeable about relevant law[77];
- be knowledgeable about simple facts about the applicants[78]; and
- be knowledgeable about relevant practice, have done research on the
  subject, have consulted the available data.[79]

Expert evidence should:

- be '[f]rank, objective and consistently based on empirical data'[80];
- be relevant to the issue, to 'the applicants' circumstances or the issue to
  be decided by the court'[81];

---

[77] Ibid. at [402]: '[Dr. Kim] has very little knowledge, if any at all, about medical assistance in
dying in Canada, the criteria of the federal or provincial legislation, local data, or even the
existence of the Commission des soins de fin de vie, one of the objectives of which is precisely
to analyze, compile and publish up-to-date data on capacity assessment.'

[78] Ibid. at [402]: '[Dr. Kim] was also unable to confirm simple facts about the applicants
themselves, such as, for example, whether they were suffering from a psychiatric condition
that could possibly defeat their application for medical assistance in dying. He even went so far
as to qualify the possibility that Mr. Truchon might be suffering from a psychiatric condition as
a "detail", even though he then added that it would not be a "trivial detail."'

[79] Ibid. at [375]: 'First, the Court is astounded by the fact that the experts for the Attorney General
of Canada had not even a basic knowledge of the practice of medical assistance in dying in
Canada, which has nonetheless been legal throughout the country since 2016. None of them
has participated in the request process for medical assistance in dying, either by assessing a
patient or by providing such medical assistance. None of them has done any research on the
subject or even tried to consult the data available in Canada'. See also at [376]: '[they compare
suicide and MAiD] without ever having analyzed, learned, or addressed the specifics of
medical assistance in dying, its parameters, its eligibility criteria, or how it is practised in
Canada.'

[80] Ibid. at [448]: 'Without taking anything away from Professor Boer and Professor Lemmens, the
first two experts called by the Attorney General of Canada, the Court particularly appreciated
Dr. van der Heide's testimony, which was frank, objective and consistently based on
empirical data.'

[81] Ibid. at [426].

- be 'findings drawn from the experience in Canada, an experience modelled on our own social and cultural reality and reflecting the successes and flaws of a regime put in place by Parliament and the legislature'[82]; and
- be 'based on practical experience' (especially when being contrasted with evidence from experts 'who practice in the field').[83]

Expert evidence should not:

- be 'merely hypotheses or extrapolations from the data'[84];
- be 'too insufficient or theoretical to be truly probative'[85];
- 'elevate anecdotal and still-marginal cases to the rank of broad principles applicable to the situation prevailing in Canada'[86];
- be based on 'mere conjecture or anecdote' described as 'robust findings'[87];
- 'go too far in the conclusions he draws from the assumptions he presented'[88]; or
- offer comparisons that are 'purely theoretical at best' and opinion 'based on biases or a practice that does not correspond to reality'.[89]

While these lessons may seem obvious, they are worth reporting on as lessons to be learned because all of them were breached (to their detriment) by the Attorney General in their use of experts.

---

[82] Ibid. at [427].

[83] Consider the comments regarding Dr. Gaind's testimony on 'vulnerable groups based on their psychiatric condition alone' at Ibid. [415]: 'he goes too far in the conclusions he draws from the assumptions he presented. In addition, they are at odds with all the testimony heard from physicians who practice in the field and are not based on practical experience.' These comments can be contrasted with those regarding Drs Rivard and Naud's testimony on differences between MAiD and suicide at [383]: 'The applicants' experts and Dr. Rivard, who all have personal experience with medical assistance in dying in their practice, all stated that they would not confuse one with the other and that they are two separate phenomena. Dr. Naud has treated many suicidal patients in his family medicine practice and does not see how one could equate the two phenomena. Moreover, Dr. Rivard seemed astonished at the hearing that anyone could associate the two.' Contrast also with the comments regarding Drs Downar and Dembo's testimony on differences between MAiD and suicide and the potential impact of removing the challenged provisions from the legislation at [384]: 'Dr. Downar and Dr. Dembo, who assess patients requesting medical assistance in dying in their medical practice, unequivocally agreed with this assessment and confirmed that the two realities are clearly dissimilar. They claim that there is nothing to indicate that removing the impugned requirement will lead to an increase in requests for medical assistance in dying, influence the suicide rate in Canada, or undermine suicide prevention efforts.'

[84] Ibid. at [400].

[85] Ibid.

[86] Ibid. at [401].

[87] Ibid. at [404].

[88] Ibid. at [405].

[89] Ibid. at [377].

Consultation

For Bill C-7, the federal government engaged in public consultation – round tables with experts and advocacy groups and an online questionnaire for the public. Notably, their online questionnaire had 300,140 responses, the largest response ever received by the Department of Justice for any public consultation ('cannabis and prostitution only netted about 30,000 responses each').[90] The results of these consultations were released in March 2020.[91] The choices made in Bill C-7 are reflective of many but not all of the opinions expressed in the consultations. For example:

- *Reflective*: 78.6 per cent supported allowing for advance requests for MAiD when a person had already been assessed and found to be eligible for MAiD at the time of making the request. Bill C-7 introduces 'final consent waivers' to achieve this result.
- *Not reflective*: 73 per cent of respondents indicated that they thought that 'the current safeguards would prevent abuse, pressure or other kinds of misuse of MAiD after eligibility is broadened to people whose deaths are not reasonably foreseeable'. Yet Bill C-7 introduces new safeguards.

It is worth noting here that the government consulted on the issues in advance of introducing the legislation but, again, did not consult with experts on the draft legislation itself. This will again result in confusion. In particular, Bill C-7 stipulates that mental illness cannot be considered a serious and incurable illness, disease or disability for the purposes of MAiD. However, it does not define 'mental illness'. It is not clear what the government thinks 'mental illness' means. Did the government think it is synonymous with 'mental disorders' (thus including cognitive disorders like dementia as well as intellectual and developmental disorders like autism)? Or did the government think it is a subcategory of mental disorders (e.g., including only anxiety, mood, psychotic, personality, and eating disorders)? If it is to be a subcategory, what disorders are included and what are not? And how is a clinician to know? If they had been consulted, clinical experts would likely have told the government that, to avoid confusion, the phrase 'mental illness' should not be used in the legislation.[92]

---

[90] Catherine Cullen, 'Online Government Survey on Medical Aid in Dying Sees Record-Breaking Response', CBC News, 23 January 2020, www.cbc.ca/news/politics/medical-assistance-dying-survey-response-1.5434832.

[91] 'What We Heard Report: A Public Consultation on Medical Assistance in Dying (MAID)', Report from the Department of Justice (March 2020 Government of Canada), www.justice.gc.ca/eng/cj-jp/ad-am/wwh-cqnae/index.html.

[92] It is reasonable to assume they would have been told this given the rejection of this terminology in the CCA Expert Panel Report on MAiD: 'The State of Knowledge on Medical Assistance in Dying Where a Mental Disorder Is the Sole Underlying Medical Condition', 6.

Legislative Drafting

Once again, with Bill C-7, there were problems with legislative drafting, and it will likely result in ambiguity and unforeseen/unintended circumstances.

First, as noted earlier, the legislation stipulates that mental illness cannot be considered a serious and incurable illness, disease or disability for the purposes of MAiD.[93] However, it does not define 'mental illness'. It is not clear what the government thinks 'mental illness' means and what conditions contained within, for example, the DSM-5 (the authoritative Diagnostic and Statistical Manual of Mental Disorders) are mental illnesses and what are not.

Second, the government opened the door for some advance requests for MAiD. It introduced 'final consent waivers' and made them available to individuals who meet the eligibility criteria for MAiD and whose natural deaths have become reasonably foreseeable.[94] It is clear that the government was responding to concerns about:

- people dying earlier than they otherwise would (accessing MAiD while they still had capacity but before they wished to die for fear of losing capacity);
- people refusing pain medication in order to avoid losing capacity before MAiD can be provided; and
- people having to suffer if they lose their access to MAiD because they unexpectedly lose capacity or they lose capacity before a provider can get to them.

The government was also responding to the scenario of a person self-administering MAiD, this failing to cause death, and physicians and nurse practitioners not being able to then administer MAiD because the self-administration had rendered the person incapable of giving final consent to the provider-administered MAiD. Bill C-7 explicitly allows for 'advance consent' to a medical or nurse practitioner administering MAiD if self-administration fails to cause death within a specified time period.

It is likely that the government thought it was not introducing advance requests for MAiD for individuals with dementia.[95] However, given that individuals with dementia have already been found to meet the eligibility criteria for MAiD under Bill C-14 (including that their natural deaths had become reasonably foreseeable),[96] some individuals with dementia under Bill C-7 will be permitted to make requests

---

[93] This exclusion will be automatically repealed on 17 March 2023: Bill C-7, ss 1(2.1) and 6.

[94] Bill C-7, s. 3.2.

[95] See, for example, public comments made by the Minister of Health at a press conference on the draft legislation: Daniel Leblanc, 'Ottawa Proposes Tweaks Rather than Sweeping Changes to Assisted-Dying Law', *The Globe and Mail*, 24 February 2020, www.theglobeandmail.com/politics/article-ottawa-proposes-tweaks-rather-than-sweeping-changes-to-assisted-dying/.

[96] Downie, 'It Can Happen Here'.

for MAiD in advance of loss of capacity.[97] This consequence was likely not intended but it is nonetheless a consequence of the way the legislation was drafted.

Staged Reform

Once again, the government took a staged reform approach, indicating that the issues of mature minors, requests made in advance of loss of decision-making capacity, and MAiD for persons with mental disorders as their sole underlying medical condition would be part of a statutorily mandated Parliamentary review of the legislation rather than taking a position on them in Bill C-7. In other words, they legislated about what was needed to respond to the *Truchon*[98] decision (i.e., removing 'reasonably foreseeable' as an eligibility criterion) and about what they had detected clear consensus from Canadians (e.g., final consent waivers for those who have been assessed and approved for MAiD) but put off for further deliberations the issues about which there was less agreement, greater complexity, or controversy, or a need for greater evidence, analysis and consultation.[99] One might have expected there to be no patience for such a staged reform process on the very issues that had been deferred with the introduction of Bill C-14. These issues were supposed to have been addressed in a five year review that was supposed to have started in June 2020 (but never did). However, this approach was likely tolerated for Bill C-7 because Parliament was once again up against a court-imposed deadline and the Bill mandated that a review start in April 2021 and report back in March 2022.

Legislative vs. Judicial Path

Post Bill C-14, law reform came again to Canada by way of both the legislative and judicial paths. Once again, litigation prompted action by Parliament. In September 2019, the judge in *Truchon* found that the 'reasonably foreseeable' provision in the federal legislation and the 'end of life' provision in the Québec legislation violate the *Charter*.[100] In response to *Truchon*, on 24 February 2020, the federal government introduced Bill C-7, An Act to Amend the Criminal Code (Medical Assistance in

---

[97] Jocelyn Downie and Stefanie Green, 'For People with dementia, changes in MAiD law offer new hope', Policy Options, Institute for Research on Public Policy, 21 April 2021, policyoptions. irpp.org/magazines/april-2021/for-people-with-dementia-changes-in-maid-law-offer-new-hope/.

[98] *Truchon* [2019] QCCS 3792

[99] Department of Justice Canada, 'Government of Canada Proposes Changes to Medical Assistance in Dying Legislation: News Release', Government of Canada, 24 February 2020, www.canada.ca/en/department-justice/news/2020/02/government-of-canada-proposes-changes-to-medical-assistance-in-dying-legislation.html.

[100] *Truchon* [2019] QCCS 3792.

Dying).[101] Once again, the federal legislation was drafted against a deadline (the court had given the government six months – later extended four times (because of an election[102] and the COVID pandemic[103]) for an additional total of 12 months - before the declaration of invalidity would take effect).

This time, however, the legislative process was partially reactive (removing 'reasonably foreseeable' as an eligibility criterion) but it was also partially proactive (most notably, introducing a 'final consent waiver' which, in effect, allows for MAiD that was requested in advance of loss of capacity in some limited circumstances). It remains to be seen whether it will be regarded as a better process leading to better results as a result of not being entirely driven by the courts.

CONCLUSIONS

Countries considering the decriminalization of MAiD would certainly do well to reflect on the Canadian experience of moving from the unsuccessful constitutional challenge of the absolute prohibition to the permissive legislation found in Québec and at the federal level. Key lessons include: advocates should be alert to changes in the law and in the empirical evidence throughout the world; advocates should develop skills with respect to the use of social sciences evidence; legislators should consult widely and deeply before and while drafting legislation; legislators can take a staged approach to legislative reform, dealing immediately with the least contentious aspects and then studying further and acting upon the more complex and contentious aspects; and legislatures should be proactive. By reflecting on the Canadian experience, countries considering lifting prohibitions on MAiD can potentially realise the benefits and avoid the pitfalls experienced along the Canadian path from *Rodriguez*[104] to Bill C-14 and beyond.

---

[101] See Bill C-7.
[102] *Truchon v. Canada (Attorney General)* [2020] QCCS 772.
[103] *Truchon v. Canada (Attorney General)* [2020] QCCS 2019 5 months; *Truchon v. Canada (Attorney General)* [2020] QCCS 4388 2 months; *Truchon v. Canada (Attorney General)* [2021] QCCS 590 1 month.
[104] *Rodriguez* [1993] 3 SCR 519.

Appendix: Chronology*

1990	Legislative path	Judicial path	Expert input
		30/09/1993 *Rodriguez* v. *Canada (Attorney General)* [1993] 3 SCR 519.	
			16/10/2009 Collège des Médecins du Québec discussion paper, Physicians, Appropriate Care and the Debate on Euthanasia.[1]
	22/03/2012 Québec Select Committee Dying with Dignity Report.[3]		
		15/06/2012 *Carter* v. *Canada (Attorney General)* [2012] BCSC 886.	**15/11/2011** The Royal Society of Canada Expert Panel: End-of-Life Decision Making Report.[2]
	05/06/2014 Québec Act Respecting End-of-Life Care passed.[4]		
		10/10/2013 *Carter* v. *Canada (Attorney General)* [2013] BCCA 435.	
	10/12/2015 Québec Act Respecting End-of-Life Care came into force.[6]	**06/02/2015** *Carter* v. *Canada (Attorney General)* [2015] 1 SCR 331.	**30/11/2015** Provincial-Territorial Expert Advisory Group on Physician-Assisted Dying Final Report.[5]
	25/02/2016 Special Joint Committee [House and Senate] on Physician-Assisted Dying, 'Medical Assistance In Dying: A Patient-Centred Approach', Report of the Special Joint Committee on Physician Assisted Dying.[8]	**15/01/2016** *Carter* v. *Canada (Attorney General)* [2016] 1 SCR 13. **27/06/2016** *Julia Lamb and BCCLA* v. *Canada (Attorney General)* [2016] Supreme Court of British Columbia, No. S-165851 filed.	**15/12/2015** External Panel on Options for a Legislative Response to *Carter* v. *Canada*, Consultations on Physician-Assisted Dying: Summary of Results and Key Findings: Final Report.[7]
	17/06/2016 Federal Bill C-14, An Act to Amend the Criminal Code and to Make Related Amendments to Other Acts (Medical Assistance in Dying) passed and came into force.[9]	**19/06/2017** *AB* v. *Canada (Attorney General)* [2017] ONSC 3759. **11/09/2019** *Truchon* v. *Canada (Attorney General)* [2019] QCCS 3792.	
	01/11/2018 Federal Regulations for the Monitoring of Medical Assistance in Dying came into force.[10]	**18/09/2019** *Julia Lamb and BCCLA* v. *Canada (Attorney General)* [2016] Supreme Court of British Columbia, No. S-165851 adjourned. **11/10/2019** Appeal deadline for *Truchon* v. *Canada (Attorney General)* [2019] QCCS 3792 passed with no appeal.	**12/12/2018** Council of Canadian Academies Expert Panel on Medical Assistance in Dying Reports.[11]
	24/02/2020 Federal Bill C-7, An Act to Amend the Criminal Code (Medical Assistance in Dying) introduced.[12]	Four extensions on suspension of declaration of invalidity granted: **03/03/2020** *Truchon* v. *Canada (Attorney General)* [2020] QCCS 772 **29/06/2020** *Truchon* v. *Canada (Attorney General)* [2020] QCCS 2019 **17/12/2020** *Truchon* v. *Canada (Attorney General)* [2020] QCCS 4388 **25/2/2021** *Truchon* v. *Canada (Attorney General)* [2021] QCCS 590.	
2021	**17/03/2021** An Act to Amend the Criminal Code (Medical Assistance in Dying) passed and came into force.[13]		

---

* See Chapter 8 for a chronology focusing on Québec and including further discussion of developments.

1   'Physicians, Appropriate Care and the Debate on Euthanasia: A Reflection', Discussion Paper from the Collège des médecins du Québec (16 October 2009 CMQ).
2   Report from the Royal Society of Canada Expert Panel: End-of-Life Decision Making (November 2011 Royal Society of Canada).
3   Report from the Select Committee on Dying with Dignity (March 2012 National Assembly of Québec).
4   Act Respecting End-of-Life Care, RLRQ, c. S-32.0001 (2014) (Québec).
5   Final Report from the Provincial/Territorial Expert Advisory Group on Physician-Assisted Dying (30 November 2015 Government of Ontario, Ministry for Health and Long-Term Care).
6   Act Respecting End-of-Life Care, RLRQ, c. S-32.0001 (2014) (Québec).
7   'Consultations on Physician-Assisted Dying: Summary of Results and Key Findings', Final Report from the External Panel on Options for a Legislative Response to *Carter* v. *Canada* (15 December 2015 Government of Canada, Department of Justice).
8   'Medical Assistance in Dying: A Patient-Centred Approach', Report from the Special Joint Committee on Physician-Assisted Dying (2016 Parliament of Canada, House of Commons and Senate).
9   An Act to Amend the Criminal Code and to Make Related Amendments to Other Acts (Medical Assistance in Dying), SC 2016, c. 3.
10 Regulations for the Monitoring of Medical Assistance in Dying: Ginette Petitpas Taylor, Minister for Health, 'Registration: SOR/2018-166: Criminal Code', in *Canada Gazette*, pt. 2, vol. 152, no. 16, 27 July 2018, at 3077.
11 'The State of Knowledge of Medical Assistance in Dying for Mature Minors', Report from the Expert Panel Working Group on MAID for Mature Minors (2018 Council of Canadian Academies); 'The State of Knowledge on Advance Requests for Medical Assistance in Dying', Report from the Expert Panel Working Group on Advance Requests for MAID (2018 Council of Canadian Academies); Council of Canadian Academies 'The State of Knowledge on Medical Assistance in Dying Where a Mental Disorder is the Sole Underlying Medical Condition'.
12 Bill C-7, An Act to Amend the Criminal Code (Medical Assistance in Dying), SC 2020 died on the order paper.
13 Bill C-7, An Act to Amend the Criminal Code (Medical Assistance in Dying), SC 2021, c. 2.

3

The Extension of the Belgian Euthanasia Law to Minors in 2014

Kasper Raus, Luc Deliens and Kenneth Chambaere

INTRODUCTION

In 2002, Belgium passed the Law of 28 May 2002 on Euthanasia (hereafter referred to as the '2002 euthanasia law') which legalised euthanasia, making Belgium one of only a handful of countries where this is the case. It is important to note at the outset that this law only legalises euthanasia, which it defines as 'intentionally terminating life *by someone other than the person concerned*, at the latter's request'.[1] This formulation means that physician-assisted suicide ('PAS') was not legalised since in PAS the final act (i.e. the taking of lethal medication) is performed by the patient themselves. The Belgian context is thus different from that in the Netherlands (where both euthanasia and PAS are legal) and several states in the United States (where only PAS is legalised).[2] For this reason, this chapter will only discuss euthanasia and *not* PAS. How this 2002 law came to pass will be discussed more in detail later on in the chapter.

Twelve years later, on 13 February 2014, the Belgian Chamber of Representatives voted on a legislative proposal to amend the 2002 euthanasia law.[3] With eighty-eight votes in favour of the proposal, twelve abstentions, and forty-four votes against the proposal, it was approved. Two weeks later the new law was ratified and became the

---

[1] Judgement 153/2015, Constitutional Court of Belgium (29 October 2015) [English translation] at 3. No official English translation of the Belgian euthanasia law exists. However, in 2015 the Constitutional Court of Belgium issued a ruling concerning the 2014 extension of the euthanasia law (discussed below). In the English version of this ruling, the Court provides a complete translation of the Belgian euthanasia law into English. As the Constitutional Court is a high-level Belgian Court and there exists no official translation of the euthanasia law, we will use the Court's translation as authoritative. Therefore, when we quote from the euthanasia law, we will use the Constitutional Court's translation.

[2] See Chapters 4 and 7 for a discussion of the relevant law in the Netherlands and the United States, respectively.

[3] Bill Amending the Law of 28 May 2002 on Euthanasia, to Enable Euthanasia on Minors, S 5-2170/1.

Law of 28 February 2014 amending the Law of 28 May 2002 on Euthanasia to Extend Euthanasia to Minors.[4] This new law legally extended the use of euthanasia to non-emancipated minors (it was already legal for emancipated minors under the 2002 law), making it possible for those non-emancipated minors to legally receive euthanasia when several criteria of due care were met. When it comes to euthanasia, the difference between emancipated and non-emancipated minors in Belgium is a particularly important distinction that will be elaborated on further below.

This chapter deals specifically with the legislative process leading up to the Belgian law on euthanasia and particularly its extension to minors. This is a particularly important and interesting topic since it concerns a unique extension of a euthanasia law that is itself already very distinctive. Unlike PAS, which is legal in several countries around the world, euthanasia is legal in only six countries.[5] Euthanasia for non-emancipated minors was, until the Belgian extension, only legal in the Netherlands from the age of twelve.[6]

To fully understand the importance of the extension to minors and the process leading up to it, we will first briefly discuss the original 2002 law, the Law of 28 May 2002 on Euthanasia.[7] Second, we will focus more specifically on the 2014 extension. Here we will discuss the content of the 2014 law, how it is different from the 2002 euthanasia law and how it has been used in practice since it was passed. Then we will discuss the legislative process in detail and the reception of the law. Finally we will look at several arguments that were raised in the legal and moral debate on whether or not the euthanasia law should be extended to include minors.

TERMINOLOGY

We first make two preliminary notes about terminology. First, throughout this chapter we will refer only to 'minors' and not 'children'. Both terms are found in the literature with several commentators and journalists choosing to refer to

---

[4] Law of 28 February 2014 Amending the Law of 28 May 2002 on Euthanasia to Extend Euthanasia to Minors, *Belgian Official Gazette* (12 March 2014) 2014/009093, 21053.

[5] The countries where euthanasia is legal are the Netherlands (2001), Belgium (2002), Luxembourg (2009), Canada (federally from 2016 and in Québec from 2014), Australia (Victoria from 2017, Western Australia from 2019 and Tasmania in 2021), and Colombia where euthanasia was decriminalised via a Constitutional Court decision (Sentence C-239 (1997), Ref. Expedient D-1490 (Constitutional Court of the Republic of Colombia, 20 May 1997), with regulations in 2015). Assisted dying laws in the Netherlands (Chapter 4), Canada federally (Chapter 2), Québec, Canada (Chapter 8) and Victoria, Australia (Chapter 5) are discussed further in this book.

[6] For completeness it should be noted that in 2018 Colombia passed a resolution allowing euthanasia for children aged seven or older, making it the third country where euthanasia for minors is allowed.

[7] Law of 28 May 2002 on Euthanasia, *Belgian Official Gazette* (22 June 2002) 2002/09590, 28515, art. 1.

'euthanasia for children' or 'child euthanasia'.[8] We believe the difference between the two is not just semantic, partly because of the imagery they invoke. The word 'child' could be argued to invoke the more emotively relevant idea of younger and innocent human beings, whereas 'minor' is a more legalistic and neutral term that invokes the image of a somewhat older person. We observe it is not surprising that many opponents of the law's extension talk about 'children'.[9] The reason we opt for the term 'minor' is that it is the more correct legal term and best translates the term used in the 2014 extension (*minderjarige*).

Second, when it comes to the Belgian euthanasia law there is a crucial difference between emancipated minors and non-emancipated minors. The 2002 euthanasia law not only legalised euthanasia for adult patients but also for emancipated minors. Emancipation is a legal mechanism whereby minors become legally competent to autonomously (i.e. without permission from a parent or guardian) make their own legal decisions (e.g. make financial decisions or enter into legal contracts). Only minors over the age of fifteen can become emancipated and they can become emancipated in one of two ways. First, minors who marry and have their marriage approved before a juvenile court become emancipated. Second, minors over the age of fifteen can become emancipated through the order of a juvenile court. Although such emancipation rarely occurs, the 2002 euthanasia law did make it possible for a certain category of minors to legally receive euthanasia. The 2014 extension thus made euthanasia a legal possibility for all minors, emancipated and non-emancipated. As minors are, by default, non-emancipated until they explicitly become emancipated and because emancipation is so rare we will for the remainder of the chapter simply use 'minor' to refer to non-emancipated minors. When discussing emancipated minors, we will mention this explicitly.

THE 2002 LAW ON EUTHANASIA

The Legislative Process

In 2002 Belgium adopted the Law of 28 May on Euthanasia which legalised euthanasia for adults and emancipated minors. Much has already been written about the legislative process that preceded the passing of the law.[10] As the focus in

---

[8] Luc Bovens, 'Child Euthanasia: Should We Just Not Talk about It?' (2015) 41 *Journal of Medical Ethics* 630–4. See also Geoff Keeling, 'The Sensitivity Argument against Child Euthanasia' (2018) 44 *Journal of Medical Ethics* 143–4.

[9] Charles Lane, 'Children Are Being Euthanized in Belgium', *Washington Post*, 7 August 2018, www.washingtonpost.com/opinions/children-are-being-euthanized-in-belgium/2018/08/06/ 9473bac2-9988-11e8-b60b-1c897f17e185_story.html.

[10] An excellent and thorough overview can be found in John Griffiths, Heleen Weyers and Maurice Adams, *Euthanasia and Law in Europe* (Oxford: Hart Publishing, 2008).

this chapter lies primarily on the 2014 extension we will only highlight a few relevant issues.

The first relevant point to make is that the 'original' 2002 euthanasia law was preceded by ethical and societal debate. In its very first advice in 1997, the Belgian Advisory Committee on Bioethics discussed the moral and legal issues of euthanasia.[11] As it was impossible to reach agreement within the Advisory Committee, they instead drafted four possible positions regarding the legal regulation of euthanasia. Three of these positions allowed for euthanasia in some cases. Although this advice was of course not legally binding, it was still regarded as highly important since it helped spark societal and political debate. The final euthanasia law was certainly inspired or catalysed by this advice.

The inability of the Advisory Committee to reach agreement also shows that opinions were divided on the issue. On the one hand, there were, of course, debates about whether or not euthanasia should be legalised. On the other hand, from the very start there was also disagreement between the proponents of euthanasia concerning how euthanasia should be legally regulated and in which cases it should be allowed. The eventual 2002 law, with its criteria of due care, should thus be considered a compromise between various different positions. With respect to minors, several politicians wanted the 2002 law to include access to euthanasia for non-emancipated minors, but no majority for this position could be found. This will be discussed more extensively below.

A second important point is that the debate preceding the 2002 euthanasia law was not just ideological but was informed by empirical research. In the process leading up to the euthanasia law, hearings were held with experts who made clear that euthanasia was already occurring in Belgium. Important empirical work had shown that there were cases of euthanasia (and also of termination of life without explicit request[12]) in Belgium before the passing of the euthanasia law.[13] Part of the

---

[11] Raadgevend Comité voor Bioethiek, *Advies nr. 1 d.d. 12 mei 1997 betreffende de wenselijkheid van een wettelijke regeling van euthanasie* (1997).

[12] Termination of life without explicit request refers to those cases where physicians gave lethal doses of medication to patients *without* there being an explicit request. In literature this is sometimes referred to as involuntary euthanasia, but since the Belgian law includes in its definition of euthanasia that it happens at the person's request, cases without consent cannot, by definition, be categorised or labelled as euthanasia. Termination of life without explicit request is a broad category that may include cases where life-ending drugs were administered: (1) against the patient's wishes; (2) without asking the patient their views (and it was possible to ask them); (3) when it was impossible to ask the patient's views; or (4) when there was a request but this was not put into writing.

[13] See Luc Deliens, Freddy Mortier, Johan Bilsen, Marc Cosyns, Robert Vander Stichele, Johan Vanoverloop and Koen Ingels, 'End-of-Life Decisions in Medical Practice in Flanders, Belgium: A Nationwide Survey' (2000) 356 *The Lancet* 1806–11. It should be noted that this is hardly surprising since later research suggests that euthanasia occurs in nearly all countries, even countries where the practice is illegal. One important study looked at six European countries (Belgium, Denmark, Italy, the Netherlands, Sweden and Switzerland) and found that although the incidence of euthanasia differs, euthanasia occurs in each of these countries:

reason for passing the 2002 law was thus that it would bring into the open a practice that, until 2002, was happening without oversight.

It should also be stressed that the 2002 euthanasia law created the legal possibility for physicians to perform euthanasia, but in no way created a legal obligation to perform euthanasia or even to explore the grounds for a request. The law explicitly provides that no person can be forced to be involved in a euthanasia procedure and this includes not only doctors but also includes nurses, psychologists, pharmacists and other health professionals. Also, around the same time as the 2002 law was passed, the Law of 14 June 2002 Concerning Palliative Care was passed.[14] This law guarantees palliative care as a right for every patient, with the intention, among others, that no patient opts for euthanasia because palliative care is unavailable.

The Criteria of Due Care

Like the legislative process, the content of the 2002 law has also been amply discussed.[15] In order to fully understand the 2014 amendment, it is relevant here to briefly describe several criteria of due care that have to be met for euthanasia to be legal. We will distinguish between criteria that concern the patient and their (clinical) condition, criteria that deal with the procedure that should be followed, and criteria about how euthanasia should be reported when performed.

Conditions of the Euthanasia Request

Because the Belgian euthanasia law defines euthanasia as the intentional termin-ation of a person's life by a physician *at that person's explicit request*, every case of euthanasia starts from a request by the patient. Concerning this request, the law stipulates that the request should be 'voluntary, well-considered and repeated, and ... not the result of any external pressure'.[16] Every physician faced with a euthanasia request by a patient (and who is willing to explore this request) is required to ascertain that these conditions are met. How these criteria should be

---

Agnes van der Heide, Luc Deliens, Karin Faisst, Tore Nilstun, Michael Norup, Eugenio Paci, Gerrit van der Wal and Paul J van der Maas, 'End-of-Life Decision-Making in Six European Countries: Descriptive Study' (2003) 361 *The Lancet* 345–50.

[14] Law of 14 June 2002 Concerning Palliative Care, *Belgian Official Gazette* (26 October 2002) 2002/022868, 49160.

[15] T. Vansweevelt, 'De euthanasiewet: de ultieme bevestiging van het zelfbeschikkingsrecht of een gecontroleerde keuzevrijheid?' (2003) 4 *Tijdschrift voor Gezondheidsrecht* 216–78. See also Evelien Delbeke, *Juridische aspecten van zorgverlening aan het levenseinde* (Antwerp: Intersentia, 2012); Herman Nys, 'A Discussion of the Legal Rules on Euthanasia in Belgium Briefly Compared with the Rules in Luxembourg and the Netherlands', in David Albert Jones, Chris Gastmans and Calum MacKellar (eds.), *Euthanasia and Assisted Suicide: Lessons from Belgium* (Cambridge: Cambridge University Press, 2017), 7–25.

[16] Judgement 153/2015, Constitutional Court of Belgium (29 October 2015) (English translation) at 3.

assessed is not stipulated explicitly in the law, but physicians are assumed to have the required skills to assess competence.

It is also possible to draft an advance directive for euthanasia, which takes effect after patients enter a state of permanent unconsciousness such as a permanent vegetative state. Contrary to what is sometimes assumed by the general public, advance directives cannot be relied upon for patients in states of permanent *incompetence* (e.g. advanced dementia). Because the advance directive only applies in the less common event of irreversible unconsciousness, euthanasia is rarely performed following such a direct-ive. In 2016 and 2017, for example, euthanasia following an advance directive accounted for only 1.3 per cent of all reported euthanasia cases.[17] The Federal Control and Evaluation Commission for Euthanasia ('FCECE') has also released some data from which it is clear that in 2018 euthanasia following an advance directive accounted for 0.9 per cent of all reported euthanasia cases,[18] and in 2019 this was 1 per cent.[19]

Medical Condition of the Patient
Second, even when a request is made voluntarily, repeatedly and without external pressure, it can only be legally granted when the patient 'is in a medically futile condition of constant and unbearable physical or mental suffering that cannot be alleviated, resulting from a serious and incurable condition caused by illness or accident'.[20] Relevant here is that this formulation legally allows euthanasia for physical suffering, but also for mental suffering, provided of course that the mental suffering is due to a serious and incurable condition. Also, the law does not require patients receiving euthanasia to be close to death, so that patients suffering from, for example, psychiatric conditions or degenerative diseases such as amyotrophic lateral sclerosis can also receive euthanasia. However, as will be made clear below, when patients are not close to death, additional procedural requirements apply.

Procedural Requirements
Third, the law prescribes several procedural requirements which must be satisfied in order to move from a request for euthanasia to the actual performance of euthanasia. The most relevant requirements are, first, as mentioned above, the treating phys-ician who is faced with a request and is willing to explore this request should first

---

[17] Report from the Federal Control and Evaluation Commission for Euthanasia (2018 Federal Public Service).

[18] 'Euthanasie – Cijfers voor het jaar 2018', Report from the Federal Control and Evaluation Commission for Euthanasia (2019 Federal Public Service), https://overlegorganen.gezondheid .belgie.be/nl/documenten/euthanasie-cijfers-voor-het-jaar-2018.

[19] 'Euthanasie – Cijfers voor het jaar 2019', Report from the Federal Control and Evaluation Commission for Euthanasia (2020 Federal Public Service), https://overlegorganen.gezondheid .belgie.be/sites/default/files/documents/fcee_cijfers-2019_persbericht.pdf.

[20] Judgement 153/2015, Constitutional Court of Belgium (29 October 2015) (English translation) at 3.

ascertain that the criteria regarding the voluntary nature of the patient's request and her medical condition are met. Second, the physician needs to 'consult another physician about the serious and incurable nature of the condition and inform him about the reasons for this consultation'.[21] This consulted physician should be independent from both the patient and the treating physician and 'must ascertain the patient's constant and unbearable physical or mental suffering that cannot be alleviated'.[22] The consulted physician should physically examine the patient, make a written report on their findings and provide this to the treating physician.

If, however, the patient is not expected to die within the foreseeable future (e.g. patients with psychiatric illnesses or degenerative diseases), there is an additional legal requirement to consult a further physician who should be a psychiatrist or a specialist in the condition from which the patient is suffering. Like the first consulted physician, this second consulted physician must check whether the criteria of due care (person has made a free and voluntary request and is suffering from constant and unbearable suffering) are indeed met. In cases of patients who are not expected to die within the foreseeable future, there should also always be at least one month between the patient's written request and the actual act of euthanasia.

Societal Control (Reporting and Reviewing Euthanasia Cases)

Finally, the Belgian euthanasia law creates a control mechanism that involves reviewing cases of euthanasia after it has been provided. All physicians who have performed euthanasia must file an official report to the FCECE. The FCECE reviews all reports of euthanasia and checks whether the criteria of due care were indeed met. If the FCECE judges that in a certain case the legal criteria for euthanasia were not met, it should send the report to the Public Prosecutor who can then judge whether or not to file charges.

Since the legalisation of euthanasia in 2002, the FCECE has referred one report to the Public Prosecutor. In that case, it was ultimately decided not to prosecute because the patient took the lethal medication herself, which meant that it was not euthanasia but rather a case of PAS that was not regulated by the euthanasia law.[23] In 2019 there was also a Court of Assizes trial, which was the subject of extensive media coverage, where three physicians (one treating physician and two consulting physicians) were indicted for allegedly incorrectly performing euthanasia. All three physicians were ultimately acquitted.[24] Of note is that this euthanasia case had been

[21] Ibid. at 4.
[22] Ibid.
[23] Beau Wauters, 'Arts niet vervolgd wegens toedienen gifbeker: "Geen illegale euthanasie, maar hulp bij zelfdoding"', *De Morgen*, 29 April 2019, www.demorgen.be/nieuws/arts-niet-vervolgd-wegens-toedienen-gifbeker-geen-illegale-euthanasie-maar-hulp-bij-zelfdoding~b52446b9/.
[24] Douglas De Coninck, 'Vrijspraak voor drie artsen: doek valt over euthanasieproces in Gent', *De Morgen*, 31 January 2020, www.demorgen.be/nieuws/vrijspraak-voor-drie-artsen-doek-valt-over-euthanasieproces-in-gent~beb843c0/.

fully approved by the FCECE but the legal investigation was initiated following a complaint by the family.

THE CONTENT AND USE OF THE 2014 EXTENSION

Having discussed the 2002 euthanasia law, we now examine the 2014 extension which made euthanasia legal for non-emancipated minors provided they have 'capacity for discernment' (discussed below). However, the 2014 law is not a simple extension of euthanasia to non-emancipated minors. There remain some significant differences between euthanasia for non-emancipated minors, on the one hand, and for adults and emancipated minors, on the other hand. First, we will briefly discuss the crucial concept of capacity for discernment and, subsequently, we will highlight the relevant differences between the 2002 euthanasia law and the 2014 extension. Finally, we will discuss the extent to which the 2014 extension has been used in practice.

Minors with the 'Capacity for Discernment'

The 2014 extension does not create a whole new law, but rather amends the original 2002 law. Key to the 2014 extension is a small amendment it makes to article 3.1 of the 2002 law which now states that a physician performing euthanasia commits no criminal offence if he or she has ascertained that:

> the patient is a legally competent person of age, a legally competent emancipated minor, **or a minor with the capacity for discernment**, and conscious at the moment of making the request [emphasis added].[25]

This provision is the first to introduce the concept of 'capacity for discernment' (*oordeelsbekwaamheid* in Dutch). The use of this new terminology, a first in Belgian medical law, is significant.[26] The 2002 Belgian Patients' Rights Law[27] already recognised the rights of minors to decide on medical decisions, including far-reaching decisions where death would follow (e.g. refusing life-sustaining treatment), according to their age and maturity. Euthanasia was an exception to this law as non-emancipated minors could not legally receive euthanasia, regardless of their age and maturity. In the 2014 euthanasia extension there is no reference to the criteria mentioned in the patient rights law ('age and maturity'); instead, the choice was for eligibility to depend on a minor's capacity for discernment.

[25] Judgement 153/2015, Constitutional Court of Belgium (29 October 2015) (English translation) at 3.
[26] Kristof Van Assche, Kasper Raus, Bert Vanderhaegen and Sigrid Sterckx, '"Capacity for Discernment" and Euthanasia on Minors in Belgium' (2019) 27 *Medical Law Review* 242–66.
[27] Law of 22 August 2002 concerning the Rights of the Patient, *Belgian Official Gazette* (26 September 2002) 2002/22737, 43719.

Legislators could have chosen to reform by simply removing any reference to adult patients and emancipated minors in the euthanasia law. If that had been done, the patient rights law would apply and grant eligibility to minors of sufficient age and maturity according to general principles, and all the other criteria of due care in the euthanasia law would then apply to this cohort. However, this was not done and the fact that 'minors with capacity for discernment' were added to the list of those potentially eligible for euthanasia suggests that the new terminology – 'capacity for discernment' – has a different meaning.

As a novel term, the meaning and application of 'capacity for discernment' are a matter of debate, particularly since it is clear from the parliamentary proceedings that the term was specifically intended as a *medical* term rather than a legal term. Physicians working with minors – the argument goes – are both trained and experienced in assessing how well a minor is able to judge their own situation and make their own decision.[28] Others argue that the concept is vague and potentially arbitrary since there is no agreed upon way to measure it.[29]

The Differences between Euthanasia for Adults and Euthanasia for Non-emancipated Minors

As was remarked several times, the 2014 extension is more than a simple extension of euthanasia to non-emancipated minors with capacity of discernment. There remain important differences between euthanasia for adults and emancipated minors, on the one hand, and non-emancipated minors, on the other hand. We will highlight these differences here.

First, a relevant difference relates to when advance directives for euthanasia can take effect. Adults and emancipated minors can make an advance directive for euthanasia to operate should they ever find themselves in a permanent state of unconsciousness (e.g. a permanent vegetative state). As noted above, euthanasia is rarely performed relying on an advance directive, but the possibility exists. For non-emancipated minors, it is not possible to make such an advance directive, meaning they have to be conscious at the time of the euthanasia request (and probably[30] also at the time when euthanasia is performed).

---

[28] See, for example, Freddy Mortier, 'Euthanasie bij minderjarigen', in Maurice Adams, John Griffiths and Govert den Hartogh (eds.), *Euthanasie: nieuwe knelpunten in een voortgezette discussie* (Leuven: Kok Publishing, 2003), 199–218.

[29] Stefaan Van Gool and Jan De Lepeleire, 'Euthanasia in Children: Keep Asking the Right Questions', in David Albert Jones, Chris Gastmans and Calum MacKellar (eds.), *Euthanasia and Assisted Suicide: Lessons from Belgium* (Cambridge: Cambridge University Press, 2017), 173–87.

[30] We write 'probably' as there is some room for legal debate here. Both the original euthanasia law and the 2014 extension stipulate that a physician who performs euthanasia does not commit a crime when they have assured themselves that the patient is an adult, emancipated minor or minor with capacity of discernment 'who is conscious at the time of his request' (Law of 28 May

Second, euthanasia is only legal for minors who are expected to die within the foreseeable future. Minors who have a serious and incurable condition but a longer life-expectancy are unable to legally receive euthanasia. It is clear that some parties in the parliamentary proceedings were concerned that including the possibility of euthanasia for minors with a longer life expectancy would open the possibility of euthanasia for love-sick minors or 'confused teenagers'[31] who feel heartbroken but who will recover from this in time. It should be remarked, however, that it is very unlikely that a love-sick teenager would be able to satisfy the other euthanasia criteria, such as the need for a 'serious and incurable condition caused by illness or accident'.

Third, minors are able to receive euthanasia only for physical suffering and not, like adults, also for mental suffering. This excludes the possibility of euthanasia resulting solely from psychological or psychiatric conditions. The difference between physical and mental suffering has, however, been the topic of some debate.[32] Empirical research into why people ask for euthanasia indicates that 'pain' is seldom the sole reason. The most cited reasons for asking for euthanasia could be classified as mental or psychological and include 'loss of dignity' and 'fear of future suffering'.[33] This indicates that the line between physical and psychological suffering is often very thin and complex. It is unclear what this means for minors requesting euthanasia. It is possible that, because euthanasia for purely physical suffering is less common, minors are less likely than adults to meet the legal criteria for euthanasia. This could perhaps offer an additional explanation[34] for why there have been so few cases of euthanasia for minors (as discussed below).

2002 on Euthanasia, ch. 2, art. 3, para. 1). The particular legal phrasing raises the question of whether patients requesting euthanasia have to be conscious when euthanasia is actually performed. It should be noted that nowhere in the law is this explicitly mentioned. However, the law also stipulates that 'the patient can at all times revoke the request, after which the document [i.e. the written request] is taken out of the medical file and returned to the patient' (Law of 28 May 2002 on Euthanasia, ch. 2, art. 3, para. 4). One could argue that patients with a written request who become unconscious are no longer able to meet this legal requirement as they can no longer revoke their request. This might imply that patients have to be conscious when euthanasia is performed.

[31] 'Verslag namens de verenigde commissies voor de justitie en voor de sociale aangelegenheden', Belgian Senate (2013d, document number 5-2170/4) at 66.

[32] See, for example, Kasper Raus and Sigrid Sterckx, 'Euthanasia for Mental Suffering', in Michael Cholbi and Jukka Varelius (eds.), *New Directions in the Ethics of Assisted Suicide and Euthanasia* (Cham: Springer, 2015), 79–96.

[33] For the Belgian data, see Kenneth Chambaere, Johan Bilsen, Joachim Cohen, Bregje D. Onwuteaka-Philipsen, Freddy Mortier and Luc Deliens, 'Physician-Assisted Deaths under the Euthanasia Law in Belgium: A Population-Based Survey' (2010) 182 *Canadian Medical Association Journal* 895–901. For the Dutch data see Judith A. C. Rietjens, Johannes J. M. van Delden, Agnes van der Heide, Astrid M. Vrakking, Bregje D. Onwuteaka-Philipsen, Paul J. van der Maas and Gerrit van der Wal, 'Terminal Sedation and Euthanasia: A Comparison of Clinical Practices' (2006) 166 *Archives of Internal Medicine* 749–53.

[34] The other explanation of course being that there is a significantly higher percentage of sudden deaths among minors compared to the adult population. See Geert Pousset, Johan Bilsen,

Fourth, an important extra criterion of due care is that when the patient is a non-emancipated minor there has to be a consultation not only with another physician (as in all cases of euthanasia), but also an additional consultation with a child and adolescent psychiatrist or psychologist. This psychiatrist or psychologist also examines the patient, 'ascertains the minor's capacity for discernment, and certifies this in writing'.[35] This is intended to provide an extra check to guarantee that the minor indeed possesses the crucial capacity for discernment.

Fifth, and finally, minors require the consent of their legal representative in order to legally qualify for euthanasia, even when they are judged to possess capacity for discernment. This legal representative can be a parent or a legal guardian who thus has the power to veto the euthanasia request. In this respect, the euthanasia law deviates from the general Belgian patients' rights law which stipulates that minors who are judged to have sufficient age and maturity are legally allowed to enforce their patient rights independently from their legal representatives. In effect, this means that minors who meet these criteria are allowed to refuse, for example, life-sustaining treatments without their parents' consent, but legally require their parents' consent to receive euthanasia.

The Practice of Euthanasia for Minors 2014–2019

The *Washington Post* published an opinion piece in August 2018 entitled 'Children Are Being Euthanized'.[36] Around the same time, many other international papers discussed the occurrence of euthanasia for minors. The reason for this sudden attention was the then-latest report of the FCECE (reporting on the years 2016–2017) which made clear that since the extension of euthanasia to minors, the FCECE had received three cases of euthanasia for minors.[37] The FCECE has since released data on the years 2018–2019 showing there were no cases of euthanasia for minors in 2018,[38] and one reported case of euthanasia for a minor with capacity for discernment in 2019.[39] Since 2014, there have thus been only four reported cases. As nothing is yet known about the 2019 case, we will focus on the three earlier cases.

Joachim Cohen, Kenneth Chambaere, Luc Deliens and Freddy Mortier, 'Medical End-of-Life Decisions in Children in Flanders, Belgium: A Population-Based Postmortem Survey' (2010) 164 *Archives of Pediatrics & Adolescent Medicine* 547–53.

[35] Judgement 153/2015, Constitutional Court of Belgium (29 October 2015) (English translation) at 3.

[36] Lane, 'Children Are Being Euthanized in Belgium'.

[37] 'Achtste verslag aan de wetgevende kamers (2016–2017)', Report from the Federal Control and Evaluation Commission for Euthanasia (2018 Federal Public Service), https://overlegorganen .gezondheid.belgie.be/sites/default/files/documents/8_euthanasie-verslag_2016-2017-nl.pdf.

[38] 'Euthanasie – cijfers voor het jaar 2018', Report from the Federal Control and Evaluation Commission for Euthanasia (2019 Federal Public Service), https://overlegorganen.gezondheid .belgie.be/nl/documenten/euthanasie-cijfers-voor-het-jaar-2018.

[39] 'Euthanasie – cijfers voor het jaar 2019', Report from the Federal Control and Evaluation Commission for Euthanasia (2020 Federal Public Service), https://overlegorganen.gezondheid .belgie.be/nl/documenten/euthanasie-cijfers-voor-het-jaar-2019.

In any case, as was predicted when the 2014 extension was discussed, the law is not used frequently.

The three cases involved minors aged nine, eleven and seventeen who had received euthanasia and whose cases were subsequently reported to the FCECE. In each of the three cases, the minors suffered from a serious condition (as is required by law): cystic fibrosis, a glioblastoma brain tumour and the degenerative muscle disease Duchenne muscular dystrophy. As the FCECE only publishes limited information about individual cases, very little is known about them.

However, what is known is that all three cases were reviewed by the FCECE which decided that they met the legal requirements and were therefore approved. Despite these approvals by the FCECE, the cases did generate some international debate, particularly concerning the nine-year-old and the eleven-year-old. As remarked above, the Netherlands also allows euthanasia for minors but only from the age of twelve and both Belgian cases fell below this Dutch threshold.

Much of the controversy about these two cases seemingly revolved around two issues. The first is whether nine- and eleven-year-olds are old and mature enough to have the required 'capacity for discernment'. The second issue dealt with the prognosis of the minors. Although the FCECE report mentions the minors' age and disease, it does not specify which minor suffered from which disease. Several news channels, including the *Washington Post*, claimed to have talked to insiders and found out that it was the eleven-year-old who suffered from cystic fibrosis. The criticism voiced at this case was that people with cystic fibrosis have been known to reach the age of thirty in relatively good health. This raises the question of whether the eleven-year-old could have been expected to die in the foreseeable future.

We consider that the starting point for considering this question is that the FCECE evaluated this case and concluded that the criteria for euthanasia were met. Cystic fibrosis is an incurable condition and is capable of causing unbearable suffering. Although some people with cystic fibrosis may live for a longer period, others may not and it is reasonable to assume that the minor in this case was close to death. Without further evidence, and in light of the FCECE's approval of this case, it is difficult to suggest it fell outside the euthanasia law.

OVERVIEW OF THE LEGISLATIVE PROCESS

This chapter has thus far discussed the content of both the 2002 euthanasia law and the 2014 extension. In this part we will discuss more in detail how the 2014 extension came to pass.

Potential Catalysts for Reform

The extension to minors should not be seen as unexpected. As mentioned above, several politicians and policymakers had wanted the 2002 euthanasia law to cover euthanasia for minors.[40] Ever since the enactment of the 2002 euthanasia law, legislative proposals to extend euthanasia to minors were submitted periodically.[41] The relevant question to ask is perhaps not so much why the amendment was passed at all, but rather why it was passed in 2014.

Determining with certainty why the 2014 amendment was passed when it did is difficult. Various factors seemed to be at play. First, it has been argued that some impetus for legislative change came from the medical profession.[42] Already in 2003 the Belgian Order of Physicians officially took the position that: 'From a deontological point of view the mental age of a patient is more important than his calendar age'.[43] Furthermore, it became clear that in some cases involving non-emancipated minors, paediatricians and oncologists were resorting to the use of lethal doses in order to accelerate the dying process in minors. An important and much quoted empirical study confirmed this in 2010.[44] Other empirical research in this period also indicated that there was considerable support among physicians,[45]

[40] See, for example, an amendment to the 2002 euthanasia law that was submitted when the original euthanasia law was being discussed but was eventually voted down. See: Amendment to Law Proposal Concerning Euthanasia, 2000, S 2-244/3.

[41] The proposals that were submitted are: Bill Supplementing the Law of 28 May 2002 on Euthanasia as Concerns Minors, 15 June 2006, K. 51-2553/1; Bill Supplementing the Law of 28 May 2002 on Euthanasia as Concerns Minors, 12 December 2006, S 3-1993; Bill Supplementing the Law of 28 May 2002 on Euthanasia, Concerning Minors, 28 November 2007, S 4-431; Bill Amending the Law of 28 May 2002 on Euthanasia as Concerns Minors, 19 December 2007, K. 52-611; Bill Supplementing the Law of 28 May 2002 on Euthanasia, Concerning Minors, 26 May 2008, S 4-785; Bill Amending art. 3 of the Law of 28 May 2002 on Euthanasia, Concerning Euthanasia on Minors, 16 September 2008, S 4-920; Bill Amending art. 3 of the Law of 28 May 2002 on Euthanasia, Concerning Euthanasia on Minors, 16 August 2010, S 5-21; Bill Amending the Law of 28 May 2002 on Euthanasia as Concerns Minors of 15 Years and Older, 23 September 2010, S 5-179; Bill Supplementing the Law of 28 May 2002 on Euthanasia, Concerning Minors, 28 October 2010, K 53-496; Bill Supplementing the Law of 28 May 2002 on Euthanasia, Concerning Minors, 9 May 2012, S 5-1610; Bill on the Extension of the Law of 28 May 2002 on Euthanasia to Minors, the Medical Assistance to the Patient Who Performs the Life-Terminating Action Himself or Herself and the Punishment of Assisted Suicide, 25 January 2013, S 5-1947; Bill Amending the Law of 28 May 2002 on Euthanasia, Concerning Euthanasia on Minors, 7 February 2013, K 53-2633. The Bill that eventually was adopted was the Bill Amending the Law of 28 May 2002 on Euthanasia, to Enable Euthanasia on Minors, S 5-2170/1.

[42] Van Assche et al., 'Capacity for Discernment'.

[43] Orde der Artsen, 'Advies betreffende palliatieve zorg, euthanasie en andere medische beslissingen omtrent het levenseinde' (2003) doc. a100006 at 6, www.ordomedic.be/nl/adviezen/advies/advies-betreffende-palliatieve-zorg-euthanasie-en-andere-medische-beslissingen-omtrent-het-levenseinde.

[44] Pousset et al., 'Medical End-of-Life Decisions in Children'.

[45] Geert Pousset, Freddy Mortier, Johan Bilsen, Joachim Cohen and Luc Deliens, 'Attitudes and Practices of Physicians Regarding Physician-Assisted Dying in Minors' (2011) 96 *Archives of Disease in Childhood* 948–53.

adolescent cancer survivors[46] and secondary school students[47] for euthanasia for minors.

Second, it has been argued that another factor in the decision was the fact that the Belgian Senate (the Belgian Higher House of the Parliament) was set to have its role changed and political power diminished in a next governing period. It has been suggested that the Senate thus saw the extension of euthanasia to minors as a last chance for an important achievement.[48] This perhaps influenced the Belgian Senate to take the initiative towards the end of this governing period, although the extent to which this is true cannot be definitively established.

Third, political parties in Belgium view the ethical issue of euthanasia as an opportunity to gain public profile and standing, and this, along with the wider political situation at the time, may have influenced the 2014 law extension. When the original 2002 euthanasia law was passed, it was the first time in a considerable period that the Belgian Christian Democratic Party ('CVP') was not part of the multi-party government coalition. The government at that time consisted of liberal and socialist parties which, as has been argued, aimed to present themselves publicly as ethically progressive.[49] This has been identified as perhaps one of the reasons why euthanasia was originally legalised. As will be discussed below, for the 2014 extension, two Christian Democratic parties ('CD&V' on the Flemish side and 'CDH' on the Walloon side) were part of the government coalition but refused to support the extension. Other political parties within the government then had to look for support amongst the opposition, something which rarely happens in Belgium.

That a political stance on euthanasia is part of public profiling for political parties is also evidenced by the fact that after a highly publicised Court of Assizes case in Belgium in 2019, all political parties took a formal public stance on euthanasia and whether or not the law should be extended further (e.g. to patients with dementia). This later development provides support for the argument that such political profiling already functioned as a catalyst for the 2014 extension. Finally, another relevant political factor is that it is customary that laws concerning delicate and controversial ethical subjects are passed towards the end of a governing period as a final symbolic act, as it were, before new elections take place. This was the case for both the original 2002 euthanasia law and the 2014 extension.

---

[46] Geert Pousset, Johan Bilsen, Joke De Wilde, Yves Benoit, Joris Verlooy, An Bomans, Luc Deliens and Freddy Mortier, 'Attitudes of Adolescent Cancer Survivors toward End-of-Life Decisions for Minors' (2009) 124 *Pediatrics* e1142–48.

[47] Geert Pousset, Johan Bilsen, Joke De Wilde, Luc Deliens and Freddy Mortier, 'Houding van Vlaamse leerlingen uit het secundair onderwijs ten opzichte van euthanasie en andere beslissingen aan het levenseinde bij minderjarigen' (2009) 10 *Tijdschrift voor Jeugdrecht en Kinderrechten* 282–92.

[48] Ludo M. Veny and Pieter Goes, 'Een wereldprimeur: de uitbreiding van de Euthanasiewet naar niet-ontvoogde minderjarigen' (2014) 5 *Rechtskundig Weekblad* 163–72.

[49] Griffiths et al., *Euthanasia and Law in Europe*, 275–94.

Legislative Process

What can at least be confidently posited is that the number of different legislative proposals over time concerning the extension of the euthanasia law to minors submitted was so high that the Senate determined to act upon this. Generally speaking, since 2002 there had been three categories of legislative proposals. The first category suggested the extension of euthanasia to minors from the age of fifteen, thus maintaining a strict age limit.[50] The second suggested the extension to all minors who, regardless of age, possessed capacity of discernment.[51] A third category proposed not only extending euthanasia to all minors with capacity of discernment, regardless of age, but also sought to allow euthanasia for minors *without* capacity of discernment when requested by parents or legal guardians.[52]

In deciding how to pursue the issue, the Belgian Senate organised several hearings where many legal and medical experts confirmed what was known from empirical research and spoke in favour of extending the euthanasia law to minors.[53] Subsequently, the Senate took one particular legislative proposal as the one to pursue and to guide the debates. This proposal was from the second category outlined above and thus suggested allowing euthanasia for minors regardless of age who possess the necessary capacity for discernment and are seen by a psychiatrist.[54] Although the proposal mentioned the capacity of discernment, it did not include any of the other safeguards in the eventual law extension. The proposal was thus to simply extend the existing law to that cohort.

The legislative proposal was first extensively discussed in a smaller senatorial commission,[55] informed by the hearings that were held. During these debates it became clear that the Flemish Christian Democratic Party ('CD&V'), who was part of the government majority, was not willing to support an extension of euthanasia for all minors. A political party that was in the opposition (the Flemish Nationalist Party ('N-VA')) was willing to support, but only if several additional safeguards were put into the legislation. The final text thus differed from the initial legislative proposal, as it now included the safeguards discussed above. The discussions in this smaller

---

[50] Bill Amending the Law of 28 May 2002 on Euthanasia as Concerns Minors of 15 years and Older, 23 September 2010, S 5-179.

[51] See, for example, the Bill Amending the Law of 28 May 2002 on Euthanasia as Concerns Minors, 7 July 2004, S 3-804/1. See also: Bill Amending art. 3 of the Law of 28 May 2002 on Euthanasia, Concerning Euthanasia on Minors, 16 August 2010, S 5-21993.

[52] Bill Supplementing the Law of 28 May 2002 on Euthanasia as Concerns Minors, 12 December 2006, S 3-1993; Bill Supplementing the Law of 28 May 2002 on Euthanasia, Concerning Minors, 9 May 2012, S 5-1610.

[53] Annex to Bill Supplementing the Law of 28 May 2002 on Euthanasia as Concerns Minors, 4 December 2013, S 5-2170/8.

[54] Bill Amending the Law of 28 May 2002 on Euthanasia, to Enable Euthanasia on Minors, S 5-2170/1.

[55] Report on Behalf of the Joint Commissions of Justice and Social Affairs (4 December 2013, S 5-2170/4).

commission proved crucial. The text agreed upon by the Senatorial commission was subsequently discussed in a plenary session of the Senate, which approved the text and sent it to the Belgian Chamber of Representatives (the Belgian Lower House of Parliament). Here, similar to the Senate, the text approved by the Senate was first discussed in a smaller Commission of Justice where it was again approved. Finally, the text was discussed in a plenary session of the Belgian Chamber of Representatives where it was voted into law. Importantly, in none of these subsequent discussions were any substantial changes made to the text agreed upon by the first Senatorial commission. Only smaller linguistic changes were made. The compromise reached in the initial smaller Senatorial commission could thus be argued to have remained intact through all subsequent steps.

During the discussion of the legislative proposal in the Commission of Justice of the Belgian Chamber of Representatives, it became clear that several Belgian political parties additionally wanted the document to be checked by another Parliamentary commission or by the Council of State (Belgium's highest advisory organ on legal affairs). However, this request was perceived as a deliberate move to stall the approval of the bill proposal and was subsequently dismissed. As mentioned above, the 2014 extension to the euthanasia law was passed towards the end of a governing period. A delay meant that the possibility would have existed that the law could not be passed before new elections, after which political support for the law may have become uncertain. Those parties who supported the law thus had an incentive to avoid delay. As such the text was only sent out for linguistic revision and subsequently (in a Chamber of Representatives plenary session) passed into law.

What is noteworthy about these debates is that the Christian Democratic political party, which formed part of Belgium's multi-party government coalition, was in fact against the extension. This meant that the other coalition members had to look for support amongst members of the opposition in order to pass the bill. Such a procedure, where a legislative proposal is passed using opposition votes and with a government coalition partner voting *against* the proposal (so-called *wisselmeerderheid*), rarely occurs in Belgian politics. It is often used on moral issues where political parties allow their members to vote according to their own conscience, even when their vote is not in accordance with the official party stance. For this reason, the procedure was also used in 1990 when abortion was decriminalised. Such a procedure gives considerable power to the opposition party supporting the law, since their support is absolutely crucial. One can read in the publicly available proceedings that this party (the Flemish Nationalist Party ('N-VA')) explicitly prided itself on the fact that all its suggested additional safeguards were accepted into the final law.[56]

---

[56] Parliamentary Proceedings, K 5-130, 12 December 2013, at 6.

Reception and Judgement by the Constitutional Court on the Amendment

Reception of the 2014 extension, both nationally and internationally, was mixed. Within Belgium there was considerable support, but there was equally strong criticism of the law. For example, the then-head of the Belgian Catholic Church, Archbishop André Leonard, spoke out publicly against the amendment of the euthanasia law, and several churches held masses in protest before the amendment was voted on.[57] Internationally, the 2014 extension was, for many, regarded as a sure sign that Belgium had started down the slippery slope.[58] However, some commentators also defended the extension.[59]

The extension also faced legal challenge. Not long after the 2014 extension was passed, several Belgian organisations and private persons filed an action for annulment of the amendment by the Constitutional Court.[60] They argued that the 2014 euthanasia extension was unconstitutional. The extension, they argued, raised serious human rights concerns and was a violation of the state's obligation: '(i) to protect the right to life of their citizens; and (ii) to respect their citizens' moral and physical integrity, especially if they are minors'.[61] The obligations that the applicants argued were violated, are enshrined in articles 22 (right to respect for private life), 22*bis* (right to respect for children's integrity) and 23 (right to lead a dignified life) of the Belgian Constitution and should be read in conjunction with articles 2, 3 and 8 of the European Convention on Human Rights and article 6 of the United Nations Convention on the Rights of the Child.[62] The Constitutional Court was thus asked to determine whether the 2014 euthanasia extension was a violation of the Belgian Constitution and the European Convention on Human Rights. If the Court should determine this is the case, the law would effectively be annulled.

In essence, the applicants argued that the 2014 extension did not contain sufficient safeguards to protect minors. The Belgian Constitutional Court's task was to consider whether the additional safeguards that were installed by the 2014 extension were sufficient. Ultimately, the Court ruled that the 2014 extension was constitutional and thus allowed to stand. The content of this ruling has been

---

[57] Ian Traynor, 'Belgian Law on Euthanasia for Children, with No Age Limit, Will Be First in World', *The Guardian*, 13 February 2014, www.theguardian.com/world/ 2014/feb/12/belgium-legalise-euthanasia-children-age-limit.

[58] Carly Andrews, 'Child Euthanasia Bill Is "Counsel of Despair", Says Bioethicist', Aleteia, 14 February 2014, www.aleteia.org/en/society/article/child-euthanasia-is-council-of-despair-says-bioethicist-5289790371004416. See also Wesley J. Smith, 'A Bioethicist's Farcical Case for Child Euthanasia', Life Site, 17 June 2014, www.lifesitenews.com/opinion/a-bioethicists-farcical-case-for-child-euthanasia.

[59] Tom Riddington, 'Euthanasia for Children Is Hard to Contemplate – But We Must Talk about It', *The Guardian*, 17 February 2014, www.theguardian.com/commentisfree/2014/feb/17/euthanasia-for-children-belgium-law-terminally-ill-die.

[60] Judgement 153/2015, Constitutional Court of Belgium (29 October 2015) (English translation).

[61] Van Assche et al., 'Capacity for Discernment' at 245.

[62] General Assembly Resolution 44/25, 20 November 1989.

amply discussed elsewhere,[63] so we will merely discuss the main thrust of the arguments here.

First, the applicants argued that the 'capacity for discernment' criterion was vague and arbitrary. However, the Court ruled that 'capacity for discernment' is very clear and that the legislature was justified in not setting out more specific criteria to determine that capacity. They pointed out that assessing whether a minor possesses capacity for discernment does not require legal data but medical data and can be determined by physicians in every case '*in concreto*'.[64] With regard to the child and adolescent psychiatrist or psychologist who needs to assess whether the minor has capacity for discernment, the Court remarked:

> In view of the fact that the term 'capacity for discernment' is essentially medical in scope, the circumstance that the psychiatrist or psychologist being consulted does not need to have had any legal training does not prevent the practitioners in question from judging the minor's ability to understand the real implications of his euthanasia request and its consequences.[65]

To support its interpretation the Court referred to the Parliamentary proceedings, for example where the then-Minister of Justice remarked that 'it is reserved to the physicians to evaluate the request of a terminally ill minor on a case by case basis'.[66] Another example is from a member of the Chamber of Representatives who during the discussions explicitly remarked that: 'Capacity for discernment is a clinical criterium which is preferable over a purely legal concept'.[67] Because of these reasons, the Court believed that it was appropriate for lawmakers to not fully explain and define capacity for discernment in law.

The second important remark concerning the ruling by the Court concerns the additional consultation by the child and adolescent psychiatrist or psychologist. The applicants argued that this could not be considered a safeguard since this consultation and the child and adolescent psychiatrist or psychologist opinion would most likely not be binding. The original euthanasia law required that a physician has to consult a second independent physician who examines that patient and files a report. However, the law does not indicate or require that this report be *positive* (i.e. when the opinion of the consulted physician is that all legal criteria are met), merely that there is a report. This is confirmed from the parliamentary proceedings and by legal experts.[68] Euthanasia after a negative report or opinion by a consulted physician is perfectly legal and does occur, although rarely so. For instance, Van

---

[63] Van Assche et al., 'Capacity for Discernment'.

[64] Judgement 153/2015, Constitutional Court of Belgium (29 October 2015) (English translation) at 34.

[65] Ibid. at 46.

[66] Report on Behalf of the Commission of Justice (7 February 2013, K 53-3245/004) at 4.

[67] Ibid. at 36.

[68] Delbeke, *Juridische aspecten van zorgverlening aan het levenseinde*, 72. See also Vansweevelt, 'De euthanasiewet', 253.

Wesemael et al. found that in four of 363 studied cases of euthanasia involving adults, euthanasia was performed in spite of a negative report or opinion from the consulted physician.[69]

If this is true for the consulted physician, the applicants argued, this could also be the case for the additional consultation with the child and adolescent psychiatrist or psychologist. Their report could then be advisory and thus ignored, in which case it would not be a sufficient safeguard. In this case, however, the Court ruled that the wording of the 2014 extension differs in important respects from the wording regarding the second consulted physician. The second consulted physician has to 'report his findings', but the additional psychiatrist or psychologist has to 'certify in writing' that the minor has capacity for discernment. The Court thus ruled that, unlike the report from the second consulted physician, the report of the additional child and adolescent psychiatrist or psychologist is *binding* and thus has to be positive for euthanasia to be legally performed.[70] Although not explicit in the 2014 extension of the law, this was clarified by the Court's decision. A positive report or opinion from the child and adolescent psychiatrist or psychologist confirming a minor's capacity for discernment is thus mandatory.

KEY ARGUMENTS RAISED IN THE DEBATE

In this section, we analyse various arguments that were used in the political and public debates to provide insight into the reasons why euthanasia in Belgium was extended to minors. Determining exactly which arguments were key is difficult since in various discussions of the 2014 extension in both Senate and Chamber of Representatives, many arguments were raised. However, every legislative proposal in Belgium is accompanied by an explanation and argumentation for why the proposal is submitted. This provides valuable information as to the reasoning of those who submitted the proposal. When relevant, we will refer to this explanation and argumentation by the persons submitting the original proposal in our discussion of the arguments.

Congruence with the Law Concerning Rights of Patients

A commonly voiced argument in favour of euthanasia for minors is that it would be respectful of minors' autonomy and would bring euthanasia more in line with other significant medical decisions.[71] This argument is also explicitly mentioned in the

---

[69] Yanna Van Wesemael, Joachim Cohen, Johan Bilsen, Tinne Smets, Bregje Onwuteaka-Philipsen and Luc Deliens, 'Process and Outcomes of Euthanasia Requests under the Belgian Act on Euthanasia: A Nationwide Survey' (2011) 42 *Journal of Pain and Symptom Management* 721–33.

[70] Judgement 153/2015, Constitutional Court of Belgium (29 October 2015) (English translation).

[71] Mortier, 'Euthanasie bij minderjarigen'.

explanation accompanying the legislative proposal that was ultimately passed.[72] Around the time the 2002 euthanasia law was passed, Belgium also passed an important law concerning the rights of patients, namely the Law on Patients' Rights of 22 August 2002. This law provided that in medical decisions minors should always be involved according to their age and maturity. Minors who are able to reasonably assess their own interests should be able to exercise their patient rights independently. This effectively means that competent minors are able to take significant medical decisions, including decisions that inevitably lead to death (e.g. refusal of care or refusing a transplant). As mentioned above, from 2003 the Belgian Order of Physicians officially took the position that a patient's mental age is more important than calendar age.

The argument that is made is that if minors are already able to make such life and death medical decisions, why would they not be able to make a voluntary and well-considered request for euthanasia? For example, before the 2014 law extension, minors were able to stop all food and fluids, thereby dying of dehydration,[73] but were unable to choose euthanasia. This, many commentators argue, is unjustified.[74] By extending euthanasia to minors the law is brought more into line with the patient rights law.[75]

Opponents, however, raised the argument that it is not strange for the law to set an age limit, since this is a common thing to do. The law sets the legal age for, for example, drinking alcohol, driving, or having consensual sex. What would be unjustified, these opponents claim, is that without an age criterion in the euthanasia law, a fifteen-year-old would be legally allowed to request euthanasia but not to drive a car or buy alcohol.[76]

Practice

Explicitly mentioned during the hearing organised in the Belgian Senate and emphasised in the explanation to the legislative proposal is that life-shortening or life-ending acts on minors are a practical reality.[77] During the hearings various experts confirmed that such practices already occur, despite being currently illegal. The politicians submitting the initial legislative proposal judged that there had been a societal evolution and an increased acceptance of terminating life on patients'

---

[72] Bill Amending the Law of 28 May 2002 on Euthanasia, to Enable Euthanasia on Minors, S 5-2170 at 2–3.

[73] Robert Pool, '"You're Not Going to Dehydrate Mom, Are You?": Euthanasia, Versterving, and Good Death in the Netherlands' (2004) 58 *Social Science & Medicine* 955–66.

[74] Peter Singer, 'Voluntary Euthanasia: A Utilitarian Perspective' (2003) 17 *Bioethics* 526–41.

[75] Annex to Bill Supplementing the Law of 28 May 2002 on Euthanasia as Concerns Minors, 4 December 2013, S 5-2170/8 at 17.

[76] Parliamentary Proceedings, K 5-130, 12 December 2013, at 94.

[77] Bill Amending the Law of 28 May 2002 on Euthanasia, to Enable Euthanasia on Minors, S 5-2170/1 at 2.

explicit request, thereby sparing them an undignified death. Extending the euthanasia law to minors would bring these practices into the open and regulate them since as euthanasia they would have to be officially reported.[78]

Additionally, it was claimed in the Senate debates that as long as euthanasia for minors is illegal, some physicians might be overly cautious with sedatives and painkillers for minors out of fear for prosecution.[79] The evidence for this position is anecdotal since no empirical research exists confirming the underuse of palliative medication.

In general, however, it was known from empirical research that euthanasia for minors is extremely rare. A study showed that in 2007–2008 there had been no cases of euthanasia on minors in Belgium.[80] Data from the Netherlands, where euthanasia is legal for minors above the age of twelve, also show that euthanasia is rarely used for minors. So, from the very start it was clear that for the most part the extension to minors was 'symbolic' and would not be frequently used. Indeed, as was discussed above, there have been only four reported cases of euthanasia for minors since the extension.

By contrast, opponents of the extension argued that it was dangerous to extend the euthanasia law precisely because it was known that it would be rarely used. In Belgium, like in other countries, there is the defence of 'necessity' where someone (here the physician) has two conflicting duties they cannot meet at the same time. Exceptional cases of euthanasia for minors could then, opponents argued, be captured under this necessity defence. However, this would still require a physician to be willing to risk prosecution and stand trial. Legal trials in Belgium are also known to last a long time, during which the physician would be subject to considerable uncertainty and would be provisionally banned from practising. A better solution, argued the proponents, was to extend the euthanasia law.

Competence and Capacity for Discernment

Many national and international commentators have questioned whether minors are ever able to formulate a voluntary and well-considered request for euthanasia. To what degree they can be competent to make such a decision is a topic of considerable debate.[81]

---

[78] Annex to Bill Supplementing the Law of 28 May 2002 on Euthanasia as Concerns Minors, 4 December 2013, S 5-2170/8 at 118.

[79] Ibid. at 14–15. See also Kasper Raus, 'The Extension of Belgium's Euthanasia Law to Include Competent Minors' (2016) 13 *Journal of Bioethical Inquiry* 305–15.

[80] Pousset et al., 'Medical End-of-Life Decisions in Children'.

[81] Roger Palmer and Gareth Gillespie, 'Consent and Capacity in Children and Young People' (2014) 99 *Archives of Disease in Childhood: Education & Practice Edition* 2–7; Andrew M. Siegel, Dominic A. Sisti and Arthur L. Caplan, 'Pediatric Euthanasia in Belgium: Disturbing Developments' (2014) 311 JAMA 1963–4.

Opponents of the extension argued that the concept of capacity for discernment is not defined or explained further, meaning it is possible that different physicians will interpret this concept in different ways. It has also been argued that minors suffering from a terminal illness might be especially willing to please their parents, and so request euthanasia because they think that is what they should do. Finally, opponents argue that the psychological, cognitive and moral development of minors is complex and lasts into adulthood. This makes it difficult if not impossible for minors to make a well-considered decision about euthanasia.[82]

Proponents counter this argument by positing that the maturity of a severely ill minor is not to be underestimated.[83] In the hearings held with experts, several emphasised that faced with a terminal illness minors can develop high levels of maturity and 'capacity for discernment' more quickly than healthy minors.[84] The explanation accompanying the legislative proposal also mentions that minors with terminal conditions can often exhibit maturity far exceeding that of their healthy peers. Dying minors may both feel that they suffer unbearably and understand that their condition and suffering is never going to improve. Euthanasia, for proponents, might give these minors a way to end their suffering and have a dignified death.

CONCLUDING REMARKS

The 2014 extension to the Belgian euthanasia law was a significant amendment to the existing law. It made it possible for minors of any age (provided they possess capacity for discernment), to legally receive euthanasia. While euthanasia for minors was already possible in the Netherlands, this was only for minors aged twelve and above. What is unique about the Belgian extension is that it contains no specific age limit.

In this chapter, we have discussed the legislative process as to how and why Belgium came to extend its euthanasia law to competent minors. The reasons were numerous, and identifying the main catalysts and determining their influence on changing the law is difficult. We have shown that support for euthanasia for minors was already relatively high in Belgium. The Belgian Order of Physicians had long taken the official position that using calendar age as a cut-off point is problematic. Also, proposals to extend euthanasia to minors were regularly submitted after the original euthanasia law passed in 2002. Following various such proposals, the Senate, which was set to have its role diminished in the next legislature, finally, decided to pursue this topic and to organise hearings. These hearings consulted several experts and led to a new legislative proposal that was eventually turned into

---

[82] Van Gool and De Lepeleire, 'Euthanasia in Children'.
[83] Mortier, 'Euthanasie bij minderjarigen'.
[84] Annex to Bill Supplementing the Law of 28 May 2002 on Euthanasia as Concerns Minors, 4 December 2013, S 5-2170/8 at 47.

law. An important contextual element for why the extension passed when it did was political momentum and a drive amongst parties to present themselves as socially progressive. Nevertheless, the passing of the amendment was controversial. One of the political parties that was part of the multi-party majority in Parliament did not support the amendment, meaning that support from the opposition had to be sought, something which is rare in Belgian politics.

We have also shown in this chapter how the 2014 extension is not simply a removal of the age limit for euthanasia. Considerable differences remain between euthanasia for non-emancipated minors and euthanasia for adults and emancipated minors. For example, non-emancipated minors can only receive euthanasia for physical suffering and when they are close to death. Furthermore, an additional child and adolescent psychiatrist or psychologist has to be consulted, who then needs to certify that the minor indeed possesses the capacity for discernment. The opinion of the psychologist or psychiatrist is also binding, meaning that when the psychiatrist or psychologist provides a negative report, the euthanasia cannot proceed.

This chapter has also suggested that while the extension was heavily debated, so far it could be argued to have predominantly symbolic value. Although effectively legal since 2014, euthanasia for minors has been rarely used. Currently there have only been four reported cases of euthanasia for minors. How this law will be used in practice remains to be seen and should be the topic of further monitoring and research.

4

The Role of Scientific Evaluations of the Dutch Termination of Life on Request and Assisted Suicide (Review Procedure) Act

Old Law, New Boundaries

Agnes van der Heide, Johan Legemaate, Johannes (Hans) J. M. van Delden and Bregje Onwuteaka-Philipsen

INTRODUCTION

Ending the life of a person upon his or her own request constituted a crime under the first Dutch Penal Code that came into force in 1886. Articles 293 and 294 of the Code prohibited actively ending a person's life and providing assistance for a person to commit suicide, respectively. The societal, political and professional debate in the Netherlands about legalising these acts started in the 1960s, at a time when medicine's motto gradually changed from 'prolonging life whenever possible' to 'prolonging life whenever possible and beneficial'.[1] During this debate, the medical profession and case law contributed to the development of criteria that delineated the circumstances in which ending of life could be acceptable. These criteria were finally embedded in the Termination of Life on Request and Assisted Suicide (Review Procedures) Act[2] that came into force in 2002. Since then, physicians providing a patient with assistance to die, at the patient's request, either by injecting lethal medication or by providing lethal medication to enable the patient to end their own life, will be exempt from legal prosecution if they adhere to the criteria as defined in the law.

The Termination of Life on Request and Assisted Suicide (Review Procedures) Act[3] is one of several laws that have been developed in recent decades to promote the quality of health care and regulate the rights of patients. These laws and associated regulations often have far-reaching consequences for the practice of health care and, as an important mechanism to explore the effectiveness and (side) effects of legislation in practice, the regime is scientifically evaluated every five years.

---

[1]   Jan Hendrik van den Berg, *Medical Power and Medical Ethics* [*Medische Macht en Medische Ethiek*] (Nijkerk: Callenbach, 1969).

[2]   Termination of Life on Request and Assisted Suicide (Review Procedures) Act of 1 April 2002 (the Netherlands).

[3]   Ibid.

In the past, this evaluation has been undertaken by an independent multidisciplinary team of scientific researchers.[4] This research is regarded as an important instrument to inform regulation, including whether legislation should be revised, or other (policy) measures taken. Since the introduction of the legislation in 2002, three evaluation studies have been performed. Each of them has attracted considerable attention within society, politics and the medical profession, both nationally and internationally.

This chapter focuses on the findings and impact of the third and most recent evaluation study that was performed in 2015–2016, with results being published in a Dutch report in 2017.[5] Although there is an abundance of literature on the development, content and interpretation of the law, for international readers of this book, we begin this chapter with a summary of the developments that resulted in the enactment of legislation in 2002. We also briefly summarise the findings of the first two evaluations of the Termination of Life on Request and Assisted Suicide (Review Procedures) Act.[6]

THE EVOLVING REGULATION OF EUTHANASIA AND PHYSICIAN-ASSISTED SUICIDE[7]

The debate about euthanasia and physician-assisted suicide in the Netherlands was triggered in 1973 by the 'Postma case'.[8] In this case, a physician helped her dying mother to end her own life following repeated and explicit requests for euthanasia. While the court concluded that the physician had committed murder, the physician

---

[4] Brochure from the Programme for the Evaluation of Health Law [Programma Evaluatie Regelgeving] (2013 The Netherlands Organisation for Health Research and Development ('ZonMw')) at 2.

[5] Bregje Onwuteaka-Philipsen, Johan Legemaate, Agnes van der Heide, Hans van Delden, Kirsten Evenblij, Inssaf El Hammoud, Roeline Pasman, Corrette Ploem, Rosalie Pronk, Suzanne van de Vathorst and Dick Willems, 'Third Evaluation of the Termination of Life on Request and Assisted Suicide (Review Procedure) Act' ['Evaluatie Wet Toetsing Levensbeëindiging op Verzoek en Hulp bij Zelfdoding'], Report from The Netherlands Organisation for Health Research and Development (May 2017 ZonMw).

[6] Termination of Life on Request and Assisted Suicide (Review Procedures) Act of 1 April 2002 (the Netherlands).

[7] This section is a modified version of a previously published chapter in: Agnes van der Heide, 'Physician-Assisted Suicide and Euthanasia', in Matthew K. Nock (ed.), *The Oxford Handbook of Suicide and Self-Injury* (New York: Oxford University Press, 2014), 460–78.

[8] Netherlands Jurisprudence [Nederlandse Jurisprudentie] (1973) District Court of Leeuwarden, 21 February 1973, No. 183 ('Postma case'). An English translation of the Postma case is available at: Walter Lagerwey [Translator], 'Euthanasia Case Leeuwarden – 1973' (1987–8) 3 *Issues in Law and Medicine* 439–42. See also Heleen Weyers, *Euthanasia: The Process of Legal Reform* [*Euthanasie: Het Proces van Rechtsverandering*] (Amsterdam: Amsterdam University Press, 2004).

only received a short, suspended sentence. In its verdict, the court effectively opened the door to regulating physician assistance in dying by acknowledging that a physician does not always have to keep a severely suffering patient alive against his or her will. As the first public test case, the Postma case broke social taboos in a country with strong Christian traditions. It also reflected the growing awareness among many young medical professionals of the limits of medical care and the importance of patients' self-determination.

During the 1980s, the debate in the Netherlands regarding euthanasia and physician-assisted suicide progressed and was formalised. In 1980, the national Committee of Attorneys General took a formal interest in physicians' end-of-life decisions. To achieve uniformity in the legal policy concerning assistance in dying by physicians, it decided to review every case of euthanasia to determine whether the attending physician should be legally prosecuted. In 1982, the government established a committee of experts to study and give advice on the permissibility and possibilities of regulating assistance in dying by physicians. The Committee issued its report in 1985[9] and established the definitions of euthanasia and physician-assisted suicide that have been used in the Netherlands ever since: euthanasia is the administration of lethal drugs with the aim of ending the life of a person upon his or her explicit request; assisting in suicide is supplying or prescribing lethal drugs with the aim of enabling a person to end his or her own life.[10] The committee proposed criteria for 'due care' that had to be met in every case to avoid legal prosecution. These criteria were further developed through case law.

An important euthanasia case, the 'Schoonheim case', occurred in 1984.[11] It was the first euthanasia case that was evaluated by the Dutch Highest Criminal Court. In this case, Schoonheim, a general practitioner, performed euthanasia at the explicit request of a ninety-five-year-old patient who suffered unbearably from a combination of deteriorating eyesight, hearing and speech, as well as being bedridden; the patient exhibited general decline and loss of dignity. The physician voluntarily reported his act to the police and was charged with ending a patient's life upon her explicit request. The Highest Criminal Court concluded that the physician had acted in a situation of 'necessity', that is, the physician had been confronted with a conflict of duties: the duty to relieve unbearable suffering and the duty to do no harm.[12] The defence of necessity was held to apply, and the physician was acquitted.

---

[9] Report from the State Euthanasia Commission [Staatscommissie Inzake Euthanasie] (1985 Government of the Netherlands).
[10] Ibid. at 26.
[11] Netherlands Jurisprudence [Nederlandse Jurisprudentie] (1985) Supreme Court, 27 November 1984, No. 106 ('Schoonheim case'). See also Weyers, *Euthanasia: The Process of Legal Reform*.
[12] Ibid.

In the 'Chabot case', a decade later in 1994, a Dutch psychiatrist ended the life of a competent woman who was suffering from depression.[13] The Highest Criminal Court held that suffering due to psychological problems can also be unbearable and may result in a situation of necessity. In 2002 in the 'Brongersma case', this was further clarified in the sense that suffering could originate from a medically classifiable disease, from either a somatic or psychiatric origin.[14] Brongersma was an eighty-six-year-old male who suffered mainly from loneliness and had relatively minor health problems due to his advanced age. He was assisted in suicide by his general practitioner who was prosecuted for the offence of assisting a suicide on the basis that his patient's suffering did not originate from a medically classifiable cause. The Highest Criminal Court held that the general practitioner had committed an offence, but did not impose a sentence.[15]

The Royal Dutch Medical Association was highly influential in the process that resulted in the legalisation of euthanasia and physician-assisted suicide in the Netherlands. In 1984, shortly after the verdict in the Schoonheim case, it officially took a supportive position regarding the legalisation of euthanasia and physician-assisted suicide, and called for the clarification of the circumstances under which ending a patient's life could be lawful for physicians who were willing to report and account for their life-ending acts. They rephrased the due care criteria obtained from case law into medical-professional requirements that had to be met when performing euthanasia or assisting in a suicide. These criteria provided that before complying with a request for euthanasia or physician-assisted suicide, the physician should take the following steps: assess that the patient's request is voluntary and well considered, the patient's suffering is unbearable and hopeless, the patient is adequately informed about his or her situation and prospects, and that there are no reasonable alternatives to relieve the suffering. Further, a second independent physician should be consulted and the termination of life should be performed with due medical care and attention.[16]

Since the start of the debate on euthanasia and physician-assisted suicide, some physicians have been willing to have their cases reviewed, but their number was very limited until the mid-1980s. The Royal Dutch Medical Association considered formal societal control of the practice of euthanasia and physician-assisted suicide to be of extreme importance and encouraged physicians to report their cases. In 1985, the Ministry of Justice explicitly declared that, as a general rule, physicians

[13] *Office of Public Prosecutions* v. *Chabot*, Netherlands Jurisprudence [Nederlandse Jurisprudentie] (1994) Supreme Court, 21 June 1994, No. 656 ('Chabot case'). For an English summary of this case see: John Griffiths, Alex Bood and Heleen Weyers, *Euthanasia and Law in the Netherlands* (Amsterdam: Amsterdam University Press, 1998), 80–2.

[14] Netherlands Jurisprudence [Nederlandse Jurisprudentie] (2003) Supreme Court, 24 December 2002, No. 167 ('Brongersma case'). For an English summary and discussion of this case see: John Griffiths, Heleen Weyers and Maurice Adams, *Euthanasia and Law in Europe: With Special Reference to the Netherlands and Belgium* (OR: Hart Publishing, 2008), 35–9.

[15] Ibid.

[16] Jurriaan de Haan, 'The New Dutch Law on Euthanasia' (2002) 10 *Medical Law Review* 57–75.

who had complied with the due care criteria for euthanasia or physician-assisted suicide that had been developed in case law would not be prosecuted.

In 1990, the Dutch government appointed a committee to investigate the practice of medical end-of-life decisions. The committee, named after its chairman, Professor Jan Remmelink, who was at that time the Attorney General of the High Council of the Netherlands, tasked an independent group of researchers to investigate the practice of life-ending acts carried out by physicians around the world. In 1991, the Remmelink Committee presented a report containing the results of the empirical research including a finding that life-ending acts were a clinical reality, but that they were rarely reported as unnatural causes of death. In response to this finding, the government expressed the view that transparency around the nature of life-ending medical practices was of great importance and, for the sake of effective protection of human life, it was appropriate for assessment of life-ending practices to occur within a criminal framework.[17] In 1993, the Ministry of Justice proclaimed a formal notification and review procedure for life-ending acts, to harmonise regional prosecution policies and eliminate practices that were perceived to be hampering physicians' willingness to report, such as police interrogating relatives shortly after a patient had died of euthanasia. The procedure was accepted by parliament in February 1993.[18] This notification procedure required the physician performing euthanasia or assisting in suicide to inform the local medical examiner about his or her act through filling out an extensive questionnaire. Subsequently, the medical examiner informed the Public Prosecution Service who considered whether the physician had adhered to the due care criteria and made a determination about prosecution.

As a next step, in 1998, the government established a system of multidisciplinary review. All cases were, from that time forward, first reviewed by one of five Regional Euthanasia Review Committees, each consisting of a lawyer, a physician and an ethicist. The Regional Euthanasia Review Committees advised the Public Prosecution Service about whether the due care requirements had been fulfilled, and the Public Prosecution Service subsequently decided about prosecution. While this practice has been amended since the enactment of the legislation (discussed further below), review of each case of euthanasia and physician-assisted suicide remains central to the current regulatory framework in the Netherlands.

THE DUTCH TERMINATION OF LIFE ON REQUEST AND ASSISTED SUICIDE (REVIEW PROCEDURES) ACT

In 1994, an important change occurred in the composition of the national Dutch Government following the election: the Christian Democratic Party, which had

---

[17] See Weyers, *Euthanasia: The Process of Legal Reform*, 318.
[18] Minutes of Parliament, House of Representatives [Handelingen Tweede Kamer], 1991–2, 3404–5.

been the majority party within all governing coalitions for decades, no longer formed part of the government. Instead, government was formed by a coalition of liberals and social democrats, and they remained in power for seven years. In 2001, this government proposed a law that defined the circumstances in which physicians would not be prosecuted for providing their patients with lethal drugs. The criteria for due care that had been formulated by the Royal Dutch Medical Association and the multidisciplinary review system were important elements of the proposed law. On 1 April 2002, the Dutch Termination of Life on Request and Assisted Suicide (Review Procedures) Act[19] came into force. It regulated the ending of life by a physician (or with the assistance of a physician) at the request of a patient who was suffering unbearably without hope of relief. The law includes an exemption from criminal liability under the Criminal Code for physicians who terminate life on request or assist in a patient's suicide. This means that such physicians can no longer be prosecuted, provided they satisfy the statutory due care criteria and notify the case, via the local medical coroner, to the appropriate Regional Euthanasia Review Committee. The main aim of the law is to bring medical practices into the open, to apply uniform criteria in assessing every case in which a doctor terminates life upon request or assists in a suicide, and to ensure that maximum care is exercised in such cases. A distinct feature of the due care criteria is that they are articulated rather broadly on the understanding that further content will be given to these criteria in the review procedures and by case law.

The due care criteria specified in the legislation are:[20]

- The physician must be satisfied that the patient's request is voluntary and well-considered;
- The physician must be satisfied that the patient's suffering is unbearable, with no prospect of improvement;
- The physician must have informed the patient about their situation and prognosis;
- The physician must have come to the conclusion, together with the patient that there is no reasonable alternative in the patient's situation;
- The physician must have consulted at least one other, independent physician, who must see the patient and give a written opinion on whether the due care criteria set out above have been fulfilled;
- The physician must have exercised due medical care and attention in terminating the patient's life or assisting in the patient's suicide.

[19] Termination of Life on Request and Assisted Suicide (Review Procedures) Act of 1 April 2002 (the Netherlands).
[20] See 'Due Care Criteria', Regional Euthanasia Review Committees, 2020, https://english .euthanasiecommissie.nl/due-care-criteria.

The first four of these criteria are regarded as 'substantive' criteria while the last two are 'procedural' criteria.[21]

In addition, the law facilitates patients who are sixteen years of age or older to complete a written statement requesting termination of life at some time in the future when the patient is no longer able to express their will (sometimes referred to as an advance directive requesting euthanasia). This can replace a contemporaneous oral request provided the patient had decisional capacity at the time the statement was completed. The physician must also ensure that the other due care criteria have been met.

Finally, physicians can also respond to a request for termination of life or assisting a suicide of a minor patient between sixteen and eighteen years of age if the minor can appreciate their own interests. The parents who exercise authority over them must have been consulted in the decision-making process, but have no decision-making authority for this age group. For minor patients between twelve and sixteen years of age, termination of life or assisting a suicide is only possible if the parents agree with the decision.

An important feature of the law is that physicians are not obliged to comply with a request for euthanasia or physician-assisted suicide, even if all of the due care criteria are satisfied. The basic principle underlying physicians' ability to refuse such a request is that assistance in dying is an option, if certain conditions are met, and not an entitlement of patients. Physicians do not have a duty to provide such assistance. The Netherlands was one of the first countries in the world to legalise euthanasia.[22] However, by passing legislation, it in fact predominantly regulated existing practice. The major change introduced by the Act was the requirement for the Regional Euthanasia Review Committees to forward to the Public Prosecution Service only those cases for which the due care criteria have not been met. Further, the Act specified the criteria for patients below eighteen years of age.

Under the law, both euthanasia and physician-assisted suicide are subject to the same criteria for due care. Further, the law allows only physicians to be involved in these practices. A very important feature of the Dutch regulation is the requirement that euthanasia and physician-assisted suicide only occur on the explicit request of the patient. Ending someone's life in the absence of an explicit request is illegal and

---

[21] Hilde Buiting, Joseph Gevers, Judith Rietjens, Bregje Onwuteaka-Philipsen, Paul van der Maas, Agnes van der Heide and Hans van Delden, 'Dutch Criteria of Due Care for Physician-Assisted Dying in Medical Practice: A Physician Perspective' (2008) 34 *Journal of Medical Ethics* 1–5 at 4.

[22] Legislation was enacted in the Northern Territory (Australia) in 1995, Rights of the Terminally Ill Act 1995 (NT), although this Act was only in force for a short time before being overturned by the Australian Commonwealth Government; and also in Oregon's Death with Dignity Act, or Rev Stat §§ 127.800–127.995 (1994) in 1994 (although as a result of legal challenges, this legislation did not become operative until 1997: David Sclar, 'U.S. Supreme Court Ruling in *Gonzales v. Oregon* Upholds the Oregon Death with Dignity Act' (2006) 34 *Journal of Law and Medical Ethics* 639–46).

not considered to be a form of euthanasia. The definitions of euthanasia and
physician-assisted suicide do not include the withdrawal or withholding of (potentially) life-prolonging treatments, nor the alleviation of pain or other symptoms with
medication that may hasten death as an unintended but foreseen side effect. Both
these practices are considered to be part of normal medical practice and are subject
to regular professional and legal regulation.

EVALUATION STUDIES[23]

The goals of the euthanasia and physician-assisted suicide law are to provide legal
security for all those involved in physician assistance in dying upon the request of
the patient; to assure prudent practice; and to provide a framework for physicians to
be accountable and thus enable transparency and societal control. Every five years
the law is evaluated to examine whether its objectives are (still) being met and, if
not, whether reform of the way in which euthanasia and physician-assisted suicide
are regulated should be considered.

The first evaluation study was performed in 2005–2006, the second in 2010–2011
and the third in 2015–2016. The evaluation studies are government funded and
performed by an independent, multidisciplinary research team that is selected based
upon submitted research proposals. The review includes an analysis of developments in the interpretation and conceptualisation of the legal criteria (which are
broadly articulated in the legislation), empirical assessments of clinical practices,
and identification of potential complexities of the review system. This chapter will
focus predominantly on the results of the most recent evaluation study, but the main
findings and impact of the first and second evaluations are first summarised to
provide a historical context.

The First Evaluation Study 2005–2006[24]

One of the most remarkable findings of the first evaluation study, undertaken after
the law came into force, was the decrease in frequency of euthanasia and physician-
assisted suicide: in 2005, the total number of cases was 2,400, although there had
been 3,800 cases in 2001. The majority of the physicians thought there was an
association between improvements in palliative care and the decrease in life-
terminating action taken by physicians. Another explanation may be uncertainty

---

[23] All authors of this chapter were involved in one or more evaluation studies.
[24] A full account of the study can be found in: Bregje Onwuteaka-Philipsen, Joseph Gevers,
Agnes van der Heide, Hans van Delden, Roeline Pasman, Judith Rietjens, Mette Rurup, Hilde
Buiting, Johanna Hanssen-de Wolf, Gerard Janssen and Paul van der Maas, 'Evaluation of the
Termination of Life on Request and Assisted Suicide (Review Procedure) Act' ['Evaluatie Wet
Toetsing Levensbeëindiging op Verzoek en Hulp bij Zelfdoding'], Report from the
Netherlands Organisation for Health Research and Development (May 2007 ZonMw).

among physicians about the obligations imposed by the new legal regime. As in previous studies, euthanasia and physician-assisted suicide appeared to be carried out predominantly by general practitioners, in relation to patients with cancer and patients younger than eighty years of age. The most frequently cited reasons for administering euthanasia and physician-assisted suicide were patients' hopeless situation, their loss of dignity and unbearable suffering due to serious symptoms.

The evaluation study showed that the majority of physicians were of the opinion that the law had improved their legal certainty and contributed to the carefulness of life-terminating acts. Physicians almost always adhered to the due care requirements and they reported about 80 per cent of cases to the Regional Euthanasia Review Committees. This represented a marked increase from 54 per cent in 2001. The five Regional Euthanasia Review Committees assessed non-compliance to be evident in fifteen cases during the three years from 2003 to 2005. The Public Prosecution Service indicated in 2003 that they would only initiate a legal inquiry if a Regional Euthanasia Review Committee assessed that one or more of the substantive due care requirements (unbearable and hopeless suffering, voluntary and well-considered request) had not been complied with.[25]

The overall conclusion of the first evaluation study was that the objectives of the law were achieved. The researchers nevertheless formulated a number of recommendations. The first related to the criminal law. It was recommended that a clause should be inserted in the Criminal Code to clarify that a life-terminating act was different from the indicated and proportional use of medicines to alleviate suffering, even if this means that the physician is hastening the death of the patient. Such an amendment would provide greater certainty for physicians. Further, consequences other than criminal sanctions should operate for failing to report acts to the Regional Euthanasia Review Committees or failure to comply with the requirement of due medical care. Secondly, some recommendations concerned procedural issues to enhance the quality of physicians' reports and the review process. Finally, better education of physicians and the general public about specific aspects of the law, such as the role of written statements requesting euthanasia completed in advance of losing decision-making capacity, was recommended.

The Second Evaluation Study 2010–2011[26]

An important finding of the second evaluation study was that the recommendations from the first evaluation study regarding procedural issues and education were

---

[25] 'Designation of Prosecution Decision Regarding Active Termination of Life on Request (Euthanasia and Assisted Suicide)' ['Aanwijzing Vervolgingsbeslissing Inzake Actieve Levensbeëindiging op Verzoek (Euthanasie en Hulp bij Zelfdoding)'], *Staatscourant* (23 December 2003), No. 248, 19.

[26] A full account of the study can be found in: Agnes van der Heide, Johan Legemaate, Bregje Onwuteaka-Philipsen, Eva Bolt, Ineke Bolt, Hans van Delden, Eric Geijteman, Marianne

followed, but those in relation to amending the Criminal Code were ignored. The arguments underlying these recommendations remained valid: the distinction between life-terminating acts and the indicated and proportional use of medication to relieve suffering remained confusing for physicians, and criminal sanction for a violation of the requirement that termination of life should be performed with due care still seemed inappropriate.

The second evaluation found that the number of cases of euthanasia and physician-assisted suicide, approximately 4,050 cases in 2010, had increased to the level that existed before enactment of the law. The main characteristics of the practice remained unaltered, that is, the practice mainly involved patients with end-stage cancer who were provided with euthanasia by the general practitioner, but the study suggested that there was a tendency towards more liberal positions of both physicians and Regional Euthanasia Review Committees towards requests for assistance in dying from patients with dementia or psychiatric diagnoses and persons who were weary of life without having a serious illness. During the years 2007–2011, the Regional Euthanasia Review Committees found that the due care criteria had not been complied with in thirty-six cases, yet none of these cases resulted in a formal legal proceeding. The findings of the research indicate that very few cases are assessed as being non-compliant and, where there is non-compliance, violations virtually always relate to the non-substantive criteria. As such, some suggest that the criminal law may not be the appropriate framework to regulate this medical practice.

The overall conclusion of the second evaluation was again that the Act had succeeded in improving the carefulness of clinical practices and in providing a transparent and consistent legal framework for this practice. The researchers again recommended including an explicit statement in the Criminal Code by way of clarification that a life-terminating act was a different practice from the indicated and proportional use of medication to relieve suffering, even if such medication hastens death. They also repeated their recommendation that the requirement concerning due medical care when performing euthanasia or assisting in suicide should be assessed outside the context of criminal law. Another recommendation emerging from the second evaluation was the implementation of structures to support and educate physicians in complex cases. A few years later, this recommendation resulted in the publication of the so-called code of practice that summarised the Regional Euthanasia Review Committees' interpretation of the criteria of due care. Finally, recommendations were made relating to measures to increase the

Snijdewind, Donald van Tol and Dick Willems, 'Second Evaluation of the Termination of Life on Request and Assisted Suicide (Review Procedure) Act' ['Tweede Evaluatie Wet Toetsing Levensbeëindiging op Verzoek en Hulp bij Zelfdoding'], Report from the Netherlands Organisation for Health Research and Development (December 2012 ZonMw).

efficiency of the Regional Euthanasia Review Committees which were assessing increasing numbers of reported cases.

The Third Evaluation Study 2015–2016[27]

The third evaluation study was performed in 2015–2016 and comprised a legal study, a study of clinical practices and an analysis of the review procedure. Some parts of these studies were similar to the studies performed in previous evaluations; other parts were new.

Legal Study
The design of the legal study was comparable to the design of the studies that were performed in 2005–2006 and 2010–2011, with the analysis focusing on developments that occurred after the first two evaluation studies. Written documents from the period 2012 through 2016 were studied, files of cases of euthanasia and physician-assisted suicide that were forwarded by the Regional Euthanasia Review Committees to the Public Prosecution Service because of violations of the criteria of due care were analysed, and experts involved in the review procedure for termination of life or assisting in suicide were interviewed.

It appeared that during the study period no new developments occurred in the interpretation of the criteria of due care. There were, however, intensive discussions during the study period, both within the medical field and in society as a whole, on a number of specific themes. These discussions did not primarily pertain to the law as such; they predominantly focused on the (moral) acceptability and desirability of some practices. Topics that were discussed included: the circumstances in which a written statement seeking euthanasia when the patient later has dementia and becomes incapacitated should operate; and the possibility of physician assistance in dying on the request of competent children under twelve years of age, people with a psychiatric illness, and older people who consider their life completed. These debates have not ended yet and have not resulted in law reform thus far.

The number of cases where Regional Euthanasia Review Committees assessed that the physician did not fully meet the due care criteria remained very low. Out of 25,930 cases that were reported during 2012–2016, the due care criteria were not met in thirty-three cases. In a substantial number of these cases, the problem did not relate to the substantive criteria of due care (the first four due care requirements

[27] A full account of the study can be found in: Bregje Onwuteaka-Philipsen, Johan Legemaate, Agnes van der Heide, Hans van Delden, Kirsten Evenblij, Inssaf El Hammoud, Roeline Pasman, Corrette Ploem, Rosalie Pronk, Suzanne van de Vathorst and Dick Willems, 'Third Evaluation of the Termination of Life on Request and Assisted Suicide (Review Procdure) Act' ['Derde Evaluatie Wet Toetsing Levensbeëindiging op Verzoek en Hulp bij Zelfdoding'], Report from the Netherlands Organisation for Health Research and Development (May 2017 ZonMw).

listed above that include the request, the suffering, and the availability of alternative treatment options), but to the procedural criteria (the fifth and sixth criteria regarding consultation and medically prudent administration of euthanasia or physician-assisted suicide). All cases in which the due care criteria are not met are forwarded to the Health Care Inspectorate (a government department charged with public health responsibilities) and the Public Prosecution Service. These authorities initiated further formal steps in only three cases: the Health Care Inspectorate started a disciplinary procedure in two out of these thirty-three cases.[28] The Public Prosecution Service is even more reluctant to initiate a legal investigation: it initiated the first criminal procedure in 2013. This legal proceeding did not relate to potentially unjustified termination of life, but to the physician's refusal to submit a detailed report about his act, which is a separate and distinct violation.[29]

The use of written statements requesting termination of life, completed by patients in advance of losing decision-making capacity, was rarely considered in the early years after the enactment of legislation. In 2017, however, after reports from the Regional Euthanasia Review Committees that they observed an increase of euthanasia among dementia patients in the Netherlands,[30] a group of more than 200 doctors signed a letter urging against euthanasia based on advance directives from patients.[31] These doctors argued that they were reluctant to end the life of people who could not confirm that they still wanted to die. In that same year, the Public Prosecution Service, for the first time, commenced legal proceedings in a potential case of unjustified euthanasia. The case concerned an elderly care physician who had administered a lethal injection to a seventy-four-year-old patient with advanced dementia. The patient had asked her physicians in writing to end her life if she had to be admitted to a nursing home, and 'if she [the patient] thought the time was right'. The Prosecutor argued that the physician had acted with good intentions, but had not complied with Dutch law by failing to ensure the woman had consented at the time of euthanasia. It was argued that this constituted a major breach of the legal criteria because she displayed 'mixed signals' about dying. Before

---

[28] Regional Disciplinary Tribunal for Healthcare Amsterdam, 20 August 2013, ECLI:NL: TGZRAMS:2013:26; Regional Disciplinary Tribunal for Healthcare Amsterdam, 12 November 2013, ECLI:NL:TGZRAMS:2013:55.

[29] Annex 1 to the Annual Report from the Regional Euthanasia Review Committees (2014 Regional Euthanasia Review Committees) at 76–8 (overview of procedures of Public Prosecution Service and Health Inspectorate). In this case, the right to prosecute expired after three years and was barred mid-2014. The case was therefore closed. However, a medical prosecutor pointed out the defects in his actions to the physician and explained that these breaches, in principle, justified legal prosecution.

[30] Annual Report from the Regional Euthanasia Review Committees (2016 Regional Euthanasia Review Committees) at 5.

[31] See 'Media', Niet Stiekem bij Dementie, 2019, www.nietstiekembijdementie.nl/. See also Palko Karasz, 'Dutch Court Clears Doctor in Euthanasia of Dementia Patient, *New York Times*, 11 September, www.nytimes.com/2019/09/11/world/europe/netherlands-euthanasia-doctor.html.

administering the lethal injection, the physician slipped a sedative into the woman's coffee, as the patient was held down by her family and seemed to struggle against the injection.[32] The regional court in The Hague ruled that the euthanasia was carried out with proper care and that the physician did not have to verify her patient's wish to die with the patient because it was clear that she was incapable of responding. In addition, the court said it supported the doctor's decision to put a sedative in the woman's coffee to calm her before lethal drugs could be administered because it had made her as comfortable as possible. The Public Prosecution Service asked the Highest Criminal Court for a judgement, not to dispute the verdict, but to clarify the law. Rather than to punish the physician, whose motives they said were blameless, the Public Prosecution Service sought to clarify how doctors should deal with patients who are not in a position to confirm their wish to die and seemed to resist an injection. In June 2020, the Highest Criminal Court ruled that the regional court, in finding that the physician had acted with due care and so was not punishable by law, did not constitute an error of law.[33]

Assistance in suicide from non-physicians was also extensively considered in the evaluation review, partly in response to the facts revealed in the 'Heringa case'. In the Netherlands, assistance in dying can only be provided by physicians. Albert Heringa (who is not a physician) assisted his stepmother, who was ninety-nine years of age and felt that her life was completed and no longer worth living, in ending her life. The Dutch Regional Court found Heringa guilty of unlawful assistance in suicide, but did not impose a penalty.[34] However, an Appeals Court cleared him of all criminal responsibility because it accepted that he had to choose between two conflicting duties, that is, his duty to adhere to the law and his duty to help his mother to have a peaceful and dignified death.[35] In March 2017, the Highest Criminal Court ruled that the judgement of the Appeals Court could not be upheld and referred the case back to another Appeals Court.[36] In December 2017, the Public Prosecution Service before the second Appeals Court acknowledged that Heringa's motives were pure, but added that only doctors are allowed to assist with suicides. The Appeals Court then ruled that Heringa was guilty of assisting a suicide

---

[32] Regional Euthanasia Review Committee, Judgement No. 2016-85, 5–6; Regional Disciplinary Tribunal for Healthcare The Hague, 24 July 2018, ECLI:NL:TGZRSGR:2018:165, r.o. 2.24, 2.25. See also, in less detail, District Court of The Hague, 11 September 2019, ECLI:NL: RBDHA:2019:9506, final para., r.o. 4.4.1.

[33] Supreme Court, 21 April 2020, ECLI:NL:HR:2020:712.

[34] Gelderland District Court, 22 October 2013, ECLI:NL:RBGEL:2013:397. Notably, action taken by the Public Prosecution Service against Heringa responded to the national broadcast of a documentary on his case: Nan Rosens, *Moek's Final Wish*, The End: Levenseinde Documentaires and Film, 2010, www.thisistheend.nl/kijk-online/de-laatste-wens-van-moek/; Merel Kristi Schoonman, Ghislaine José Madeleine Wilhelmien van Thiel and Johannes Jozef Marten van Delden, 'Non-Physician-Assisted Suicide in The Netherlands: A Cross-Sectional Survey among the General Public' (2014) *Journal of Medical Ethics* 842–8.

[35] Court of Appeal Arnhem-Leeuwarden, 13 May 2015, ECLI:NL:GHARL:2015:3444.

[36] Supreme Court, 14 March 2017, ECLI:NL:HR:2017:418.

and could not invoke the defence of necessity on the basis of having an irresolvable conflict of the duty to relieve unbearable suffering and the duty to do no harm.[37] In April 2019, the Dutch Supreme Court upheld this ruling.

The public discourse in recent years seems to reflect greater societal emphasis on individual autonomy and self-determination. This is most evident in the debate on the desirability of enabling older people who consider their life completed to receive assistance in dying. In early 2016, an advisory committee established by the government concluded that the law on euthanasia and physician-assisted suicide functions adequately and provides sufficient options for the large majority of people who wish to receive assistance in dying.[38] To the surprise of many, the government responded to this conclusion by recommending the enactment of new legislation designed to respect older people's autonomy. This change would represent a shift in the traditional underpinning of legislation, namely the professional responsibility of physicians to express compassion and respond to the suffering of their patients. However, after the national election in March 2017, the political landscape was fragmented with thirteen political parties represented in parliament. The coalition government consisted of four parties, two of which have a Christian denomination. The newly formed government decided not to discuss major medical-ethical issues until the next parliamentary elections. Legislation regarding physician assistance in dying remains unchanged.

A final observation from the legal evaluation study is whether reform of the review procedure itself is needed. Some commentators have called for a central (appeal) commission as physicians cannot currently appeal against a judgement of the Regional Euthanasia Review Committees. There have also been calls for a legal pathway to seek the opinion of the Dutch Highest Criminal Court on the judgement of a Regional Euthanasia Review Committee.

Clinical Practices Study

In this component of the third evaluation study, developments in the practice of end-of-life decision-making were analysed. The emphasis was on euthanasia and physician-assisted suicide, but attention was also paid to other medical decisions that can have a life-shortening effect. Data were collected through the following questionnaire studies involving:

1. a sample of over 1,900 adults who were representative of the Dutch population ('*general public study*');
2. attending physicians of a sample of over 7,000 deceased people ('*death certificate study*');

---

[37] Court of Appeal of 's-Hertogenbosch, 31 January 2018, ECLI:NL:GHSHE:2018:345.
[38] 'Completed Life: On Assistance to Die for People Who Consider Their Life Completed' ['Voltooid Leven: Over Hulp bij Zelfdoding aan Mensen Die hun Leven Voltooid Achten'], Report from the Advisory Committee on Completed Life [Adviescommissie Voltooid Leven] (January 2016 Adviescommissie Voltooid Leven).

3. a sample of 2,500 physicians of specialties that regularly care for patients in the last phase of life (general practitioners, clinical specialists, and elderly care physicians) ('*physicians study*'); and
4. a sample of about 500 psychiatrists, followed by in-depth interviews with fifteen psychiatrists ('*psychiatrists study*').

The *death certificate study* and the *physicians study* were largely similar to studies performed in previous evaluations, while the *general public study* and the *psychiatrists study* were new.

The *general public study* revealed wide public support for the law on euthanasia and physician-assisted suicide. The public's knowledge of the law is generally good, although there are misunderstandings about specific details. The principle of compassion, that is, addressing unbearable suffering, is the central principle of the euthanasia and physician-assisted suicide law according to most members of the general public, but the right of self-determination is also important to many. Depending on exactly what is asked, 40–50 per cent of the general public support allowing physician assistance in dying for people with a psychiatric illness, 60–80 per cent support it for people with advanced dementia (based on an advance directive requesting euthanasia), 40–60 per cent support it for older people who consider their life completed, and 40 per cent support it for children under twelve years of age. In general, public support for allowing physician assistance in dying for these special groups has grown somewhat compared to earlier years. Finally, a large majority of the Dutch public has a positive attitude towards the End of life Clinic, which has recently changed its name to Centre of Expertise for Euthanasia. This Centre of Expertise counsels and supports physicians who have doubts about or cannot grant requests for euthanasia or physician-assisted suicide from their patients, for whatever reason. The Centre consists of a network of 140 physicians and nurses throughout the Netherlands who are willing to provide assistance in dying in complex cases, while adhering to the legal criteria of due care.[39]

In the *death certificate study*, cases are classified as euthanasia if physicians report that the death of the person was the result of medication that they administered with the explicit intention of hastening death and at the explicit request of the patient. Cases are classified as physician-assisted suicide if physicians report that death was the result of the patient taking medication that they provided with the explicit intention of enabling the patient to hasten his or her own death. The study showed that the frequency of physician assistance in dying had increased again, from 4,000 cases in 2010 to 6,800 in 2015. Euthanasia was performed on 6,650 persons or 4.5 per cent of all deceased persons in 2015 (2010: 3,850 cases or 2.8 per cent). The

---

[39] See 'Careful and Caring', Expertisecentrum Euthanasie, 2019, https://expertisecentrumeuthanasie .nl/en/.

frequency of physician-assisted suicide remained relatively low in 2015: 150 cases or 0.1 per cent of all deaths (2010: 200 cases or 0.1 per cent).

The study shed some light on the reasons for the increase in euthanasia. First, the total number of deceased people who had requested physician assistance in dying was higher in 2015 (8.4 per cent) than in 2010 (6.7 per cent).[40] Further, the percentage of requests that resulted in performing euthanasia or physician-assisted suicide increased, from 45 per cent in 2010 to 55 per cent in 2015. Compared to earlier years, there seems to be a trend towards a more substantial estimated shortening of life, which suggests that some patients ask or receive euthanasia somewhat earlier in their disease trajectory. However, the percentage of patients for whom the estimated shortening of life is longer than half a year is still less than 10 per cent. In about 20 per cent of the cases that were classified as euthanasia or physician-assisted suicide based on the answers of the physicians in our question-naire, the physicians themselves would not classify their act as such. This percentage is comparable to previous years. Physicians regarded these acts as regular 'comfort care', and as a consequence, these cases are not reported to the Regional Euthanasia Review Committees. Physicians typically use opioids in these cases, instead of muscle relaxants and barbiturates, and the extent to which life is shortened is mostly limited to less than twenty-four hours. This suggests a lack of clarity by physicians regarding the demarcation between physician assistance in dying, on the one hand, and regular comfort care for dying patients, on the other hand.

The frequencies of other end-of-life decisions, that is, hastening of death not at the explicit request of the patient, alleviation of symptoms with medication that may have hastened death without hastening of death being the intention, and the withholding or withdrawing of potentially life-prolonging treatment, remained simi-lar in 2015 as compared to 2010. This is not the case for continuous deep palliative sedation, which was provided to 12 per cent of all deceased patients in 2010 compared with 18 per cent in 2015. In continuous deep palliative sedation, physicians provide patients with medication to deeply and continuously sedate them until death. Continuous deep sedation may or may not involve (potential) hastening of death and therefore, depending on the facts of the particular case, death may or may not be the result of an end-of-life decision.

The majority of patients who request and receive physician assistance in dying have cancer (4,100 or 64 per cent of all reported cases in 2019). The number of patients who request and receive physician assistance in dying because of dementia (162 or 2.5 per cent), a psychiatric disease (68 or 1.0 per cent) or because they feel

---

[40] The main explanation for the gap between 8.4 per cent of people who requested and 4.6 per cent of people who received physician assistance in dying is that either the physician had considered the criteria of due care not applicable or the patient had died before the procedure of discussing the request and involving an independent advisor could be completed. See: Onwuteaka-Philipsen et al., 'Third Evaluation of the Termination of Life on Request and Assisted Suicide (Review Procedure) Act', 108–9.

that their life is completed without having a serious illness (172 or 2.7 per cent) remained relatively small.[41]

The *physicians study* explored the percentage of physicians who can conceive of ever granting a request where a person has dementia, a psychiatric disease or feel their life is completed. The percentage of doctors who could conceive of ever granting a request varies from 16 per cent for older people who feel their life is completed to 42 per cent for competent patients with early-stage dementia. The majority of physicians have a positive attitude towards the Centre of Expertise for Euthanasia, the network that provides assistance in complex cases; 18 per cent have referred a patient to this Centre and two-thirds of the physicians can imagine doing so in an appropriate case.

The *psychiatrists study* showed an increase in the estimated total annual number of explicit requests for physician-assisted suicide made to psychiatrists from 320 in 1995, to 500 in 2008, and 1,100 in 2016. In 2016, 4 per cent of psychiatrists reported that they had granted such a request. Although the number of requests that were granted increased from 14 in 2012[42] to 60 in 2016,[43] psychiatrists have reported becoming more reluctant about assisting their psychiatric patients to commit suicide. In 1995, 53 per cent of psychiatrists found it inconceivable to ever do so, and this had increased to 63 per cent in 2015. After 2016, the number of reported cases remained stable, with 68 reported cases in 2019.[44] Psychiatrists provided arguments both in favour of and against allowing assistance in suicide for psychiatric patients. The arguments in favour included: it is unfair to exclude them if it is possible to fulfil the due care criteria, psychiatric suffering might be worse than somatic suffering, patients with a psychiatric disease also have a right to self-determination, physician assistance in dying might offer a dignified end of life to patients who otherwise might commit suicide, and seriously considering a request for assistance in suicide is considered to be part of the professional responsibility of a physician. Arguments against assistance in suicide for psychiatric patients included: the risk of counter-transference, arguments related to the due care criteria such as doubts about the extent to which a request of a psychiatric patient can be voluntary and well-considered, and concerns about the quality of mental health care in the Netherlands. Although assistance in dying for patients with psychiatric diseases is relatively rare, when it is provided, it is often by physicians within the Centre of Expertise for Euthanasia.

The Review Procedure Study

The Dutch legal framework requires physicians to report any acts of physician assistance in dying to a Regional Euthanasia Review Committee. This requirement

---

[41] Annual Report from the Regional Euthanasia Review Committees (2019 Regional Euthanasia Review Committees) at 17.

[42] Annual Report from the Regional Euthanasia Review Committees (2012 Regional Euthanasia Review Committees) at 12.

[43] Annual Report from the Regional Euthanasia Review Committees (2016) at 13.

[44] Annual Report from the Regional Euthanasia Review Committees (2019) at 13.

is designed to achieve a transparent and controlled practice. After ending the life of a patient on their explicit request, the physician must report their act to the municipal coroner who has to confirm the (unnatural) death of the patient. The physician must submit a detailed report regarding their compliance with the due care criteria. The municipal coroner hands over the report to the eligible Regional Euthanasia Review Committee. All five Regional Euthanasia Review Committees consist of a lawyer who also acts as chairman, a physician and an expert on ethical issues. The Committee assesses every notification of termination of life on request as to whether the doctor has acted in accordance with the statutory due care requirements. If necessary, the committee may request further information from the reporting physician or others. The committee must inform the physician of its reasoned opinion within six weeks. If it concludes that the doctor has acted with due care, that is, has complied with all the relevant criteria, the procedure is ended. If the committee judges that the doctor has not complied with one or more of the due care criteria, the committee must send the case to the Public Prosecution Service and the Health Inspectorate. These two authorities then determine whether further steps are necessary.

The study of the review procedure and the functioning of the Regional Euthanasia Review Committees, a component of the broader evaluation of the euthanasia and physician-assisted suicide law, included an analysis of a database of all reported cases between 2002 and 2015, a questionnaire study of a sample of physicians who had reported a case, an analysis of a sample of files of reported cases, observations of meetings of Regional Euthanasia Review Committees, and a questionnaire study of and in-depth interviews with (former) members of the Regional Euthanasia Review Committees.

In 2015, it was found that 81 per cent of all cases were actually reported. (The figure of 81 per cent is an estimate based on the data from the *death certificate study*.) This percentage is comparable to the findings in 2010 and 2005. The annual number of reported cases increased from 2,819 in 2010 to 5,089 in 2015. Not reporting is predominantly related to the fact that physicians think the cases they do not report do not constitute euthanasia.

In the period from 2002 to 2015, the Regional Euthanasia Review Committees assessed that the physician did not act in accordance with the due care criteria in seventy-six cases. This represents 0.2 per cent of all reported cases (43,171) in that period. While the number of reported cases has risen, the risk of a judgement 'not in accordance with the due care criteria' has decreased over the years.

The questionnaire study of physicians who had reported a case of euthanasia or physician-assisted suicide to the Regional Euthanasia Review Committees showed that most of them experienced the procedure around reporting and reviewing as positive or neutral. In 4 per cent of all reported cases the Regional Euthanasia Review Committee asked the physician to provide extra clarification; in 1 per cent of reported cases the physician was invited to give this clarification in a personal meeting with the committee.

The approach taken by the Regional Euthanasia Review Committees when assessing reported cases is to have trust in the physician, at least unless there is reason not to have such trust. The Committees prefer an educational approach towards physicians who they assess as intending to act in their patient's best interest and to adhere to the legal criteria, but are judged not to have fully done so. They understand the difficult position of physicians in complex cases and prefer to support and inform them so that they can adjust their decision-making for future cases. Researchers who attended these meetings observed that the Regional Euthanasia Review Committee members seemed to be willing to assess a case as 'not in accordance with the due care criteria' only if they thought that there had been a serious violation of the criteria.

Members of the Regional Euthanasia Review Committees were satisfied with how the Committees functioned. They consider the current review system sustainable, despite the increasing workload due to the increasing number of reported cases. The fact that the Public Prosecution Service has rarely initiated legal prosecution in cases where the Regional Euthanasia Review Committees came to the conclusion that the physician had not acted in accordance with the due care criteria is not considered a problem by most Committee members. Nevertheless, some of them would appreciate receiving legal guidance from the court in relation to difficult legal points that arise. Some support creating a pathway so a Regional Euthanasia Review Committee can apply to a court to receive legal guidance in interpreting the law (and what is required to satisfy due care requirements), without the need to involve a particular physician.

Recommendations from the Third Evaluation Study

The third evaluation study, unlike the first two studies, did not make recommendations to amend the law itself. Instead, recommendations to address continued confusion of physicians regarding the distinction between life-terminating acts, on the one hand, and regular symptom control and palliative sedation, on the other hand, focused on better education of physicians on this distinction. The recommendations mainly focused on the emerging complexities of regulation. These included the need for increased transparency and understanding of how the Regional Euthanasia Review Committees interpret the legal requirements for physician assistance in dying in complex cases, and how they assess whether physicians comply with these criteria in the context of quite sharply increased numbers. Timely initiation of open communication about the expectations and preferences of people with a severe incurable illness was advocated as a strategy to avoid complex decision-making at a later time when patients are no longer able to carefully consider their options. Further, greater efforts could be made to implement easily accessible structures for support or advice from peers or experts when considering requests for physician assistance in dying from patients in complex situations.

CONCLUSION

All three of the evaluation studies demonstrate that the goals of the Termination of Life on Request and Assisted Suicide (Review Procedures) Act[45] are, to a large extent, met. All stakeholders appear to be satisfied with the content of the law and how it is implemented. The evaluation studies have had a clear and important impact on debates in the political, societal and medical arena. They have provided robust, scientific evidence that inform deliberations on complex issues. The law in the Netherlands has, for quite some time, been widely endorsed. It is likely that this is for a combination of reasons: the long-term societal debate that preceded the enforcement of the law; the emphasis on compassion and relief of unbearable suffering as an important rationale for the law; and the availability of evidence as provided by the evaluation studies.

Recommendations from the first and second evaluation studies to reform the criminal law by (1) including a provision that clarifies the distinction between physician assistance in dying and regular alleviation of patients' suffering and (2) exempting the clinical performance of the administration of assistance in dying from criminal liability, were not followed. In contrast, important aspects of the notification and review procedures were adapted as a result of findings from the studies. There is currently pressure on certain aspects of the regulatory framework. Concerns are less about the actual content of the law itself, but rather other factors including inconsistencies in interpretations of the criteria of due care, the workload of the Regional Euthanasia Review Committees due to the increased number of reported cases, and debates about whether additional groups should qualify for access to physician assistance in dying. Nevertheless, the evaluation studies have identified one aspect of the law that may need further consideration: in what circumstances will a physician be permitted to comply with a request for euthanasia contained in a written statement made when the patient was still able to appreciate their interests? The Highest Criminal Court recently held that a lower court's finding that a physician exercised due care in the controversial case of a patient with dementia did not constitute an error of law. Despite that finding, it is likely that the ruling will have only a limited effect on clinical practice as physicians are known to be very reluctant to provide assistance in dying in comparable cases.

The Dutch regulatory framework reflects the societal and political debates that have occurred over many decades. What sets the Dutch framework apart from many other legislative regimes is the extensive and regular reviews of the regime by a team of independent multidisciplinary researchers. The findings of these rigorous evaluation studies inform decisions of parliament about the content of the law, as well as

---

[45] Termination of Life on Request and Assisted Suicide (Review Procedures) Act of 1 April 2002 (the Netherlands).

decisions about how review bodies should operate. The outcome of current debates on whether or not ending of life on request should be regulated for situations that currently fall outside the law, such as requests from older people who feel their life is completed, requests from competent minors under twelve years of age and assistance in dying by non-physicians, remains to be seen.

5

The Challenging Path to Voluntary Assisted Dying Law Reform in Australia

Victoria as a Successful Case Study

Lindy Willmott and Ben P. White

INTRODUCTION

In November 2017, Victoria enacted the Voluntary Assisted Dying Act 2017 (Vic) (the 'VAD Act'). After an eighteen-month implementation period, the Act commenced operation in June 2019 making voluntary assisted dying ('VAD') lawful in Australia's second most populous State. More than two decades earlier, in 1995, the Northern Territory, the least populous of Australia's eight States and Territories, was the first jurisdiction in the world to have operative legislation allowing VAD. This legislation was short-lived however, being overturned by the Commonwealth approximately nine months after it commenced operation. Since 1993, there have been dozens of unsuccessful attempts to legalise VAD in almost all Australian jurisdictions.[1]

This chapter explores the Victorian experience as a successful model for VAD law reform. Why did the Victorian Bill pass while previous reform attempts failed? The Victorian reform process had some key features which distinguished it from earlier efforts. It was instigated, supported and funded by the government. The law reform process was thorough, methodical, considered and included leadership from key influential individuals. The process was also very consultative and occurred over an extended period. This combination proved to be a successful formula for legislative reform in a country where ongoing and high-level public support for change has been met, at least until recently, by equivalent ongoing political resistance to reform. This approach has also proven successful in Western Australia, which has recently

---

[1] Lindy Willmott, Ben White, Christopher Stackpoole, Kelly Purser and Andrew McGee, '(Failed) Voluntary Euthanasia Law Reform in Australia: Two Decades of Trends, Models and Politics' (2016) 39 *University of New South Wales Law Journal* 1–46; Ben White and Lindy Willmott, 'Future of Assisted Dying Reform in Australia' (2018) 42 *Australian Health Review* 616–20.

passed its own Voluntary Assisted Dying Act 2019 (WA) after a Victorian-style reform process.

This chapter has three sections. It commences with a brief review of the history of law reform attempts in Australia since the first bill was introduced into the Australian Capital Territory Parliament in 1993, and notes the characteristics and trends of these reform attempts. The second section then describes the Victorian reform process: establishment of the Parliamentary Committee and the work undertaken by that Committee; the nature of the governmental response to the recommendations made in the Committee's Report; and establishment of the Ministerial Advisory Panel and its activities including recommendations about the nature of a legislative regime. It also describes the parliamentary path to changing the law. The third and final section considers the reform process overall and identifies further features of that process that we consider distinguish it from previous ones, and which may have also contributed to its success in achieving reform.

BRIEF HISTORY OF AUSTRALIAN EXPERIENCE

The VAD Act was passed following numerous previously unsuccessful attempts to legalise the practice in Australia. Reform attempts have occurred at all levels of government – the Commonwealth, States and Territories – since the first attempt in the Australian Capital Territory in 1993. As mentioned, the legislation that was enacted in the Northern Territory, the Rights of the Terminally Ill Act 1995 (NT), was overturned by the federal Euthanasia Laws Act 1997 (Cth), pursuant to its constitutional powers relating to Territory laws. The Commonwealth legislation is still in force today and prevents the Northern Territory or the Australian Capital Territory parliaments from reforming law on this topic.[2] It is important to note, however, that the Commonwealth does not have equivalent powers to overturn any VAD legislation enacted by the States.

Despite the inability of Australian Territories to reform their laws, there has been ongoing legislative activity over the past three decades, with reform attempts intensifying over recent years. This has primarily been at the State level given how legislative powers are shared between State and Commonwealth governments in Australia. A comprehensive review of reform attempts up until 31 December 2015 revealed that fifty-one bills about VAD had been introduced into various Australian parliaments.[3] The bills generally proposed the introduction of a comprehensive VAD regime, but some proposed more limited alterations to criminal law statutes to introduce a defence, a referendum on whether there should be reform, or to overturn the Commonwealth legislation that limits Territorial rights. There have

[2]   Report from the Select Committee on End of Life Choices in the Australian Capital Territory (2019 Parliament of the Australian Capital Territory) at 75–81.
[3]   Willmott et al., '(Failed) Voluntary Euthanasia'.

been ongoing reform attempts since this review and, as at 30 June 2020, a further eight bills have been tabled (including the Victorian VAD Bill and the WA VAD Bill that ultimately became law).[4]

That 2015 review also examined characteristics of the bills as well as the prevailing political context in which the reform attempts occurred, and some interesting themes were revealed.[5] The first was to note that reform attempts were largely removed from party politics. All bills were introduced as private member's bills, and all parliamentarians were given a conscience vote. The proponents of the bills were mainly independents or members of socially progressive political parties, the Australian Democrats and the Australian Greens. A small number of bills were proposed by members of the Australian Labor Party (Australia's mainstream left-leaning party), and only one bill was proposed by a member of the Country Liberal Party (Australia's mainstream conservative party, as it was then known). At the time of the review, the major parties, the Australian Labor Party, the Liberal Party and the National Party (the latter two are both conservative parties and generally act in coalition with each other), did not have policies on VAD, while the Australian Greens Party had supported reform since the party was formed in 1992. Despite the major parties, at the time, not having formal policies on the topic and also allowing a conscience vote, for the most part there were correlations between party affiliations and voting preferences. This was particularly the case for members of conservative political parties where the members generally voted against VAD.

The second important observation from this review was how difficult it was to bring about reform. In most Australian States, a bill must be passed by their two Houses of Parliament, the 'Lower House' and the 'Upper House'.[6] To become law, the bill must progress through various phases: it must first be introduced into each House of Parliament and then be formally 'read' before it is considered in detail. If not defeated early in the process, it is formally voted upon by all members of parliament.[7] As part of the 2015 review, fifty bills[8] were examined in detail to determine how far through the legislative process, as described above, it had progressed. From this review, the authors determined whether or not the bill was 'close to passing',[9] and concluded that only seven of the fifty bills fell into that category. Surprisingly, all of these bills originated in small States or Territories:

---

[4] White and Willmott, 'Future of Assisted Dying'.
[5] Willmott et al., '(Failed) Voluntary Euthanasia'.
[6] In one Australian State (Queensland) and two Territories (the Northern Territory and the Australian Capital Territory), there is only one House of Parliament, so passage of a bill into law may be easier to achieve in those jurisdictions.
[7] After the bill is passed by both Houses of Parliament, it is then signed into law by the Governor of the State.
[8] Although fifty-one bills had been introduced, at the time of the review, one bill had not yet been disposed of in parliament so was not included in this analysis.
[9] To be 'close to passing', the bill had to be voted on and supported by at least 70 per cent of the number of members required for it to pass through the House.

Northern Territory (one bill that ultimately was enacted),[10] Tasmania (one bill) and South Australia (five bills). It may be, however, that VAD bills being introduced now are more likely to pass. Although only a small sample, of the eight bills introduced from the beginning of 2016 until 30 June 2020 (and the one bill that was introduced prior to 2016 but resolved in 2018), five would be 'close to passing' as described above (indeed the Victorian and WA VAD Acts did pass).[11] Further, since 30 June 2020, VAD legislation has also been enacted in Tasmania.[12]

Finally, the authors of the 2015 review attempted to explain why those seven, rather than the other forty-three bills, were close to passing. Interestingly, this was not due to any unique *content* of the seven bills as they were no more or less conservative than the other forty-three bills. The first possible explanation was the profile of the proponent of the bill. For example, the Northern Territory Bill which was ultimately enacted was championed by a former Chief Minister of the Northern Territory, Marshall Perron, who was highly regarded in the Territory and a charismatic advocate of the Bill. The second possible explanation was the power and influence of interest groups. For example, in South Australia, there had been a long history of advocates actively campaigning for reform. Plumb commented that one of the well-known interest groups regularly appeared on the steps of parliament with placards and information pamphlets.[13]

Since the 2015 review, party politics appears to have played a greater role in bringing about reform. As described below, over recent years, we have seen sitting governments in four States (Victoria, Western Australia, Queensland and South Australia) and one Territory (the Australian Capital Territory) becoming more proactive in the reform process.[14] The Victorian process, the subject of this chapter, is considered in more detail below, but commenced with an inquiry by a parliamentary committee in 2015 followed by a Ministerial Advisory Panel in late 2016. This approach seems to have been influential elsewhere in Australia. Western Australia held an inquiry by a parliamentary committee that recommended reform[15] and, as occurred in Victoria, this was followed by the appointment of a Ministerial Expert Panel that was tasked

---

[10] Note that this Bill was enacted before the Commonwealth passed legislation to prohibit Territories from enacting law about VAD.

[11] White and Willmott, 'Future of Assisted Dying', 618. The bills were the Restoring Territory Rights (Assisted Suicide Legislation) Bill 2015 (Cth), Voluntary Assisted Dying Bill 2017 (NSW), Death with Dignity Bill 2016 (SA), Voluntary Assisted Dying Bill 2017 (Vic) and Voluntary Assisted Dying Bill 2019 (WA) (the latter two bills ultimately becoming law).

[12] End-of-Life Choices (Voluntary Assisted Dying) Act 2021 (Tas).

[13] Alison Plumb, 'The Future of Euthanasia Politics in the Australian State Parliaments' (2014) 29 *Australasian Parliamentary Review* 67–86 at 73, which considered the role of politics and political affiliation in this context in South Australia and Tasmania.

[14] As a further example of the infusion of VAD into the political arena, in July 2017, the Queensland Branch of the Australian Labor Party voted to support the introduction of VAD legislation.

[15] 'My Life, My Choice', First Report from the Joint Select Committee on End of Life Choices (2018 Parliament of Western Australia).

with developing legislation for consideration by Parliament.[16] Queensland also set up a parliamentary committee inquiry which recommended reform and proposed a draft bill for consideration.[17] Unlike Western Australia and Victoria, however, the Queensland government responded to this committee's report by a referral to the Queensland Law Reform Commission, tasking the Commission to draft legislation for consideration by the Queensland Parliament.[18] The South Australian parliament also established a parliamentary committee[19] to review this issue, with that Committee producing its final Report in October 2020.[20] Finally, a parliamentary committee in the Australian Capital Territory reviewed its end-of-life care framework, even though it is prohibited from passing VAD legislation.[21]

Despite sitting governments being more at the forefront of reform over recent years, a role may still exist for independent Members of Parliament initiating reform. In Tasmania, for example, VAD legislation has been enacted following a bill being tabled by Michael Gaffney, an Independent Member of Parliament.[22] And a New South Wales Independent Member of Parliament, Alex Greenwich, has indicated that he will table a VAD bill in the near future.[23]

Nevertheless, as we explain further below, the Victorian experience which comprised a Parliamentary Committee and Ministerial Advisory Panel may have been influential in a bill successfully navigating the parliamentary process.[24]

THE VICTORIAN LAW REFORM PROCESS

Prior to 2016, Victoria had not experienced significant formal agitation for legislative change of the law on VAD in the form of bills. The review referred to above revealed that, up until the end of 2015, there had only been one Victorian bill out of a total of

[16] Government of Western Australia, Department of Health, *Ministerial Expert Panel on Voluntary Assisted Dying* (Final Report, July 2019).

[17] 'Voluntary Assisted Dying', Report No. 34 from the Health, Communities, Disability Services and Domestic and Family Violence Prevention Committee (2020 Parliament of Queensland). The Bill recommended by the Committee is published in Ben White and Lindy Willmott, 'A Model Voluntary Assisted Dying Bill' (2019) 7(2) *Griffith Journal of Law and Human Dignity* 1.

[18] Queensland Law Reform Commission, Queensland's Laws Relating to Voluntary Assisted Dying (Terms of Reference, 2020).

[19] Terms of Reference of the Joint Committee on End of Life Choices (2019 Parliament of South Australia).

[20] Report from the Joint Committee on End of Life Choices (2020 Parliament of South Australia).

[21] Report from the Select Committee on End of Life Choices in the Australian Capital Territory (2019 Parliament of the Australian Capital Territory) at 74–96.

[22] End-of-Life Choices (Voluntary Assisted Dying) Act 2021 (Tas).

[23] 'New South Wales Parliament set to debate voluntary assisted dying legislation in 2021', SBS News, 13 December 2020, www.sbs.com.au/news/nsw-parliament-set-to-debate-voluntary-assisted-dying-legislation-in-2021.

[24] For a consideration of the reform process in Victoria, see also Margaret M. O'Connor, Roger W. Hunt, Julian Gardner, Mary Draper, Ian Maddocks, Trish Malowney and Brian K. Owler, 'Documenting the Process of Developing the Victorian Voluntary Assisted Dying Legislation' (2018) 42 *Australian Health Review* 621–6.

fifty-one bills relating to the legalising of VAD.[25] Despite this lack of legislative activity though, concern about the state of the law had been expressed in Victoria from time to time. For example, in 1995 seven doctors wrote an open letter to *The Age* newspaper calling for VAD law reform.[26] More recently in 2013, one of those seven doctors, Dr Rodney Syme, publicly admitted to assisting terminally ill patients to end their lives in an attempt to bring the issue to public attention and to challenge authorities to respond to his admittedly illegal activity.[27] No criminal charges were laid. At the same time, at a national level, a high-profile media personality, Andrew Denton, began conducting a public campaign to legalise VAD. This campaign attracted a great deal of media coverage.

Parliamentary Committee Inquiry into End-of-Life Choices (7 May 2015–9 June 2016)

The real momentum for reform came on 7 May 2015 when the Victorian Special Minister of State, Gavin Jennings, under pressure from other members of parliament,[28] moved a motion to refer the topic of end-of-life choices to the Legislative Council Standing Committee on Legal and Social Issues. The terms of reference required the Committee 'to inquire into, consider and report on the need for laws in Victoria to allow citizens to make informed decisions about their own end-of-life choices'.[29] In particular, the Committee was required to:

---

[25] Willmott et al., '(Failed) Voluntary Euthanasia', 11.

[26] The doctors wrote: 'It cannot be right to tolerate this totally unsatisfactory situation, where it is a matter of chance whether patients will receive the treatment which they so desperately seek and where it must be only a matter of time before some doctor is prosecuted by the state for following the dictates of his conscience' in Nick Davies, 'Helping Patients to Die', *The Age*, 25 March 1995, 1.

[27] 'Melbourne Doctor, Rodney Symes, Attempting to Provoke Prosecution for Euthanasia to Spur Test Case', ABC News, 10 November 2015, www.abc.net.au/news/2015-11-10/doctor-provoking-euthanasia-prosecution-to-spur-test-case/6925964.

[28] Hansard, Victoria, Legislative Council, 7 May 2015, 1278–82 (Gavin Jennings). Although the motion was moved by a senior Labor Government minister in the Upper House, Gavin Jennings, pressure to take action had been applied by other members of parliament. In April, Colleen Hartland, from the Australian Greens Party, had tabled a motion to refer VAD to the Victorian Law Reform Commission: Hansard, Victoria, Legislative Council, 15 April 2015, 946–7 (Colleen Hartland), and Fiona Patten who was then a member of the Australian Sex Party (later renamed the Reason Party) tabled a motion to investigate VAD through a joint investigative committee: Hansard, Victoria, Legislative Council, 15 April 2015, 962–4 (Fiona Patten). When the government introduced its motion for the inquiry, Gavin Jennings acknowledged that Fiona Patten's motion was the template for their own motion: Hansard, Victoria, Legislative Council, 7 May 2015, 1280 (Gavin Jennings). Mr Jennings also acknowledged Colleen Hartland's motion to refer the matter to the Law Reform Commission: Hansard, Victoria, Legislative Council, 7 May 2015, 1278, 1280 (Gavin Jennings).

[29] Final Report from the Legal and Social Issues Committee's Inquiry into End of Life Choices (2016 Parliament of Victoria) at xiii.

1. assess the practices currently being utilised within the medical community to assist a person to exercise their preferences for the way they want to manage their end of life, including the role of palliative care;
2. review the current framework of legislation, proposed legislation and other relevant reports and materials in other Australian states and territories and overseas jurisdictions; and
3. consider what type of legislative change may be required, including an examination of any federal laws that may impact such legislation.

The terms of reference required the Committee to deliver its Report by no later than 31 May 2016.

These terms of reference were wide and obliged the Committee to look broadly at the health services available, with a particular focus on palliative care services, and the experiences of people at the end of life. Whether the criminal law in Victoria that prohibits VAD should be reformed was situated within this broader inquiry.[30]

The Committee comprised eight members of parliament: three from the Australian Labor Party (the incumbent governing party), three from the Liberal Party (one of whom chaired the Committee), one from the Australian Greens Party and one from the Australian Sex Party (as it was then known). The Australian Greens and the Australian Sex Party (both minor parties) had policies that supported VAD, while the Australian Labor Party and the Liberal Party (both major parties) did not have policies on the topic. The Committee was supported by a Secretariat comprising a Secretary, Inquiry Officers and Legal Interns.[31]

The Inquiry process was thorough and comprised four components:

1. Research: The Committee undertook extensive research from academic literature and reports from other similar inquiries nationally and internationally.[32]
2. Submissions:[33] The Committee invited submissions and received 1,037 (925 from individuals and 112 from organisations). The submissions were from individuals and organisations who had very different perspectives including individuals facing their own death, health professionals (including palliative care specialists), legal experts, religious and faith-based organisational leaders and members of the public who wished to offer their opinion on the topic. The overwhelming majority of the individual submissions related to VAD rather than broader issues about palliative care services. Submissions relating to VAD were also received from religious organisations and lobby groups including the Australian

---

[30] Ibid.
[31] Ibid. at iv.
[32] Ibid. at 2.
[33] Those making submissions are listed in the Final Report from the Legal and Social Issues Committee's Inquiry into End of Life Choices (2016 Parliament of Victoria) at appendix 1.

Catholic Bishops Conference, Australian Christians, Australian Christian Lobby, Catholic Archdiocese of Melbourne and Catholic Health Australia, as well as organisations associated with medical and health services including the Royal Australasian College of Physicians, the Royal Australian and New Zealand College of Psychiatrists, the Australian and New Zealand Society for Geriatric Medicine, the Australian and New Zealand Society of Palliative Medicine, the Australian College of Nursing and the Australian Nursing and Midwifery Federation (Victorian Branch).

3. Public hearings, site visits and briefings: The Committee also informed itself through other means. Between July 2015 and February 2016, the Committee undertook public hearings (over seventeen days, hearing from 154 witnesses) and site visits in seven locations around the State including rural and regional health services. The Committee heard from various governmental agencies as well as individuals. It was also briefed by departmental experts in end-of-life care, the peak palliative care body for the State and legal academics. Representatives of religious and medical organisations also gave evidence at public hearings (although fewer than those who provided submissions).

4. International visits: Finally, in 2016 a five-person delegation visited the Netherlands, Switzerland, Canada (including Québec) and Oregon, jurisdictions where VAD is lawful.

Committee's Report (9 June 2016)

The Committee's Report was tabled in Parliament on 9 June 2016. It comprised 444 pages and included forty-nine recommendations. Forty-eight of these recommendations related to system and other issues concerning the delivery of health care services at the end of life. Its forty-ninth recommendation was to legalise VAD in limited circumstances. In this short chapter, it is not possible to comprehensively review the reasoning underpinning the Committee's recommendation to legalise VAD. But there are four key points worthy of mention. The first is to note that the Committee proposed twelve core values that should underpin end-of-life care, and which were shared by all the Committee members, including the two who ultimately delivered a minority report in relation to legalising VAD. They are:

- Every human life has value.
- Open discussion about death and dying should be encouraged and promoted.
- People should be able to make informed choices about the end of their life.
- End-of-life care should be person-centred.
- End-of-life care should address the needs of families and carers.

- Pain and suffering should be alleviated for those who are unwell.
- Palliative care is an invaluable, life-enhancing part of end-of-life care.
- High-quality end-of-life care should be available to all people in all settings.
- Each person should be entitled to core rights in end-of-life care.
- Vulnerable people should be supported and protected.
- The law should be coherent and transparent.
- The law should be followed and enforced.

These values were based on what the Committee learnt throughout the Inquiry process,[34] and were stated to underpin the Committee's approach to the review. These principles, therefore, ultimately, underpinned its decision – by majority – to recommend reform to permit VAD.

The second point is that the Committee considered the evidence presented about the implications of the current legal framework, and concluded that 'the current legal framework is not serving Victorians well'.[35] The Committee noted that 'Victorians with serious and incurable conditions and irremediable suffering are exposed to the possibility of a traumatic death'.[36] The Committee appeared to be particularly persuaded by the evidence of the Victorian Coroner which highlighted some of the 'horrific ways people are currently dying under our current law, particularly frail, elderly and vulnerable Victorians'.[37] The Coroner advised the Committee that some people were ending their own lives in dreadful ways, in pain and dying alone so as not to implicate their relatives.[38] Drawing on this and other evidence about the impact of the current law, the Committee then articulated the options: to maintain the status quo; enforce the current framework, for example, by ensuring individuals assisting others to die are charged and prosecuted; or change the law. The first option was not acceptable as it would ignore the evidence of harm that is currently occurring.[39] The Committee did not consider the consequence of stricter enforcement was one that would serve Victorians well. It therefore recommended the introduction of VAD laws.

The third point, related to the second point above, is the relatively scant engagement with the arguments raised by individuals and organisations in favour of or opposing reform. More is said about this later in this chapter, but the Report's focus

---

[34] Ibid. at 15.

[35] Ibid. at 207.

[36] Ibid. at 204.

[37] Ibid. at 206.

[38] Ibid.

[39] For a consideration of the extent to which the Voluntary Assisted Dying Act 2017 (Vic) would have provided another option to the suicides referred to by the Coroner or to the assisted suicides or 'mercy killings' that led to criminal prosecution, see Katrine Del Villar, Lindy Willmott and Ben White, 'Suicide, Assisted Suicides and "Mercy Killings": Would Voluntary Assisted Dying Prevent These "Bad Deaths"?' (2021) 46 *Monash University Law Review* (forthcoming, available at www://eprints.qut.edu.au/199576/).

is on the fact that change is needed rather than the pros and cons of VAD reform. As a result of this approach, the arguments offered by organisations that are traditionally influential in the debate, such as religious and lobby groups, did not receive much traction. Indeed, in its Report, the Committee expressly rejected the assertion of various religious groups that a VAD regime could not provide adequate protection to the vulnerable (drawing in part on the empirical social science evidence about this).[40]

The fourth and final point is to note that the Committee was divided over recommendation forty-nine: six members (two from the Australian Labor Party, two from the Liberal Party, one from the Australian Greens and one from the Australian Sex Party, as it then was) were in favour, and two (one from the Australian Labor Party and one from the Liberal Party) opposed it. The model ultimately recommended was a narrow (and some would describe as a conservative) one, both in terms of eligibility requirements and the nature of the assistance that could be provided by a doctor to a person assessed as eligible. Key features of the proposed legislation included:

- A person is eligible if they are a competent adult and suffering from a serious and incurable condition that is causing enduring and unbearable suffering and that person is at the end of life.
- The person's request must be voluntary and repeated, and the person must be informed about aspects of their condition and treatment options.
- Assistance permitted from a doctor is in the form of prescribing a lethal drug (and in most circumstances the doctor is not permitted to administer the drug).
- Establishment of a Voluntary Assisted Dying Review Board to ensure (retrospectively) compliance with the legislation.[41]

Victorian Government's Response to the Report (8 December 2016)

Six months later, the Government responded to the Committee's recommendations. In relation to the first forty-eight recommendations about the delivery of health services generally, the government supported forty-two, supported two in part, did not support two and put two recommendations 'under review'. In relation to recommendation forty-nine, the Government responded that the Report lacked 'legal, clinical and organisational detail about the implementation, practicalities and issues relating to introducing an assisted dying framework'.[42] It continued that a 'rigorous review of the assisted dying framework should be undertaken including safety and

---

[40] Final Report from the Legal and Social Issues Committee's Inquiry into End of Life Choices (2016 Parliament of Victoria) at 212–13 (see also xxviii).

[41] Ibid. at 239.

[42] Government Response to the Final Report from the Legal and Social Issues Committee's Inquiry into End of Life Choices (2016 Victorian Government) at 17.

quality considerations and the impact on wider health care delivery including resource implications for palliative and end-of-life care'.[43]

At the same time that the Government's Report was released, the Premier, the Honourable Daniel Andrews publicly announced that his government would be introducing VAD legislation in the second half of 2017. He also announced that he was setting up a Ministerial Advisory Panel headed by Professor Brian Owler, a neurosurgeon and former Federal President of the powerful Australian Medical Association, to advise on the drafting of the legislation.[44]

Ministerial Advisory Panel (December 2016–21 July 2017)

The Ministerial Advisory Panel comprised seven members, bringing together a variety of expertise, perspectives and experiences: Professor Brian Owler (Chair); Professor Margaret O'Connor (Deputy Chair, professor emeritus of Nursing with palliative care expertise); Ms Mary Draper (expertise in health administration in quality and safety); Mr Julian Gardner (a lawyer and former Public Advocate, a statutory role safeguarding adults with impaired decision-making capacity); Dr Roger Hunt (palliative medicine consultant); Professor Ian Maddocks (professor emeritus in palliative care) and Ms Tricia Malowney (health advocate for women with disabilities).

The terms of reference for the Panel were very narrow. It was directed to take the VAD framework as recommended by the Parliamentary Committee as a 'starting point' and its task was 'to provide advice to government about how a compassionate and safe legislative framework for voluntary assisted dying could be implemented'.[45] The terms of reference included a statement that the government wanted advice on 'how it could be implemented in Victoria to provide access to eligible people while minimising risk to potentially vulnerable people'.

The Panel was directed to provide an interim report within three months and a final report within six months. These tight time frames constrained the extent to which the Panel was able to consult. To briefly summarise the Panel's process:

- Release of a Discussion Paper:[46] On 25 January 2017, the Panel released a Discussion Paper that sought input on specific issues such as: how to

[43] Ibid.

[44] Richard Willingham and Rania Spooner, 'Euthanasia Bill: Victorian Parliament to Vote on Assisted Dying Laws Next Year', *The Age*, 8 December 2016, www.theage.com.au/national/victoria/victorian-parliament-to-vote-on-assisted-dying-laws-next-year-20161208-gt6tow.html.

[45] Final Report from the Ministerial Advisory Panel on Voluntary Assisted Dying (2017 Victorian Government) at 5.

[46] 'Voluntary Assisted Dying Bill', Discussion Paper from the Department of Health and Human Services (2017 Victorian Government). The Discussion Paper is available from: www2.health.vic.gov.au/about/publications/researchandreports/voluntary-assisted-dying-bill-discussion-paper.

define a 'serious and incurable' condition; what safeguards are necessary to ensure that a request is voluntary, and how they should they be assessed; how should conscientious objection operate under the regime; and specifics about where the lethal medication should be administered and how handling of the medication should be monitored. The questions were framed to elicit detailed responses, and were also constrained by the scope of the framework recommended by the Parliamentary Committee. The Panel received 176 submissions in response to the Discussion Paper.

- Consultation: The Panel conducted fourteen forums and roundtables and heard from more than 300 stakeholders across Victoria.
- Release of the Interim Report:[47] The Panel's Interim Report was released publicly on 17 May 2017 and it summarised the feedback the Panel received from the consultation process and submissions. Notably, the identities of individuals and organisations making submissions, and participating in forums and roundtables were not included in the Interim Report.
- Release of the Final Report:[48] The Panel released its Final Report on 31 July 2017.

The Final Report was comprised of four parts: Part A on eligibility; Part B on the request and assessment process; Part C on oversight and governance arrangements; and Part D on various implementation issues to ensure the framework was resourced appropriately. Case studies were used throughout the Report to illustrate how the proposed legislation would work in practice, or to justify why particular provisions were needed.

By and large, the legislative framework recommended by the Panel was consistent with that recommended by the Parliamentary Committee and, for the most part, provides greater detail on how the legislation might operate in practice. The Panel's Report also contained a set of guiding principles to shape its decision-making, which was largely similar to those outlined by the Parliamentary Committee, though couched in different language.[49] The principles are:

- Every human life has equal value.
- A person's autonomy should be respected.

---

[47] 'Consultation Overview', Interim Report from the Ministerial Advisory Panel on Voluntary Assisted Dying (2017 Victorian Government). The Interim Report is available from: www2 .health.vic.gov.au/searchresults?q=ministerial%20advisory%20panel%20interim%20report %20voluntary%20assisted%20dying.

[48] Final Report from the Ministerial Advisory Panel on Voluntary Assisted Dying (2017 Victorian Government). The Final Report is available from: www2.health.vic.gov.au/about/publications/ researchandreports/ministerial-advisory-panel-on-voluntary-assisted-dying-final-report.

[49] Ibid. at 11.

- A person has the right to be supported in making informed decisions about their medical treatment and should be given, in a manner that they understand, information about medical treatment options, including comfort and palliative care.
- Every person approaching the end of life should have access to quality care to minimise their suffering and maximise their quality of life.
- The therapeutic relationship between a person and their health practitioner should, wherever possible, be supported and maintained.
- Open discussions about death and dying and peoples' preferences and values should be encouraged and promoted.
- Conversations about treatment and care preferences between the health practitioner, a person and their family, carers and community should be supported.
- Providing people with genuine choice must be balanced with the need to safeguard people who might be subject to abuse.
- All people, including health practitioners, have the right to be shown respect for their culture, beliefs, values and personal characteristics.[50]

Changes from the Parliamentary Committee Report were recommended, however, in relation to eligibility. The first was that the Committee's recommendation that the person be at the 'end of life' was altered to the requirement that 'death was likely to occur within 12 months'. This was suggested for the purpose of clarity. The second alteration was more significant. The Committee's recommendation was that the person be suffering from 'a serious and incurable condition' which is causing enduring and unbearable suffering. There was no causal requirement between the condition and death (although the person had to be at the end of life). By contrast, the Panel required that the incurable disease would result in death. This may have been due to the desire to make clear that the requisite medical condition was terminal. This was presumably less of an issue for the Parliamentary Committee whose recommendation that the person be at the 'end of life' meant that assistance to die would only be available for a very short period prior to death.

The appendices of the Report are worthy of comment. Appendix 1 provided a summary of the legislative framework. While it did not attempt to draft provisions, this appendix along with the detail in the body of the Report, provided clear guidance to parliamentary drafters. Appendix 2 explored how the Panel's

---

[50] These principles were adopted by the Voluntary Assisted Dying Act 2017 (Vic) with s. 5(1) using very similar language. The Act contains ten principles instead of the report's nine because it separated out the eighth principle into two: one about genuine choice (s. 5(1)(h)) and one about protecting individuals from abuse (s. 5(1)(i)). Whether the Act's ten guiding principles have been reflected in the drafting of the Victorian legislation is considered in Ben P. White, Katrine Del Villar, Eliana Close and Lindy Willmott, 'Does the *Voluntary Assisted Dying Act 2017* (Vic) Reflect Its Stated Policy Goals' (2020) 43 *University of New South Wales Law Journal* 417–51.

recommendations related to Victoria's human rights framework. At the time the Report was published, Victoria was one of only two Australian jurisdictions that had human rights legislation,[51] so framing or justifying recommendations within a human rights framework was important. Appendix 3 was also significant as it listed sixty-eight separate safeguards that were embedded within the Panel's recommendations. It also compared the recommended safeguards with those in Canada and the United States (Oregon, Washington, Vermont, California and Colorado) and Europe (the Netherlands and Belgium), jurisdictions in which VAD was lawful at the time of the publication.[52]

Enactment of the Voluntary Assisted Dying Act 2017 (Vic) (20 September–29 November 2017)

The final phase of the Victorian law reform process was, of course, the enactment of the VAD Act. The VAD Bill was passionately and extensively debated in both the Legislative Assembly (the Lower House) and the Legislative Council (the Upper House) of the Victorian Parliament over a two-month period. The Bill, closely modelled on the recommendations of the Ministerial Advisory Panel, was introduced into the Lower House by the then Minister for Health, the Honourable Jill Hennessy, on 20 September 2017. After an extended debate, the Bill was passed with forty-seven members voting in favour and thirty-seven voting against the Bill. The Bill was not amended during this phase of deliberation.

The Bill was then introduced into the Upper House on 20 October 2017, and again, an extended debate followed. To secure the necessary votes to pass the Bill, amendments to the Bill were adopted. These amendments had the effect of narrowing an already narrow Bill. There were, broadly, three types of variation. The first, and most significant, related to eligibility. The Bill, as passed by the Lower House, required that a person have a disease, illness or medical condition that was expected to cause death within twelve months.[53] This time period was reduced to six months except for a person with a neurodegenerative condition in which case it remained twelve months.[54] An amendment was also made regarding residency in

---

[51] Since then, Queensland has also passed human rights legislation with the enactment of the Human Rights Act 2019 (Qld).

[52] Final Report from the Ministerial Advisory Panel on Voluntary Assisted Dying (2017 Victorian Government). The Final Report specified that it did not undertake comparisons with jurisdictions 'that legalise voluntary assisted dying through more minimal legislation (such as Switzerland) or through court decisions': at 180, 216.

[53] The disease also had to be incurable, advanced, progressive and would cause the person's death: Voluntary Assisted Dying Bill 2017 (Vic), cl. 9(1)(d)(i) and (ii).

[54] In addition, the Bill was amended so that if the person had a neurodegenerative disease and their death was expected in a period of between six and twelve months, their diagnosis must be confirmed by a specialist in that particular disease: Voluntary Assisted Dying Act 2017 (Vic), s. 18(4).

Victoria. Although the Bill already required the person to be 'ordinarily resident in Victoria' to be eligible, an additional requirement was added for the person to have been ordinarily resident in Victoria for at least twelve months from the time of making a first request for assistance to die.[55]

The second kind of variation related to safeguards. It is beyond the scope of this chapter to detail all of the additional safeguards that were added at this stage, but the following are illustrative:

- The Bill, as passed by the Lower House, required the relevant medical practitioners to refer a person to a health practitioner with appropriate skills and training if they were uncertain as to the person's capacity to make a decision about VAD. An additional safeguard was introduced that if uncertainty related to a person's past or current mental illness, a psychiatrist would be a health practitioner with appropriate skills and training.[56]
- The Bill, as passed by the Lower House, provided for any unused VAD substance to be returned to a pharmacy by a person appointed for the purpose. This requirement was to ensure the substance is accounted for at all times. The Upper House proposed an amendment to reduce the time frame within which the substance needed to be returned from one month to fifteen days after the person's death.[57]

The final kind of variation related to sundry matters that did not go directly to eligibility or to safeguards. The following are illustrative of the amendments made by the Upper House:

- Once satisfied of eligibility, the co-ordinating medical practitioner is to encourage the person requesting VAD to inform any other treating medical practitioners of their request to access VAD.[58]
- Once satisfied of eligibility, the co-ordinating medical practitioner should, if the person consents, take all reasonable steps to fully explain to a member of the person's family the plan for self-administration of the VAD substance.[59]
- In addition to recording the cause of death as the disease, illness or medical condition that was the reason for a person to access VAD, the relevant documentation should record VAD as the manner of death.[60]

[55] Ibid., s. 9(1)(iii).
[56] Ibid., ss. 18(1), 27(1).
[57] Ibid., ss. 39(2)(a), 45(c), 89.
[58] Ibid., ss. 19(1)(g), 28(1)(g).
[59] Ibid., s. 19(2).
[60] Ibid., pt. 11 through consequential amendment to the Births, Deaths and Marriages Registration Act 1996 (Vic), s. 119.

The revised Bill was passed by the Upper House on 22 November 2017,[61] and returned to the Lower House where it was passed with no further amendments on 29 November 2017.

Prior to the Bill's enactment, and before it was further narrowed by the amendments of the Legislative Council, the Bill was described by the Victorian Government as the safest and most conservative VAD model in the world.[62] The Act, as ultimately passed, permits access to VAD after a rigorous process that requires at least three requests from an eligible patient and at least two assessments by qualified and trained medical practitioners. VAD is intended usually to be self-administration (i.e. medication taken by the patient themselves) as practitioner administration is permitted only where a person is physically incapable of taking or digesting the medication themselves.[63]

The Act also has restrictive eligibility criteria. Section 9(1) outlines the primary eligibility criteria and states that '[f]or a person to be eligible for access to voluntary assisted dying':

(a) the person must be aged 18 years or more; and
(b) the person must –
   (i) be an Australian citizen or permanent resident; and
   (ii) be ordinarily resident in Victoria; and
   (iii) at the time of making a first request, have been ordinarily resident in Victoria for at least 12 months; and
(c) the person must have decision-making capacity in relation to voluntary assisted dying; and
(d) the person must be diagnosed with a disease, illness or medical condition that –
   (i) is incurable; and
   (ii) is advanced, progressive and will cause death; and
   (iii) is expected to cause death within weeks or months, not exceeding 6 months [or 12 months if the disease, illness or medical condition is neurodegenerative[64]]; and
   (iv) is causing suffering to the person that cannot be relieved in a manner that the person considers tolerable.

Section 9 also clarifies that mental illness and/or disability alone are not grounds to access VAD.[65] As a matter of statutory interpretation, however, the fact that a person

---

[61] Note that the Upper House also made further clerical corrections on 28 November 2017.
[62] Premier Daniel Andrews, 'Voluntary Assisted Dying Model Established Ahead of Vote in Parliament', Office of the Premier of Victoria, 25 July 2017.
[63] Voluntary Assisted Dying Act 2017 (Vic), ss. 46, 48.
[64] Ibid., s. 9(4) (the words in square brackets have been added by the authors).
[65] Ibid., ss. 9(2) and 9(3) respectively.

has a mental illness or disability will not preclude them from accessing VAD if the eligibility criteria are met.[66]

The legislation contains a myriad of other safeguards including the need for medical practitioners who assess eligibility to have particular expertise and experience[67] and to have undertaken mandatory training;[68] prohibitions against health practitioners raising the possibility of VAD with a patient even if he or she may think this would be an option that the patient may wish to consider;[69] and the requirement for the medical practitioner to obtain a permit from the government before being able to prescribe the VAD substance for an eligible patient.[70]

Also of importance, and relatively unique to this legal framework, the Act provided for an eighteen-month implementation period between enactment of the legislation and commencement of its operation. This period enabled the Victorian Department of Health and Human Services to ensure the health system was equipped to provide this new health service.[71]

To conclude this review of the Parliamentary process, we comment briefly on the nature of the Parliamentary debate. Not surprisingly, the debate was highly charged with politicians bringing their own experiences to the table. The debate was long and extended well into (or through) the night on occasions.[72] As has been the universal experience in Australia on VAD bills, politicians were permitted a conscience vote and this saw sharp conflict within members of the same parties. And

[66] This outcome is consistent with the Ministerial Advisory Panel's Recommendations Five (in respect of mental illness) and Six (in respect of disability) in the Final Report from the Ministerial Advisory Panel on Voluntary Assisted Dying (2017 Victorian Government) at 80–2, 83–5.

[67] Voluntary Assisted Dying Act 2017 (Vic), s. 10 requires the medical practitioner to hold a fellowship with a specialist medical college or be a vocationally registered general practitioner. In addition, one of the two practitioners who is involved with the eligibility assessment must have practised as a medical practitioner for at least five years after completing a fellowship or vocational registration. One of the two practitioners must also have relevant expertise and experience in the relevant condition which is the subject of the assessment.

[68] Both medical practitioners must undertake mandatory training prior to making an eligibility assessment: Voluntary Assisted Dying Act 2017 (Vic), ss. 17, 26.

[69] Ibid., s. 8. For a consideration of the provision and the implications on the doctor/patient relationship, see Lindy Willmott, Ben White, Danielle Ko, James Downar and Luc Deliens, 'Restricting Conversations about Voluntary Assisted Dying: Implications for Clinical Practice' (2020) 10 BMJ Supportive and Palliative Care 105–10.

[70] See Voluntary Assisted Dying Act 2017 (Vic), ss. 47, 48, which set out the process for applying for a self-administration and practitioner administration permit respectively.

[71] The implementation work was undertaken under the guidance of the Voluntary Assisted Dying Implementation Taskforce whose terms of reference are available here: Terms of Reference of the Voluntary Assisted Dying Implementation Task Force (2018 Victorian Government), www2 .health.vic.gov.au/about/publications/factsheets/vad-implementation-taskforce-terms-of-reference.

[72] For commentary on the time frames of the debates in the Lower and Upper Houses, see Stephen Duckett, 'The Long and Winding Road to Assisted Dying in Australia' (2019) 54 Australian Journal of Social Issues 1–15.

despite this being a conscience vote (or perhaps because of this), Hansard[73] reflects that many politicians consulted widely within their electorates to determine their constituents' attitudes to the proposed reform. Hansard also revealed how politicians were moved by personal stories of bad deaths where pain was not or could not be relieved, of suicides by individuals diagnosed with terminal illnesses, and the enduring effect of these bad deaths on families and friends.

It is likely that some politicians knew how they would vote from the beginning of the reform process, and the reasons underpinning their stance. As can be gleaned from public comments, however, some politicians appeared to struggle to make their decision, and engaged deeply with the evidence to inform their position. It is impossible to know the extent of private lobbying that occurred and how successful that was. However, one piece of advocacy may have been particularly effective during this period, and is worthy of reflection. The Chair of the Ministerial Advisory Panel, Professor Brian Owler, gave an address at the National Press Club. 'National Press Club Addresses' are high-profile events which are disseminated by Australia's national broadcaster and reach wide audiences. Professor Owler's address outlined the reason reform was needed, the nature of the proposed legislation and why the community can have confidence that the safeguards contained within the Bill would protect the vulnerable within the community. The address was factual, articulate and highly persuasive. Given Professor Owler's medical expertise and background as former President of the Australian Medical Association, the presentation also had commensurate authority and credibility. The date of the address, 12 October 2017, was also pivotal – after the introduction of the Bill into the Lower House (20 September 2017) but before it was debated in detail (17–19 October). Undoubtedly, the date of the address was calculated to have the greatest impact both on the members of the public and members of parliament.

ANALYSIS OF VICTORIA'S VAD REFORM PROCESS

As described earlier, there have been many unsuccessful legislative attempts to legalise VAD in Australia. There are several aspects of the Victorian experience which distinguish it from other reform attempts and may have contributed to its success in achieving reform.

Government-Supported Reform Process and Bill

In Victoria, the review was first initiated by the government.[74] While the Parliamentary Committee Inquiry which produced a Report recommending reform

---

[73] Hansard is the official record of the Parliamentary debate.
[74] As observed earlier, however, we note that the establishment of Parliamentary Committee may have occurred as a result of the agitation of other members of parliament.

was a genuinely cross-party review, the government response to the recommendations, namely the establishment of the Ministerial Advisory Panel tasked with the
development of legislation to be tabled in the second half of 2017, reflected government leadership in the reform process to legalise VAD. The support for legalisation
of VAD by the Premier of Victoria, Daniel Andrews, as evidenced by the establishment of the Panel to draft legislation, was also shared by other senior government
ministers including Jill Hennessy, the then Minister for Health.

Having government support for reform resulted in a reform process that differed
in a number of ways from other attempts to enact VAD legislation. The first is that
the reform process was well-resourced. For example, this enabled the Parliamentary
Committee to be well-supported by a secretariat which included research officers.
Members of the Parliamentary Committee also had an opportunity to travel across
Victoria as well as internationally to jurisdictions where VAD is lawful. This high
level of resourcing also facilitated comprehensive and high-quality publications.
The recommendations in the Parliamentary Committee's Report were based on
detailed engagement with a range of evidence, and arguments on all sides were
considered so it was apparent to all stakeholders and activists that the Committee
had a sound understanding of all aspects of the debate. This high level of resourcing
is further illustrated by the Panel's work, which was established and supported by the
Government including in relation to staff of the Victorian Department of Health
and Human Services.

The second consequence of the reform being led by the government is that it
attracted a high level of publicity. While proposals to legalise VAD will generally
attract attention, this is especially so when the government of the day is taking the
process forward. Prominent media coverage occurred at important stages in
the review, for example, announcing the review, noting the Final Report of the
Parliamentary Committee, announcing the Government Response, establishing the
Ministerial Advisory Panel, accepting the recommendations of the Panel, and then
drafting a bill to give effect to them. This publicity ensured the fact that the law on
VAD that was being reviewed was in the public consciousness for an extended
period. The publicity attracted public attention, and drew responses from both those
in favour of and opposed to reform. Regardless of a person's perspective, it was
difficult not to notice that reform was on the political agenda and was possible in the
foreseeable future. This persistence of the issue in the public domain helped
normalise reform as something that was going to happen.

A third consequence of a government-initiated review, and subsequent support for
changing the law, is that it lent credibility to VAD law reform. In the past, agitation
for change came from independents, minority parties or a member of a major party
acting in a 'private member' capacity. Advocacy from the fringes of politics, in
particular where an individual or party may have policies in general that are
regarded by the community as controversial, lends a tone to those efforts to change
the law. If VAD is part of a wider policy platform of a minor party that includes a

range of social policy reforms that are not widely supported by the community, this frames VAD as a questionable reform. However, the perception can be quite different when it is the elected government of the day that is identifying this as a legitimate and appropriate policy direction to take.

Two-Staged Review

We consider that the two stages of the review – the Parliamentary Committee followed by the Ministerial Advisory Panel – had two strategic advantages. The first is that VAD reform (through the Parliamentary Committee, the Government Response and the Panel) took place over a two-year period (from when the Committee was established on 7 May 2015 until the Panel's Report was handed down in July 2017). Over this extended period, VAD was being normalised as a possible policy option (as noted above). While there continued to be strident opposition over this time, the conversation about possible reform continued in public forums.

The second observation is that the nature of the debate shifted after the Parliamentary Committee announced its support for reform, and the recommendation was accepted by the government. At this point, the Panel was appointed with a very specific brief – to advise the government on the specific nature of VAD legislation that it would introduce into Parliament in the second half of 2017. For a seven-month period (January–July 2017), all Victorians knew that draft legislation was being developed, and a bill would soon be introduced. It was no longer a matter of arguing for and against reform – that decision had been made. Instead, debate was then confined to the *nature* of that reform. Stakeholders had a choice to be involved in the design of that bill, or be completely locked out of the reform process. This meant that stakeholders who did not support VAD legislation needed to engage with the Panel to at least have some impact on the nature of the model.

Extensive Consultation

A significant feature of the Victorian VAD process was the breadth and depth of its consultation. This is linked with the two preceding points in that the high level of government support meant that wide and inclusive consultation was possible. The two-staged review also provided multiple opportunities for input and, as noted above, both the Panel and particularly the Parliamentary Committee took a consultative approach.[75]

---

[75] The wide, inclusive and staged process described above contributed to this reform process being highly rated against the 'Wiltshire Test: Ten Criteria for a Public Policy Business Case': Matthew Lesh, 'Evidence Based Policy Research Project' (2018 Institute of Public Affairs) at 60–1.

Consultation has long been regarded as an important part of effective law reform.[76] While the primary purpose of consultation is often framed as ensuring optimal design of law and policy, another key purpose is gathering support through involvement of key stakeholders in the process. The collective breadth of consultation by the Parliamentary Committee and the Panel ensured that any individual or organisation who wished to express a view about these reforms had ample opportunity to do so. Indeed, it could be argued that the public nature of the consultation was integral to building a community consensus that reform was needed. A good example of this is the public airing of personal stories about cases where current end-of-life care was insufficient. Consultation provided a public forum for these stories to be heard, and then reported by the media and others. But these stories were also influential on the policy decision-makers, firstly in shaping the decision to permit reform (Parliamentary Committee) and then in deciding on the form that reform should take (Panel). These stories were also arguably significant for the parliamentarians when ultimately deciding whether to vote in favour of the Bill.[77]

Despite the many opportunities for input that the reform process afforded, an important feature of the Victorian experience is the apparent lack of influence exercised by groups traditionally opposed to reform, in particular religiously aligned organisations. This was apparent at both stages of the review. As explored further below, in its Report, the Parliamentary Committee did not engage with the usual arguments in favour of and opposing reform. While the Committee reported that these arguments were considered in depth in making its recommendations, they were summarised and included as an appendix to the Report.[78] To an extent, this strategy deprived religious organisations and other opponents of reform of the usual platform of opposition.

The approach taken by the Ministerial Advisory Panel also deprived the usual protagonists of influence, at least so far as can be gleaned from the Panel's publications. While the publicly released material discloses that the Panel received 176 submissions, conducted fourteen forums and roundtables and heard from more than 300 stakeholders across Victoria, the Panel's publications do not disclose who those individuals or organisations were, or what particular individuals or organisations

---

[76] See, for example: Peter M. North, 'Law Reform: Processes and Problems' (1985) 101 *Law Quarterly Review* 338–58; Peter M. North, 'Law Reform: The Consultation Process' (1982) 6 *Trent Law Journal* 19–31. See also the extended discussions of the importance of consultation for law reform in a range of settings in Brian Opeskin and David Weisbrot (eds.), *The Promise of Law Reform* (Leichhardt: The Federation Press, 2005).

[77] See also Duckett, 'Long and Winding Road', regarding the significance of the stories and submissions that were provided to both the Parliamentary Committee and the Ministerial Advisory Panel; Stephen Duckett, 'Pathos, Death Talk and Palliative Care in the Assisted Dying Debate in Victoria, Australia' (2020) 25 *Mortality* 151–66.

[78] Final Report from the Legal and Social Issues Committee's Inquiry into End of Life Choices (2016 Parliament of Victoria) at 9.

said. The Panel's Final Report did not contain any detail of the consultation, except to say that it had occurred. The input from consultation was instead summarised and outlined in the Panel's Interim Report, so far as it assisted the Panel in designing a VAD legislative regime.[79] But importantly, as noted by the Panel in its Final Report, 'the Panel did not consider opinions for or against voluntary assisted dying – this question was beyond the scope of the Panel's terms of reference, which are about developing a safe and compassionate framework'.[80] In other words, the very nature of the Panel's task rendered arguments opposing law reform irrelevant.

A final point to note about the consultation process is that it facilitated reform by flushing out issues of concern and providing an opportunity for the policy process to specifically address them. The Panel's process is perhaps the best example of this. By the time it began its work, the question was not if VAD should be legalised, but how. Through its consultation, the Panel identified the range of objections and concerns that people and organisations had concerning VAD. This consultation (building on that by the Parliamentary Committee) ensured that all arguments were laid open for discussion, and enabled the Panel to craft responses to them. The example of addressing concerns about 'doctor shopping' given below is one example of this.

Membership of the Parliamentary Committee and the Ministerial Advisory Panel

The composition of both the Committee and Panel was effective in minimising criticism of their respective reports. The Parliamentary Committee was a Standing Committee, with members appointed for the life of the Parliamentary term. The membership of the Committee is balanced to reflect the composition of Parliament, with members being nominated by their respective parties. At the time of its review, it comprised members from both major parties as well as from the Australian Greens Party and the Australian Sex Party. The Committee deals with any matter referred to it by the Legislative Council. As it is a Standing Committee, it could not be 'stacked' to ensure reform was recommended. Indeed, the findings of the Committee (six in favour of and two opposing reform), reflected that its membership had divergent views on VAD.

The Panel was tasked with drafting VAD legislation, so its composition was even more critical to ensure its recommendations had legitimacy and credibility, particularly with health professionals and opponents to reform whose stated concerns related to protecting the vulnerable in the community. We consider that the composition of the Panel achieved this outcome. As mentioned earlier, it was

---

[79] 'Consultation Overview', Interim Report from the Ministerial Advisory Panel on Voluntary Assisted Dying (2017 Victorian Government).
[80] Final Report from the Ministerial Advisory Panel on Voluntary Assisted Dying (2017 Victorian Government) at 11.

chaired by Professor Brian Owler, a neurosurgeon and former national president of the Australian Medical Association, a powerful and influential medical organisation in Australia. The Panel's Deputy Chair was professor emeritus Margaret O'Connor, a professor of Nursing with particular expertise in palliative care. Importantly, two members of the Panel (one a lawyer who was formerly the Public Advocate of Victoria, Julian Gardner, and one a health advocate, Tricia Malowney) had experience in advocating for those with disabilities, and two members were palliative care physicians. In other words, the Panel was comprised of eminent professionals with considerable and relevant experience both in health care and also in protecting the vulnerable within the community. They were from key stakeholder and mainstream organisations. Despite the controversial nature of the Panel's brief, namely the recommendation of VAD legislation, there was no suggestion in the media that this group were ill-equipped to undertake their task.

Nature of the Reports of the Parliamentary Committee and Ministerial Advisory Panel

The Reports of both the Parliamentary Committee and the Panel were politically strategic and crafted in ways that increased the prospect of law reform. As noted above, the Parliamentary Committee Report was of a very high quality in that it carefully engaged with a range of evidence including peer-reviewed scholarly work. But that aside, there were other features of the Committee Report that were significant from a law reform perspective. The first is that the Report reached a concrete view that reform should occur. The Committee made specific recommendations that VAD should be allowed in certain circumstances, and outlined the reasonably narrow parameters within which it should operate. The two members who did not agree provided a Minority Report. Importantly, the fact that there was not unanimous support for reform did not prevent the majority from making a recommendation. This can be contrasted with other reviews of controversial topics where the review bodies stopped short of making recommendations because of disagreement between the members. The Report of the Health Committee to the New Zealand House of Representatives in August 2017 is an example where, after a long review, the majority on the Committee concluded that: 'We have not made any recommendations about introducing assisted dying legislation.'[81] There was a brief (one paragraph) dissent from the New Zealand First party who considered that the matter should be decided through a referendum.[82]

---

[81] 'Petition 2014/18 of Hon Maryan Street and 8,974 Others' from the Health Committee (2017 Parliament of New Zealand) 47.

[82] In this regard, we note that the New Zealand Parliament passed its End of Life Choice Act 2019 (NZ) in late 2019, but the law only came into effect because it was approved by a public referendum which took place in late 2020.

Secondly, as noted above, in its Report the Parliamentary Committee did not engage afresh with the well-trodden arguments for and against VAD reform. Instead, it noted that these issues had been canvassed sufficiently in jurisdictions internationally and also that they were considered by the Committee throughout its deliberations.[83] The Report contained a summary of these arguments in one of its Appendices. In this way, it did not need to take a view on which of the arguments it supported more than others. Instead, the Committee took the view that palliative care is not always the solution to managing pain and suffering at the end of life, and noted that the current legal framework that governs end-of-life care was not working. In particular, the Committee was moved by the Coronial evidence of some (often frail, elderly and vulnerable Victorians) who were dying in awful ways (through suicide) because of the current law; that some were dying in pain despite high-quality palliative care; that some were breaching the criminal law to assist their loved ones to die; and that some were being assisted to die unlawfully by doctors.[84] As noted above, in response to these findings, it put forward three options. They were: to maintain the status quo (which it did not see as an option); to enforce the current framework (which was not advocated during the review); and to reform the law. Framed in this way, the choice to change the law to permit VAD appeared to be a logical conclusion. This was a very practical approach that did not require the 'in principle' case for reform to be made but rather demonstrated clearly that the current approach was flawed and change was needed for pragmatic reasons.

Thirdly, both the Committee and the Panel recommended a conservative VAD model, hence more likely to attract the necessary support to become law. After examining all of the options, the Committee recommended adopting a limited model where VAD would occur primarily through doctors prescribing medication and eligible individuals self-administering. The Panel's brief was to operationalise this recommendation, and they did so by suggesting a model that is more conservative than any other in operation. The Panel recommended sixty-eight safeguards. All sixty-eight of these safeguards are then strategically listed in an appendix, and this list is followed by a comparison of these safeguards with the safeguards in other jurisdictions. The strategy behind this is obvious – to demonstrate that the model recommended was by far the most conservative of all VAD models in operation around the world. And this approach continued to be emphasised by the government when the Panel's Report was released with Premier Daniel Andrews proclaiming the proposed model as the 'safest, and most conservative model in the world'.[85]

---

[83] Final Report from the Legal and Social Issues Committee's Inquiry into End of Life Choices (2016 Parliament of Victoria) at 9.
[84] Ibid. at 206–7. For a consideration of whether such deaths would be avoided by legalising VAD, see Del Villar et al., 'Suicide, Assisted Suicides and "Mercy Killings"'.
[85] Premier Daniel Andrews, 'Voluntary Assisted Dying Model Established Ahead of Vote in Parliament', Office of the Premier of Victoria, 25 July 2017.

Fourthly, the 'balancing of principles' approach taken by the Panel in its Report may have increased the prospect of reform by demonstrating a principled and measured decision-making process that took account of a tension specifically named by the Panel – 'the need to balance respect for autonomy with safeguarding individuals and communities'.[86] The Report continued that the 'Panel is of the view that the eligibility criteria, the process to access voluntary assisted dying, and the oversight measures recommended appropriately balance these aims'.[87] This approach in its decision-making was reiterated regularly throughout the Report and this balancing exercise was transparently described for the specific aspects of the VAD system proposed.[88] To illustrate, below are some examples of where the Panel took a specific position (e.g. through a recommendation regarding the proposed VAD law) after balancing 'autonomy' with the need for 'safeguards' for individuals or the community:

- *Recommendation 2* [part of]: To be eligible, a person must be an adult, 18 years and over: 'the Panel considers that requiring a person to be at least 18 years to access voluntary assisted dying represents an appropriate safeguard by striking a balance between providing choice for adults who are at the end of their life and protecting young people who do not have the appropriate level of maturity, capacity for abstract reasoning, or life experience to make the decision to access voluntary assisted dying'.[89]
- *Recommendation 3*: To be eligible, a person must have decision-making capacity: 'balancing principles of respecting individual autonomy and the need to ensure effective safeguards for people without decision-making capacity requires that requests for voluntary assisted dying in advance care directives are invalid'.[90]
- *Recommendation 5*: Mental illness does not satisfy the eligibility criteria for access, nor does it exclude a person from eligibility to access: 'strikes an appropriate balance between providing a necessary safeguard to protect people who may be vulnerable without unreasonably restricting the opportunity to access ... for people with mental illness who meet all of the eligibility criteria'.[91]
- *Recommendation 7*: Request for information about VAD can only be initiated by the person, not by others; *Recommendation 8*: A health practitioner cannot initiate a discussion about VAD with a person with whom they have a therapeutic relationship: '... the request and

---

[86] Final Report from the Ministerial Advisory Panel on Voluntary Assisted Dying (2017 Victorian Government) at 11.
[87] Ibid.
[88] Ibid. at 15, 22, 43, 46, 48, 82, 87, 210–13.
[89] Ibid. at 54.
[90] Ibid. at 62.
[91] Ibid. at 82.

assessment process should strike a balance between providing protection from abuse and not being unduly burdensome for a person who is suffering from an incurable disease, illness or medical condition that is advanced, progressive and will cause their death'.[92]

Finally, the Panel tackled squarely a number of concerns that are often raised in opposition to VAD, and dealt with them carefully and comprehensively when designing the specifics of the VAD framework. By developing concrete solutions to address likely problems, the Panel provided responses to many of the objections that have impeded prior reform efforts. An example is concerns about 'doctor shopping'. The Panel explicitly acknowledged this as a potential issue but also normalised the idea of seeking other medical advice and contextualised this within the standard medical practice to seek second opinions as appropriate.[93] The Panel also outlined how the safeguards included in its Report would make potential doctor shopping transparent and how it would be dealt with.[94]

CONCLUDING OBSERVATIONS ABOUT VICTORIAN VAD LAW REFORM

This chapter has described the lengthy and extensive process that was undertaken in Victoria that ultimately led to the enactment of the VAD Act. Given the nature of political and policy decision-making, it is difficult to determine the impact of this reform process, or any particular component of that process, on the ultimate enactment of the legislation. Some politicians no doubt had entrenched views leading into the reform process which were based on deeply held values, so were unlikely to shift regardless of the findings of the Parliamentary Committee or Ministerial Advisory Panel, the evidence they presented, or even personal stories of individuals affected. However, we consider that there are three further aspects of the Victorian experience that may have been particularly influential and are worthy of comment.

The first is the influence of particular individuals in the reform process. Premier Daniel Andrews played a significant role during this time, from the announcement of the Parliamentary Review in May 2015 until the final passage of the legislation through the Lower House in November 2017. Andrews spoke publicly of his father's death, and how that experience changed his view about having other choices at the end of life.[95] Work done by other members of the Victorian parliament, Fiona

---

[92] Ibid. at 87.
[93] Ibid. at 16.
[94] Ibid. at 122.
[95] Jon Faine and Jean Edwards, 'Euthanasia Debate: How the Death of His Father Changed Daniel Andrews' Mind about Euthanasia', ABC News, 17 October 2017, www.abc.net.au/news/2017-10-17/death-father-changed-daniel-andrews-mind-about-euthanasia/9053002.

Patten and Colleen Hartland, were also important as they brought pressure to bear on the government to refer the issue to the Parliamentary Committee. Brian Owler, Chair of the Ministerial Advisory Panel, also had an important leadership role in the process, being a highly credible and articulate voice of reason in prosecuting the case for change. The Victorian Coroner, John Olle, gave evidence to the Parliamentary Committee about bad deaths that were occurring in the absence of VAD legislation. This evidence was relied upon by the Committee in making its recommendations and also by politicians during Parliamentary debates. And during the entire reform process, the media personality, Andrew Denton, maintained an effective media campaign in support for law reform. Although this chapter has primarily been a story of reform effected through Committees, Panels and Parliament, individuals have also played an important role in shaping debate and changing minds.

The second, and associated, factor that appeared to resonate with the Committee, Panel and members of parliament was the recounting of personal stories of people who had experienced the death of a loved one or were themselves terminally ill.[96] These stories were movingly given in evidence before the Parliamentary Committee including by the Coroner, who repeated the tragic cases of suicide that had come before him. Denton's book, circulating during the period, also recounted in a moving and accessible way, the circumstances surrounding terrible deaths. These stories were written from the perspective of friends and families as well as individuals who were dying.[97] The stories of members of parliament themselves also seemed to factor in their decisions to support reform. When the VAD Bill was debated in the Lower and Upper Houses of Parliament, many politicians gave emotionally charged addresses that included personal experiences of death and dying, and explained how important those experiences had been in shaping their views. Taken together, these personal stories may have been effective in moving the reform agenda forward.

Finally, it may have been that 'the time had come' for reform. While the careful design of the Victorian process is likely to have been influential in the law passing, it also appears that the timing and circumstances in Victoria created an environment that was ripe for reform.[98] The media was keenly interested in the issue and reported on developments as well as engaged in editorial commentary.[99] One major Victorian newspaper, *The Age*, was openly supportive of reform.[100] This seemed to

---

[96] Duckett, 'Long and Winding Road', 10; Duckett, 'Pathos, Death Talk and Palliative Care'.

[97] Andrew Denton, *The Damage Done* (Sydney: Go Gentle Australia, 2016).

[98] As commented by Stephen Duckett, 'assisted dying was an idea whose time had come in Victoria': Duckett, 'Long and Winding Road', 12.

[99] See, for example: Gay Alcorn, 'Victoria's Proposal on Assisted Dying Is Careful and Rigorous. Let the Debate Begin', *The Guardian*, 21 July 2017; Naaman Zhou, 'Assisted Dying: States Rally as Bills Offer Chance to Legalise Voluntary Euthanasia', *The Guardian*, 17 May 2017; John Lyons, 'The Debate that Simply Refuses to Die Quietly', *The Australian*, 24 September 2016, 21.

[100] 'Proposed Assisted Dying Law Is Decent and Safe', *The Age*, 22 July 2017, 28.

reflect but perhaps also generated broader public interest in the issue.[101] At the same time, as mentioned above, Andrew Denton was receiving a great deal of publicity for his 'Go Gentle' campaign to introduce VAD laws. Denton is a polished media personality who engaged in a high-profile and effective campaign which included a series of podcasts, publishing a book, appearances on popular and well-regarded television panel sessions, and national press addresses.[102] Also, a well-known VAD advocate and retired urologist, Dr Rodney Syme, had publicly admitted to assisting a named individual to die and challenged police to charge him.[103] The decision of police not to do so rightly sparked further public debate about the efficacy of the criminal law. And finally, the review of VAD took place at a time when Victoria was considering how care should be delivered to individuals at the end of life more generally. As we have seen, a consideration of whether there should be laws allowing VAD was positioned within a broader review of end-of-life practices (including the broader legal framework governing end-of-life care). Implicit in the referral to the Legislative Council Standing Committee on Legal and Social Issues was that it was time to reconsider all aspects of end-of-life care. The experiences of Victorians at the end of their lives needed to be improved.

Although as might be expected, some disagree with the Committee's and Panel's recommendations and the enactment of the VAD Act, there has not been widespread criticism of the Victorian reform process.[104] This model has since been successfully replicated in Western Australia, leading to its Voluntary Assisted Dying Act 2019 (WA) being enacted in December 2019 and due to commence operation in June 2021. Queensland has also embarked on a similar extensive reform process that included a Parliamentary Committee review, although its findings were

---

[101] See, for example: Sunrise, 'Should the Bill be Passed, Terminally Ill Patients Could Be Given Access to Lethal Drugs within 10 Days of Asking. Where Do You Stand on Assisted Dying?', Facebook, 24 July 2017, www.facebook.com/Sunrise/posts/10154700908585887, which had received over 1,000 comments and been shared 5,000 times by 25 August 2017; ABC News, 'Doctors are Divided about Whether They'd Want to Help Someone Die If Victoria's Proposed Voluntary Assisted Dying Legislation Is Passed. Could You Do It?', Facebook, 21 August 2017, www.facebook.com/abcnews.au/videos/10155670570059516/, which included a video that had been viewed over 75,000 times by 25 August 2017.

[102] Simon Canning, 'Ad Industry Has "Vital Role" in Changing Law on Assisted Dying, Says Andrew Denton', Mumbrella, 15 August 2016, mumbrella.com.au/ad-industry-vital-role-changing-law-assisted-dying-says-andrew-denton-387969; See also Andrew Denton's speech, 'Assisted Dying', which was delivered at National Press Club in Canberra on 10 August 2016 and the Go Gentle Australia website at www.gogentleaustralia.org.au/.

[103] 'Melbourne Doctor, Rodney Symes, Attempting to Provoke Prosecution for Euthanasia to Spur Test Case', ABC News, 10 November 2015.

[104] Indeed, the review process undertaken in Victoria has been positively rated in a recent review of twenty public policy processes (in top three): Lesh, 'Evidence Based Policy Research Project'. One notable exception to this is John Keown's extensive critique of the Victorian reform process, particularly the work of the Parliamentary Committee: John Keown, '"Voluntary Assisted Dying" in Australia: The Victorian Parliamentary Committee's Tenuous Case for Legalisation' (2018) 33 *Issues in Law and Medicine* 55–81.

referred not to an expert panel for consideration but rather to another independent body, the Queensland Law Reform Commission.

VAD reform is likely to continue in other Australian States, although it is notoriously difficult to predict the timing and success for such efforts.[105] Despite VAD legislation being enacted in Victoria, Western Australia and Tasmania, reform continues to be controversial and difficult. While that continues to be the case, the Victorian process used to change its law may represent a suitable model in the political context of other Australian States, at least where the government of the day is open to reform. Such an approach may also be worth consideration internationally in those jurisdictions where reform attempts have repeatedly failed and a different approach is needed to engage politicians, interested groups and the community in VAD reform. However, it is also possible in the future that such an extensive reform process may not be required. There is a case to be made, at least in Australia given the extensive work that has occurred in Victoria, Western Australia and now Queensland, for a more modest reform exercise in other States that are contemplating reform.[106] That exercise could utilise the substantial body of work already done by reform committees and panels, and focus instead on the lessons learnt from practice in those States where VAD is lawful and any significant local considerations important for implementing VAD. It may also be that with experience and practice of VAD in Australia, this issue becomes a less divisive topic, and the political need for such an extensive reform process diminishes.

---

[105] White and Willmott, 'Future of Assisted Dying'.

[106] Indeed, Tasmania is the most recent state to enact VAD legislation and the review that was established in that state occurred after the End-of-Life Choices (Voluntary Assisted Dying) Act 2021 (Tas) had already passed the upper house of parliament. The review was undertaken by an independent panel from the University of Tasmania, which was tasked to report within a three month period. This required a narrower review and a more targeted consultation process than was undertaken in Victoria, Western Australia and Queensland.

6

Should Assisted Dying Require the Consent of a High Court Judge?

Penney Lewis

INTRODUCTION

A consensus has recently developed within the UK Parliamentary debate over the legalisation of assisted dying that the consent of a High Court judge should be required as part of a future regulatory regime. I question the basis of this consensus, arguing that it is neither evidence-based nor required by the decision of the UK Supreme Court in *Nicklinson*,[1] as has been suggested by Parliamentarians both in favour of and against legalisation.[2] The chapter begins with a brief sketch of the approach of permissive regulatory regimes to the evaluation of cases of assisted dying which demonstrates the dearth of direct experience of judicial approval of such cases. I next consider the recent calls for prospective judicial approval in two jurisdictions then contemplating legalisation – Canada (which did indeed legalise) and England and Wales (which has not done so). I demonstrate that these calls are tactical and lack substantive argument.

The efficacy of a judicial approval requirement is difficult to assess in the absence of experience. I examine the data from permissive regimes to describe those persons most likely to seek assistance in dying. Using a representative person, I evaluate the extent to which a prospective judicial approval requirement would meet the likely legislative goals, and then recommend an alternative approach. Finally, I seek to draw some broader lessons from this recent experience for legislative change on assisted dying.

In previous work,[3] recently updated,[4] I have examined the impact on the resulting regulatory regime of the choice of a particular legal route towards legalisation of

---

[1]   *R (Nicklinson)* v. *Ministry of Justice* [2015] AC 657 ('Nicklinson').
[2]   See text accompanying note 84.
[3]   Penney Lewis, *Assisted Dying and Legal Change* (Oxford: Oxford University Press, 2007).
[4]   Penney Lewis, 'Legal Change on Assisted Dying', in S. Westwood (ed.), *Regulating the Ending of Life: Death Rights* (London: Routledge, 2021) (in press).

assisted dying, including: constitutionally entrenched human rights; the duty-based defence of necessity; and legislative approaches. Unlike regulatory regimes implementing judicial decisions vindicating patients' rights[5] or doctors' duties,[6] which are shaped by one primary goal, those regulatory regimes which have their genesis in a legislature tend to be shaped by multiple goals.[7] In this chapter, I adopt Karen Yeung's tripartite description of the multiple, possibly conflicting goals of a (legislature-initiated) regulatory regime for lawful assistance in dying: respect for individual autonomy; protection of the vulnerable; and compassion in response to unbearable suffering.[8] Yeung's summary of what makes a regulatory regime legitimate is also useful:

> [A] regulatory regime's legitimacy depends upon whether it achieves its stated goals effectively (with a minimum of administrative costs),[9] and whether, in both its design and implementation, it conforms with principles of good governance such as transparency, accountability, due process, and the requirements of substantive fairness (including proportionality, consistency and equality of treatment).[10]

EXISTING REGULATORY REGIMES

Retrospective Scrutiny

There is widespread agreement that a reporting obligation with retrospective assessment is necessary for a regime regulating assisted dying to be transparent and accountable. Almost all such regulatory regimes impose such an obligation, including the Netherlands, Belgium, Oregon[11] and the states following its model

---

[5] One example is *Baxter v. State*, 224 P 3d 1211 (Mont. 2009). See more generally, Lewis, *Assisted Dying and Legal Change*, 118–24.

[6] For example, the Dutch regime. An unofficial English translation of the Dutch statute is 'Review Procedures for the Termination of Life on Request and Assisted Suicide and Amendment of the Criminal Code and the Burial and Cremation Act (Termination of Life on Request and Assisted Suicide (Review Procedures) Act) 2001' (2001) 8 *European Journal of Health Law* 183–91. See also, Lewis, *Assisted Dying and Legal Change*, 124–36.

[7] Lewis, *Assisted Dying and Legal Change*, 149–58.

[8] Karen Yeung, 'Regulating Assisted Dying' (2012) 23 *King's Law Journal* 163–79 at 168.

[9] I will not here consider the resource implications of a judicial approval requirement for the health care, coronial and judicial systems. For such an analysis in a different end-of-life context, see Simon Halliday, Adam Formby and Richard Cookson, 'An Assessment of the Court's Role in the Withdrawal of Clinically Assisted Nutrition and Hydration from Patients in the Permanent Vegetative State' (2015) 23 *Medical Law Review* 556–87.

[10] Yeung, 'Regulating Assisted Dying', 165.

[11] For an evaluation of this aspect of the regimes in the Netherlands, Belgium, Switzerland and Oregon, see Penney Lewis and Isra Black, 'Adherence to the Request Criterion in Jurisdictions Where Assisted Dying Is Lawful? A Review of the Criteria and Evidence in the Netherlands, Belgium, Oregon, and Switzerland' (2013) 41 *Journal of Law, Medicine and Ethics* 885–98.

(Washington,[12] California,[13] Colorado,[14] Hawaii,[15] New Jersey,[16] Maine,[17] Vermont[18] and the District of Columbia[19]), Luxembourg,[20] Québec,[21] Canada,[22] Western Australia[23] and Victoria, Australia.[24] In Colombia, a reporting requirement is imposed by the 2015 Ministry of Health resolution which finally implements the 1997 decision of the Constitutional Court vindicating the fundamental right to die with dignity.[25] In that decision the Court ruled that a physician should not be prosecuted for ending life at the repeated request of a terminally ill patient who is suffering unbearably because the physician's action 'is justified'.[26] There was originally no requirement for physicians to report prescriptions written under the Vermont statute or deaths resulting from the ingestion of prescribed medication.[27] A reporting requirement was added in 2015.[28] Most proposals for regulatory regimes also require

[12] Death with Dignity Act, Wash Rev Code § 70.245.150 (2008) (Washington).
[13] End of Life Option Act, Cal Health and Safety Code § 443.9 (2015) (California)
[14] End-of-Life Options Act, Colo Rev Stat §§ 25-48-101-123, 111 (2016) (Colorado); Reporting and Collecting Medical Aid-in-Dying Medication Information, 6 CCR 1009-4 (2017) (Colorado, Department of Public Health and Environment).
[15] Our Care, Our Choice Act, Haw Rev Stat Ann § 14 (2018) (Hawaii) ('Our Care, Our Choice Act (Haw)').
[16] Medical Aid in Dying for the Terminally Ill Act, NJ Stat Ann § 26:16–13 (2019) (New Jersey).
[17] An Act to Enact the Death with Dignity Act, 22 Me Rev Stat Ann § 17 (2019) (Maine).
[18] Patient Choice and Control at the End of Life Act, 18 Vt Stat Ann § 5293 (2013, as amended 2015) (Vermont). See text accompanying notes 27 and 28.
[19] Death with Dignity Act of 2016, DC Code §§ 7–661, 661.07 (2017) (District of Columbia).
[20] Loi du 16 Mars 2009 sur l'euthanasie et l'assistance au suicide [Law of 16 March 2009 on Euthanasia and Assisted Suicide], art. 5: Memorial Journal Officiel du Grand-Duché de Luxembourg (2009) A no. 46, 615–19 ('Law on Euthanasia and Assisted Suicide (Luxembourg)').
[21] Act Respecting End-of-Life Care, RSQ 2014, c. S-32.0001, s. 34 (2014) (Québec) (End-of-Life Care Act (Québec)').
[22] An Act to Amend the Criminal Code and to Make Related Amendments to Other Acts (Medical Assistance in Dying), SC 2016, c.3, s. 4 (Canada) ('Medical Assistance in Dying Act (Canada)'), amending the Criminal Code, RSC 1985, c. C-46 ('Criminal Code (Canada)') and inserting s. 241.31.
[23] Voluntary Assisted Dying Act 2019 (WA), ss. 29(2), 33(1), 40(2), 46, 50, 52(4), 60, 61(4) (Australia). The Act will not come into force until the second half of 2021 at the earliest.
[24] Voluntary Assisted Dying Act 2017 (Vic), ss. 21(2), 30(1)(b)(i), 30(2), 41(2), 49(4)(b), 51(3), 52(b), 60(2), 63(2), 66(2), 69(c), 90 (Australia) ('VAD Act (Vic)'). The Act came into force on 19 June 2019.
[25] República de Colombia Ministerio de Salud y Protección Social, Resolución 1216 de 2015 por medio de la cual se da cumplimiento a la orden cuarta de la sentencia T-970 de 2014 de la Honorable Corte Constitucional en relación con las directrices para la organización y funcionamiento de los Comités para hacer efectivo el derecho a morir con dignidad (2015), art. 16 (Colombia) ('Resolution 1216 of 2015 (Colombia)').
[26] Sentence C-239 (1997), Ref. Expedient D-1490 (Constitutional Court of the Republic of Colombia, 20 May 1997).
[27] Patient Choice and Control at the End of Life Act, 18 Vt Stat Ann §§ 5281–93 (2013) (Vermont).
[28] Ibid. § 5293 (as amended 2015).

reporting.[29] Where required, retrospective assessment will decide whether the substantive and procedural criteria were met, and (if needed) whether the terms of any prospective approval were satisfied.[30]

Prospective Scrutiny

There is far less agreement on the extent of prospective scrutiny needed. Such scrutiny could range from prospective consultation or independent peer review – adopted by most current regulatory regimes – to prospective evidence-taking, or approval by a civil servant, regulatory body, panel, tribunal or court. Although they have been considered either at the time of legalisation[31] or since, few existing regimes include such formal prospective approval mechanisms.

Consultation[32]

In most regulatory regimes, including the Netherlands,[33] Belgium,[34] Luxembourg,[35] Canada[36] and Québec,[37] an independent physician must see the patient and give a written opinion on whether the requirements are met. The most well-established

[29] See, for example, Voluntary Assisted Dying Bill 2013 (Tas), cl. 28; Voluntary Assisted Dying Bill 2016 (Tas), cl. 28; Voluntary Assisted Dying Bill 2017 (NSW), cls. 27–29, sch. 2 cl. 2.1; Assisted Suicide (Scotland) Bill, Bill 40, Scottish Parliament, Sess. 4 (2013), cl. 20. An exception is found in End of Life Assistance (Scotland) Bill (2010) [38].

[30] See Roger Brownsword, Penney Lewis and Genevra Richardson, 'Prospective Legal Immunity and Assistance with Dying: Submission to the Commission on Assisted Dying' (2012) 23 *King's Law Journal* 181–93 at 188.

[31] In Belgium, see 'Avis No.1 du 12 Mai 1997 concernant l'opportunité d'un règlement légal de l'euthanasie', Report from the Comité Consultatif de Bioéthique de Belgique (1997 Service Public Fédéral) IV; É. Montero, 'La genèse, la mise en œuvre et les développements de la loi belge relative à l'euthanasie' (2018) 75 *Droit et Cultures* 141 at [42].

[32] See the discussion of the consultation requirement in the Netherlands, Belgium, Switzerland and Oregon in Penney Lewis and Isra Black, 'The Effectiveness of Legal Safeguards in Jurisdictions that Allow Assisted Dying', Briefing Paper from the Commission on Assisted Dying (2012) at 21–3, 32–3, 40–3, 48–9, 58–9, 65–7; John Griffiths, Heleen Weyers amd Maurice Adams, *Euthanasia and Law in Europe: With Special Reference to the Netherlands and Belgium* (Oxford: Hart, 2008), 139–40.

[33] 'Review Procedures for the Termination of Life on Request and Assisted Suicide and Amendment of the Criminal Code and the Burial and Cremation Act (Termination of Life on Request and Assisted Suicide (Review Procedures) Act) 2001' (2001) 8 *European Journal of Health Law* 183–91. See also, Lewis, *Assisted Dying and Legal Change*, 124–36 at s. 2(1)(e); 'Euthanasia Code 2018: Review Procedures in Practice' (April 2018 Regional Euthanasia Review Committees) at 27–33 [3.6] ('Euthanasia Code 2018 (Netherlands)').

[34] See Law of 28 May 2002 on Euthanasia (Belgium); Judgement 153/2015, Constitutional Court of Belgium (29 October 2015) [English translation], § 2(3), www.const-court.be/public/e/2015/2015-153e.pdf ('Law on Euthanasia (Belgium)').

[35] Law on Euthanasia and Assisted Suicide (Luxembourg), art. 2(1)(3).

[36] Medical Assistance in Dying Act (Canada), s. 3, inserting s. 241.2(3) into the Criminal Code (Canada).

[37] End-of-Life Care Act (Québec), ss. 26, 29(3).

consultation model is found in the Netherlands, where the state-funded programme Support and Consultation on Euthanasia in the Netherlands ('SCEN') trains physicians to be consultants and to provide support and advice for doctors treating patients at the end of life. The 'vast majority' of reported euthanasia cases involve a SCEN consultant.[38] A non-binding protocol containing guidelines for good consultation has been implemented among SCEN consultants.[39] In a review of the empirical evidence on the effectiveness of safeguards in permissive regimes, Isra Black and I concluded that specially trained consultants may improve the quality of consultations.[40] Attending physicians appear to have welcomed the availability of such specially trained consultants via the SCEN and Life End Information Forum ('LEIF')[41] networks in the Netherlands and Flanders. In one study, such consultations were judged by attending physicians to be of good quality in 97.2 per cent of cases.[42] The positive evaluation of SCEN consultations is supported by previous research, which found that 'SCEN physicians more frequently meet the criteria for good consultation and GPs attach some more importance to consultant's judgement when the consultant is a SCEN physician'.[43]

More stringent consultation requirements exist in the Netherlands if the patient's suffering is the result of a psychiatric disorder,[44] and in Belgium if the patient 'is clearly not expected to die in the near future'[45] or is a minor.[46]

In Oregon and the states following its model, the attending physician must refer the individual requesting assisted death to a physician who is qualified to make a professional diagnosis and prognosis of the patient's disease. The physician must also

---

[38] Euthanasia Code 2018 (Netherlands), 27–33 [3.6].

[39] 'Goede Steun en Consultatie bij Euthanasie' ['Good Support and Consultation for Euthanasia'], Guidelines from the Koninklijke Nederlandse Maatschappij ter Bevordering van de Geneeskunst (KNMG) (2012 Royal Dutch Medical Association).

[40] Lewis and Black, 'Effectiveness of Legal Safeguards', 22.

[41] Life End Information Forum ('LEIF'), a service similar to the Dutch SCEN service has been developed in Flanders. LEIF consultants are trained using guidelines based on the SCEN protocol. Most LEIF consultants have undertaken additional training in end-of-life care, and have experience caring for incurably ill patients: ibid.

[42] Yanna Van Wesemael, Joachim Cohen, Johan Bilsen, Bregje D. Onwuteaka-Philipse, Wim Distelmans and Luc Deliens, 'Consulting a Trained Physician When Considering a Request for Euthanasia: An Evaluation of the Process in Flanders and the Netherlands' (2010) 33 *Evaluation and the Health Professions* 497–513 at 506, table 3.

[43] Marijke Catharina Jansen-van der Weide, Bregje Dorien Onwuteaka-Philipsen and Gerrit van der Wal, 'Quality of Consultation and the Project "Support and Consultation on Euthanasia in the Netherlands" (SCEN)' (2007) 80 *Health Policy* 97–106 at 104.

[44] 'Standpunt Federatiebestuur KNMG iIzake Euthanasie' from the Koninklijke Nederlandse Maatschappij ter Bevordering van de Geneeskunst (KNMG) (2003 Royal Dutch Medical Association) at 12–13 [5.1.1]; 'Richtlijn Omgaan met het Verzoek om Hulp bij Zelfdoding door Patiënten met een Psychiatrische Stoornis', Guideline from the Nederlandse Vereniging voor Psychiatrie (2009 Dutch Association for Psychiatry) at 21–3 [5] ('Dutch Association for Psychiatry Guideline').

[45] Law on Euthanasia (Belgium) § 3(3).

[46] Ibid. §§ 3(1), 3(2)(7), 3(4).

determine that the patient is capable and acting voluntarily.[47] In most Oregon-model states, a counselling referral must be made if the attending or consulting physician suspects the patient may have a mental disorder or depression impairing their judgement, and the request may proceed only if the counsellor determines that such a condition does not exist.[48] In Hawaii, such a counselling referral is mandatory.[49]

The Swiss 'right to die' organisations use their own internal protocols to determine whether an individual is eligible for suicide assistance from the organisations.[50] Two doctors are involved, one of whom has a pre-existing treating relationship with the patient.[51]

Approval by a Civil Servant, Regulatory Body, Panel or Tribunal

Two examples exist of formal prospective approval mechanisms, although in neither case is there evidence of the effectiveness of the mechanism. Victoria, Australia requires prospective approval by a civil servant; Colombia requires approval by a local panel.

The Victorian statute requires the Secretary (a senior civil servant in the state Department of Health and Human Services) to issue a voluntary assisted dying permit for either self- or practitioner-administration of a voluntary assisted dying substance. The co-ordinating medical practitioner can apply for a permit by submitting a statutory form accompanied by forms documenting the process of assessment of the patient's request for voluntary assisted dying.[52] As John Keown notes, this appears to be a purely 'bureaucratic' prerequisite: 'If the required forms have been submitted with the appropriate boxes ticked, will the application not automatically be approved?'[53]

---

[47] Death with Dignity Act, Or Rev Stat §§ 127.800–127.995, 127.820 § 3.02 (1994) (Oregon) ('Death with Dignity Act (Oregon)').

[48] Ibid. § 127.825 § 3.03.

[49] Our Care, Our Choice Act (Haw) § 4(5).

[50] Stephen J. Ziegler and Georg Bosshard, 'Role of Non-Governmental Organisations in Physician Assisted Suicide' (2007) 334 *British Medical Journal* 295–8 at 295. See, for example, 'Frequently Asked Questions', Exit, 2020, www.exit.ch/en/en/faq/; 'How Dignitas Works', Brochure from Dignitas, 3rd ed. (2014 Dignitas), www.dignitas.ch/images/stories/pdf/so-funktio nicrt-dignitas-e.pdf; 'The Foundation', Document from the Eternal Spririt Foundation (2020 Life Circle), www.lifecircle.ch/pdf/EternalSPIRIT_Foundation.pdf.

[51] Georg Bosshard, 'Switzerland', in John Griffiths, Heleen Weyers and Maurice Adams (eds.), *Euthanasia and Law in Europe: With Special Reference to the Netherlands and Belgium* (Oxford: Hart, 2008) 463–81 at 475; Lewis and Black, 'The Effectiveness of Legal Safeguards', 23.

[52] VAD Act (Vic), ss. 47–52.

[53] John Keown, '"Voluntary Assisted Dying" in Australia: The Victorian Parliamentary Committee's Tenuous Case for Legalization' (2018) 33 *Issues in Law and Medicine* 55–81 at 79. The requirement was proposed by the Final Report from the Ministerial Advisory Panel on Voluntary Assisted Dying (2017 Victorian Government) at 131–4 ('Ministerial Advisory Panel Report (Victoria)').

Colombia requires the approval of a special three-person multi-disciplinary hospital-based committee, which also bears responsibility for ensuring that the assistance in dying is provided within strict time-limits, and for accompanying the patient and their family members.[54] The regulation creating this regime dates from 2015 and no official information has been made available on the decisions taken by such committees. As very few cases have proceeded to euthanasia, the functioning of the committees is difficult to evaluate.[55]

In Luxembourg, the national Commission to which euthanasia and assisted suicide must be reported refused a request for prospective approval in the form of an advance opinion, on the grounds that the legislature had neither envisaged nor desired such a procedure, which would disturb the unique physician–patient relationship at the heart of therapeutic decision-making. Moreover, it would risk considerably slowing the response to the patient's request.[56]

Approval by a Court

No regulatory regime currently requires judicial approval, so no direct evidence exists about how it would work. Judicially crafted constitutional exemptions requiring judicial approval did exist in Canada for a four-month period in 2016, but this was not a fully–fledged regulatory regime, and the small number of reported cases involved (eighteen) makes generalisation from this experience difficult.[57] The

---

[54] Resolution 1216 of 2015 (Colombia). See also, República de Colombia Ministerio de Salud y Protección Social, Protocolo para la aplicación del procedimiento de eutanasia en Colombia (2015) (Colombia). (On accompaniment within hospital-based palliative care, see Bernard J. Lapointe and Dawn Allen, 'Hospital-Based Palliative Care', in Judith M. Stillion and Thinas Attig (eds.), *Death, Dying, and Bereavement: Contemporary Perspectives, Institutions, and Practices* (New York, NY: Springer, 2015), 158.

[55] 'Un Derecho Muerto: Es Inconcebible que la Decisión de la Corte Constitucional Sobre la Eutanasia siga Incumpliéndose', *El Tiempo*, 24 August 2017, www.eltiempo.com/opinion/editorial/un-derecho-muerto-eutanasia-en-colombia-122934 (stating that eighteen cases had been officially registered since the regulation came into force in 2015).

[56] 'Troisième rapport à l'attention de la Chambre des Députés (Années 2013 et 2014)', Report from the Commission Nationale de Contrôle et d'Évaluation de la loi du 16 Mars 2009 sur l'euthanasie et l'assistance au suicide (2015 Luxembourg Government) at 12.

[57] *Canada (Attorney General)* v. *EF* [2016] ABCA 155 (Alberta Court of Appeal); *HS (Re)* [2016] ABQB 121 (Alberta Queen's Bench); *AB* v. *Canada (Attorney General)* [2016] ONSC 1912 (Ontario Superior Court of Justice); *Patient* v. *Canada (Attorney General)* [2016] MBQB 63 (Manitoba Queen's Bench); *AA (Re)* [2016] BCSC 570 (British Columbia Supreme Court); *AB* v. *Ontario (Attorney General)* [2016] ONSC 2188 (Ontario Superior Court of Justice); *CD* v. *Canada (Attorney General)* [2016] ONSC 2431 (Ontario Superior Court of Justice); *HH (Re)* [2016] BCSC 971 (British Columbia Supreme Court); *Tuckwell (Re)* [2016] ABQB 302 (Alberta Queen's Bench); *Patient 0518* v. *RHA 0518* [2016] SKQB 176 (Saskatchewan Queen's Bench); *MN* v. *Canada (Attorney General)* [2016] ONSC 3346 (Ontario Superior Court of Justice); *EF* v. *Canada (Attorney General)* [2016] ONSC 2790 (Ontario Superior Court of Justice); *IJ* v. *Canada (Attorney General)* [2016] ONSC 3380 (Ontario Superior Court of Justice); *WV* v. *Canada (Attorney General)* [2016] ONSC 2302 (Ontario Superior Court of Justice); *XY* v. *Canada (Attorney General)* [2016] ONSC 2585 (Ontario Superior Court of Justice); *GH* v. *Canada (Attorney General)* [2016] ONSC 2873 (Ontario Superior Court of Justice); *BC*

system was created by the 2016 decision of the Supreme Court of Canada in *Carter v. Canada (Attorney General)* ('*Carter*'), granting a four-month extension to the one year suspension of the declaration of invalidity the Court had originally granted in 2015.[58] In the original case, the Court struck down the criminal prohibition on assisted suicide on the grounds that it infringed section 7 of the Canadian Charter of Rights and Freedoms which provides that: 'Everyone has the right to life, liberty and security of the person and the right not to be deprived thereof except in accordance with the principles of fundamental justice.' In the 2016 decision, a majority of the Court created a constitutional exemption for those meeting the 2015 *Carter* criteria: competence; adulthood; consent; and a grievous and irremediable medical condition causing enduring and intolerable suffering. During the period of the extension, such persons could apply for judicial agreement that their request met these criteria. The Court stated that '[r]equiring judicial authorization during that interim period ensures compliance with the rule of law and provides an effective safeguard against potential risks to vulnerable people.'[59]

On the expiry of the four-month period, in most provinces patients were able to seek medical assistance in dying *without* judicial approval.[60] In Ontario, judicial approval continued to be required until the national regulatory regime was in place. While judicial authorisation was considered a *sufficient* safeguard during this period in Ontario (in the absence of other safeguards), it was not seen as a *necessary* one:

> The situation of the need for court authorizations persists in the third phase of the legal history of physician-assisted death and may persist until Parliament enacts legislation without any constitutional deficiencies. I wish to be clear, however, that there is nothing in this decision … that mandates that future phases of the legal history of physician-assisted death will require judicial authorizations. Arguably, the medical establishment is far better situated to supervise this constitutionally protected right, but pending a constitutionally-sound enactment, it falls on the court to protect a constitutional right.[61]

---

v. *Canada (Attorney General)* [2016] ONSC 3231 (Ontario Superior Court of Justice); FG v. *Canada (Attorney General)* [2016] ONSC 3099 (Ontario Superior Court of Justice).

[58] *Carter v. Canada (Attorney General)* [2016] 1 SCR 13; *Carter v. Canada (Attorney General)* [2015] SCR 331.

[59] *Carter v. Canada (Attorney General)* [2016] 1 SCR 13 at [6].

[60] Director of Public Prosecutions (Newfoundland and Labrador), Interim Practice Directive: Physician-Assisted Death (PAD) (9 June 2016); Director of Public Prosecutions (Nova Scotia), DPP Directive: Physician-Assisted Death (16 June 2016); Minister of Health (Alberta), Order in Council Respecting Medical Assistance in Dying Standards of Practice, OC 142/2016 (10 June 2016); Terry Lake (British Columbia (BC) Minister of Health) and Suzanne Anton (BC Attorney General), 'Ministerial Statement on Medical Assistance in Dying', Government of British Columbia, 6 June 2016.

[61] OP v. *Canada (Attorney General)* [2016] ONSC 3956 (Ontario Superior Court of Justice) at [56].

Some British legislators have sought to draw analogies between prospective judicial approval of assisted dying and judicial involvement in other end-of-life decisions[62] – most of which involve patients who lack capacity.[63] These analogies fail to recognise that patients in those cases are not expected to bring legal proceedings.[64] Any analysis of how a prospective judicial approval requirement would work in assisted dying cases is therefore necessarily speculative.

In the next section I consider the recent calls for prospective judicial approval in two jurisdictions then contemplating legalisation – Canada and England and Wales. I demonstrate that these calls are tactical and lack substantive argument.

CALLS FOR PROSPECTIVE APPROVAL

Calls for prospective approval in the recent public and legislative debates in Canada and England and Wales have come predominantly from two different groups. First, from opponents of legalisation seeking to prevent legalisation. Second, from proponents of legalisation seeking either to bring opponents with them, or to reach a compromise to avoid a judicial approval system advocated by opponents they see as unworkable.

Canada

Within the first category, those groups seeking prior judicial approval in the recent Canadian national consultation all opposed legalisation primarily on religious grounds.[65] Their stated reasons included the need to verify that the criteria are met, protecting doctors, and avoiding bias by other possible decision-makers including doctors and tribunal members.[66] The Vulnerable Persons Standard,[67] which contains a requirement for prospective approval by a judge or independent body,

---

[62] See, for example, Hansard, HL, vol. 756, col. 1853, 7 November 2014 (Lord Pannick); Hansard, HL, vol. 756, col. 1879, 7 November 2014 (Lord Faulks); Hansard, HL, vol. 756, col. 1854, 7 November 2014 (Lord Carlile); Hansard, HL, vol. 756, col. 1858, 7 November 2014 (Baroness Butler-Sloss); Stage 1 Report on Assisted Suicide (Scotland) Bill from the Health and Sport Committee (2015 SP 712) at [190]–[193].

[63] See, for example, *Airedale NHS Trust v. Bland* [1993] AC 789; *Re A (Children) (Conjoined Twins: Surgical Separation)* [2001] Fam 147.

[64] *Re B (Adult: Refusal of Medical Treatment)* [2002] EWHC 429 at [88], [98], [100(ix)] ('*Re B*').

[65] Association for Reformed Political Action (Reformed Christians); Euthanasia Prevention Coalition; Christian Legal Fellowship; Evangelical Fellowship of Canada; Christian Medical and Dental Society of Canada; Physicians' Alliance against Euthanasia.

[66] Consultations on Physician-Assisted Dying: Summary of Results and Key Findings', Final Report from the External Panel on Options for a Legislative Response to *Carter v. Canada* (15 December 2015 Government of Canada, Department of Justice) at 93–4 ('External Panel Report on Legislative Response to *Carter*').

[67] Vulnerable Persons Standard (2016), standard 5: Arms-Length Authorization (2017 Vulnerable Persons Standard).

was created by 'a coalition of professional, faith, and advocacy organisations'.[68] Less onerous prospective approval models (e.g. tribunals or panels) were also favoured by groups not opposed in principle to legalisation, relying on similar reasons.[69]

A number of proponents of legalisation participating in the national consultation described prospective approval as a 'barrier' to access.[70] This description has particular significance in the Canadian constitutional context following the Supreme Court of Canada's 1988 decision on abortion, *Morgentaler*, in which the court struck down as unconstitutional provisions in the Criminal Code requiring prospective approval by hospital committees which prevented women from accessing abortion services.[71] The view of prospective approval as a 'barrier' was echoed during the consultation by most of the provincial bodies regulating and representing doctors.[72] In its report, the Special Joint Committee (of the Parliament of Canada) agreed:

> requiring a review by either a panel or a judge would create an unnecessary barrier to individuals requesting [medical assistance in dying]. The Committee recommends therefore: ... [t]hat the Government of Canada work with the provinces and territories, and their medical regulatory bodies to ensure that the process to regulate medical assistance in dying *does not include a prior review and approval process*.[73]

The second category of calls for prospective approval – proponents of legalisation seeking compromise – did not feature in the Canadian debate, perhaps because proponents' reliance on *Morgentaler* strengthened their arguments against prospective approval, making compromise on this point unnecessary. Instead, proponents of legalisation called for retrospective scrutiny only. Most medical organisations and professional regulatory bodies saw prospective approval as an unnecessary interference in the doctor–patient relationship, although in the recent national consultation two such bodies did suggest that a formal process might improve patients' ability to obtain needed assessments.[74]

---

[68] Harvey Max Chochinov and Catherine Frazee, 'Finding a Balance: Canada's Law on Medical Assistance in Dying' (2016) 388 *The Lancet* 543–5 at 544.
[69] Canadian Association of Community Living; Canadian Psychiatric Association; Canadian Association for Spiritual Care: 'External Panel Report on Legislative Response to *Carter*', 94–95.
[70] These proponents included the British Columbia Civil Liberties Association, Dying with Dignity Canada and the Association Québécoise Pour le Droit de Mourir Dans la Dignité: Ibid., 96–7.
[71] *R v. Morgentaler* [1988] 1 SCR 30 (Canada).
[72] 'External Panel Report on Legislative Response to *Carter*', 96–7.
[73] 'Medical Assistance in Dying: A Patient-Centred Approach', Report from the Special Joint Committee on Physician-Assisted Dying (2016 Parliament of Canada) at 30 [emphasis added]. The Provincial-Territorial Expert Advisory Group on Physician-Assisted Dying also recommended only retrospective review (in addition to prospective consultation): Final Report from the Provincial-Territorial Expert Advisory Group on Physician-Assisted Dying (30 November 2015 Government of Ontario, Ministry for Health and Long-Term Care) at 38 (Recommendation 22), 41–2 (Recommendation 29).
[74] 'External Panel Report on Legislative Response to *Carter*', 96–7.

Following lengthy and acrimonious negotiations between the House of Commons and the Senate, an Act inserting a defence into the Criminal Code received Royal Assent on 17 June 2016.[75] The criteria for the defence do not include prospective judicial or quasi-judicial approval.[76] The parameters of the defence are more limited than those drawn from the Supreme Court of Canada's decision in *Carter*, which were applied in the constitutional exemption cases earlier in 2016.[77] Additional criteria were added to the definition of a 'grievous and irremediable medical condition': the person requesting assistance in dying must be 'in an advanced state of irreversible decline in capability' and 'their natural death must have become reasonably foreseeable, taking into account all of their medical circumstances, without a prognosis necessarily having been made as to the specific length of time that they have remaining.'[78] Whether these additional criteria require that the person be terminally ill and whether the Act should so require was the subject of much Parliamentary and public debate during the passage of the Act. A constitutional challenge to the statute and a similar provision in the Québec statute succeeded at trial in Québec, and neither the federal nor provincial governments appealed this decision.[79] The federal statute has now been amended in light of this litigation.[80]

United Kingdom

All of the ten legalisation attempts in Parliament since 1936 have been unsuccessful. The modern attempts have all been restricted to the terminally ill. The most recent three Bills incorporate prospective approval by a judge of the High Court (Family Division). Different versions of this requirement were proposed as amendments by both opponents and proponents of legalisation during debate at the Committee stage of the Assisted Dying Bill (2014–15) introduced by Lord Falconer in the House of Lords.[81] The proponents' version was agreed and added to the Bill,[82] which subsequently failed. It was also included in both 2015–16 Bills, both of which failed.[83]

---

[75] See Chapter 2 for an examination of the Canadian assisted dying law reform process.
[76] Medical Assistance in Dying Act (Canada), amending the Criminal Code (Canada) and inserting s. 241.31.
[77] See above, text accompanying notes 57–59.
[78] Medical Assistance in Dying Act (Canada), s. 3, inserting s. 241.2(2) into the Criminal Code (Canada).
[79] *Truchon v. Canada (Attorney General)* [2019] QCCS 3792 (CanLII).
[80] Bill C-7, An Act to Amend the Criminal Code (Medical Assistance in Dying), SC 2021 c. 2 (Canada).
[81] Assisted Dying HL Bill (2014–15) 6.
[82] Hansard, HL, vol. 756, col. 1885, 1906, 7 November 2014.
[83] Assisted Dying HL Bill (2015–16) 25; Assisted Dying (No. 2) HC Bill (2015–16) [7].

According to both the proponents and opponents, the requirement for judicial approval was explicitly based on a judicial suggestion by three Supreme Court judges in *Nicklinson*, one of a series of rights-based challenges to the blanket ban on assisted suicide arguing that it is incompatible with the right to respect for the patient's private life in Article 8 of the European Convention on Human Rights.[84] Such reliance on *Nicklinson* is at best misplaced and at worst disingenuous. In *Nicklinson*, Lord Neuberger wrote:

> A system whereby a judge or other independent assessor is satisfied in advance that someone has a voluntary, clear, settled, and informed wish to die and for his suicide then to be organised in an open and professional way, would, at least in my current view, provide greater and more satisfactory protection for the weak and vulnerable, than a system which involves a lawyer from the [Director of Public Prosecutions'] office inquiring, after the event, whether the person who had killed himself had such a wish, and also to investigate the actions and motives of any assister, who would, by definition, be emotionally involved and scarcely able to take, or even to have taken, an objective view.[85]

Lord Neuberger's suggestion was intended to rebut the Secretary of State's argument that the issue should be left to Parliament, in part because 'any legalisation of euthanasia would require a surrounding framework with appropriate procedural safeguards which it would be impossible for the courts to introduce, still less monitor'.[86] Lord Neuberger was simply pointing out that the court would not need to *create* such a framework in order to conclude that it would be possible to do so. 'For the purpose of deciding that article 8 is infringed, the court needs to consider that aspect no further than is necessary to satisfy itself that some such scheme or schemes could be practically feasible.'[87] Lady Hale's discussion of the possibility of a judicial approval requirement is similarly contingent, and she makes explicit reference to the possibility of decision-makers other than the courts: '[O]ther bodies, sufficiently neutral and independent of anyone involved with the applicant, and skilled at assessing evidence and competing arguments, could be envisaged.'[88] Moreover, both Lord Neuberger and Lord Wilson explicitly envision such a judicial approval scheme applying only to cases where the patient is not terminally ill,[89] yet the Bill and its successors apply *only* to the terminally ill.

What of the two versions? The opponents' version falls into the first category described above – it sought to prevent legalisation. Lord Carlile introduced a set of amendments which he described as requiring a 'merits-based' assessment by a court

---

[84] Hansard, HL, vol. 756, col. 1853, 7 November 2014 (Lord Pannick); Hansard, HL, vol. 756, col. 1879 (Lord Faulks); Hansard, HL, vol. 756, col. 1855–6 (Lord Carlile).

[85] *Nicklinson* [2015] AC 657 at 791 [108].

[86] Ibid. at 758.

[87] Ibid. at 790 [107].

[88] Ibid. at 863 [315]. And at 864 [318] Lady Hale mentions a 'judge or other tribunal'.

[89] Ibid. at 795 [123], 820 [197(g)], 822 [205].

based on the evidence. (He contrasted this with the proponents' amendments, which he described as a 'medical model of decision-making' in which the court's more limited role is to 'verify that a process has been followed'.[90]) The opponents' amendments would permit the High Court (Family Division) to make an order permitting assistance in dying only if satisfied *beyond reasonable doubt* (i) that the criteria are satisfied (capacity; clear, settled, informed and voluntary intention; written and witnessed declaration; age; and residence) and (ii) that to refuse the order would amount to a breach of *both* Article 3 *and* Article 8 of the European Convention on Human Rights. The Court would also be required to consider not only the rights of the applicant but 'also the rights of others who may be affected by the applicant's suicide'.[91] The opponents' amendments also included an alternative approach to capacity and decision-making:

> an applicant has capacity commensurate with a decision to end his or her own life and a clear, settled, informed and voluntary intention to do so if he or she—
> (a) is not suffering from any impairment of, or disturbance in, the functioning of the mind or brain or from any condition which might cloud or impair his or her judgement;
> (b) is able to communicate clearly an intention to end his or her life;
> (c) has maintained over a reasonable period of time a firm and unchanging intention to end his or her life; [and]
> (d) is not the subject of influence by, or a sense of obligation or duty to, others.[92]

This provision would impose much higher standards than those used for assessing the capacity and voluntariness of other decisions, including decisions to refuse life-saving or life-sustaining medical treatment.[93]

In relation to capacity, a person will be assessed as unable to make a decision for themselves under the Mental Capacity Act 2005 (England and Wales) only if an impairment or disturbance in the functioning of the mind or brain causes them to be unable to understand, retain or use or weigh the information relevant to the decision.[94] Under Lord Carlile's proposal, the mere presence of an impairment or disturbance in the functioning of the mind or brain prevents the person from having capacity regardless of its effect, as does 'any condition which *might* cloud or impair his or her judgement'. It will be an unusual person who has a prognosis of three

---

90 Hansard, HL, vol. 756, col. 1854–8, 7 November 2014.
91 Assisted Dying HL Bill (2014–15) 6, 6 November 2014, List of Marshalled Amendments, Amendment 64 (Lords Carlile, Darzi and Harries).
92 Assisted Dying HL Bill (2014–15) 6, 6 November 2014, List of Marshalled Amendments, Amendment 65 (Lords Carlile, Darzi and Harries).
93 See, for example, *Re B* [2002] EWHC 429 (ventilation); *Re T (Adult: Refusal of Medical Treatment)* [1993] Fam 95 ('*Re T*') (blood transfusion). For a more recent example, see *King's College Hospital NHS Foundation Trust v. C* [2015] EWCOP 80 (refusal of dialysis).
94 Mental Capacity Act 2005 (England and Wales), ss. 2–3.

months to live[95] who does not have a condition which *might* cloud their judgement. Indeed it might well be argued that we all suffer regularly from one or more conditions which *might* cloud our judgement!

In relation to voluntariness, the common law position is that only *undue* influence prevents a decision from being made voluntarily.[96] Under Lord Carlile's proposal, *any* influence by others on the person will do so, as will the person feeling 'a sense of obligation or duty to others'. If most terminally ill persons will be unable to meet the opponents' capacity standard, even fewer will be able to prove beyond a reasonable doubt that they are not subject to the influence of others.[97] Indeed most people whether ill or well would be unable to do so. Nor would they want to.[98]

Even if a person could meet both the capacity and voluntariness tests, they must also satisfy the court beyond a reasonable doubt that both their right to be free from inhuman and degrading treatment (Article 3) and their right to respect for their private and family life (Article 8) would be breached if an order were not made. No court has ever found that Article 3 (or its counterparts in other constitutionally entrenched human rights documents) is breached in this context,[99] although Lady Hale did express some sympathy with the Article 3 claim in *Nicklinson*.[100]

The use of the criminal standard of proof, impossibly high standards for capacity and voluntariness, and an extraordinary requirement that the applicant satisfy the High Court that *two* of their rights under the European Convention would be breached, for one of which there is no precedent, compel the conclusion that this set of amendments is not intended to provide for prospective judicial approval of cases meeting the criteria for assistance, but instead to prevent any such approval being given.

In contrast, the simpler set of amendments successfully introduced by proponents of legalisation incorporates the existing legal standards of capacity and voluntariness. Assistance would be lawful if the High Court (Family Division) is satisfied that the criteria are met: capacity; voluntary, clear, settled and informed wish; written and witnessed declaration; age and residence.[101]

This set of amendments falls into the second category set out above – proponents of legalisation sought either to bring opponents with them, or to reach a compromise to avoid the judicial approval system advocated by their opponents (led by Lord

---

[95] Assisted Dying HL Bill (2014–15) 6, 6 November 2014, List of Marshalled Amendments, Amendment 17 (Lords Carlile, Darzi and Harries).
[96] *U v. Centre for Reproductive Medicine* [2002] EWCA Civ 565; *Re T* [1993] Fam 95.
[97] Eric J. Cassell, 'Unanswered Questions: Bioethics and Human Relationships' (2007) 37 *Hastings Center Report* 20–3 at 22.
[98] See the discussion of the communitarian critique of rights discourse in the context of assisted dying in Lewis, *Assisted Dying and Legal Change*, 67–8.
[99] See ibid., 20, n. 54.
[100] *Nicklinson* [2015] AC 657 at 863 [313].
[101] Assisted Dying HL Bill (2014–15) 6, 6 November 2014, List of Marshalled Amendments, Amendment 4 (Lord Pannick, Baronesses Neuberger and Mallalieu).

Carlile) that they saw as unworkable. The importance of this aim to proponents is clear from the short introduction to the amendments given by Lord Pannick, who stated that the Bill 'would be improved, and some of those who are concerned about it may be reassured, if judicial safeguards were to be added'.[102] Two aims were therefore identified. The first is some kind of improvement to the Bill. The second, which falls squarely into the second category, is reassurance of opponents.

The only improvement mentioned by Lord Pannick related to the protection of the vulnerable based on the misunderstanding of Lord Neuberger's judgement in *Nicklinson*.[103] The Bill's sponsor, Lord Falconer, also described the protection of the vulnerable as the aim of the amendments, in addition to the reassurance-related aim of giving 'much greater confidence regarding the Bill'.[104] Lord Falconer, who endorsed Lord Pannick's amendments during the debate,[105] had earlier rejected the argument that prospective judicial approval was needed to protect the vulnerable. As Chair of the Commission on Assisted Dying, Lord Falconer had considered extensive arguments on the issue of prospective approval by a court or tribunal and whether this would provide better protection for the vulnerable. The Commission on Assisted Dying concluded that assisted suicide for the terminally ill could safely be legalised with safeguards to protect the vulnerable which did not include prospective judicial approval:

> Our assessment of the body of evidence overall has convinced us that it is health and social care professionals who have the knowledge, skills and training structures that would be needed to implement a safeguarded system to permit assisted dying in the UK. Therefore, we do not consider that it would be necessary or desirable to involve a tribunal or other legal body in decision-making, as proposed by some of those who gave evidence to the Commission.[106]

Improving the Bill to protect the vulnerable does not appear to be the primary motivation of the proponents. On the basis of the unconvincing reliance on *Nicklinson* by Lord Pannick, and the earlier reasoned and evidence-based rejection of a prospective judicial approval requirement by Lord Falconer, it seems more likely that reassurance of opponents was their primary aim. Yet the inclusion of this requirement did not reassure sufficient Parliamentarians at the time or for the subsequent two Bills, all of which failed.

Nonetheless, the repeated adoption of this requirement along with the misleading claim by both sides[107] that it was required by the judges of the Supreme Court in *Nicklinson* have created a Parliamentary consensus that will make it difficult for

---

[102] Hansard, HL, vol. 756, col. 1853, 7 November 2014.
[103] See above, text accompanying notes 84–89.
[104] Hansard, HL, vol. 756, col. 1880, 7 November 2014 (Lord Falconer).
[105] Hansard, HL, vol. 756, col. 1881, 7 November 2014 (Lord Falconer).
[106] Final Report form the Commission on Assisted Dying (2011 Demos) at 28–9.
[107] See Hansard, HL, vol. 756, col. 1853, 7 November 2014 (Lord Pannick); Hansard, HL, vol. 756, col. 1879 (Lord Faulks); Hansard, HL, vol. 756, col. 1855–6 (Lord Carlile).

Parliamentarians to resist including it in future Bills. It is, therefore, important to ascertain whether such a requirement would meet the regulatory goals identified for this and future Bills.

WOULD A PROSPECTIVE JUDICIAL APPROVAL REQUIREMENT MEET THE REGULATORY GOALS?

The Typical Condition of a Patient Who Requests Assistance in Dying

The data from retrospective reporting in permissive regimes indicate that the typical request for assisted dying is made by an individual who is dying of cancer. To establish this we can look first at the data on diagnosis, and then at the data on time to death, which are less well-reported.

First, what do the available data tell us about the diagnosis of those seeking assistance to die? Although the legal requirements relating to the requesting person's condition and/or experience of suffering vary widely across permissive jurisdictions, both in regimes which impose a 'terminal illness' requirement (e.g. Oregon and the states which follow its model) and those that use an 'unbearable suffering' requirement not limited to terminal illness (e.g. the Netherlands, Belgium and Luxembourg), Emanuel and colleagues reported in 2016 that over 70 per cent of all reported cases of euthanasia or physician-assisted suicide involved cancer patients.[108] Very recently that rate has been declining, although it remains above 60 per cent in all jurisdictions with a statutory regime, and in some it is substantially higher than 70 per cent.[109] The data are less comprehensive for Switzerland, but it is

---

[108] Ezekiel J. Emanuel, Bregje D. Onwuteaka-Philipsen, John W. Urwin and Joachim Cohen, 'Attitudes and Practices of Euthanasia and Physician-Assisted Suicide in the United States, Canada, and Europe' (2016) 316 *Journal of the American Medical Association* 79–90.

[109] Taking the most recent year for which data are available in each jurisdiction: in the Netherlands the rate in 2018 was 66 per cent: 2018 Annual Report from the Regionale Toetsingscommissies Euthanasie (2019 Regional Euthanasia Review Committees) at 12 ('RTE 2018 Annual Report'). In Belgium in 2016–17 it was 64 per cent. The Belgian rate has declined steadily since 2008–9 when it dropped below 80 per cent for the first time since legalisation in 2002: 'Huitième Rapport aux Chambres Législatives (années 2016–2017)', Report from the Commission fédérale de Contrôle et d'Évaluation de l'Euthanasie (2018 Belgian Federal Public Service, Health, Food Chain Safety and Environment) at 3 ('Annual Report on Euthanasia 2016–17 (Belgium)'). In 2018 in the US states modelled on Oregon for which data are available, it was 62.5 per cent in Oregon, 75 per cent in Washington, and 69 per cent in California: 'Oregon Death with Dignity Act: 2018 Data Summary', Annual Report from the Oregon Public Health Division, Centre for Health Statistics (15 February 2019 Oregon Government) at 3 ('2018 Data Summary (Oregon)'); '2018 Death with Dignity Act Report', Report from the State Government) at 5; 'California End of Life Option Act 2018 Data Report', Report from the California Department of Public Health (July 2019 California Government) at 4. The most recent rate in Vermont is 83 per cent (from 2013 to 2017): 'Report Concerning Patient Choice at the End of Life', Report from the Vermont Department of Health (15 January 2018 Vermont Government) at 4. In Luxembourg, 82 per cent of all reported cases from 2009 to 2018 involved cancer patients. However, the number of reported cases is so tiny that – unlike

clear that significantly lower than 70 per cent of all reported cases in Switzerland involve cancer patients.[110] The data nonetheless allow us to conclude with certainty that a typical patient requesting assistance to die will be a cancer patient.

Second, what does the available data tell us about how close to death those seeking assistance to die are? The data are less clear on closeness to death. If the patient 'is clearly not expected to die in the near future', the Belgian statute requires a mandatory additional consultation with either a psychiatrist or relevant specialist and a waiting period of at least one month.[111] (No such requirement exists in the other jurisdictions employing an unbearable suffering criterion: the Netherlands and Luxembourg.) The Belgian data indicate that the patient *is* expected to die in the near future in well over 80 per cent of reported cases.[112] In the Netherlands, the most recent data from 2015 indicate that in 36 per cent of cases, the patient is expected to die within a week, and in additional 36 per cent of cases, the patient is expected to die within one to four weeks. Thus in 72 per cent of cases, the patient is expected to die within four weeks.[113]

A patient who requests assistance in dying is most commonly dying of cancer and likely to die soon. Bearing this typical patient in mind, how would a prospective judicial approval requirement contribute to achieving the regulatory goals of

the other permissive jurisdictions – the rate varies markedly over time, from a high of 100 per cent in 2009, 2010 and 2016, to a low of 63 per cent in 2013: 'Cinquième rapport à l'attention de la Chambre des Députés (Années 2017 et 2018)', Report from the Commission Nationale de Contrôle et d'Évaluation de la loi du 16 mars 2009 sur l'euthanasie et l'assistance au suicide (2019 Luxembourg Government) at 6 ('Cinquième rapport à l'attention de la Chambre des Députés 2017–18').

[110] Cancer was the underlying diagnosis in 42 per cent of reported assisted suicide cases of Swiss residents in 2014: 'Assisted Suicide and Suicide in Switzerland: Cause of Death Statistics 2014', Report from the Federal Department of Home Affairs, Statistical Office (October 2016 Swiss Confederation) at 2. The rate of cancer was 46.5 per cent among Swiss residents assisted by right to die associations from 2003 to 2008: Nicole Steck, Christopher Junker, Maud Maessen, Thomas Reisch, Marcel Zwahlen and Matthias Egger, 'Suicide Assisted by Right-to-Die Associations: A Population Based Cohort Study' (2014) 43 *International Journal of Epidemiology* 614–22. The rate among non-residents is likely lower: 37 per cent of assisted suicides of non-residents in Zürich from 2008 to 2012 had underlying cancer diagnoses. This is likely due to the shorter prognoses of cancer patients coupled with the difficulty of travelling at the very end of life: Saskia Gauthier, Julian Mausbach, Thomas Reisch and Christine Bartsch, 'Suicide Tourism: A Pilot Study on the Swiss Phenomenon' (2015) 41 *Journal of Medical Ethics* 611–17.

[111] Law on Euthanasia (Belgium) § 3.

[112] The percentage of reported Belgian euthanasia cases where the patient is expected to die in the near future slowly declined from its highest point of 94 per cent in 2006–7, stabilising recently at 85 per cent between 2013 and 2017: 'Annual Report on Euthanasia 2016–17 (Belgium)' at 3. For earlier data, see the previous biannual reports.

[113] Bregje Onwuteaka-Philipsen, Johan Legemaate, Agnes van der Heide, Hans van Delden, Kirsten Evenblij, Inssaf El Hammoud, Roeline Pasman, Corrette Ploem, Rosalie Pronk, Suzanne van de Vathorst and Dick Willems, 'Third Evaluation of the Termination of Life on Request and Assisted Suicide (Review Procedure) Act' ['Evaluatie Wet Toetsing Levensbeëindiging op Verzoek en Hulp bij Zelfdoding'], Report from The Netherlands Organisation for Health Research and Development (May 2017 ZonMw) at 104–5, table 4.14.

respecting autonomy, protecting the vulnerable, and responding compassionately to unbearable suffering?

Respecting Autonomy

As Lord Pannick noted during the 2014 House of Lords debate over the Assisted Dying Bill, the imposition of extra substantive or procedural requirements could interfere with an individual's autonomy if the requirements prevent her from obtaining assistance in dying or make it significantly more difficult to do so.[114] Of course, this will only constitute an interference with autonomy if the individual's request for assistance is made autonomously.

Concerns raised about the second regulatory aim, protecting the vulnerable, focus primarily on capacity and voluntariness,[115] which have the potential to undermine autonomy. As Eric Cassell writes, 'sick persons require the help of others to make autonomous decisions.'[116] Separating out this much-needed help from undue influence is difficult. Interestingly, though, particular characteristics of those who seek assistance in dying may correlate positively with an autonomously made request when compared with other (much more common) serious and difficult medical decisions made by sick persons.[117] There is some evidence from Oregon that individuals who request assistance in dying are characterised by a need to retain control and independence.[118] 'Losing autonomy' is the most-cited reason for a request in Oregon, mentioned by 95.5 per cent of the 1,459 patients who died following the ingestion of medication prescribed under the Death with Dignity

[114] Hansard, HL, vol. 756, col. 1882, 7 November 2014.
[115] Hansard, HL, vol. 756, col. 1853, 7 November 2014 (Lord Pannick); Hansard, HL, vol. 756, col. 1859–60, 7 November 2014 (Lord Deben); Hansard, HL, vol. 756, col. 1860, 7 November 2014 (Baroness Mallalieu); Hansard, HL, vol. 756, col. 1862, 7 November 2014 (Lord Condon); Hansard, HL, vol. 756, col. 1866, 7 November 2014 (Baroness Finlay); Hansard, HL, vol. 756, col. 1869, 7 November 2014 (Lord Campbell-Savours); Hansard, HL, vol. 756, col. 1880, 7 November 2014 (Lord Faulks); Hansard, HL, vol. 756, col. 1880–81 (Lord Falconer).
[116] Cassell, 'Unanswered Questions', 23.
[117] For an overview of the comparative prevalence data on end-of-life decisions made by doctors, see Penney Lewis, 'Assisted Dying Regimes', Briefing Note from the Oireachtas Committee on Justice (22 November 2017 Houses of the Oireachtas), in 'Report on the Right to Die with Dignity', Report from the Joint Committee on Justice and Equality (June 2018, 32/JAE/18 Houses of the Oireachtas) at 74–80, table 2.
[118] Linda Ganzini, Steven K. Dobscha, Ronald T. Heintz and Nancy Press, 'Oregon Physicians' Perceptions of Patients Who Request Assisted Suicide and Their Families' (2003) 6 *Journal of Palliative Medicine* 381–90 at 388; Linda Ganzini, Elizabeth R. Goy and Steven K. Dobscha, 'Oregonians' Reasons for Requesting Physician Aid in Dying' (2009) 169 *Archives of Internal Medicine* 489–92; Kathryn A. Smith, Theresa A. Harvath, Elizabeth R. Goy and Linda Ganzini, 'Predictors of Pursuit of Physician-Assisted Death' (2015) 49 *Journal of Pain and Symptom Management* 555–61 at 559.

Act between 1998 and 2018.[119] There may therefore be some correlation between the making of a request, and acting autonomously, including acting with capacity and voluntarily.[120]

Isra Black and I reviewed the criteria in respect of requests for assisted dying in the Netherlands, Belgium, Oregon, and Switzerland, and the empirical evidence of adherence to those criteria. We concluded that the evidence suggests that the legal criteria governing requests are well-respected, and that individuals who receive assistance in dying do so on the basis of valid requests. Both the capacity and voluntariness criteria are used by doctors to weed out invalid requests. Retrospective review bodies have not found substantive problems with the validity of requests in reported cases.[121]

This review suggests that a prospective judicial approval requirement is not routinely needed to ensure that requests are granted only when made voluntarily by individuals with capacity. It would be more useful to focus such approvals on cases in which the treating or consulting doctors or the patient's loved ones have concerns about the patient's capacity or voluntariness by permitting a referral for judicial determination in such cases. A recent private members' Bill in New South Wales took this approach, permitting close relatives to challenge the patient's 'request certificate' in court, not only on the grounds that the request was not made autonomously, but also on the grounds that the patient does not meet the eligibility requirements in relation to age, terminal illness and residence.[122] The Bill was narrowly defeated on second reading in November 2017. This approach would mirror the referral of cases where there are doubts or disputes about a patient's capacity to refuse life-saving, life-sustaining or other serious treatment.[123] Applying a judicial approval requirement more selectively would contribute to the regulatory goal of respecting autonomy.

Protecting the Vulnerable

Aside from capacity and voluntariness issues, are some or all patients in this group presumptively 'vulnerable', so that imposing a judicial approval requirement might protect them? In 2007, researchers examined data from the Netherlands and Oregon in order to see if members of vulnerable groups were more likely to receive assistance in dying. They examined the frequency of such assistance in ten groups of potentially vulnerable patients, defined by gender, age, ethnicity, educational and socio-economic status, psychiatric illness (including depression), chronic illness and

---

[119] '2018 Data Summary (Oregon)', 12.
[120] Lewis and Black, 'Adherence to Request Criterion', 889.
[121] Ibid., 893–4.
[122] Voluntary Assisted Dying Bill 2017 (NSW), cl. 21 (Australia).
[123] *St George's Healthcare NHS Trust* v. *S* [1998] 3 WLR 936 (Court of Appeal) at 969–70; 'Mental Capacity Act 2005: Code of Practice', Code of Practice from the Department of Constitutional Affairs, issued by Lord Falconer, Secretary of State for Constitutional Affairs and Lord Chancellor (2007 UK Government) at 142 [8.16]; *An NHS Trust* v. *Y* [2018] UKSC 46 ('*Re Y*').

disability. They found 'no evidence of heightened risk . . . with the sole exception of people with AIDS',[124] though the lack of Oregon data on pre-existing disabilities weakens the force of this conclusion with respect to disability.[125] The presumptive vulnerability premise is further undermined by the researchers' conclusion that 'the available data . . . shows that people who died with a physician's assistance were more likely to be members of groups enjoying comparative social, economic, educational, professional and other privileges'.[126]

In addition to capacity and voluntariness, depression is an issue often raised in relation to protection of the vulnerable. While capacity may be doubted in patients with a depressive disorder, a majority of depressed patients have capacity.[127] Although doubts have been raised about the generalisability of these findings to patients with treatment-resistant depression, most terminally ill cancer patients will not have been diagnosed with treatment-resistant depression.[128] For patients with a terminal illness, the prevalence of depression in granted requests is lower than in ungranted requests in Oregon,[129] Belgium[130] and the Netherlands.[131]

---

[124] Margaret P. Battin, Agnes van der Heide, Linda Ganzini, Gerrit van der Wal and Bregje D. Onwuteaka-Philipsen, 'Legal Physician-Assisted Dying in Oregon and the Netherlands: Evidence Concerning the Impact on Patients in "Vulnerable" Groups' (2007) 33 *Journal of Medical Ethics* 591–7.

[125] Charles E. Drum, Glen White, Genia Taitano and Willi Horner-Johnson, 'The Oregon Death with Dignity Act: Results of a Literature Review and Naturalistic Inquiry' (2010) 3 *Disability and Health Journal* 3–15 at 7, 12.

[126] Battin et al., 'Legal Physician-Assisted Dying in Oregon'.

[127] Thomas Grisso and Paul S. Appelbaum, 'The MacArthur Treatment Competence Study III: Abilities of Patients to Consent to Psychiatric and Medical Treatments' (1995) 19 *Law and Human Behaviour* 149–74; J. Vollmann, A. Bauer, H. Danker-Hopfe and H. Helmchn, 'Competence of Mentally Ill Patients: A Comparative Empirical Study' (2003) 33 *Psychological Medicine* 1463–71.

[128] See Martin R. Broome and Angharad de Cates, 'Choosing Death in Depression: A Commentary on "Treatment-Resistant Major Depressive Disorder and Assisted Dying"' (2015) 41 *Journal of Medical Ethics* 586–7 at 586.

[129] Lewis and Black, 'Adherence to Request Criterion', 889, 893–4, discussing Linda Ganzini, Elizabeth R. Goy and Steven K. Dobscha, 'Prevalence of Depression and Anxiety in Patients Requesting Physicians' Aid in Dying: Cross Sectional Survey' (2008) 337 *British Medical Journal* 973–5; Ilana Levene and Michael Parker, 'Prevalence of Depression in Granted and Refused Requests for Euthanasia and Assisted Suicide: A Systematic Review' (2011) 37 *Journal of Medical Ethics* 205–11; Battin et al., 'Legal Physician-Assisted Dying in Oregon; Linda Ganzini, 'Commentary: Assessment of Clinical Depression in Patients Who Request Physician-Assisted Death' (2000) 19 *Journal of Pain and Symptom Management* 474–8; Ilora G. Finlay and Rob George, 'Legal Physician-Assisted Suicide in Oregon and the Netherlands: Evidence Concerning the Impact on Patients in Vulnerable Groups – Another Perspective on Oregon's Data' (2011) 37 *Journal of Medical Ethics* 171–4.

[130] Yanna Van Wesemael, Joachim Cohen, Johan Bilsen, Tinne Smets, Bregje Onwuteaka-Philipsen and Luc Deliens, 'Process and Outcomes of Euthanasia Requests under the Belgian Act on Euthanasia: A Nationwide Survey' (2011) 42 *Journal of Pain and Symptom Management* 721–33 at 721, 726, 731–2.

[131] Bregje D. Onwuteaka-Philipsen, Mette L. Rurup, H. Roeline, W. Pasman and Agnes van der Heide, 'The Last Phase of Life: Who Requests and Who Receives Euthanasia or

For typical patients who are dying of cancer, the relationship between depression and requests for assistance in dying is unclear.[132] One Dutch study looking at depression and explicit requests made to general practitioners for euthanasia or assisted suicide among sixty-four cancer patients with a terminal prognosis of six months or less found that

> none of the patients with an explicit EAS [euthanasia or assisted suicide] request [N=17] suffered from a definite major depression... Furthermore, no relationship was found between depressed mood and explicitly requesting EAS. This outcome was based on results from the [Hospital Anxiety and Depression Scale] (all scales), as well as the single-item depression screener.[133]

This finding differed from an earlier Dutch study which found that in a group of terminally ill cancer patients, those with depressed mood were four times more likely to request euthanasia.[134] A recent Oregon study compared the characteristics of patients seeking physician-assisted death with those who were not interested in physician-assisted death. The former group had 'higher levels of depression'.[135]

It is possible that a small number of individuals requesting assistance in dying will be suffering from treatable depression which is not identified by their treating physician or the reviewing consulting physician. Additional evaluation by a mental health professional would be more likely to identify these individuals than a requirement for judicial approval. This could be achieved either by requiring such an evaluation for all patients seeking assistance, as is required in Hawaii[136] and was proposed in Scotland,[137] or by setting out specific circumstances in which physicians

---

Physician-Assisted Suicide?' (2010) 48 *Medical Care* 596–603 at 601, table 4; Marijke C. Jansen-van der Weide, Bregje D. Onwuteaka-Philipsen and Gerrit van der Wal, 'Granted, Undecided, Withdrawn, and Refused Requests for Euthanasia and Physician-Assisted Suicide' (2005) 165 *Archives of Internal Medicine* 1698–704 at table 1 (depression present in 0.01 per cent of granted euthanasia requests and 21.3 per cent of refused requests); Johanna H. Groenewoud, Agnes van der Heide, Alfons J. Tholen, W. Joost Schudel, Michiel W. Hengeveld, Bregje D. Onwuteaka-Philipsen, Paul J. Van Der Maas and Gerrit Van Der Wal, 'Psychiatric Consultation with Regard to Requests for Euthanasia or Physician-Assisted Suicide' (2004) 26 *General Hospital Psychiatry* 323–30; Ilinka Haverkate, Bregje D. Onwuteaka-Philipsen, Agnes van der Heide, Piet J. Kostense, Gerrit van der Wal and Paul J. van der Maas, 'Refused and Granted Requests for Euthanasia and Assisted Suicide in the Netherlands: Interview Study with Structured Questionnaire' (2000) 321 *British Medical Journal* 865–6.
[132] Smith et al., 'Predictors of Pursuit of Physician-Assisted Death'.
[133] Cees D. M. Ruijs, A. J. F. M. Kerkhof, G. van der Wal and B. D. Onwuteaka-Philipsen, 'Depression and Explicit Requests for Euthanasia in End-of-Life Cancer Patients in Primary Care in the Netherlands: A Longitudinal, Prospective Study' (2011) 28 *Family Practice* 393–9 at 396. Data collection took place from 2003 to 2006 with follow-up in 2007.
[134] Marije L. van der Lee, Johanna G. van der Bom, Nikkie B. Swarte, A. Peter, M. Heintz, Alexander de Graeff and Jan van den Bout, 'Euthanasia and Depression: A Prospective Cohort Study among Terminally Ill Cancer Patients' (2005) 23 *Journal of Clinical Oncology* 6607–12.
[135] Smith et al., 'Predictors of Pursuit of Physician-Assisted Death', 558.
[136] Our Care, Our Choice Act (Haw) § 4(5).
[137] End of Life Assistance (Scotland) Bill (2010) [38], cl. 9 (requiring a psychiatric report).

must refer the patient for an evaluation. An example of the latter approach is found in the Oregon statute, which requires a counselling referral to be made if either the attending or consulting physician suspects that the patient 'may be suffering from a psychiatric or psychological disorder, or depression causing impaired judgment'. (A physician may prescribe 'medication to end a patient's life in a humane and dignified manner' only if the counsellor determines that the patient is not suffering from such a condition.)[138] In light of the characteristics of the group of patients most likely to seek assistance, the former blanket approach may infringe on patient autonomy and cause additional suffering with little advancement of the aim of protecting the vulnerable. The latter, more focused approach seems more attractive, but evidence of its effectiveness is questionable. In Oregon, only a very small percentage of patients seeking assistance are referred to a mental health professional: 4.5 per cent or 65 of 1,459 patients who died as a result of ingesting medication prescribed under the statute between 1998 and 2018.[139] There is a downward trend in the rate of such referrals over time. In recent years the rate has remained below 4 per cent. The small numbers involved mean that the fluctuations are not statistically significant.[140] If this approach is to be effective, those caring for patients at the end of life, including nurses, general practitioners, specialists and palliative care teams should be trained to assess patients for possible symptoms of depression.[141] This would better achieve the regulatory aim of protecting the vulnerable than a requirement for judicial approval.

Compassionate Response to Unbearable Suffering

In the group of patients dying of cancer, the cumbersome and bureaucratic nature of the judicial process[142] will be particularly acute, for two reasons. First, such persons are likely to be frail and physically weak, finding the rigours of the judicial

---

[138] Death with Dignity Act (Oregon) §§ 127.800–127.995, 127.815 § 3.01, 127.825 § 3.03.
[139] '2018 Data Summary (Oregon)', 11.
[140] Lewis and Black, 'Effectiveness of Legal Safeguards', 48.
[141] Helen Scott, 'Assessment of Depression When Patients Desire a Hastened Death' (2011) 1 *End Life Journal* 1–16; Simon Dein, 'Psychiatric Liaison in Palliative Care' (2003) 9 *Advances in Psychiatric Treatment* 241–8; Ann Payne, Sandra Barry, Brian Creedon, Carol Stone, Catherine Sweeney, Tony O'Brien and Kathleen O'Sullivan, 'Sensitivity and Specificity of a Two-Question Screening Tool for Depression in a Specialist Palliative Care Unit' (2007) 21 *Palliative Medicine* 193–8; Lewis and Black, 'The Effectiveness of Legal Safeguards', 67. A good recent summary of the literature on treating depression in the palliative care setting is found in Felicity Ng, Gregory B. Crawford and Anna Chur-Hansen, 'Treatment Approaches of Palliative Medicine Specialists for Depression in the Palliative Care Setting: Findings from a Qualitative, In-Depth Interview Study' (2016) 6 *BMJ Supportive and Palliative Care* 186–93, 186–7.
[142] See Margaret Otlowski, 'Active Voluntary Euthanasia: Options for Reform' (1994) 2 *Medical Law Review* 161–205 at 182; Maurice Adams and Heleen Weyers, 'Supervision and Control in Euthanasia Law: Going Dutch?' (2012) 23 *King's Law Journal* 121–39 at 133; Yeung, 'Regulating Assisted Dying', 179.

process, however sympathetically handled, too much for them. (For instance, the judge may visit the patient rather than requiring the patient to come to the Court.)[143] If they are willing and able to, they may seek judicial approval earlier than they would wish while still strong enough to go through the process, just as patients in prohibitive jurisdictions kill themselves or seek assistance in doing so earlier than they would wish while still mentally and physically strong enough to do so. Evidence from or about individuals who have killed themselves or sought assistance in doing so earlier than they would have wished as a result of a criminal prohibition on assisting suicide has been accepted by courts in the United Kingdom, Canada, the United States and New Zealand.[144] A select committee of the Victorian Parliament recently took evidence from the state Coroners Court describing cases of individuals who took their own lives earlier than they would have wished as a result of the criminal prohibition on assisting suicide. The Report concluded:

> The Coroner's [sic] Court told the Committee that some Victorians are ending their lives in dreadful ways. Many of these people identified by the Coroner are dying alone and in pain. They are often dying earlier than they desire because they believe they must act alone, before they are no longer capable, and so that their loved ones are not implicated in their death.[145]

There are numerous published accounts of patients who ended their lives with or without assistance earlier than they would have wished to do so had assisted dying been lawful.[146]

---

[143] See, for example, *Re B* [2002] EWHC 429.

[144] *Nicklinson* [2015] AC 657 at 788 [96]; *R (Purdy)* v. *Director of Public Prosecutions* [2010] 1 AC 345 at [31], [38] ('*Purdy*'); *Ross* v. *Lord Advocate* [2016] CSIH 12 at [3] ('*Ross*'); *Carter* v. *Canada (Attorney General)* [2012] BCSC 886 at [1048], [145], [277], [324]–[325]; *Carter* v. *Canada (Attorney General)* [2013] BCCA 435 at [119]–[21]; *Carter* v. *Canada (Attorney General)* [2015] 1 SCR 331 (Supreme Court of Canada) at [1], [15], [57]–[58], [90]; *Rodriguez* v. *Canada (Attorney General)* [1993] 3 SCR 519 (Supreme Court of Canada) at [62] ('*Rodriguez*'); *Compassion in Dying* v. *Washington* 79 F 3d 790 (9th Cir. 1996) at 824 n 98; *Baxter* v. *State*, No. ADV-2007-787, 2008 WL 6627324 (Mont. Dist. Ct., 5 December 2008) at 20; *Seales* v. *Attorney-General* [2015] 3 NZLR 556 at 593–4 [165]–[166] ('*Seales*').

[145] Final Report from the Legal and Social Issues Committee's Inquiry into End of Life Choices (2016 Parliament of Victoria) at 197–200, 206. Similar evidence was given to the Health Committee of the New Zealand Parliament: 'Petition 2014/18 of Hon Maryan Street and 8,974 Others', Report from the Health Committee (2017 New Zealand Parliament, House of Representatives) at 43–4.

[146] See, for example, Sherwin B. Nuland, *How We Die: Reflections on Life's Final Chapter* (New York: Vintage Books, 1994), 152–3 (describing the death of the Nobel Prize winning physicist Percy Bridgman); Marcia Angell, 'The Supreme Court and Physician-Assisted Suicide – The Ultimate Right' (1997) 336 *New England Journal of Medicine* 50–3 at 50–3 (describing the death of the author's father); Mark Colvin, 'Euthanasia Advocate Given Suspended Sentence', ABC National Radio, 24 May 2004 (discussing the assisted death of Elizabeth Godfrey); Hansard, HL, vol. 681, col. 1184, 12 May 2006 (Lord Joffe), debating the Assisted Dying for the Terminally Ill HL Bill (2006–7) 36 (assisted death of Dr Anne Turner); Richard Savill, 'By the Time You Read This, I Will Be Dead', *Telegraph*, 25 January 2006, www.telegraph.co.uk/news/uknews/1508714/By-the-time-you-read-this-I-will-be-dead.html (assisted death of Dr Anne

If approval is granted, these patients may activate the assistance earlier than they would wish to avoid a real or perceived expiration of the approval. A similar argument is sometimes made against the Dutch requirement that the physician be present during the entirety of an assisted suicide.[147]

Second, they lack time. This may make it difficult to find a doctor who is both willing to assist *and* willing to go to court. It is possible that doctors may be more willing to assist if the judicial stamp of approval is perceived as lessening the risk of prosecution. The evidence from permissive jurisdictions, though, is that even without judicial approval, the risk of prosecution is tiny. In the Netherlands, for example, 111 cases were referred to prosecutors by the reporting bodies between 1999 and 2018 (0.16 per cent of all reported cases).[148] Only one prosecution (recently ending in an acquittal) has been brought following these referrals,[149] although from 2016, the *Annual Report* no longer contains follow-up information on the outcome of cases referred to the Public Prosecution Service and to the Healthcare

Turner); Charlie Russell, *Terry Pratchett: Choosing to Die*, KEO Films, 2011 (documenting the death of Peter Smedley); Jonathan Owen, 'Jeffrey Spector: The 54-Year-Old Father Who Killed Himself at Dignitas – In His Own Words: "I Am Going Too Early Because of the Law in the UK"', *Independent*, 26 May 2015, www.independent.co.uk/news/people/jeffrey-spector-the-54-year-old-father-who-killed-himself-at-dignitas-in-his-own-words-10276671.html; Louise Dickson, 'Victoria Right-to-Die Activist Felt Pressure to Take His Own Life', *Times Colonist*, 9 April 2016, www.timescolonist.com/news/local/victoria-right-to-die-activist-felt-pressure-to-take-his-own-life-1.2227757 (Life Circle Switzerland death of John Hofsess); Melissa Davey, 'Police Raid Pushed Academic to End Her Life, Says Euthanasia Advocate', *The Guardian*, 23 April 2016, www.theguardian.com/society/2016/apr/22/police-raid-pushed-academic-to-end-her-life-euthanasia-advocate-philip-nitschke (suicide of Avril Henry).
[147] See, for example, 'Dutch Association for Psychiatry Guideline', 70; Griffiths et al., *Euthanasia and Law in Europe*, 101; Lewis and Black, 'Effectiveness of Legal Safeguards', 95.
[148] Penney Lewis and Isra Black, 'Reporting and Scrutiny of Reported Cases in Four Jurisdictions Where Assisted Dying Is Lawful: A Review of the Evidence in the Netherlands, Belgium, Oregon and Switzerland' (2013) 13 *Medical Law International* 221–39 at 225; 2013 Annual Report from the Regionale Toetsingscommissies Euthanasie (2014 Regional Euthanasia Review Committees): see cases 15, 16, 18, 19, 20 ('RTE 2013 Annual Report'); 2014 Annual Report from the Regionale Toetsingscommissies Euthanasie (2015 Regional Euthanasia Review Committees): see cases 1, 2, 4, 5; 2015 Annual Report from the Regionale Toetsingscommissies Euthanasie (2016 Regional Euthanasia Review Committees): see cases 1, 28, 29, 81; 2016 Annual Report from the Regionale Toetsingscommissies Euthanasie (2017 Regional Euthanasia Review Committees): see cases 21, 23, 24, 37, 45, 53, 57, 85–87 ('RTE 2016 Annual Report'); 2017 Annual Report from the Regionale Toetsingscommissies Euthanasie (2018 Regional Euthanasia Review Committees): see cases 2, 10, 11, 24, 28, 31, 36, 40, 73, 79, 103, 118; 'RTE 2018 Annual Report': see cases 4, 23, 42, 69, 70, 75.
[149] 'RTE 2016 Annual Report': see case 2016-85; David Gibbes Miller, Rebecca Dresser and Scott Y. H. Kim, 'Advance Euthanasia Directives: A Controversial Case and Its Ethical Implications' (2019) 45 *Journal of Medical Ethics* 84–9; Daniel Boffey, 'Doctor to Face Dutch Prosecution for Breach of Euthanasia Law', *The Guardian*, 9 November 2018, www.theguardian.com/world/2018/nov/09/doctor-to-face-dutch-prosecution-for-breach-of-euthanasia-law; Stephanie van den Berg, 'Dutch Doctor Acquitted in Case of Euthanasia of Patient with Dementia', *Reuters*, 11 September 2019, www.reuters.com/article/us-netherlands-euthanasia/dutch-doctor-acquitted-in-case-of-euthanasia-of-patient-with-dementia-idUSKCN1VW1IN.

Inspectorate.[150] In Belgium, the first referral to prosecutors occurred only in late 2015.[151] This case was discontinued in 2019 because it involved physician-assisted suicide which the prosecutorial authorities decided was not a criminal offence.[152] A separate criminal investigation recently resulted in acquittal in a case instigated by the family of a young woman diagnosed with autism, which the Federal Control and Evaluation Commission for Euthanasia did not refer to the prosecutorial authorities.[153] No cases have been referred to prosecutors in Oregon[154] or Luxembourg.[155]

Although the absence of such a requirement in any permissive jurisdiction results in a lack of direct evidence in support of the claim that a judicial approval requirement would discourage terminally ill patients from seeking assistance in dying, it is worth noting that in the small number of cases in which persons with capacity have sought judicial assistance in defending their rights to make their own end-of-life decisions including assisted dying, almost all of them have not been likely to die in the near future, with most suffering from progressive neurological diseases,[156] severe

---

[150] 'RTE 2016 Annual Report'.

[151] Dateline, *Allow Me to Die*, SBS, 2015, www.sbs.com.au/guide/video/517459523808/Dateline-S2015-Ep31-Allow-Me-To-Die; 'Belgian Euthanasia Doctor Could Face Criminal Charges', *SBS News*, 19 November 2015, www.sbs.com.au/news/dateline/article/2015/10/29/belgian-euthanasia-doctor-could-face-criminal-charges; Lewis and Black, 'Reporting and Scrutiny of Reported Cases', 228; 'Sixième Rapport aux Chambres Législatives (2012–2013)', Report from the Commission fédérale de Contrôle et d'Évaluation de l'Euthanasie (2014 Belgian Federal Public Service, Health, Food Chain Safety and Environment); Montero, 'La genèse, la mise en œuvre et les développements de la loi belge relative à l'euthanasie', [41].

[152] 'Arts Niet Vervolgd voor Hulp bij Zelfdoding [Doctor Not Prosecuted for Assistance with Suicide]', *De Standaard*, 26 April 2019, www.standaard.be/cnt/dmf20190426_04353439.

[153] Maria Cheng, 'Belgium Investigates Doctors Who Euthanized Autistic Woman', *Associated Press*, 27 November 2018, www.apnews.com/249a8067af6740d2af22ed66fc9e1a90; Charles Lane, 'More Trouble for Belgium's System of Euthanasia', *Washington Post*, 29 November 2018, www.washingtonpost.com/blogs/post-partisan/wp/2018/11/29/more-trouble-for-belgiums-system-of-euthanasia/?noredirect=on&utm_term=.d3a541f942b4; Elian Peltier, 'Belgium Acquits Three Doctors in Landmark Euthanasia Case', *New York Times*, www.nytimes.com/2020/01/31/world/europe/doctors-belgium-euthanasia.html.

[154] Lewis and Black, 'Adherence to Request Criterion', 229; 'Oregon's Death with Dignity Act – 2013', Annual Report from the Oregon Public Health Division (22 January 2014 Oregon Government); 'Oregon's Death with Dignity Act – 2014', Annual Report from the Government); 'Oregon Death with Dignity Act: 2015 Data Summary', Annual Report from the Oregon Public Health Division (2016 Oregon Government); 'Oregon Death with Dignity Act: 2017 Data Summary', Annual Report from the Oregon Public Health Division (2018 Oregon Government).

[155] 'Cinquième rapport à l'attention de la Chambre des Députés 2017–18', 8.

[156] See, for example, *Rodriguez* [1993] 3 SCR 519 (Supreme Court of Canada) (amyotrophic lateral sclerosis (ALS)); *Carter v. Canada (Attorney General)* [2015] 1 SCR 331 (Supreme Court of Canada) (ALS); *Pretty v. United Kingdom* (2002) 25 EHRR 1 (ECHR) (motor neurone disease); *Purdy* [2010] 1 AC 345 (multiple sclerosis); *In Re Z (Local Authority: Duty)* [2004] EWHC 2817 (cerebellar ataxia); *R (Burke) v. General Medical Council* [2005] EWCA Civ 1003 (cerebellar ataxia); *Ross* [2016] CSIH 12 (diabetes, cardiac problems, Parkinson's disease, and peripheral neuropathy).

disabilities,[157] or psychiatric conditions.[158] When terminally ill patients have been involved in such challenges, they have all died before the case was finally resolved. The three patient plaintiffs in the US Supreme Court case of *Washington* v. *Glucksberg* died of cancer, AIDS and emphysema respectively before the case reached the Ninth Circuit.[159] The lawyer Robin Stransham-Ford died of prostate cancer just before a judge of the High Court of South Africa ruled in favour of his 'urgent application' that a doctor be permitted to provide him with euthanasia or assistance in suicide.[160] Lecretia Seales died of a brain tumour the day after the New Zealand High Court ruled against her application that her doctor be permitted to assist her suicide.[161]

Of the eighteen patients who applied to the Canadian courts for constitutional exemptions under the temporary *Carter* regime in 2016,[162] only six were dying of cancer,[163] with most of the twelve others dying of progressive neurological diseases.[164] The diagnosis for two cases is unknown,[165] and one case involved a

---

[157] *Carter* v. *Canada (Attorney General)* [2015] 1 SCR 331 (Supreme Court of Canada) (spinal stenosis); *Nicklinson* [2015] AC 657 (stroke); *Nicklinson and Lamb* v. *United Kingdom* (2015) 61 EHRR SE7 (ECHR) (stroke; paralysis); *Re B* [2002] EWHC 429 (paralysis); *Koch* v. *Germany* (2013) 56 EHRR 6 (ECHR) (paralysis); *Sanles Sanles* v. *Spain* [2001] EHRLR 348 (ECHR) (the Ramón Sampedro case, paralysis).

[158] *Haas* v. *Switzerland* (2011) 53 EHRR 33 (ECHR); *Gross* v. *Switzerland* (2014) 58 EHRR 7 (ECHR).

[159] *Washington* v *Glucksberg*, 521 US 702 (1997) (US Supreme Court).

[160] *Stransham-Ford* v. *Minister of Justice and Correctional Services* [2015] ZAGPPHC 230 (South Africa High Court).

[161] *Seales* [2015] 3 NZLR 556. Publication of the judgement was delayed until after her death.

[162] See note 57 and accompanying text.

[163] *AB* v. *Canada (Attorney General)* [2016] ONSC 1912 (Ontario Superior Court of Justice) (lymphoma); *CD* v. *Canada (Attorney General)* [2016] ONSC 2431 (Ontario Superior Court of Justice) (breast cancer); *EF* v. *Canda (Attorney General)* [2016] ONSC 2790 (Ontario Superior Court of Justice) (renal cancer); *GH* v. *Canada (Attorney General)* [2016] ONSC 2873 (Ontario Superior Court of Justice) (lung cancer); *MN* v. *Canada (Attorney General)* [2016] ONSC 3346 (Ontario Superior Court of Justice) (ampullary cancer); *WV* v. *Canada (Attorney General)* [2016] ONSC 2302 (Ontario Superior Court of Justice) (ovarian cancer). It is possible that the applicant in *Patient* v. *Canada (Attorney General)* [2016] MBQB 63 (Manitoba Queen's Bench) was also dying of cancer, as the details of the applicant's two terminal diseases were withheld on grounds of privacy.

[164] *AA (Re)* [2016] BCSC 570 (British Columbia Supreme Court) (multiple sclerosis); *AB* v. *Ontario (Attorney General)* [2016] ONSC 2188 (Ontario Superior Court of Justice) (confidential progressive irreversible disease); *HH (Re)* [2016] BCSC 971 (British Columbia Supreme Court) (mitochondrial encephalomyopathy, lactic acidosis, and stroke-like episodes (MELAS)); *HS (Re)* [2016] ABQB 121 (Alberta Queen's Bench) (ALS); *IJ* v. *Canada (Attorney General)* [2016] ONSC 3380 (Ontario Superior Court of Justice) (spinal stenosis; discogenic disease; neurogenic claudication; lumbosacral facet osteoarthropathy; spondylolisthesis; rotoscoliosis; major kyphosis; sacroiliac joint complex pain disorder); *Patient 0518* v. *RHA 0518* [2016] SKQB 176 (Saskatchewan Queen's Bench) at [27]–[30] (ALS with metastatic bone cancer; primary cause of suffering appears to be ALS); *Tuckwell (Re)* [2016] ABQB 302 (Alberta Queen's Bench) (ALS); *XY* v. *Canada (Attorney General)* [2016] ONSC 2585 (Ontario Superior Court of Justice) (ALS).

[165] *BC* v. *Canada (Attorney General)* [2016] ONSC 3231 (Ontario Superior Court of Justice); *FG* v. *Canada (Attorney General)* [2016] ONSC 3099 (Ontario Superior Court of Justice).

severe psychiatric disorder.[166] The proportion of patients dying of cancer was much lower than would be expected based on the experience of permissive jurisdictions[167] which could indicate that the requirement for judicial approval was seen as a barrier by cancer patients who will be more frail and closer to the end of life than those with progressive neurological diseases.

These arguments and evidence suggest that many terminally ill patients will be discouraged from applying for judicial approval. Evidence from prohibitive jurisdictions indicates that they will instead take their own lives without assistance, or seek assistance underground or offshore, again possibly earlier than they would otherwise wish.[168] Imposing a prospective judicial approval requirement on the terminally ill is not a compassionate response to unbearable suffering.[169]

CONCLUSION

A highly formal system of prospective judicial approval fails to meet the regulatory aims of respecting autonomy, protecting the vulnerable and responding compassionately to unbearable suffering in the typical case where the person seeking assistance has cancer and is close to the end of life. Such an approach is unlikely to work; instead it would incentivise premature, offshore and underground deaths, or alternatively preclude access to any form of assisted dying. Highly formal prospective judicial approval mechanisms should not form a routine part of regimes restricted to the terminally ill. Further assessment of different models of decision-making is needed to determine their impact on the quality of decision-making. Prospective approval could be studied as part of such an assessment, but should be reserved for more complex cases.

The Dutch Regional Review Committees have recently adopted a distinction between reported cases that are 'straightforward' and those which are not. In the first category, if all committee members reviewing the case agree that the due care criteria are met, the case is approved without discussion. In the second category, all cases are discussed. First category 'cases are often cases where the patient is terminally ill with a short period of time left to [live], for instance, patients with cancer, with a short life expectancy, who are suffering from severe pain and other physical symptoms such as nausea, extreme fatigue and functional loss.'[170]

---

[166] *Canada (Attorney General)* v. *EF* [2016] ABCA 155 (Alberta Court of Appeal) (severe conversion disorder).

[167] See text accompanying notes 108–110.

[168] Penney Lewis, 'Informal Legal Change on Assisted Suicide: The Policy for Prosecutors' (2011) 31 *Legal Studies* 119–34; *Carter* v. *Canada (Attorney General)* [2015] 1 SCR 331 (Supreme Court of Canada) at [1], [57]–[58].

[169] Hansard, HL, vol. 756, col. 1859–60, 7 November 2014 (Baroness Wheatcroft).

[170] Marianne C. Snijdewind, Donald G. van Tol, Bregje D. Onwuteaka-Philipsen and Dick L. Willems, 'Developments in the Practice of Physician-Assisted Dying: Perceptions of Physicians

The academic and professional literature, public discourse and retrospective review bodies have identified three types of cases as particularly complex:[171] those involving dementia,[172] psychiatric illness,[173] and existential suffering ('tired of life').[174] Snijdewind and others' qualitative interviews with doctors and family members identify underlying characteristics which contribute to complexity, and which may be more prevalent in these three types of particularly complex cases. The researchers divided '[c]omplex situations … into relational complexities and complexities that arise from the occurrence of unexpected situations.'[175]

Relational complexities could occur due to (i) the absence of a process of growth together toward the decision to perform euthanasia, 'for instance when a patient asked a physician for EAS while there had been no previous care relation between them'; (ii) pressure from the patient or relatives on the physician to perform euthanasia, or miscommunication stemming from 'a difference in expectations: patients and relatives did not understand why [euthanasia] was not or not yet an option'; or (iii) invisible or hidden suffering, 'when the patient's apparent condition seemed a lot better than it really was, when there was incongruence between the medical state of the patient and his/her appearance or the story he/she told'.[176]

Who Had Experience with Complex Cases' (2018) 44 *Journal of Medical Ethics* 292–6 at 295; Euthanasia Code 2018 (Netherlands), 11–15 [2.3]; 'RTE 2013 Annual Report', ch. 3, 36–7.

[171] Marianne C. Snijdewind, Donald G. van Tol, Bregje D. Onwuteaka-Philipsen and Dick L. Willems, 'Complexities in Euthanasia or Physician-Assisted Suicide as Perceived by Dutch Physicians and Patients' Relatives' (2014) 48 *Journal of Pain and Symptom Management* 1125–34 at 1126.

[172] Lewis and Black, 'Adherence to Request Criterion', 887–8. See also, Eva Elizabeth Bolt, Marianne C. Snijdewind, Dick L. Willems, Agnes van der Heide and Bregje D. Onwuteaka-Philipsen, 'Can Physicians Conceive of Performing Euthanasia in Case of Psychiatric Disease, Dementia or Being Tired of Living?' (2015) 41 *Journal of Medical Ethics* 592–8.

[173] Lewis, *Assisted Dying and Legal Change*, 78–81, 124–7; Sigrid Dierickx, Luc Deliens, Joachim Cohen and Kenneth Chambaere, 'Euthanasia for People with Psychiatric Disorders or Dementia in Belgium: Analysis of Officially Reported Cases' (2017) 17 *BMC Psychiatry* 1–9 at 7, doi: https://doi.org/10.1186/s12888-017-1369-0. See also, Scott Y. H. Kim, Raymond G. De Vries and Johan R. Peteet, 'Euthanasia and Assisted Suicide of Patients with Psychiatric Disorders in the Netherlands 2011 to 2014' (2016) 73 *JAMA Psychiatry* 362–8; Paul S. Appelbaum, 'Physician-Assisted Death for Patients with Mental Disorders – Reasons for Concern' (2016) 73 *JAMA Psychiatry* 325–6; Reginald Deschepper, Wim Distelmans and Johan Bilsen, 'Requests for Euthanasia/Physician-Assisted Suicide on the Basis of Mental Suffering: Vulnerable Patients or Vulnerable Physicians?' (2014) 71 *JAMA Psychiatry* 617–18.

[174] Lewis, *Assisted Dying and Legal Change*, 99–101. See also, Snijdewind et al., 'Developments in the Practice of Physician-Assisted Dying', 294; Natasja J. Raijmakers, Agnes van der Heide, Pauline S. C. Kouwenhoven, Ghislaine J. M. W. van Thiel, Johannes J. M. Delden and Judith A. C. Ruietjens, 'Assistance in Dying for Older People without a Serious Medical Condition Who Have a Wish to Die: A National Cross-Sectional Survey' (2015) 41 *Journal of Medical Ethics* 145–50; Suzanne Ost and Alexandra Mullock, 'Pushing the Boundaries of Lawful Assisted Dying in the Netherlands? Existential Suffering and Lay Assistance' (2011) 18 *European Journal of Health Law* 163–89.

[175] Snijdewind et al., 'Complexities in Euthanasia', 1129.

[176] Ibid., 1129–30.

Complexities that arise from the occurrence of unexpected situations reflect the physician's 'need for control':

> The capricious progress of a disease sometimes created a sense of haste and the idea of being overtaken by the disease: the patient's condition was rapidly deteriorating, which complicated the procedure and/or the assessment of the due care criteria. From that moment on, the performance of [euthanasia] was no longer possible . . .. Another event that created a complex situation was the unexpected necessity to move the patient to another place to perform [euthanasia].[177]

Clearly strong associations exist between the complexities identified by Snijdewind and her colleagues, and the complex cases associated with particular causes of suffering: dementia, psychiatric illness and existential suffering.[178] Pressure from relatives to perform euthanasia often occurred after the patient had lost capacity, for example due to the progression of dementia. Rapid deterioration in the patient's condition or progression of the disease caused sudden loss of capacity which made assessment of the criteria no longer possible. Hidden or invisible suffering was frequently associated with psychiatric illness or dementia.[179] Other complexities were more independent of these causes, for example the absence of a process of growth together towards the decision to perform euthanasia, or the need to move the patient.

This discussion reflects the difficulty of identifying complex cases prospectively. Snijdewind and her colleagues found that '[m]ost often it is not possible to distinguish beforehand which cases will become more complex than other cases'.[180] If an assessment of different models of decision-making is undertaken in order to determine their impact on the quality of decision-making, an alternative approach would be to define what constitutes a non-complex case, when prospective judicial approval should not generally be required. Building on the earlier discussion of respecting autonomy, the distinction in the Belgian law, the practice of the Dutch Regional Review Committees and the work of Snijdewind and her colleagues, the criteria could be: (i) the patient retains capacity, is expected to die in the near future[181] and is suffering from severe physical symptoms; (ii) the patient's relationship with their physician permits a process of growth together toward the decision to perform euthanasia; (iii) the expectations of the patient, their loved ones and the physician are consistent; and (iv) the physician and the consulting physician agree that the legal requirements are satisfied.[182] Such an

---

[177] Ibid., 1130–1.
[178] Ibid., 1131–2.
[179] Ibid., 1130.
[180] Ibid., 1132.
[181] Such a proposal was narrowly defeated in the Canadian Senate: Hansard, Senate, 42nd Parl., 1st Sess., vol. 150, no. 46 (9 June 2016) at 1720.
[182] See also Penney Lewis, 'Public Evidence before the Commission on Assisted Dying' (2011 Commission on Assisted Dying), www.commissiononassisteddying.co.uk/wp-content/uploads/

approach would help to ensure that prospective approval is only used when
necessary in order to meet the regulatory goals of respecting autonomy and
protecting the vulnerable, and does not impede those willing to provide assistance
in dying to those seeking it from responding compassionately to unbearable
suffering.

I have argued elsewhere that the greatest scope for legislative autonomy in law
reform on assisted dying is pre-emptive, avoiding judicial interpretation of constitutionally entrenched rights and/or statutory or common law defences.[183] The
Northern Territory (Australia) statute[184] which combined elements from both
rights-based and necessity-based regimes is an example of the greater freedom
possessed by legislators in comparison to judges, who may be constrained by the
way in which a claim has been brought using constitutionally entrenched human
rights, or, in the case of common law judges, the need to develop the substantive law
incrementally in a consistent and principled fashion with due regard to precedent.
Experience from Canada[185] and Colombia[186] demonstrates that legislatures in
jurisdictions with constitutionally entrenched human rights risk expansive regimes
if they fail to act. Even pro-active legislatures like Québec risk being forced by rights-
based challenges to bring their regime into line.[187]

The UK Parliamentary debates discussed in this chapter demonstrate how easily
such legislative autonomy can be directed away from the empirical evidence.
Legislative reform is often pragmatic and tactical rather than rational or principled.
In the example considered in this chapter, opponents of legalisation seeking to
prevent legalisation proposed an unworkable model. Proponents of legalisation
seeking either to bring opponents with them or to reach a compromise to avoid

---

2 at 12–13 (identifying particularly difficult cases where prospective review might be appropriate
  even though the person requesting assistance is terminally ill or expected to die in the near
  future, for example those involving: (i) conflict between the medical team and the family of the
  patient, (ii) conflict within the family, (iii) a less certain diagnosis, or (iv) disagreement between
  the treating physician and the consulting physician on whether the requirements are satisfied).

[183] Lewis, 'Legal Change on Assisted Dying'.

[184] Rights of the Terminally Ill Act 1995 (NT) (Australia).

[185] *Carter* v. *Canada (Attorney General)* [2015] 1 SCR 331; Medical Assistance in Dying Act
  (Canada). The law reform process in Canada is examined in Chapter 2.

[186] Sentence C-239 (1997), Ref. Expedient D-1490 (Constitutional Court of the Republic of
  Colombia, 20 May 1997); Sentence T-970 (2014), Ref. Expedient T-4.067.849 (Constitutional
  Court of the Republic of Colombia, 15 December 2014); 'Protocolo para la aplicación del
  procedimiento de eutanasia en Colombia República de Colombia', Protocol from the
  Ministerio de Salud y Protección Social (2015 Ministry of Health and Social Protection of
  Colombia).

[187] Act Respecting End-of-Life Care, RLRQ, c. S-32.0001 (2014) (Québec); *Truchon* v. *Canada
  (Attorney General)* [2019] QCCS 3792 (CanLII). The Québec law reform process is examined
  in Chapter 8.

that unworkable model, proposed an alternative model which fails to understand and accommodate the lived experience of those who would wish to access assistance in dying.

Rollback of proposed safeguards is difficult. The repeated adoption of the require-ment for approval by a High Court judge, along with the misleading claim by both sides[188] that it was required by the judges of the Supreme Court in *Nicklinson* have created a Parliamentary consensus that will make it difficult for Parliamentarians to resist including it in future Bills. It is also difficult to roll back actual or implemented safeguards, as the experience of Vermont demonstrates. The Vermont Act originally contained sunset clauses which would have changed the regulatory framework after three years from a regime modelled on Oregon to a professional practice standard.[189] This would have permitted physician-assisted suicide on the basis of a valid request from the physician's patient with a terminal illness, without requirements for consultation with a second physician, psychiatric evaluation or waiting periods. Effectively it would have been treated like other medical procedures which are covered by the medical exception to the criminal law.[190] In 2015 the Act was amended to remove these clauses. The inclusion of the sunset clauses reflected a compromise to accommodate more liberal or libertarian views within the Vermont state legislature. In contrast, very restrictive and bureaucratic regimes such as the one in Victoria, Australia may reflect a compromise to accommodate more conser-vative views: 'Proposing such a conservative model was a deliberate strategy to secure the required support for the bill to pass through the Victorian Parliament.'[191]

The case study in this chapter illustrates the need for rational evidence-based evalu-ation of laws and proposed laws against regulatory goals. Recent experience in Canada[192]

---

[188] See Hansard, HL, vol. 756, col. 1853, 7 November 2014 (Lord Pannick); Hansard, HL, vol. 756, col. 1879 (Lord Faulks); Hansard, HL, vol. 756, col. 1855–6 (Lord Carlile).

[189] Patient Choice and Control at the End of Life Act, 18 Vt Stat Ann §§ 5281–5293 (2013) (Vermont).

[190] The medical exception is the term used (particularly although not exclusively at common law) for the defence or exception to the criminal law which exempts medical practice from some or all offences against the person, for example, serious assault: see Penney Lewis, 'The Medical Exception' (2012) 65 *Current Legal Problems* 355–76.

[191] Ben White and Lindy Willmott, 'Future of Assisted Dying Reform in Australia' (2018) 42 *Australian Health Review* 616–20 at 618. The Victorian law reform process is examined in Chapter 5.

[192] Report from the Royal Society of Canada Expert Panel on End-of-Life Decision Making (November 2011 Royal Society of Canada); 'The State of Knowledge on Advance Requests for Medical Assistance in Dying', Report from the Expert Panel Working Group in Advance Requests for MAID (2018 Council of Canadian Academies); 'The State of Knowledge on Medical Assistance in Dying for Mature Minors', Report from the Expert Panel Working Group on MAID for Mature Minors (2018 Council of Canadian Academies); 'The State of Knowledge on Medical Assistance in Dying Where a Mental Disorder Is the Sole Underlying Medical Condition', Report from the Expert Panel Working Group on MAID Where a Mental Disorder is the Sole Underlying Medical Condition (2018 Council of Canadian Academies).

and Australia[193] suggests that an independent advisory body may be better placed to undertake some of this work, either instead of or in addition to the work of a legislative committee, not to usurp the legislature but to provide it with options which reflect the experience of permissive jurisdictions and avoid unworkable solutions which risk making some patients' experiences at the end of life worse rather than better.

[193] 'Ministerial Advisory Panel Report (Victoria)'; Final Report from the Ministerial Expert Panel on Voluntary Assisted Dying (2019 Government of Western Australia, Department of Health). See also 'Terms of Reference: Queensland's Laws Relating to Voluntary Assisted Dying' from the Queensland Law Reform Commission (21 May 2020 Queensland Law Reform Commission), www.qlrc.qld.gov.au/__data/assets/pdf_file/0004/651379/vad-tor.pdf.

7

Aid in Dying in the United States

Past, Present and Future

David Orentlicher

INTRODUCTION

Until Oregon voters approved an aid-in-dying referendum in 1994,[1] no jurisdiction in the United States had given legal approval to assisted dying. Moreover, fourteen years passed before a second state, Washington, legalised aid in dying, also by voter referendum.[2] But since then, recognition of a right to aid in dying has accelerated. In 2009, the Montana Supreme Court held that there was no legal barrier in the state to aid in dying,[3] and between 2013 and 2019, aid-in-dying statutes were enacted in seven more jurisdictions – by voter referendum in Colorado, and by legislative action in California, District of Columbia, Hawaii, Maine, New Jersey and Vermont.[4] With these recent adoptions, nearly one in four Americans lives in a state that permits its residents to choose aid in dying when they become terminally ill.

While a right to aid in dying has taken different paths – voter approval, legislative action, or judicial decision – all legalising US jurisdictions recognise the right in the same basic way: patients must be adults with decision-making capacity, they must be terminally ill, and they must self-administer the lethal dose of medication.[5]

[1] Melinda A. Lee, Heidi D. Nelson, Virginia P. Tilden, Lindy Ganzini, Terri A. Schmidt and Susan W. Tolle, 'Legalizing Assisted Suicide – Views of Physicians in Oregon' (1996) 334 *New England Journal of Medicine* 310–15. Implementation of the statute was delayed until it was reaffirmed in a second referendum in 1997: Mark A. Hall, David Orentlicher, Mary Anne Bobinksi, Nicholas Bagley and I. Glenn Cohen, *Health Care Law and Ethics*, 9th ed. (New York: Wolters Kluwer, 2018), at 594.
[2] Robert Steinbrook, 'Physician-Assisted Death – From Oregon to Washington State' (2008) 359 *New England Journal of Medicine* 2513–15.
[3] *Baxter v. State*, 224 P.3d 1211 (Mont. 2009).
[4] Paula Span, 'Making the Ultimate Decision,' *New York Times*, 9 July 2019, D1.
[5] David Orentlicher, Thaddeus Pope and Ben Rich, 'The Changing Legal Climate for Physician Aid in Dying' (2014) 311 JAMA 1961–2.

In this chapter, I will discuss why the different jurisdictions have converged on the same legal framework for a right to aid in dying. In particular, there are key reasons for limiting a right to aid in dying to patients who are terminally ill (i.e., having a life-expectancy of six months or less). I also will discuss the implications of the common legal framework for future evolution of the right to aid in dying in the United States.

Note that in other countries with aid in dying, the practice is not limited to the writing of a prescription for a lethal dose of medication that the patient would self-administer. In those countries, aid in dying also includes injection of a lethal dose of medication by a physician or other health care provider.[6] Thus, aid in dying in the United States entails what is also described as physician-assisted suicide but not what is also described as voluntary euthanasia.

AID IN DYING IN THE UNITED STATES

The Oregon aid-in-dying statute established a model for legalising the practice in the United States that has been followed by other states. Under the statute, individuals may obtain a prescription for a lethal dose of medication from their physicians if they are adults possessing decision-making capacity, have a life expectancy of no more than six months, and are legal residents of the state.[7] After filling the prescription, the patient must self-administer the medication.[8]

These eligibility standards distinguish the right to aid in dying from the right to have life-sustaining treatment withheld or withdrawn. In the United States, life-sustaining treatment may be withdrawn from patients who are children and therefore have not attained decision-making capacity, as well as from adults who have lost

---

[6] David Orentlicher, 'International Perspectives on Physician Assistance in Dying' (2016) 46 *Hastings Center Report* 6–7.

[7] Death with Dignity Act, Or Rev Stat § 127.805(1) (1994) (Oregon). The statute provides a non-exclusive list of factors demonstrating residency in § 127.860, including:

(1) Possession of an Oregon driver license;
(2) Registration to vote in Oregon;
(3) Evidence that the person owns or leases property in Oregon; or
(4) Filing of an Oregon tax return for the most recent tax year.

[8] While some statutes explicitly require the patient to self-administer the medication, as in End of Life Option Act, Cal Health and Safety Code § 443.1(b) (2015) (California), Oregon expresses its requirement less directly, by stating that:

• a patient may obtain a 'prescription for medication to end his or her life': Death with Dignity Act, Or Rev Stat § 127.800(11) (1994) (Oregon);
• the patient must understand the potential risks and probable effects of 'taking the medication to be prescribed': Ibid. § 127.800(7);
• the patient's physician must counsel the patient 'about the importance of having another person present when the patient takes the medication prescribed': Ibid. § 127.815(1)(g); and
• the 'act of ingesting medication to end his or her life in a humane and dignified manner [will] not affect the patient's] life, health, or accident insurance or annuity policy': Ibid. § 127.875.

or never possessed decision-making capacity. Treatment also may be withheld or withdrawn from patients who are not terminally ill and even those who could live for many more years. Indeed, a generally healthy person can refuse antibiotics, blood transfusions, or other relatively simple life-sustaining care.[9]

Limits on the right to aid in dying also include special steps patients and prescribing physicians must take to implement the right. For example, patients in Oregon must reaffirm their choice of aid in dying at least fifteen days after their initial request, and they must document their wishes in writing.[10] A prescribing physician must certify that the patient possesses decision-making capacity and is terminally ill,[11] a second physician must confirm the certification,[12] and both physicians have an obligation to refer the patient for an evaluation by a mental health professional if there is reason to think the patient's judgement is impaired by a psychological condition.[13] Each of these basic requirements has been broadly adopted by the other legalising states, with only minor variations (some of which are discussed later in this chapter).

THE RIGHT TO AID IN DYING AND ITS UNDERLYING MORAL PRINCIPLES

At first glance, it seems that American attitudes toward aid in dying have changed dramatically in recent years, much as attitudes toward same-sex marriage did in the run-up to the recognition of a fundamental right to same-sex marriage by the US Supreme Court in 2015.[14] But there is good reason to view the increasing acceptance of aid in dying as a natural extension of the moral principles that once led US states to reject aid in dying. That is, for the same reasons that US laws drew a distinction between the permitted practice of withdrawing life-sustaining treatment and the prohibited practice of aid in dying, laws are now recognising a right to aid in dying – but only a limited right.

We can understand the progression of end-of-life law in terms of two key considerations. First, the legal rules for dying patients reflect the important ethical view that when patients are greatly suffering from serious and irreversible illness, they may prioritise quality of life over length of life and take steps to shorten the dying process. Some fates are worse than death. Thus, for example, according to the Massachusetts Supreme Judicial Court,

---

[9] Hall et al., *Health Care Law and Ethics*, 521–4, 552, 574.
[10] Death with Dignity Act, Or Rev Stat § 127.840 (1994) (Oregon).
[11] Ibid. § 127.815.
[12] Ibid. § 127.820.
[13] Ibid. § 127.825.
[14] *Obergefell* v. *Hodges*, 576 US 644 (2015).

There is a substantial distinction in the State's insistence that human life be saved where the affliction is curable, as opposed to the State interest where, as here, the issue is not whether but when, for how long, and at what cost to the individual that life may be briefly extended.[15]

This ethical view is not peculiar to US law; rather, it is shared across national boundaries and moral frameworks. In the Netherlands, patients become eligible for aid in dying when they are experiencing suffering that is 'unbearable, with no prospect of improvement,' and there is 'no reasonable alternative'.[16] Similarly, the Roman Catholic Church, in its 1980 Declaration on Euthanasia countenancing withdrawal of treatment, concluded,

> When death is imminent in spite of the means used, it is permitted in conscience to take the decision to refuse forms of treatment that would only secure a precarious and burdensome prolongation of life, so long as the normal care due to the sick person in similar cases is not interrupted.[17]

Under this first consideration in US end-of-life law, two elements are critical. The patient must have a serious and irreversible illness. If the patient's health can be restored, then there is no reason to hasten death – in society's moral view. In addition, the patient must be suffering greatly from the grave illness, for if the suffering can be relieved, then again there is no reason to hasten death. As a practical matter, the two elements tend to coincide. Patients with a serious and irreversible illness generally experience substantial suffering, including high levels of pain, fatigue, altered mental status, shortness of breath, or nausea, whether from the disease itself or the side effects of treatment.

As indicated, the moral sentiments about grave illness and great suffering are widely shared among different nations and cultures. But there are variations in the way these sentiments are expressed. For example, while the Massachusetts Court refers to incurable illness, the Catholic Church speaks of imminent death. We can understand these kinds of variations as different ways of getting at the same concept. If one wants to be more certain that an illness is serious and irreversible, one might wait until death is imminent to conclude that the illness truly is irreversible. Regardless of the variations in language, all of the terms reflect a widely shared view that patients and doctors need not pursue the prolongation of life when a patient is suffering greatly from serious and irreversible illness.

---

[15] *Superintendent of Belchertown State School* v. *Saikewicz*, 370 NE 2d 417, 425–6 (Mass. 1977).

[16] Termination of Life on Request and Assisted Suicide (Review Procedures) Act 2001 (The Netherlands), s 2. See also Antina de Jong and Gert van Dijk, 'Euthanasia in the Netherlands: Balancing Autonomy and Compassion' (2017) 63 *World Medical Journal* 10–15. The Dutch law and its subsequent evaluation are considered further in Chapter 4.

[17] Ron P. Hamel (ed.), *Choosing Death: Active Euthanasia, Religion, and the Public Debate* (Philadelphia: Trinity Press International, 1991), at 51; Marjorie Hyer, 'Vatican Eases Its Position on the Prolonging of Life,' *Washington Post*, 27 June 1980.

It is the second consideration underlying end-of-life law that seems to be more American than European, and this second consideration has much to do with determining the exact contours of US law for end-of-life decisions. There is an American desire for 'bright line' rules rather than general principles for laws at the end of life (as well as in many other areas of law[18]). It is not readily ascertainable when a patient's illness becomes sufficiently serious or when a patient's suffering becomes sufficiently severe. Allowing the government to decide when a patient's quality of life has become intolerable would give the state power that can be exercised in arbitrary and invidious ways. Will some patients be allowed to die because their suffering is so severe, or because others devalue their race or ethnic origin? Letting the state decide who may choose death and who must choose life gives the government the kind of power that it should not have. Thus, while in the Netherlands patients may choose aid in dying if they are suffering unbearably (a more subjective standard), patients in the United States may choose aid in dying if their life expectancy is six months or less (a more objective standard).

A review of the progression of end-of-life law over the past forty-plus years illustrates the importance of the American desire for bright-line legal rules at the end of life.

EVOLUTION OF THE RIGHT TO REFUSE LIFE-SUSTAINING TREATMENT

At one time, there was much controversy over the question whether patients should be able to refuse life-sustaining treatment. In the view of many doctors, patients and scholars, withdrawing life-sustaining care constituted 'passive' euthanasia. Just as it was wrong to cause a patient's death by 'active' means, such as injecting a lethal dose of medication, so it seemed wrong to bring about a patient's death by the 'passive' means of discontinuing a ventilator, dialysis or other treatment. As one court wrote,

> [The] Appellant suggests there is a difference between passively submitting to death and actively seeking it. The distinction may be merely verbal, as it would be if an adult sought death by starvation instead of a drug. If the State may interrupt one mode of self-destruction, it may with equal authority interfere with the other.[19]

Thus, in the seminal *Quinlan* case in the 1970s,[20] Karen Quinlan's parents had to seek a court order to compel their daughter's physicians and hospital to discontinue her artificial ventilation.

---

[18] David Orentlicher, *Matters of Life and Death: Making Moral Theory Work in Medical Ethics and the Law* (Princeton, NJ: Princeton University Press, 2002), at 53–80. The next section of this chapter draws on themes in this book.

[19] *John F. Kennedy Hospital v. Heston*, 279 A 2d 670 at 672–3 (NJ 1971). Of course, one also can characterise the withdrawal of treatment as the taking of action.

[20] *In re Quinlan*, 355 A 2d 647 (NJ 1976) ('*Quinlan*').

Ultimately, in *Quinlan* and subsequently, courts and legislatures concluded that withholding or withdrawing life-sustaining treatment is permissible, and they reached that conclusion on the ground that when patients are suffering from serious and irreversible illness, it is acceptable for them to refuse further medical care by exercising their general right of self-determination and their more specific right to reject unwanted bodily intrusions.[21] At some point in the course of severe illness, further efforts to prolong life may only worsen the patient's suffering without providing meaningful benefit. As the New Jersey Supreme Court wrote in *Quinlan*, the patient's right to accept or decline life-sustaining treatment 'grows as the degree of bodily invasion increases and the prognosis dims. Ultimately there comes a point at which the individual's rights overcome the State interest' in prolonging life.[22]

Under the *Quinlan* court's approach, then, the patient's right to refuse life-sustaining treatment took effect only once the patient's prognosis became sufficiently serious. As with the right to abortion, the law employed a 'sliding scale' approach to balance the individual right to choose with the government's interest in preserving life. Just as the state's interest in protecting fetal welfare at the beginning of life depends on the viability of the fetus,[23] so did the state's interest in maintaining health at the end of life depend on the viability of the dying patient. Because Quinlan's prognosis was 'extremely poor' and the bodily invasion from treatment 'very great,'[24] her rights prevailed over the state's interests.

Over time, however, courts abandoned the *Quinlan* sliding scale in favour of a broad right of patients to refuse life-sustaining treatment. No longer did the patient's right turn on the severity of the patient's illness or the invasiveness of the treatment. As the New Jersey Supreme Court wrote in the *Conroy* case nine years after *Quinlan*, 'a young, generally healthy person ... has the same right to decline life-saving medical treatment' as an 'elderly person who is terminally ill'.[25] To be sure, added the court, patients will take into account their condition and prognosis in deciding whether to accept or refuse treatment. But the individual's right to decide does 'not depend on the quality or value of his life.'[26]

---

[21] *In re Conroy*, 486 A 2d 1209 at 1221–3 (NJ 1985) ('*Conroy*'). Courts also have extended the right to refuse treatment to patients who lack decision-making capacity, as a right to have treatment withheld or withdrawn, on the ground that the right to refuse unwanted treatment is important for all persons: at 1229 (citing Norman Cantor, '*Quinlan*, Privacy, and the Handling of Incompetent Dying Patients' (1977) 30 *Rutgers Law Review* 243 at 259 for the point that 'even if the patient becomes too insensate to appreciate the honoring of his or her choice, self-determination is important').

[22] *Quinlan*, 355 A 2d 647 at 664 (NJ 1976).

[23] Under *Roe v. Wade* and *Planned Parenthood v. Casey*, the government must permit women to choose abortion before fetal viability: *Planned Parenthood of Southeastern Pennsylvania v. Casey*, 505 US 833 (1992) at 870–1

[24] *Quinlan*, 355 A 2d 647 at 664 (NJ 1976).

[25] *Conroy*, 486 A 2d 1209 at 1226 (NJ 1985).

[26] Ibid.

Instead of the law determining how sick a patient must be before life-sustaining treatment may be withheld or withdrawn, patients decide for themselves how sick they must be before their treatment will be discontinued. In the words of a California court of appeals,

> As in all matters, lines must be drawn at some point, somewhere, but that decision must ultimately belong to the one whose life is in issue .... It is not a medical decision for her physicians to make. Neither is it a legal question whose soundness is to be resolved by lawyers or judges. . ... It is a moral and philosophical decision that, being a competent adult, is hers alone.[27]

In other words, as the analysis above has shown, legal rules at the end of life started with an approach under which patient rights to refuse treatment would be determined on a case-by-case basis according to a general balancing of individual and state interests. The sicker the patient and the more burdensome the treatment – in other words, the more serious the illness and the greater the suffering – the more likely that patient autonomy would prevail. Patients with widely metastatic cancer would have a stronger right to refuse treatment than patients with a simple pneumonia.

But it quickly became clear that such an approach relied too much on a troubling authority to make quality-of-life judgements. When patients wanted to refuse life-sustaining treatment, their doctors would have to assess their medical status and then apply legal rules that would determine whether the patients' prognoses were sufficiently promising that they had to accept treatment or sufficiently dismal that they were permitted to decline treatment.

And that kind of decision-making is highly problematic. The government, in conjunction with physicians, should not be deciding who must live and who may die based on people's quality of life. If government officials and doctors can make those decisions, they may do so in arbitrary and unfair ways. Views about older persons or those with a disability often reflect invidious bias. Moreover, whether patients live or die may turn on their race, ethnic origin, sex, and economic status rather than only on their medical condition.

Accordingly, end-of-life law took the view that health care decisions that might hasten death should be governed again by a bright-line rule. Before *Quinlan*, the law drew a clear line – no one could refuse life-sustaining treatment or choose aid in dying. After *Conroy*, the law settled on a different clear line – everyone could refuse life-sustaining treatment, and no one could choose aid in dying.

US (and other countries') law takes a similar bright-line approach with other decisions that might invite unfair bias. For example, rather than permitting people to vote when they demonstrate sufficient maturity and understanding, the law lets people vote when they reach the age of eighteen. If the government could decide

---

[27] *Bouvia v. Superior Court*, 225 Cal. Rptr. 297 (Ct App. 1986) at 304–5.

when a person becomes eligible to vote, the state might favour people based on their race, ethnic origin, sex, economic status, or political affiliation. This is especially a concern in the United States, with its history of disenfranchising voters based on their race.[28]

In addition to the influence of invidious bias, there also are concerns about inconsistency from one decision-maker to another. Under a case-by-case principle-oriented approach, the right of patients to refuse treatment often will depend on the moral views of their physicians. Some doctors will give greater weight to the individual interest in self-determination, while other doctors will weigh the state's interest in preserving life more heavily. A patient's fundamental rights should not vary according to the philosophical orientation of the patient's physician.

This concern about consistency also runs through other laws. Consider, for example, the use of speed limits rather than a more principled approach to traffic safety. The law could hold (as tried in some states in the past[29]) that people can drive at any speed that is safe under current traffic conditions. It would be permissible to drive faster on a sunny day than a rainy day and when there are few other cars on the road rather than during rush hour. But different police officers will have different views about safe speeds, and a drivers' likelihood of getting a ticket will depend on the views of the police that day rather than a clear standard of safe driving speeds.[30]

This is not to overstate the role of bright-line rules in US law. There are exceptions. For example, while the law defers to the competent patient's decision even when the decision seems inconsistent with the patient's best interests, as in a refusal of a blood transfusion, the law does not give similar decision-making autonomy when parents make decisions for children, or when other surrogate or substitute decision-makers decide on behalf of patients lacking decision-making capacity. But in those cases, it is unavoidable that decisions about a patient's quality of life will be made by another person. In addition, the law still tries to minimise the decision-making authority of the government. In the case of children, for example, the government generally will defer to the parent's assessment of the child's interests, unless the parent is making a decision that would cause clear and substantial harm to the child, as with the refusal of a blood transfusion,[31] antibiotics for bacterial meningitis,[32] or surgery for a bowel perforation.[33]

Assessments of decision making capacity that the above situations depend upon also allow for subjective determinations that are susceptible to bias. Physicians may

[28] Owen Fiss, 'The Accumulation of Disadvantages' (2018) 106 *California Law Review* 1945–76 at 1945–6.
[29] See for example, *State v. Stanko*, 974 P 2d 1132 (Mont. 1998) (finding unconstitutionally vague a law that allowed people to drive in a 'careful and prudent manner and at a rate of speed no greater than is reasonable and proper under the conditions existing at the point of operation').
[30] Ibid. at 1136–7.
[31] *In re L.S.*, 87 P 3d 521 (Nev. 2004).
[32] *Walker v. Superior Court*, 763 P 2d 852 (Cal. 1988).
[33] *Commonwealth v. Twitchell*, 617 NE 2d 609 (Mass. 1993).

be more likely to conclude that an adult patient possesses decision-making capacity or that an adolescent patient is mature enough to make medical decisions when the patient is white, well-educated or wealthy. But assessments of decision-making capacity are unavoidable, and we lack a good bright-line way to distinguish those who lack capacity from those who possess it.

As discussed, the desire for bright-line rules can explain why the right to refuse life-sustaining treatment belongs to all patients rather than only to patients deemed sufficiently ill. But what about the risk that patients will choose death even when they are not seriously ill? Bright-line rules inevitably are imperfect reflections of their underlying principles – sometimes it really is safe to drive above the speed limit – but bright-line rules cannot deviate too much from principle. If they did, the law would not serve its purposes properly. When everyone can refuse life-sustaining treatment, we run the risk that refusals of treatment will not be reserved for patients who are suffering greatly from serious and irreversible illness. The law's rules for implementing end-of-life principles might not reflect those principles very well.

A broad right to refuse treatment has not raised concerns about inappropriate decisions to hasten the dying process for the important reason that people typically do not refuse life-sustaining treatment unless they are seriously ill and suffering. Even though people can refuse antibiotics for a simple pneumonia or blood transfusions after an accidental bleed, they ordinarily do not. The typical refusal of treatment involves patients with severe and irreversible disease.

And when people do refuse treatment in the absence of a serious illness, they usually do so because of a religious belief, as with the refusal of blood transfusions by Jehovah's Witnesses. In these cases, there are fundamental moral principles at odds with each other. On one hand, there is the moral sentiment that life should be preserved absent great suffering from a grave illness. On the other hand, we have freedom of religion, which has been recognised as a fundamental constitutional right. Given the respect for religious freedom in the United States, we see acceptance of religiously based refusals of life-sustaining treatment even when good health could be restored.[34]

EVOLUTION OF THE LAW FOR AID IN DYING

In light of the history of the right to refuse treatment, it is not surprising that US law initially resisted a right to aid in dying. On one hand, the right to refuse treatment generally ensured that patients could avoid the undue suffering of a prolonged dying process. On the other hand, a right to aid in dying might be subject to considerable

---

[34] It is worth noting that courts have shown some ambivalence about religiously based refusals. For example, some courts have ordered blood transfusions over the objections of Jehovah's Witnesses. These orders have been overridden when appealed, though the transfusions cannot be undone: Hall et al., *Health Care Law and Ethics*, 525.

misuse. If individuals had the same freedom to choose aid in dying as to refuse life-sustaining treatment, then we would have to worry that people would choose aid in dying in the absence of serious illness. People might suffer from distorted thinking that should be treated by psychiatric therapy, whether in the wake of a lost job, death in the family, failed marriage, or more chronic source of despair.[35] Indeed, criticism of licit or illicit aid-in-dying practices in the United States and other countries often has focused on cases in which mental illness rather than serious physical illness seemed to be the reason for the patients' requests for aid in dying.[36] With a right to aid in dying, we do not have the same assurance that we do with refusals of treatment that the right would generally be invoked only in appropriate circumstances. Patients might not be suffering from a serious and irreversible illness, nor would they be acting on the basis of religious belief.[37]

But it also became clear to many Americans that while rejecting a right to aid in dying protected vulnerable people from a premature death, it also deprived other non-vulnerable individuals of the means necessary to relieve their suffering. A right to refuse treatment without a right to aid in dying was an effective way to limit the risks to patients, but it failed to go far enough in addressing the needs of dying patients. Many patients suffering from serious and irreversible illness are not dependent on a life-sustaining treatment that they can refuse. Hence came the pressure for extending rights at the end of life to include a right to aid in dying.

If aid in dying were to be legalised, it would have to satisfy the two key considerations discussed previously. First, it would have to be accessible only by patients who were suffering greatly because of a serious and irreversible illness. In addition, eligibility would have to be determined via a bright-line rule that would avoid case-by-case judgements as to whether a particular patient could choose to shorten the dying process or whether that patient's life had to be preserved over the patient's objection.

Limiting aid in dying to patients with a terminal illness – that is, patients with a life expectancy of six months or less – does a very good job of satisfying the two key factors. By definition, someone with a terminal illness has a serious and irreversible illness, and terminal illnesses generally entail substantial suffering. In addition, when determining eligibility for aid in dying in the United States, physicians do not have to assess the severity of a patient's suffering or the seriousness of the illness.

[35] To be sure, refusals of life-sustaining treatment also might reflect distorted thinking. But we can be more confident that a person's decision to shorten life reflects a genuine expression of self-determination when the person has a serious and irreversible illness: Orentlicher, *Matters of Life and Death*, 63–4.
[36] David Orentlicher, 'Physician Aid in Dying and Mental Illness' (2016) *Jotwell*, https://health.jotwell.com/physician-aid-in-dying-and-mental-illness/.
[37] Critics of a right to aid in dying often observe that terminally ill patients might choose aid in dying because they are depressed. In such cases, doctors should respond by providing psychiatric care rather than a lethal dose of medication. While this is a legitimate concern, the same concern exists for patients who refuse life-sustaining treatment.

Rather, physicians only need to decide whether the patient's life expectancy is more or less than six months.[38] While that judgement is not as exact as whether a potential voter is at least eighteen years old or whether a driver is going faster or slower than sixty mph, it is not the kind of judgement that invites the risk of arbitrary or inconsistent decisions that can result from judgements about a patient's quality of life.

In sum, the progression from a right to refuse treatment to a right to aid in dying in the United States can be understood not as a shift in societal attitudes about the nature of a patient's interests in avoiding the prolongation of life. Rather, the progression reflects the effort to refine the legal rules for end-of-life decisions so they do a better job of reflecting the same moral principles that led to the previous distinction between withdrawal of life-sustaining treatment and aid in dying. A limited right to aid in dying allows end-of-life law to more fully capture the universe of patients who are suffering greatly from a serious and irreversible illness, such as a patient with advanced and untreatable cancer who doesn't need a ventilator to breathe or a feeding tube to eat.

REJECTING ALTERNATIVE EXPLANATIONS FOR THE DISTINCTION BETWEEN TREATMENT WITHDRAWAL AND AID IN DYING

This chapter has described a natural progression of end-of-life law, starting with a limited right to refuse life-sustaining treatment, to a broad right to refuse life-sustaining treatment, subsequently complemented by a limited right to aid in dying. In this view, *why* people want to shorten the dying process matters much more than *how* they would do so.

Of course, it is often said that it very much matters how people would end their lives, that there are important intrinsic differences between the withdrawal of life-sustaining treatment and aid in dying.[39] But none of those differences can really explain the distinction in US law between treatment withdrawal and aid in dying.[40]

---

[38] The statutory requirements only speak to whether the patient is terminally ill. In practice, since physicians are not required to provide aid in dying, one would expect some physicians to take patient suffering into account in deciding whether to write a prescription. And data indicate that some physicians are more reluctant to write an aid-in-dying prescription for some eligible patients than for other eligible patients: Linda Ganzini, Heidi D. Nelson, Terri A. Schmidt, Dale F. Kraemer, Molly A. Delorit and Melinda A. Lee, 'Physicians' Experiences with the Oregon Death with Dignity Act' (2000) 342 *New England Journal of Medicine* 557–63. Similarly, physicians vary in their willingness to comply with a patient's or surrogate decision-maker's refusal of life-sustaining treatment.

[39] Edmund D. Pellegrino, 'Some Things Ought Never Be Done: Moral Absolutes in Clinical Ethics' (2005) 26 *Theoretical Medicine and Bioethics* (2005) 469–86 at 475.

[40] For a more detailed discussion of this point, see Orentlicher, *Matters of Life and Death*, 24–52.

For example, with withdrawal of treatment, the cause of death is supposed to be the patient's underlying illness. With aid in dying, the lethal dose of medication causes the patient's death.[41] In fact, however, turning off a ventilator or suspending dialysis does cause a patient's death[42] – therefore, it is considered a homicide to turn off a ventilator or discontinue other life-sustaining treatment without the patient's consent or other lawful basis, such as that continued treatment would be futile.

There also are problems with the argument that withdrawal of treatment allows a natural death in contrast to the unnatural death of aid in dying.[43] This argument assumes that the natural is preferable to the unnatural. However, much of what doctors do is unnatural – such as removing an inflamed appendix, dialysing blood to manage kidney failure or inserting a pacemaker to restore cardiac function. As these examples illustrate, the unnatural often can be superior to the natural. In any event, there is nothing natural about a death that comes after months of surgery, radiation therapy and aggressive chemotherapy.

Some writers distinguish between treatment withdrawal and aid in dying in terms of the physician's intent. When withdrawing treatment, the physician can hope that the patient will survive, while aid in dying is intended to end the patient's life.[44] However, physicians who write a prescription for a lethal dose of medication also can hope the patient will survive. Indeed, the patient's chances of survival often are greater with aid in dying. In Oregon, after more than twenty years of aid in dying, about 35 per cent of aid-in-dying patients never take their lethal doses but instead die from the progression of their terminal illness.[45] When ventilators are withdrawn, the chances of survival are much lower than 35 per cent. Moreover, the law often holds people responsible for the likely consequences of their actions even if those consequences were not intended. A company that skimps on safety precautions to reduce its operating costs can be held liable for harms that result to its employees or customers.

A number of suggested distinctions between aid in dying and treatment withdrawal turn on the risks of misuse. Patients may choose aid in dying because they suffer from depression, because of financial or other pressures from family or health care providers, or because they have not received good palliative care.[46] All of these risks are important, but they also exist for the withdrawal of treatment. Indeed, in terms of financial pressures, the risks are greater for withdrawals of treatment.

[41] *Vacco v. Quill*, 527 US 793 (1997) at 801 ('*Quill*').
[42] James Rachels, 'Active and Passive Euthanasia' (1975) 292 *New England Journal of Medicine* 78–80 at 79–80.
[43] *Conroy*, 486 A 2d 1209 at 1224 (NJ 1985).
[44] *Quill*, 527 US 793 (1997) at 801–2.
[45] 'Oregon Death with Dignity Act: 2019 Data Summary', Report from the Public Health Division, Center for Health Statistics (2020 Oregon Health Authority, Public Health Division) 5, www.oregon.gov/oha/PH/PROVIDERPARTNERRESOURCES/EVALUATION RESEARCH/DEATHWITHDIGNITYACT/Documents/year22.pdf.
[46] *Washington v. Glucksberg*, 521 US 702 (1997) at 730-2 ('*Glucksberg*').

Patients in a permanently unconscious state can live for years and even decades. There is much more money to be saved by terminating their care than by providing a lethal dose of medication to a patient who will live no longer than six more months. This is especially the case since the overwhelming majority of aid-in-dying patients have chosen hospice care rather than aggressive and expensive treatments to prolong life.[47]

THE TIMELINE FOR THE ADOPTION OF AID-IN-DYING LAWS

While we can explain the adoption of aid-in-dying laws as a natural progression of end-of-life principles, why has the adoption taken place in rather halting fashion instead of with a gradual and smooth uptake? One can only speculate about this, but there are some sensible explanations.

First, it is not surprising that it took until 1994 for the first aid-in-dying law to pass in Oregon. The New Jersey Supreme Court only decided the *Quinlan* case on the right to refuse life-sustaining treatment in 1976, and the US Supreme Court did not recognise a federal constitutional right to refuse life-sustaining treatment until 1990.[48] Just as the Supreme Court waited until there were many reassuring years of experience with the withdrawal of treatment before recognising a constitutional right to refuse life-sustaining care, so did the public wait until there were many reassuring years of experience with treatment withdrawal before extending end-of-life law to include a right to aid in dying.

Moreover, earlier voter referenda had included a right to both self-administration and physician-administration of the lethal dose of medication, and physician-administration was more controversial. These earlier referenda were proposed in Washington in 1991 and California in 1993.[49] When aid-in-dying advocates promoted a voter referendum in Oregon in 1994, they could defuse some of the opposition by promoting a right that was narrower and therefore less susceptible to misuse.

Once aid-in-dying advocates found a successful legislative blueprint in Oregon, it made sense to propose the same approach in other states. If Oregon voters were comfortable with a right for competent, terminally ill adults, so might voters in other states. Similarly, if Oregon was comfortable with a self-administration model for aid in dying, so might other states. When one compares aid-in-dying legislation from state to state, the similarities greatly outweigh the differences. In all of the legalising states, the patient must be an adult possessing decision-making capacity. In all of the states, the patient must be terminally ill, with terminal illness defined as a life

---

[47] In Oregon, around 90 per cent of aid-in-dying patients are enrolled in hospice care: Oregon Health Authority, 'Oregon Death with Dignity Act 2019', 10. Thanks to Thaddeus Pope for suggesting this point.
[48] *Cruzan v. Director, Missouri Department of Health*, 497 US 261 (1990) ('*Cruzan*').
[49] Hall et al., *Health Care Law and Ethics*, 583, 604.

expectancy no longer than six months. In all of the legalising states, a second physician must confirm that the patient possesses decision-making capacity and has a terminal illness. And in almost all of the legalising states, either physician must refer the patient for an evaluation by a mental health professional if there is reason to think that the patient's judgement is impaired by a psychological condition. Hawaii is the one state requiring a psychological evaluation in all cases.[50]

The statutory similarities extend to the procedural steps for exercising the right to aid in dying. In each state, the patient must request aid in dying at least twice, with the second request at least fifteen days after the first request. And in each state, the patient must make at least one of the requests in writing.

There are several variations. For example, Vermont added an additional waiting period of forty-eight hours to the standard fifteen-day waiting period for a total of seventeen days[51] while Hawaii requires a twenty-day waiting period between the initial and confirming requests.[52] Some states require the patient to 'ingest' the lethal medication, while other states only require the patient to 'take' or 'administer' the drugs.[53] In states that allow the patient to take or administer the lethal medication, that might permit the use of intravenous administration, as long as the patient opens the flow of the fluid into the catheter.[54]

Likely, the experience in Oregon with aid in dying encouraged later adoptions in other states. While initially, concerns were raised that patients would turn to aid in dying rather than more appropriate palliative care or that vulnerable patients would be at risk, the data from Oregon and other states have been reassuring. In Oregon, about one-half of 1 per cent of deaths occur via aid in dying, and aid-in-dying patients are comparable to other dying patients in terms of their sex, race, health insurance coverage and hospice enrolment. Moreover, aid-in-dying patients tend to have higher levels of education than other dying patients.[55]

Also, patients who desired aid in dying, such as Brittany Maynard, and their family members became effective advocates for adoption of a right. Maynard may have been especially influential. Young at age twenty-nine, articulate and attractive when she became terminally ill with brain cancer, Maynard became an eloquent proponent of a right to aid in dying. By the time of her death in November 2014 by aid in

[50] Our Care, Our Choice Act 2018, Haw Rev Stat § 327L-6 (2018) (Hawaii).
[51] Patient Choice and Control at End of Life Act, 18 Vt Stat Ann §§ 5283(a)(2), (a)(12) (2013) (Vermont).
[52] Our Care, Our Choice Act 2018, Haw Rev Stat § 327L-2(1) (2018) (Hawaii).
[53] Compare End-of-Life Options Act, Colo Rev Stat § 25-48-102(7) (2016) (Colorado) (aid in dying allows the patient to 'self-administer' the medication) with An Act to Enact the Maine Death with Dignity Act, 22 Me Rev Stat Ann § 2140(2)(L) (2019) (Maine) (allowing a patient 'to voluntarily ingest medication to end the ... patient's life in a humane and dignified manner').
[54] Intravenous administration has not been tried, but it is being discussed. See for example, Thaddeus Mason Pope, 'Medical Aid in Dying: Six Variations among U.S. State Laws' (2021) 14 (1) *Journal of Health and Life Sciences Law* 25–59.
[55] Orentlicher, Pope and Rich, 'Changing Legal Climate,' 1962.

dying, more than nine million people had viewed one of her videos. As Barbara Coombs-Lee, one of the leaders of the aid-in-dying movement, observed, 'Brittany Maynard is transformative for our movement. I've never felt this energy or seen this level of engagement in any of our campaigns.'[56] Maynard resided in California when she fell ill, and her family moved to Oregon where she would have access to aid in dying. At that time, only Oregon, Washington, and Vermont had passed enabling legislation. In the following year, her home state of California legalised aid in dying, with Colorado, DC, Hawaii, Maine and New Jersey following suit over the next few years.

But why did it take until 2008 – fourteen years after Oregon's adoption – for the second aid-in-dying law to pass? One might expect other states to wait some time for reassurance from Oregon's experience with legalised aid in dying, and legal challenges to the Oregon statute delayed its implementation until after a second voter referendum in 1997.[57] In addition, the federal government may have discouraged future adoptions with its challenge to the practice of aid in dying. While the US Justice Department initially did not object to physicians using federally controlled prescription drugs for aid in dying, the Justice Department changed course in 2001. The US Attorneys General in the George W. Bush Administration took the view that the federal Controlled Substances Act[58] made it illegal for physicians to comply with a patient's request for aid in dying. In 2006, the Supreme Court rejected that argument, holding that the Act does not give the Attorney General authority to declare 'illegitimate a medical standard for care and treatment of patients that is specifically authorized under state law'.[59] Two years later, Washington became the second state with a statute permitting aid in dying, and since then, the pace of adoption has quickened.

The chilling effect of federal policy also may help explain why adoption of a right to aid in dying has occurred almost exclusively through ballot referenda or legislative action rather than judicial decisions. Once the US Supreme Court rejected a right to aid in dying in 1997,[60] state supreme courts followed the Court's lead in rejecting a right to aid in dying under their state constitutions.[61] The state courts could have invoked common law principles, as they did for the right to refuse treatment, but they faced statutory bans on assisted suicide that pointed in the opposite direction.

---

[56] Josh Sanburn, 'Brittany Maynard Could Revive the Stalled "Death with Dignity" Movement', *Time*, 2 November 2014, https://time.com/3551089/brittany-maynard-death-with-dignity/.

[57] Hall et al., *Health Care Law and Ethics*, 594.

[58] Controlled Substances Act, 21 USC §§ 801–904 (2001).

[59] *Gonzales v. Oregon*, 546 US 243 (2006) at 258. For discussion of this history, see Hall et al., *Health Care Law and Ethics*, 597. Thanks to Kathryn Tucker for suggesting this factor.

[60] *Glucksberg*, 521 US 702 (1997).

[61] Erwin Chemerinsky, 'State Constitutions as the Future for Civil Rights' (2018) 48 *New Mexico Law Review* 259–66 at 264–5.

FUTURE OF AID IN DYING IN THE UNITED STATES

If the legalisation of aid in dying so far has reflected a refinement of legal rules rather than a change in society's moral views, what does that suggest for future changes in end-of-life law? Will the right to aid in dying extend to patients who are not terminally ill? Will US law allow administration of the lethal medication by health care providers?

First, the recent acceleration in adoption by states and the reassuring experience with aid in dying in Oregon and other states suggests that more states will enact a right to aid in dying. While some objections to aid in dying were based on its inherent aspects, such as the 'active' causing of a person's death, other objections were based on the risks to vulnerable populations or other misuse. As those risks have not materialised, the public becomes more receptive to legalisation. And at some point, specifically when a majority of states recognise a right to aid in dying, it becomes much more likely that the US Supreme Court will give the right consti-tutional status. When the Court rejected such a right in the *Glucksberg* case, the Justices rested their decision in large part on the ground that states widely prohibited the practice.[62] When a practice gains widespread approval, on the other hand, the Court cites that approval as a basis for recognising a constitutional right. In the Court's view, the fact that a practice has received broad acceptance is evidence of its importance. That is, if a right has fundamental value, then one would expect to see the right widely recognised.[63] Thus, when the Court recognised a right to refuse life-sustaining treatment in the *Cruzan* case, the Justices observed that state after state had concluded that the common law doctrine of informed consent encompassed a right to refuse unwanted medical treatment.[64]

Regarding extension of the right to aid in dying to patients who are not terminally ill, it is certainly the case that patients may suffer greatly from serious and irreversible illness before their life expectancy drops to less than six months. End-of-life prin-ciples therefore would support a broader right to aid in dying. But as discussed, it is not sufficient to show that under a system of case-by-case analyses, we would find many non-terminally ill patients eligible for aid in dying. Rather the question is whether there is a good bright-line rule to replace the terminal illness requirement. Of course, terminal illness could be defined as a life-expectancy of one year or less rather than six months or less, but estimates likely would become less reliable. Alternatively, perhaps there might be blood tests, diagnostic scans or other objective metrics that could be used to identify an additional group of patients who suffer

---

[62] *Glucksberg*, 521 US 702 (1997) at 716–19.

[63] When it comes to equal protection, on the other hand, widely accepted practices cut in the other direction. That is, if a racial minority or other class of persons is subject to persistent and broad discrimination, that leads courts to use the Equal Protection Clause to eliminate rather than validate the practice.

[64] *Cruzan*, 497 US 261 (1990) at 270–7.

greatly from serious and irreversible illness. If so, then it would be feasible to broaden the eligibility rules for aid in dying.

Might aid-in-dying law ultimately parallel treatment-withdrawal law and allow aid in dying for all patients, regardless of their prognosis? That is, individuals would not need to have a terminal illness to choose aid in dying. That certainly would satisfy the need for a bright-line rule. But it would not satisfy the need to limit choices that would shorten life to patients who are suffering greatly from a serious and irreversible illness. Society would worry about people choosing aid in dying because of a treatable depression or during a temporary condition of despair.

As for allowing administration of the lethal drug by health care providers, there are good arguments on both sides. On one hand, it is reasonable to think that the other safeguards for aid in dying are sufficient to protect against misuse of the practice. If patients must be terminally ill and mentally competent, then the difference between self-administration and physician-administration should not raise concerns about aid-in-dying rules deviating from end-of-life principles. Rather, allowing provider-administration would ensure that the terminally ill patient who is too debilitated to self-administer would still have recourse to an important measure for the relief of suffering. Moreover, experience with aid in dying has shown that there are fewer complications with provider-administration. Accordingly, in Canada, where self-administration and provider-administration are both permitted, some health care institutions only will offer provider-administration to their patients.[65] Provider-administration also can help ensure that the patient possesses decision-making capacity not only at the time a prescription is written but also later when the lethal medication is given.

On the other hand, it may be that the requirement of self-administration serves an important role in reinforcing the requirement that patients give truly voluntary consent to aid in dying. Patients who retain some residual ambivalence about their aid-in-dying choice may be more hesitant to postpone or cancel a scheduled provider-administration of the lethal medication than to stay their own hand. And recall that 35 per cent of aid-in-dying patients in Oregon who receive a prescription for the lethal medication do not end up taking it. Of course, a similar concern exists with the withdrawal of life-sustaining treatment. Patients might remain ambivalent even after agreeing to a withdrawal. With withdrawals, though, there often is time for reconsideration. The patients who stop dialysis or artificial feeding will still have a few days or longer to change their minds.

There are other potential evolutions in aid in dying law in the United States to consider. Some would entail expanding the class of patients eligible for the practice;

---

[65] David Orentlicher, 'Should the Right to Aid in Dying Include a Right to Euthanasia?' (2018) *Jotwell*, https://health.jotwell.com/should-the-right-to-aid-in-dying-include-a-right-to-euthanasia/.

others would involve changes in the procedural steps required before implementing a person's choice of aid in dying.

As to changes in eligibility, states might relax the requirement that patients be adults with decision-making capacity to include any person possessing decision-making capacity. That is, the government might allow some adolescents – 'mature minors' – the option of aid in dying. Such a change would not only be consistent with underlying principle, but also with the legal framework employed to reflect those principles. As discussed, the goal of end-of-life law is to permit life-shortening decisions for persons who are suffering greatly from serious and irreversible illness. That can happen to people before they reach the age of eighteen. And there would not be any relaxation of the requirement that the patient possess decision-making capacity.

Still, it seems unlikely that there would be widespread extension of aid in dying to mature minors. As scientists learn more about neurologic development, they are finding that decision-making capacity continues to evolve after age eighteen and also after age twenty-one.[66] Moreover, while most states allow minors to agree to a number of medical interventions, these generally are decisions for which it is clearly in the minor's interest to receive care, as for contraception or treatment for sexually transmitted diseases, drug abuse or mental illness.[67] While some states have recognised a right to refuse life-sustaining treatment for mature minors, it is still a limited number of states.[68] States have not developed a robust mature minor doctrine for decisions that would shorten life.

For another way to extend the right to aid in dying, the law might allow patients to use an advance directive to indicate their wishes for aid in dying if they become terminally ill and also lack decision-making capacity. Just as many people want to leave instructions on when to discontinue life-sustaining treatment, they also may wish to leave instructions on when to provide aid in dying. Or they might want to authorise a family member or other surrogate decision-maker to choose aid in dying for them once they become terminally ill.

Advance directives for aid in dying would only make sense if the requirement for self-administration was relaxed to allow for administration by a physician or other person. Even then, it is not clear that there would be a significant need for aid in dying by advance directive. By the time patients have become both terminally ill and lost decision-making capacity, they probably are dependent on a life-sustaining treatment that could be withheld.

---

[66] Leah H. Somerville, 'Searching for Signatures of Brain Maturity: What Are We Searching For? (2016) 92 *Neuron* 1164–7.

[67] Sidni Katz, 'A Minor's Right to Die with Dignity: The Ultimate Act of Love, Compassion, Mercy, and Civil Liberty' (2018) 48 *California Western International Law Journal* 219–46 at 219, 235.

[68] Ann Eileen Driggs, 'The Mature Minor Doctrine: Do Adolescents Have the Right to Die?' (2011) 11 *Health Matrix* 687–717 at 696–702.

Procedural reforms seem more likely. For example, it probably is not necessary to require a fifteen-day waiting period between the original request for aid in dying and the receipt of a prescription for the lethal medication. For many terminally ill patients, that may foreclose the opportunity to exercise the aid-in-dying option. Hence, Oregon has revised its statute to waive the waiting period when the patient's attending physician believes that the patient will die during the waiting period.[69] Similar changes seem likely in other states.

Similarly, it seems likely that health care providers other than physicians will be able to write prescriptions for the aid-in-dying medication. In its legislation, Canada included nurse practitioners along with physicians as having authority to provide aid-in-dying services,[70] and that makes sense elsewhere, particularly in areas that, like parts of Canada, are rural and have limited access to physician providers.

CONCLUSION

Since Oregon adopted the United States's first aid-in-dying law, controversy over legalisation has settled down considerably. While opponents of aid in dying still fight efforts to permit the practice, the pace of law reform has quickened in recent years. In addition, the issue does not attract the same degree of attention that it has in the past. The Oregon Health Authority issues annual reports on aid in dying in the state, and the *New England Journal of Medicine* published articles with summaries of the first two reports in 1999 and 2000.[71] For the next three years, the reports generated letters to the editor in the *Journal*.[72] Now, the annual reports barely get noticed.[73]

The diminution in controversy may reflect a few considerations. As many scholars have long argued, if the goal of end-of-life care is to relieve patient suffering, then it should not matter whether a patient dies from the withdrawal of a ventilator or from the ingestion of a lethal dose of medication. Indeed, aid in dying often can provide

---

[69] Death with Dignity Act, Or Rev Stat § 127.840(2) (1994) (Oregon).
[70] Orentlicher, 'International Perspectives', 6.
[71] Arthur E. Chin, Katrina Hedberg, Grant K. Higginson and David W. Fleming, 'Legalized Physician Assisted Suicide in Oregon: The First Year's Experience' (1999) 340 *New England Journal of Medicine* 577–83; Amy D. Sullivan, Katrina Hedberg and David W. Fleming, 'Legalized Physician-Assisted Suicide in Oregon – The Second Year' (2000) 342 *New England Journal of Medicine* 598–604.
[72] Katrina Hedberg, David Hopkins and Melvin Kohn, 'Five Years of Legal Physician-Assisted Suicide in Oregon' (2003) 348 *New England Journal of Medicine* 961–4; Katrina Hedberg, David Hopkins and Karen Southwick, 'Legalized Physician-Assisted Suicide in Oregon, 2001' (2002) 346 *New England Journal of Medicine* 450–2; Amy D. Sullivan, Katrina Hedberg and David Hopkins, 'Legalized Physician-Assisted Suicide in Oregon, 1998–2000' (2001) 344 *New England Journal of Medicine* 605–7.
[73] Summaries of the reports were published after years ten and twenty of aid in dying in Oregon: Katrina Hedberg and Craig New, 'Oregon's Death with Dignity Act: 20 Years of Experience to Inform the Debate' (2017) 167 *Annals of Internal Medicine* 579–83; Katrina Hedberg, David Hopkins, Richard Leman and Melvin Kohn, 'The 10-Year Experience of Oregon's Death with Dignity Act: 1998–2007' (2009) 20 *Journal of Clinical Ethics* 124–32.

greater relief of suffering than withdrawal of treatment,[74] as in the case of a patient with chronic kidney failure whose refusal of further dialysis may be followed by several days or more of discomfort. In addition, as mentioned, the experience in Oregon with aid in dying has proved reassuring in terms of the fears about misuse of the practice. A small number of patients use aid in dying – less than a per cent of those who die each year – it isn't used disproportionately by vulnerable populations, and it has become a supplement rather than a replacement for palliative care.

Moving forward, we can expect the right to aid in dying to become solidified in the United States, with more states permitting the practice, and the courts ultimately giving it constitutional status. Nevertheless, we also can expect US aid-in-dying law to retain a distinctive American character. While the public in other countries, such as the Netherlands, are comfortable with case-by-case, more subjective judgements as to when medications may be administered to shorten a patient's life, people in the United States are more comfortable with bright line, more objective rules that expand patient autonomy at the end of life without inviting others to decide when a patient's quality of life no longer makes living worthwhile.

POSTSCRIPT

In April 2021, New Mexico became the latest US state to legalise aid in dying, and it did so via legislative enactment.[75] As in other states, New Mexico requires aid-in-dying patients to be adults who are terminally ill, possess decision-making capacity, and are able to self-administer the lethal dose of medication.

As predicted by this chapter, New Mexico also relaxed some of the procedural safeguards. For example, the statute retains Oregon's waiting period of 48 hours between the time the aid-in-dying prescription is written and the time the prescription may be filled, but eliminates the 15-day waiting period between the initial request for aid in dying and the time the prescription may be written. The requirement for confirmation by a second physician also is less stringent. If the patient is enrolled in a Medicare-certified hospice program, confirmation by a second physician is not required. Finally, prescriptions may be written by nurse practitioners and physician assistants in addition to physicians.

Other states, such as Massachusetts and Nevada, may legalise aid in dying in 2021. Legislative proposals in those two states closely track the Oregon model.

[74] Rachels, 'Active and Passive Euthanasia', 78.
[75] Elizabeth Whitefield End-of-Life Options Act, H.B. 47, 55th Legis. (2021) (New Mexico).

8

The Medical Regulator as Law Reformer

Québec's Act Respecting End-of-Life Care

Mona Gupta*

INTRODUCTION

Law reform, in the sense of changing the law, necessarily passes through the hands of the legislator either in the sense of deciding to act by creating laws or deciding not to act.[1] Yet, understanding law reform in a given context must take into consideration the factors that led to the legislator's decisions. This chapter will focus on an actor who rarely receives much attention in the context of legislative change in end-of-life care: the medical regulator.

In Canada, a country of ten provinces and three territories, medical regulation occurs at the provincial and territorial levels. Each Canadian province and territory has its own regulatory authority for physicians. All physicians in Canada, including postgraduate medical trainees, must be licensed by their jurisdictional regulatory authority. The regulators ensure that individuals who apply for licenses to practise medicine fulfil their requirements. Once licensed, physicians become members of the regulated professional group, namely the College of Physicians and Surgeons in their province or territory. The regulator sets out policies, rules and standards designed to protect the public by ensuring safe and ethical medical practice. The regulator also maintains responsibility to discipline those members who fail to respect its policies, rules, and standards and ultimately has the authority to revoke a member's license to practise medicine.

Although not necessarily setting out to play a role in law reform as such, the medical regulator in Québec (le Collège des Médecins du Québec, hereafter the

* I am grateful to Yves Robert, Michèle Marchand and Véronique Hivon who gave their time generously to help me to understand the role of the CMQ leading to the passage of Québec's Act Respecting End-of-Life Care. I also wish to thank Vanessa Arviset for her assistance in preparing this manuscript.
[1] Of course, law can also be reformed by courts, as illustrated by the case of *Carter* v. *Canada (Attorney General)* [2015] 1 SCR 331 ('*Carter*'), which is considered in more detail in Chapter 2.

'CMQ') engaged in a process of critical reflection which led to it taking a position on the medical profession's potential involvement in euthanasia. As a result, the legislator was able to introduce a bill which already had the support of the medical profession as well as a regulatory structure in place to guide practice. In this chapter, I will discuss the analysis developed by the regulator, particularly its working group in clinical ethics, as well as the unique circumstances that allowed the CMQ to play the role that it did. These include its specific responsibilities and its role in Québec society vis-à-vis other medical organisations.

An earlier chapter[2] in this book has addressed law reform on this topic in Canada. It is worth explaining why a provincial jurisdiction within Canada requires specific treatment. In Canada, certain matters fall within the powers of the federal (national) government and others to the provincial/territorial governments. The Criminal Code[3] is a matter for the federal government while jurisdiction over health care is shared between the federal and provincial/territorial governments. Prior to, and in parallel with the developments unfolding in Canada, there was a civil society process under-way in Québec concerning assisted dying.[4] However, at the time of that process, assisting dying was a criminal offence in Canada. Law reform required at a minimum, decriminalisation of such assistance by the federal government. However, Québec wished to act on its own civil society process without having to wait for the federal government to decriminalise assistance in dying. The Québec legislator created its own assisted dying regime by exercising its jurisdiction in the area of health care delivery and framing assistance in dying as a health care act. Although there may be doubts about the constitutionality of this action in light of the division of powers between the federal and provincial/territorial governments,[5] the federal government took no action to challenge Québec's jurisdiction to pass its legislation.

CHRONOLOGY OF KEY EVENTS IN QUÉBEC AND CANADA

An Act Respecting End-of-Life Care ('the Act') was passed in the National Assembly of Québec on 5 June 2014 and came into force on 10 December 2015.[6] Some would regard the ad hoc non-partisan Select Committee on Dying with Dignity which was formed by the Québec government in December 2009 as the driving force behind the legislative reform. But the formation of this Committee was preceded by several years of civil society engagement, media reporting, and unsuccessful federal private members' bills. In this chapter, I argue that one particular aspect of the civil society

---

[2] See Chapter 2 for a discussion of the reform process at the federal level in Canada.

[3] Criminal Code, RSC 1985, c. C-46 (Canada) ('Criminal Code').

[4] For detail on that process, see the chronology of events in Appendix to this chapter.

[5] Michael Watts and David Solomon, 'The Impact of *An Act Respecting End-of-Life Care*, RSQ c S-32.0001', Osler, Hoskin and Harcourt LLP, 30 December 2015, www.osler.com/en/resources/regulations/2015/the-impact-of-an-em-act-respecting-end-of-life-ca.

[6] Act Respecting End-of-Life Care, RLRQ, c. S-32.0001 (2014) (Québec).

process in Québec, namely the work undertaken by the CMQ and its working group on clinical ethics, was an essential catalyst to the legislative process that ensued.[7]

The chronology in the Appendix to this chapter summarises the key events in the timeline leading up to the coming into force of the Act. This chapter focuses on the first three years of this timeline and the manner in which the CMQ chose to frame the issues concerning assisted dying. Roughly contemporaneously were legal developments occurring in the province of British Columbia and subsequently at the level of the Supreme Court of Canada in *Carter* v. *Canada (Attorney General)* ('*Carter*').[8] In February 2015, the Supreme Court determined that specific Criminal Code provisions which considered euthanasia and assisted suicide to be criminal offences (culpable homicide and administering a noxious thing; and counselling or aiding suicide)[9] were a violation of certain rights guaranteed under the Charter of Rights and Freedoms. Preceding the Supreme Court's decision in *Carter* by eight months, the Québec Act was not a legislative response to that decision. Nevertheless, the developments in Québec and Canada – including the later passage of a Canadian law[10] concerning assisted dying that also applies in Québec – were closely connected in time and influenced each other politically.[11]

Although not the central focus of this chapter, the eligibility criteria for access to medical assistance in dying ('MAiD') in the Québec and Canadian laws are presented below. These may help to orient the reader when reference is made to one or both laws.

Québec[12]

S. 26 Only a patient who meets all of the following criteria may obtain medical aid in dying:

(1) be an insured person within the meaning of the Health Insurance Act (chapter A-29);

(2) be of full age and capable of giving consent to care;

---

[7] In a recent public address, the lawyer Jean-Pierre Ménard, who has been heavily involved in various aspects of assisted dying in Québec, including as the litigator of the Truchon-Gladu case (*Truchon* v. *Attorney General of Canada* [2019] QCCS 3792 ('*Truchon*')), acknowledged the critical role of the CMQ: 'Le droit des patients: evolution et perspectives', Colloque Annuel du CMQ: Accompagner jusqu'à la fin (Montréal: 1 November 2019).

[8] *Carter* [2015] 1 SCR 331. See Chapter 2 for a discussion of the reform process in Canada generally including the decision in *Carter*.

[9] Criminal Code ss. 222(4), 245(1) and ss. 241(1)(a) and (b) respectively.

[10] Bill C-14, An Act to Amend the Criminal Code and to Make Related Amendments to Other Acts (Medical Assistance in Dying), SC 2016, c. 3.

[11] The division of powers between the federal and provincial governments is an ongoing source of political tension in Canada. This tension is strongest in the relationship between the federal government and Québec where there has been an active separatist movement for over fifty years. Québec's regular calls for greater or exclusive powers in various areas of public policy and in some cases its unilateral action also fosters resentment by other provinces.

[12] Act Respecting End-of-Life Care, RLRQ, c. S-32.0001 (2014) (Québec).

(3) be at the end of life[13];

(4) suffer from a serious and incurable illness;

(5) be in an advanced state of irreversible decline in capability; and

(6) experience constant and unbearable physical or psychological suffering which cannot be relieved in a manner the patient deems tolerable.

Canada[14]

S. 241.2 (1) A person may receive medical assistance in dying only if they meet all of the following criteria:

(a) they are eligible – or, but for any applicable minimum period of residence or waiting period, would be eligible – for health services funded by a government in Canada;

(b) they are at least 18 years of age and capable of making decisions with respect to their health;

(c) they have a grievous and irremediable medical condition;

(d) they have made a voluntary request for medical assistance in dying that, in particular, was not made as a result of external pressure; and

(e) they give informed consent to receive medical assistance in dying after having been informed of the means that are available to relieve their suffering, including palliative care.

Grievous and Irremediable Medical Condition

(2) A person has a grievous and irremediable medical condition only if they meet all of the following criteria:

(a) they have a serious and incurable illness, disease or disability;

(b) they are in an advanced state of irreversible decline in capability;

(c) that illness, disease or disability or that state of decline causes them enduring physical or psychological suffering that is intolerable to them and that cannot be relieved under conditions that they consider acceptable; and

(d) their natural death has become reasonably foreseeable, taking into account all of their medical circumstances, without a prognosis necessarily having been made as to the specific length of time that they have remaining.[15]

---

[13] This criterion was invalidated in the 2019 Québec Superior Court decision in *Truchon* [2019] QCCS 3792.

[14] Criminal Code.

[15] This criterion was invalidated in the 2019 Québec Superior Court in *Truchon* [2019] QCCS 3792. Bill C-7 was introduced in response to the *Truchon* decision: Bill C-7, An Act to Amend the Criminal Code (Medical Assistance in Dying), SC 2021, c. 2 ('Bill C-7'). Now that Bill C-7

COLLÈGE DES MÉDECINS DU QUÉBEC ('CMQ')

In this section I will discuss the role of the medical regulator in the civil society process preceding the creation of Québec's Select Committee on the Question of Dying with Dignity. But first, Table 8.1 shows the relationship between the CMQ and the host of other professional organisations to which physicians are required to belong or may choose to belong. Table 8.1 also sets out the equivalent organisation for the other Canadian provinces and territories for comparative purposes.

TABLE 8.1 *The relationship of the individual physician to provincial/territorial and national medical associations in Canada compared to their corresponding organisations in Québec*

Canada	Québec
Obligatory Membership	
Colleges of Physicians and Surgeons	Collège des Médecins du Québec
Provincial/Territorial Medical Associations (obligatory membership in certain provinces)	Fédération des Médecins Spécialistes du Québec (FMSQ) or Fédération des Médecins Omnipracticiens du Québec (FMOQ)
	Provincial Specialty Association
Voluntary Membership	
Canadian Medical Association	Canadian Medical Association
National Specialty Societies	National Specialty Societies
Provincial Specialty Association	
Provincial/Territorial Medical Associations (voluntary membership in certain provinces)	

The Medical Regulator in Québec

Amongst the provincial and territorial regulators, the CMQ plays a distinct role in mediating between the medical profession and the public. There are three ways in which the CMQ's role is different compared to its counterparts in other provinces/ territories. First, the CMQ acts, and is perceived by many, as speaking on behalf of the medical profession in Québec. For example, its public-facing website counts ten principal functions of which the last is particularly noteworthy:[16]

---

has passed, a person no longer has to meet the criterion of their natural death being reasonably foreseeable under section 241.2(2) of the Criminal Code to be eligible.

[16] Collège des Médecins du Québec, 'College's Mission: Quality Medicine at the Service of the Public', CMQ, 8 July 2020, www.cmq.org/page/en/mission.aspx.

- Monitors and assesses medical practice in Québec
- Makes recommendations in order to improve medical practice in Québec
- Receives and responds to complaints from the public
- Ensures and promotes the maintenance of physician competence
- Verifies the competence of future physicians and their fitness to practise medicine
- Issues permits and authorisations to practise
- Monitors the illegal practice of medicine
- Collaborates with other professional orders in order to maximise the deployment of health and social services provided to Québecers
- Develops practice guides and guidelines
- **Takes a position, including in the media, on various health topics**

While the other Colleges generally restrict their functions to those typically associated with regulation (licensure, quality assurance, and discipline), the role of position-taking, particularly in the media, is usually assumed by the provincial and territorial medical associations ('PTMAs'). The distinction between these two types of organizations is important: the PTMAs represent the interests of physicians, including in their collective bargaining with provincial governments concerning physician remuneration while the regulators act to protect the public. When the regulator takes a position regarding a health care practice, it must do so in the public's interest whereas when the PTMAs take a position, they are acting in physicians' interests (notwithstanding the fact that, on some issues, these sets of interests may overlap). A further division exists, namely that in each province outside Québec, the physicians' interest group takes the form of a single medical association for the family physicians and specialists of that province while in Québec the specialists and family physicians each have their own association ('FMSQ' and 'FMOQ', respectively). Neither group can speak for all Québec physicians creating space for the CMQ to be perceived as a single voice for the medical profession.[17]

Second, the CMQ has its own Code de Déontologie which serves as both a Code of Ethics (in advocating aspirational values and principles) as well as a Code of Conduct (in prescribing required duties or behaviours). This Code serves as the disciplinary standard for CMQ members, that is, all disciplinary actions undertaken by the regulator are in reference to breaches of its Code. Other provinces and territories rely on the Code of Ethics and Professionalism developed by the Canadian Medical Association ('CMA') as their disciplinary standard.[18] In practical

---

[17] There was a PTMA in Québec for all physicians called the Québec Medical Association. This was a much smaller, voluntary organisation that was not involved in collective bargaining. This organisation was disbanded in 2019.

[18] The CMA is a voluntary professional association. Its role is to 'unite physicians' and to engage in advocacy in the interests of health and the health care system. The CMA distinguishes its

terms, this means that the CMQ not only engages in the surveillance of practice but it establishes the very standards it oversees. The CMQ, therefore, plays a greater role in defining what constitutes good medical practice than the other regulators. Third, the CMQ is the only regulator in Canada that has a standing committee in clinical ethics[19] whose mandate is to respond to clinical ethical problems encountered by its members and to identify practical solutions to guide their practice.

It is within this organisational context that the CMQ chose the theme of assisted dying for its annual meeting on 12 May 2006. In the years preceding the meeting, there had been several cases of individuals assisting their loved ones to end their lives and who subsequently faced criminal prosecution.[20] The CMQ was also aware that there were individual practitioners hastening the deaths of dying patients under their care without guidance or constraints.[21] The risks to members of the public as well as to physicians fell squarely within the regulatory mandate, that is, public protection through practice guidance. Thus, the CMQ initiated an open discussion about assisted dying under its own aegis. A panel discussion at the meeting featured a well-known journalist, a researcher studying public views about assisted dying, a physician specialising in the care of elderly patients and palliative care, as well as a sitting federal politician who had herself one year earlier proposed a private member's bill in support of assisted dying. It was at this event that the journalist, Benoit Dutrizac, remarked upon the unique role of the CMQ:

> Mais si je ne me trompe, vous voulez être le pilier central du système de santé? Alors, agissez en conséquence. Vous êtes un lobby fort. La population a besoin et a le droit de savoir à quelle enseigne vous logez sur ce sujet crucial. Si un groupe comme le vôtre ne prend pas la parole et ne participe pas au débat sur l'euthanasie et le suicide assisté, qui le fera?
>
> But if I'm not mistaken, you want to be the central pillar of the healthcare system? Then act like it. You have a lot of influence. The public needs to know and is entitled to know what your position is on this crucial topic. If a group like you does not speak up and does not participate in the debate on euthanasia and assisted suicide, who will? *(translated by author)*

Here Dutrizac illustrates the public perception of the CMQ not only as the guardian of the quality of *established* practices but also to actively lead the profession towards *new* practices in the public interest.

---

role from that of its provincial affiliates (the PTMAs) by working on issues in which there is clear overlap between professional and public interests.

[19] The British Columbia College does have a standing committee that covers Patient Relations, Professional Standards, and Ethics.

[20] See for example the case of Marielle Houle: CBC News, 'No Jail Time for Woman Who Helped Son Commit Suicide', *CBC*, 27 January 2006, www.cbc.ca/news/canada/montreal/no-jail-time-for-woman-who-helped-son-commit-suicide-1.596806. See also, the case of André Bergeron: *R v. Bergeron* [2006] RJQ 3000.

[21] Y. Robert, *Personal Communication*, 5 July 2017.

The CMQ's Working Group on Clinical Ethics

Several months after its annual meeting in November 2006, the CMQ asked its working group on clinical ethics to develop an approach to the issue of aggressive/over-treatment. The committee however, chose the wording 'appropriate care' as better reflecting the issues at stake. The committee worked for two years, studying the academic literature and hearing from various experts and practitioners. In their final report,[22] they discussed appropriate care in three kinds of circumstances in which they believed problems related to aggressive/over-treatment were most likely to emerge: severe prematurity of newborns, the care of chronic, debilitating conditions, and the end of life. In what follows, I will lay out the key features of the group's analysis specifically as they pertain to the end of life.

As a committee focused on *clinical* ethics, the participants strove to glean insights from the clinical circumstances in which requests for assistance in dying most frequently emerged, namely patients nearing the end of life. One of the group's observations was that there were exceptional cases, even with the best palliative care, in which a patient's suffering could not be relieved through existing therapeutic means. In such cases, the committee concluded that euthanasia could be considered appropriate care if it was done to relieve suffering. In arriving at this conclusion, the group drew upon the CMQ's Code de Déontologie,[23] specifically article 58 which states that, 'A physician must, when the death of a patient appears to him to be inevitable, act so that the death occurs with dignity. He must also ensure that the patient obtains the appropriate support and relief.' The group interpreted this article as meaning that physicians had a positive duty to relieve suffering at the end of life. In restricting its analysis to the end-of-life context, the group noted that there was a degree of predictability about the course of events. That is, the patient was in a situation in which death was inevitable; the patient was suffering without relief and with no further means of relieving that suffering; and that this would continue until the time of death. No specific time frame concerning the proximity to death was indicated in their analysis however, they make reference to the patient being in a 'terminal phase'.

What was the relationship between assisting dying and the theme of the group's work, namely appropriate care? The group argued that appropriate care is necessarily individualised to a given patient and proportionate to their clinical circumstances. Understood this way, trying to establish general rules of appropriate care at the end of life would not succeed. How then to know what constitutes appropriate care in a given circumstance? Appropriate care is whatever is decided at the conclusion of a 'well-led decision-making process, namely one that is characterized

---

[22] 'Le Médecin, les Soins Appropriés et le Débat sur l'Euthanasie, Document de Réflexion' (16 October 2009 Collège des Médecins du Québec).
[23] Code of Ethics of Physicians, LRQ, c. M-9, s. 3; LRQ, C-26, s. 87 (Québec).

by open communication in which each party plays his or her role and assumes his or her responsibilities'.[24] Appropriate care does not refer to any specific act or treatment but to the plan that doctor and patient arrive at together. Thus, assistance in dying, like other accepted end-of-life practices decided within the therapeutic relationship such as withdrawing and withholding treatment (including food and hydration), and palliative sedation could constitute appropriate care.

A second major concept developed by the group was to consider assistance in dying as *un soin* (a therapeutic act). For the group, clinical decisions must be guided by a *'logique de soins'*[25] (therapeutic reasons). If it is a doctor's duty to relieve suffering at the end of life, and hastening death is the only thing that will relieve that suffering, then according to a *logique de soins*, assisted dying is a therapeutic act. Furthermore, if this therapeutic act is to be carried out by physicians then it is a medical act. As the medical regulatory authority, CMQ is entitled to determine what counts as a medical act.

A final theme underlying the working group analysis was that of collective responsibility. This was not elaborated upon in its report but later by its chair, Michèle Marchand who, at the time the report was drafted, was the clinical ethicist for the CMQ. In her 2016 book, *L'aide médicale à mourir au Québec: pourquoi tant de prudence* (*Medical Assistance in Dying in Québec: Why so Prudent*),[26] Marchand explains that during the time of the group's work, Québec faced a social problem: some people were suffering terribly before death, wanted to end their suffering through a hastened death, but could not be helped to die legally. For Marchand, a social problem requires a collective response. It cannot be solved by leaving it to individuals (individual physicians) to decide whether or not they wished to respond (provide assistance in dying). Marchand considers the physician to be a moral agent at three levels: as an individual, as a member of a profession, and as a member of a collective. A physician who is asked to provide MAiD to a patient is both an individual and a professional. The individual moral agent who does not support MAiD for moral reasons can exercise an objection of conscience, but the profession's moral agent operates within a set of duties and constraints that apply to all members of the profession. Conceiving of MAiD as a *'soin'* means it is part of medical practice and consistent with professional values, allowing it to fall within the extant framework of medical regulation. As a *soin*, MAiD also becomes a collective responsibility of the health care system, a practice it is responsible for organising and providing just as for any other medical act covered under the provincial health insurance scheme. In this way, professional values can 'mediate'

[24] 'Pour des soins appropriés, au début, tout au long et en fin de vie', Rapport du groupe de travail en éthique clinique' (17 October 2008 Collège des Médecins du Québec).
[25] Ibid.
[26] Michèle Marchand, *L'aide médicale à mourir au Québec: pourquoi tant de prudence?* (Montreal: Liber, 2017).

between individual values and social values, opening up a path towards professionally sanctioned law reform.

The working group's report was approved unanimously by the Board of the CMQ in October 2009.[27] Its analysis allowed the CMQ to take the position that from the regulatory point of view, the practice of euthanasia for capable, consenting adult patients at the end of life, with a goal of relieving their suffering, would be consistent with its Code de Déontologie. This position provided an opportunity for the Québec government to act and only one month later it created the multiparty Select Committee on the Question of the Right to Die with Dignity,[28] renamed three months later as the Select Committee on the Question of Dying with Dignity.

AN ACT RESPECTING END-OF-LIFE CARE

The civil society engagement on assisted dying led by the Select Committee continued for the next four years. The Committee undertook and completed its work over a two-year period. It held twenty-nine days of public consultation in eight cities in Québec, during which it met with 239 people and organisations, heard from 114 people during the public meetings, received 6,558 responses to its online questionnaire and more than 16,000 comments by email, mail, fax, and through the online questionnaire.[29] Its members also travelled to countries that had already legalised various forms of assisted dying in order to learn more about how to structure the practice. It tabled its report in the Québec National Assembly in 2012 which initiated the next step in the process including the drafting of legislative options, a draft bill, and a consultation process on the draft bill. The bill succeeded in a free vote (94–22, no abstentions) in the National Assembly (the provincial legislature) in which it defined medical aid in dying as 'care[30] consisting in the administration by a physician of medications or substances to an end-of-life patient, at the patient's request, in order to relieve their suffering by hastening death.' At the time of this writing, Québec is the only permissive jurisdiction in the world to explicitly define MAiD as '*un soin*', although in Belgium, whose law inspired the Québec Act, it is understood as such.[31]

---

[27] 'Le Médecin, les Soins Appropriés et le Débat sur l'Euthanasie, Document de Réflexion' (16 October 2009 Collège des Médecins du Québec).

[28] 'Dying with Dignity', Report from the Select Committee on Dying with Dignity (March 2012 Québec National Assembly) 11–12.

[29] Ibid. 13.

[30] This definition appears in the English translation of the Act: Act Respecting End-of-Life Care, RLRQ, c. S-32.0001, s. 3(6) (2014) (Québec). Care is a literal translation of the French word 'soin.' It might be better translated in English medical language as a therapeutic act or intervention.

[31] Paul Vanden Berghe, Arsène Mullie, Marc Desmet and Gert Huysmans, 'Assisted Dying: The Current Situation in Flanders: Euthanasia Embedded in Palliative Care', in David Albert Jones, Chris Gastmans and Calum MacKellar (eds.), *Euthanasia and Assisted Suicide: Lessons from Belgium* (Cambridge: Cambridge University Press, 2017) 67–78.

There are several important implications of MAiD being a medical act which are found in the Act and trace their roots back to the analysis of the CMQ's working group in clinical ethics. First, medical acts are relational. Like any other medical act, MAiD should result from a decision-making process that happens in the context of a therapeutic relationship. According to this way of thinking, assisted suicide is not a relational act because the physician cannot assume their responsibilities for an act if they are not present. Assisted suicide[32] was not considered appropriate care by the group and was indeed excluded from the Act. Second, a *'soin'* is the responsibility of the health care system not of any individual practitioner. In practice, this requires appropriate administrative structures to make MAiD provision possible. Indeed, the Minister of Health mandated the creation of the Groupe Interdisciplinaire de Soutien ('GIS') at all health care institutions, including community health centres, to provide clinicoadministrative support to the clinical teams caring for patients who request MAiD.[33] The Act also attributed certain tasks to existing administrative structures (e.g. the Council of Physicians, Dentists, and Pharmacists ('CMDP') which is found at all health care institutions). In other words, a person who requests MAiD is not dependent on an individual physician who may or may not provide it but can rely on administrative structures and procedures to ensure that MAiD can be provided if they are eligible. Finally, as a therapeutic act and specifically a medical act, deviations from good practice are to be handled by the regulator. The oversight body created in the Act, the End-of-Life Care Commission, has no disciplinary authority. If it is not satisfied that an instance of MAiD was provided in accordance with the Act, it notifies the CMQ (and the CMDP if the physician works in an institutional setting).[34] It is the CMQ that is responsible for evaluating the quality of the act and if necessary notifies the authorities in case of unlawful administration.

A note of comparison to the Canadian (federal) law on MAiD eligibility is worth mentioning here. Originating from the CMQ's work, the Act focused on end-of-life care and MAiD as part of the continuum of end-of-life care. The eligible person was the dying patient. While the Act recognises respect for dignity and the autonomy of the dying patient, the Act makes no mention, as does the Canadian law, about the need to balance autonomy and vulnerability in the matter of eligibility.[35] A central aspect of the ongoing debate about access to MAiD in Canada outside Québec has hinged on whether currently excluded subgroups – mature minors, persons for

---

[32] At this stage in the evolution of the Québec legislation, assisted suicide was conceptualised as a practice in which a physician would give a patient a prescription for a lethal dose of a medication which the patient would take (or not) at some later time of his or her choosing without the presence of the physician.

[33] La Direction des communications du ministère de la Santé et des Services sociaux, 'Soins palliatifs et fin de vie: Lignes directrices pour le cheminement d'une demande d'aide médicale à mourir: Loi concernant les soins de fin de vie' (2015 Gouvernement du Québec).

[34] Act Respecting End-of-Life Care, RLRQ, c. S-32.0001 (2014) (Québec).

[35] Bill C-14, An Act to Amend the Criminal Code and to Make Related Amendments to Other Acts (Medical Assistance in Dying), SC 2016, c. 3.

whom a mental disorder is their sole underlying medical condition and people who lack decision-making capacity but requested MAiD when still capable – are so vulnerable they should remain ineligible or whether additional safeguards might mitigate their vulnerability and allow respect for autonomy. A debate specifically on these terms has not taken place in Québec. Instead the pressure to extend access has focused on whether MAiD should be permissible to those beyond the end of life. Indeed, the 2019 case which succeeded in striking down the Canadian eligibility criterion of 'natural death reasonably foreseeable' (and the Québec eligibility criterion of 'end of life') was brought by two physically disabled persons in Québec.[36]

LESSONS FOR LAW REFORM

In this chapter, I have described the work of the medical regulator in Québec whose procedural choices and substantive positions ensured that its work became central to the ensuing law reform process. The CMQ's decisions offer a novel perspective on law reform.

The regulator chose to involve its working group in clinical ethics which included both physicians and non-physicians, a standing committee that had studied other difficult questions and had experience drafting guidance for members. This enabled the regulator to sidestep the exceptionalism often associated with assisted dying, namely that assistance in dying is a complete rupture with existing medical practice. This opened up the possibility of seeing the problem in continuity with other ethically challenging questions in clinical practice. The group chose to work from the bottom up, that is, from the insights gleaned from clinical practice. This was both intentional (so as to try to frame the discussion in a less polarising manner) and fruitful as it oriented the discussion to those circumstances in which physicians could agree they encountered a clinical problem. This process allowed for an alternative narrative (*'une logique de soins'*) to the traditional legal or philosophical euthanasia debate to emerge. Indeed, in its later communications, the CMQ characterised the traditional legal narrative – *'une logique de droit'* – as one that is rights and autonomy-based. It explained to its members that the legislator had to reconcile these two narratives, a *'logique de soins'* with a *'logique de droit,'* and would have to continue to do so in the face of public pressure to expand access.[37] This message served a dual role: as a reminder to physicians that the profession was now committed to assisted dying, but also to the legislator not to forget the integral role played by the medical profession's support of this social project.

Long before any concrete steps had been taken by the legislator, the CMQ's involvement permitted the profession to become a key player in the ensuing civil society process and pre-emptively structure the practice for physicians. More

---

[36] *Truchon* [2019] QCCS 3792.
[37] Yves Robert, 'Vers la mort à la carte?', 10 May 2017, Collège des Médecins du Québec, www .cmq.org/nouvelle/fr/vers-la-mort-a-la-carte.aspx.

specifically, its proposal to frame assisted dying as a therapeutic act ensured a certain degree of administrative support from within the health care system. In this way, the medical profession became more than a stakeholder in a process of law reform but a driver of reform itself, its work inciting and facilitating the legislative process for permitting this new medical act. This in turn eased acceptance of MAiD by the members of the medical profession which was necessary in order to achieve successful implementation of the Act. The legislator could count on the fact that the primary group being asked to apply the law were in support of it, at least as a collectivity. That said, it is worth mentioning that even five years later only 3 per cent of Québec's approximately 20,000 physicians actually provide MAiD, 80 per cent of whom are family physicians.[38]

Despite their very different trajectories, the Québec and Canadian laws are quite similar. Why might this be the case? It might mean that clinical, ethical and legal perspectives on a problem can converge on a similar solution even with distinct background analyses. But if that is true, does the background analysis matter? As Québec embarks on a new chapter in its debate about access to MAiD outside of the end of life in light of *Truchon*, and following its own initiative to permit advance requests,[39] the public response repeatedly references the extensive civil society consultation that preceded the original law as an example of good democratic process. Once again, the CMQ has been at the forefront engaging physicians and the public in the debate.[40] Contrary to those observers who believe the judicial process is the best (or only)[41] pathway to law reform in end-of-life care, Québec's recent history shows that other civil society actors – particularly the medical profession – have a morally and socially relevant leadership role to play.

---

[38] Michel A. Bureau, 'Commission sur les soins de fin de vie: Situations des soins de fin de vie au Québec 2015–2019', Forum national sur l'évolution de la Loi concernant les soins de fin de vie (27 January 2020 Commission sur les soins de fin de vie), www.msss.gouv.qc.ca/professionnels/documents/forum-national-soins-de-fin-de-vie/forum-evolution-LCSFV-pleniere-1.pdf.

[39] 'L'aide médicale à mourir pour les personnes en situation d'inaptitude: le juste équilibre entre le droit à l'autodétermination, la compassion et la prudence', Report from Le Groupe d'experts sur la question de l'inaptitude et l'aide médicale à mourir (29 November 2019 Government of Québec, Minister for Health and Social Services), www.msss.gouv.qc.ca. See also the comments made by Danielle McCann (the then Health Minister for Québec) in response to the Report from 'Le Groupe d'experts sur la question de l'inaptitude et l'aide médicale à mourir': CBC News, 'Québec to Expand Law on Medically Assisted Dying, Look at Advance Consent', *CBC*, 29 November 2019, www.cbc.ca/news/canada/montreal/medical-assistance-in-death-report-1.5377890.

[40] Ariane Lacoursière, 'Aide médicale à mourir et troubles mentaux graves : un délai à prévoir', *La Presse*, 23 January 2020, www.lapresse.ca/actualites/sante/202001/22/01-5257899-aide-medicale-a-mourir-et-troubles-mentaux-graves-un-delai-a-prevoir.php.

[41] At the plenary opening session of the conference that gave rise to this volume (2nd International Conference on End of Life Law, Ethics, Policy and Practice (Halifax: 13 September 2017)), Joe Arvay, the lead counsel in the *Carter* case stated that the best way of achieving progressive law reform is through the courts.

Appendix: Chronology[*]

2006	Legislative path	Judicial path	Expert input
			08/2006 Québec: CMQ working group on clinical ethics undertakes a project concerning appropriate care at the end of life.[1]
	04/12/2009 Québec: Select Committee on Dying with Dignity formed by Québec government.	**15/06/2012** British Columbia Supreme Court finds that criminalization of assisted dying in specific circumstances violates the rights to life, liberty and security of the person as well as the right to equality guaranteed by the Canadian Charter of Rights and Freedoms in *Carter* v. *Canada (Attorney General)* [2012] BCSC 886.	
			16/10/2009 Québec: Working Group Report adopted unanimously by the CMQ Board.[2]
	22/03/2012 Québec: Select Committee publishes its report (in which it recasts euthanasia as 'medical aid in dying').[4]	**10/10/2013** British Columbia Court of Appeal allows the appeal of *Carter* v. *Canada (Attorney General)* [2013] BCCA 435 against the decision of the lower court.	**16/10/2009** Québec: CMQ position, that euthanasia could constitute appropriate care at the end of life in exceptional cases, is made public.[3]
	12/06/2013 Québec: Draft bill presented; further consultation sought.	**06/02/2015** *Carter* v. *Canada (Attorney General)* [2015] 1 SCR 331 judgement rendered at the Supreme Court of Canada. The Court invalidates the Criminal Code provisions preventing assisted dying in certain circumstances. The declaration of invalidity is suspended for one year.	**15/01/2013** Québec: Committee of legal experts submits its report to the government on legislative options for implementing Select Committee recommendations.[5]
	05/06/2014 Québec: Bill passes in National Assembly on a free (conscience) vote.		**11/2017** Québec: Québec government convenes an Expert Panel on the question of incapacity and medical assistance in dying.
	10/12/2015 Québec: An Act Respecting End-of-Life Care comes into force (AREOLC).[6]	**15/01/2016** The Supreme Court grants a four-month extension at the Federal government's request but allows individuals to seek court-authorised exemptions from suspension of invalidity during that time: *Carter* v. *Canada (Attorney General)* [2016] 1 SCR 13.	**29/11/2019** Québec: Report of the Expert Panel on the Question of Incapacity and MAiD is made public.[10] The Report recommends that the Québec law permit access to MAiD for those who become incapable following the determination of their eligibility and that people be permitted to make an advance request for MAiD once they have been diagnosed with a serious condition that will lead to decisional incapacity during the course of illness.
	17/06/2016 Canada: Bill C-14, An Act to Amend the Criminal Code and to Make Related Amendments to Other Acts (Medical Assistance in Dying), SC 2016, c. 3, the federal law decriminalising medical assistance in dying (MAiD) comes into force.[7]	**11/09/2019** Québec: The Quebéc Superior Court finds that the eligibility criteria 'natural death has become reasonably foreseeable' (Canada) violates the rights to life, liberty and security of the person as well as the right to equality and that the criterion 'end of life' (Québec) violates the right to equality guaranteed by the Canadian Charter of Rights and Freedoms in *Truchon* v. *Canada (Attorney General)* [2019] QCCS 3792.	
	24/02/2020 Canada: Bill C-7, An Act to Amend the Criminal Code (Medical Assistance in Dying) introduced.[13]	**11/9/2019** Québec: The declaration of invalidity is suspended for six months, until 11 March 2020.[8] This suspension was subsequently extended four times.[9]	**13/01/2020–27/01/2020** Federal public consultation on existing safeguards and advance requests initiated through an online survey. Stakeholder and professional consultations are initiated.[11]
	17/03/2021 A new Federal government Bill C-7, An Act to Amend the Criminal Code (Medical Assistance in Dying) passed and came into force.[14]		**13/01/2020–03/02/2020** Québec: Public and user consultations on expanded access to MAiD for persons with mental disorder are initiated.[12]
	31/3/2021 Québec: National Assembly creates the Select Committee on the Evolution of AREOLC.	**03/10/2019** Québec: The Québec government announces it will not appeal the decision of the Québec Superior Court. The Attorney General of Canada allows the deadline for appeal (11/10/2019) to pass.	**4/12/2020** Québec: At the request of the CMQ and the Commission Soins Fin de Vie, the Québec Psychiatric Association (AMPQ) publishes its report on MAiD MD-SUMC arguing that given the existing legal and ethical landscape, there is no reason to exclude persons with a mental illness from access.
	16/4/2021 Québec: Ministry of Health issues directive stating that in cases of divergences between the Act Respecting End-of-Life Care and C-7, the stricter law applies.		**5/5/2021** Québec: CMQ takes position that a physician who provides MAiD in accordance with the Québec or the Canadian laws will not be disciplined.
2021	**11/6/2021** Québec: Law amended to allow final consent waiver, consistent with Canada's law.		

[*] See Chapter 2 for a chronology focusing on Canadian developments at a federal level.

1 'Pour des soins appropriés, au début, tout au long et en fin de vie', Rapport du groupe de travail en éthique clinique (17 October 2008 Collège des Médecins du Québec) 6.

2 'Le Médecin, les Soins Appropriés et le Débat sur l'Euthanasie', Document de Réflexion (16 October 2009 Collège des Médecins du Québec).

3 'Le médecin, les soins appropriés et le débat sur l'euthanasie', Document de réflexion, adopté par le Conseil d'administration (16 October 2009 Collège des Médecins du Québec).

4 'Dying with Dignity', Report from the Select Committee on Dying with Dignity (March 2012 Quebec National Assembly).

5 Jean-Pierre Ménard, Michelle Giroux, Jean-Claude Hébert, 'Mettre en œuvre les recommandations de la commission spéciale de l'assemblée nationale sur la question de mourir dans la dignité', Rapport du Comité de juristes experts' (January 2013 National Assembly of Québec).

6 Act Respecting End-of-Life Care, RLRQ, c. S-32.0001 (2014) (Québec).

7 An Act to Amend the Criminal Code and to Make Related Amendments to Other Acts (Medical Assistance in Dying), SC 2016, c. 3.

8 While there were claims that the applicability of the findings were restricted to Québec, this claim is contested: *Truchon v. Canada (Attorney General)* [2020] QCCS 772 [23]–[24].

9 2 March 2020 (*Truchon v. Canada (Attorney General)* [2020] QCCS 772) Extension of suspension of declaration of invalidity and constitutional exemption granted to 22 July 2020 and allowed people who met the eligibility criteria in the Criminal Code except for reasonably foreseeable natural death to go to court to seek a judicial authorisation for access to MAiD.

29 June 2020 (*Truchon v. Canada (Attorney General)* [2020] QCCS 2019) Extension of suspension of declaration of invalidity and constitutional exemption granted to 18 December 2020 and allowed people who met the eligibility criteria in the Criminal Code except for reasonably foreseeable natural death to go to court to seek a judicial authorisation for access to MAiD.

17 December 2020 (*Truchon v. Canada (Attorney General)* [2020] QCCS 4388) Extension of suspension of declaration of invalidity and constitutional exemption granted to 26 February 2021 and allowed people who met the eligibility criteria in the Criminal Code except for reasonably foreseeable natural death to go to court to seek a judicial authorisation for access to MAiD.

25 February 2021 (*Truchon v. Canada (Attorney General)* [2021] QCCS 590) Extension of suspension of declaration of invalidity and constitutional exemption granted to 26 March 2021 and allowed people who met the eligibility criteria in the Criminal Code except for reasonably foreseeable natural death to go to court to seek a judicial authorisation for access to MAiD.

10 Ministère de la santé et des services sociaux, 'L'aide médicale à mourir pour les personnes en situation d'inaptitude: le juste équilibre entre le droit à l'autodétermination, la compassion et la prudence' (2019 Government of Québec).

11 Department of Justice Canada, 'Medical Assistance in Dying: January and February 2020 Consultations', Government of Canada, 13 March 2020, www.justice.gc.ca/eng/cons/ad-am/index.html.

12 Department of Justice Canada, 'What We Heard Report: A Public Consultation on Medical Assistance in Dying (MAID)', Government of Canada, 31 May 2020, www.justice.gc.ca/eng/cj-jp/ad-am/wwh-cqnae/index.html.

13 Bill C-7, An Act to Amend the Criminal Code (Medical Assistance in Dying), SC 2020 died on the order paper; Bill C-7 repealed the criterion 'natural death has become reasonably forseeable' and added an exclusion of mental illness from 'illness disease or disability' for the purposes of determining whether the person meets the eligibility criterion of a 'serious and incurable illness, disease or disability'. Department of Justice Canada, 'Proposed Changes to Canada's Medical Assistance in Dying Legislation', Government of Canada, 31 May 2020, www.justice.gc.ca/eng/csj-sjc/pl/ad-am/index.html.

14 Bill C-7, An Act to Amend the Criminal Code (Medical Assistance in Dying), SC 2021, c. 2. Bill C-7 includes a sunset clause on the mental illness exclusion.

9

Extrajudicial Resolution of Medical Futility Disputes

Key Factors in Establishing and Dismantling the Texas Advance Directives Act

Thaddeus Mason Pope

INTRODUCTION

Increasingly, medical and legal professionals across the world have been calling for the establishment of special adjudicatory dispute resolution mechanisms to resolve intractable end-of-life medical treatment disputes.[1] Many commentators point to the conflict resolution provisions in the 1999 Texas Advance Directives Act ('TADA').[2] They regard TADA as a leading model and template.[3] This chapter elucidates strategies for enacting legislation like TADA.

Other scholars and I have already written extensively about the fairness and constitutionality of TADA.[4] This chapter takes a different approach. It is an examination of the conditions for the rise and fall of TADA. Instead of focusing on *whether* to copy TADA, it focuses on *how* to copy it. Instead of focusing on the content and merits of TADA, I examine its origins and history. Specifically, I first discuss how Texas lawmakers enacted the statute. I then discuss why, more recently, they have been slowly dismantling it. This inquiry is valuable, because it highlights lessons for other jurisdictions considering law reform on end-of-life medical treatment.

I begin by briefly explaining how TADA's dispute resolution mechanism works. A basic and elementary understanding is sufficient because the purpose of this chapter is to identify the conditions that enabled lawmakers to enact the TADA in the first place. The reader can look elsewhere for an explanation of the law's

---

[1] Thaddeus Mason Pope, 'Procedural Due Process and Intramural Hospital Dispute Resolution Mechanisms: The Texas Advance Directives Act' (2016) 10 *Saint Louis University Journal of Health Law and Policy* 93–158.
[2] Texas Advance Directives Act, Tex Health and Safety Code § 166.046 (1999) (Texas).
[3] See Pope, 'Procedural Due Process'.
[4] See, for example, Thaddeus Mason Pope, 'The Texas Advance Directives Act: Must a Death Panel Be a Star Chamber?' (2015) 15 *American Journal of Bioethics* 41–3; Thaddeus Mason Pope, 'The Growing Power of Healthcare Ethics Committees Heightens Due Process Concerns' (2014) 15 *Cardozo Journal of Conflict Resolution* 425–47.

requirements, implementation and impact.[5] Having equipped the reader with a fundamental understanding of TADA, I then briefly examine its legislative history and identify five key factors that facilitated TADA's enactment in 1999.

Policymakers can draw law reform lessons not only from TADA's original enactment but also from its subsequent history. I therefore turn from TADA's rise to its fall. I examine how Texas lawmakers have begun to dismantle TADA. Remarkably, despite numerous attempts to amend, repeal or judicially challenge TADA, the statute remained largely unchanged for sixteen years. Then, the tide turned. Since 2015, lawmakers have twice narrowed the scope of hospital authority to self-adjudicate end-of-life treatment disputes. Moreover, not only is a lawsuit challenging TADA's constitutionality pending before the Texas courts but also that lawsuit is supported by the state's attorney general.[6]

THE TEXAS ADVANCE DIRECTIVES ACT PROVIDES A UNIQUE DISPUTE RESOLUTION MECHANISM FOR CONFLICTS OVER LIFE-SUSTAINING TREATMENT

Before examining how legislators enacted TADA, we should first establish what exactly it is. While TADA is a comprehensive health care decisions statute, our focus is on only its dispute resolution provisions. These provisions are important, because conflicts over life-sustaining medical treatment are common.[7] Indeed, some commentators have characterised them as reaching 'epidemic proportions'.[8]

TADA's conflict resolution provisions address the situation in which 'an attending physician refuses to honor a patient's advance directive or a health care or treatment decision made by or on behalf of a patient'.[9] Patient–clinician conflicts are rare. Most end-of-life treatment conflicts involve incapacitated patients who cannot make

---

[5]   For a thorough explanation of the TADA dispute resolution procedures, see Pope, 'Procedural Due Process'.

[6]   *T.L. v. Cook Children's Medical Center*, 607 S.W.3d 9 (Tex. App. 24 July 2020), rev. denied, No. 20-0644 (Tex. 16 October 2020), cert. denied, 141 S. Ct. 1069 (11 January 2021), on remand, No. 048-112330-19 (Tarrant County Dist. Ct. Tex.).

[7]   See, for example, Terrah J. Paul Olson, Karen J. Brasel, Andrew J. Redmann, G. Caleb Alexander and Margaret L. Schwarze, 'Surgeon Reported Conflict with Intensivists about Postoperative Goals of Care' (2013) 148 *JAMA Surgery* 29–35 at 29 ('[M]ore than 70% of ICU clinicians report experiencing conflict weekly.'); John M. Luce and Douglas B. White, 'The Pressure to Withhold or Withdraw Life-Sustaining Therapy from Critically Ill Patients in the United States' (2007) 175 *America Journal of Respiratory and Critical Care Medicine* 1104–8 at 1104–7 ('[D]isagreements between families and clinicians on end-of-life care are commonplace in the United States.').

[8]   A. C. Long and J. Randall Curtis, 'The Epidemic of Physician-Family Conflict in the ICU and What We Should Do about It' (2014) 42 *Critical Care Medicine* 461–2.

[9]   Texas Advance Directives Act, Tex Health and Safety Code § 166.046(a) (1999) (Texas); see also § 166.002(7) (defining 'health care or treatment decision' to include 'consent, refusal to consent, or withdrawal of consent to health care, treatment, service, or a procedure to maintain, diagnose, or treat an individual's physical or mental condition').

their own decisions. Consequently, a surrogate or substitute decision-maker makes treatment decisions on the patient's behalf.

In Texas there are four types of surrogates. First, parents are surrogates for their minor children. Second, adults can use an advance directive to appoint other adults to be their health care agent. Third, courts can appoint individuals to serve as guardians for incapacitated patients. Fourth, if none of the foregoing applies, Texas statutes specify a hierarchical sequence of default surrogates.

Whichever type of surrogate acts on a patient's behalf, there are two main types of conflict between surrogates and clinicians. First, the surrogate may be requesting treatment that the physician thinks is inappropriate, such as dialysis for a permanently unconscious patient. Second, the surrogate may be refusing treatment that the physician thinks they should provide.[10] The former situation (a medical futility dispute) is the one for which TADA was designed and is most commonly used.

TADA encourages the 'physician's refusal' to 'be reviewed by an ethics or medical committee.'[11] In practice, the available evidence suggests that the committee usually agrees with the judgement of the referring physician.[12] This review process comprises six steps that proceed in a roughly chronological order:

(1) The attending physician refers the dispute to a review committee.
(2) The hospital provides the surrogate with notice of committee review.
(3) The review committee holds an open meeting.
(4) The review committee makes its decision and provides a written explanation.
(5) The hospital attempts to transfer the patient to a willing facility (if requested).
(6) The hospital may stop treatment.[13]

The Attending Physician Refers the Dispute to a Review Committee

In a futility dispute, at some point, the attending physician determines that one or more forms of life-sustaining medical treatment are inappropriate. Since the default presumption is that all physiologically effective treatment will be provided, the physician ordinarily seeks the consent of the patient's surrogate to a proposed plan to withhold or withdraw treatment. The surrogate refuses consent.

---

[10] TADA's notice provisions specify separate notice statements for each situation: see Pope 2016, § IV.C.2.
[11] Texas Advance Directives Act, Tex Health and Safety Code § 166.046(a) (1999) (Texas).
[12] See, for example, Richard J. Castriotta, 'Protecting Patients: The TADA, and the Limits of Surrogate Directives', paper presented at the American College of Chest Physicians Annual Meeting, Chicago, Illinois (2013); Becca Aaronson, 'A Texas Senate Bill Would Revise the State's End-of-Life Procedure', *New York Times*, 30 March 2013.
[13] Texas Advance Directives Act, Tex Health and Safety Code § 166.046(a)–(e) (1999) (Texas).

TADA includes no requirement that hospitals first exhaust less restrictive alternatives before invoking its formal process. But while not required by TADA, the attending physician will typically work on obtaining the surrogate's consent through additional family meetings and the intervention of other specialists like chaplains and ethics consultants. Such communication and mediation typically resolve the dispute. But if none of this works (or even if it was never tried), then the attending physician may invoke TADA's formal dispute resolution provisions.

TADA's dispute resolution procedures are written such that they could be invoked by patients, surrogates or physicians,[14] but they are typically invoked by the attending physician.[15] They are triggered when the attending physician 'refuses to honor a patient's advance directive or a health care or treatment decision made by or on behalf of a patient'.[16] The attending physician notifies the review committee of their refusal, effectively asking or petitioning it to adjudicate the dispute.

The Hospital Provides the Surrogate with Notice of Committee Review

Once the attending physician refers the case to the review committee, the committee convenes a 'meeting' to consider the case.[17] Presumably to enable the surrogate to attend and meaningfully participate at the committee hearing, the hospital must inform the surrogate of the committee review process at least two days in advance.[18]

The Review Committee Holds an Open Meeting

At this point, at least forty-eight hours before the review committee hearing, three things have happened. First, the attending physician has refused to honour the surrogate's treatment decision for continued life-sustaining treatment. Second, the physician has referred the case to the hospital review committee. Third, the surrogate has been apprised of their rights.

With respect to the meeting itself, TADA provides that the surrogate is entitled to attend,[19] but it does not specify any other rules or procedures. TADA is silent on who else the surrogate may bring (e.g. an attorney, a religious adviser). It is also silent on the scope of the surrogate's participation (e.g. right to ask questions).

---

[14] See Thomas William Mayo, 'The Baby Doe Rules and Texas's "Futility Law" in the NICU' (2009) 25 *Georgia State University Law Review* 1003–18 at 1005 ('[I]t can be invoked by patients, surrogates and physicians alike.').

[15] Texas Advance Directives Act, Tex Health and Safety Code § 166.046(a) (1999) (Texas) ('If an attending physician refuses to honor . . . .').

[16] Ibid.

[17] Ibid. § 166.046(b)(4).

[18] Ibid. § 166.046(b)(2).

[19] Ibid. § 166.046(b)(4)(A).

The meeting typically proceeds in two stages. It 'begins with a presentation from the attending physician and other members of the health care team'.[20] During this presentation, clinicians 'provide reasoning and evidence to support why they believe further curative care would be medically futile'.[21] Most committees then 'allow the patient and family to present their arguments and evidence'.[22]

The Review Committee Makes Its Decision and Provides a Written Explanation

After the meeting, the review committee usually deliberates in private, separate from the treating clinicians and family. Once it reaches a decision, the committee must prepare a 'written explanation of the decision reached during the review process' and provide the surrogate with a copy.[23] This 'written explanation' must also be included in the patient's medical record.[24]

A hospital review committee's consideration of a medical futility dispute typically results in one of three main outcomes. First, the committee can agree with the surrogate. Second, it can agree with the referring physician. Third, sometimes the conflict is mooted by the patient's death or by subsequent family–clinician agreement.

If the committee agrees with the referring physician (and it usually does), then the dispute resolution process may continue. Published studies indicate that review committees agree with referring physicians in more than 70 per cent of cases.[25]

The Hospital Attempts to Transfer the Patient to a Willing Facility

If the review committee agrees with the referring physician and the surrogate does not agree with that decision, then the facility's personnel must assist the physician in

---

[20] Robert W. Painter, 'Developments in Texas Advance Directives' (2009) September–October *Houston Lawyer* 20 at 20 (Painter also maintains a website, 'Surviving Hospitals': www .survivinghospitals.com/).

[21] Ibid.

[22] Ibid.

[23] Texas Advance Directives Act, Tex Health and Safety Code § 166.046(b)(4)(B) (1999) (Texas). TADA does not specify any particular format or minimum length or detail. See also below: 'Enabling Factor Five: Lawmakers Used to Trust Physicians and Hospitals to Adjudicate Treatment Disputes'.

[24] Texas Advance Directives Act, Tex Health and Safety Code § 166.046(c) (1999) (Texas).

[25] See, for example, Castriotta, 'Protecting Patients' (reporting that the Memorial Hermann review committee agreed in thirty of thirty-four cases); see also Becca Aaronson, 'A Texas Senate Bill Would Revise the State's End-of-Life Procedure' (reporting 70 per cent agreement in a survey of 200 Texas hospitals over six years and that this rate of agreement is not unique to Texas review committees). See, for example, Andrew M. Courtwright, Sharon Brackett, Wendy Cadge, Eric L. Krakauer and Ellen M. Robinson, 'Experience with a Hospital Policy on Not Offering Cardiopulmonary Resuscitation When Believed More Harmful than Beneficial' (2015) 30 *Journal of Critical Care* 173–7 (reporting that the Optimum Care Committee at the Massachusetts General Hospital agreed with physicians in 75 per cent of futility cases).

arranging the patient's transfer '[to] another facility'.[26] Yet, just because the hospital must search for a transfer does not mean that it will find one. It is difficult to find another facility willing to accept a patient who was the subject of the TADA process. Few hospitals are willing to accept the transfer of a patient after another hospital's review committee has already determined that continuing life-sustaining treatment is inappropriate.[27]

The Hospital May Stop Life-Sustaining Treatment

The transfer period is not indefinite. After being served with the review committee's 'written explanation', the surrogate has only ten days to accomplish a transfer.[28] The patient must continue to be given life-sustaining treatment until they can be transferred to a willing provider. But the waiting period to find a transfer lasts for only ten days from the time the surrogate was given the committee's 'written explanation' that life-sustaining treatment is not appropriate. If a willing provider cannot be found within ten days, then the treating facility may withdraw the treatment.

Summary of the TADA Dispute Resolution Process

Other jurisdictions specify similar dispute resolution mechanisms.[29] But three features make TADA unique. *First*, the final step of the statutorily specified process explicitly permits the hospital to stop the disputed treatment, if the surrogate cannot

---

[26] Texas Advance Directives Act, Tex Health and Safety Code § 166.046(d) (1999) (Texas).

[27] See Gabriel T. Bosslet, Thaddeus M. Pope, Gordon D. Rubenfeld, Bernard Lo, Robert D. Truog, Cynda H. Rushton, J. Randall Curtis, Dee W. Ford, Molly Osbourne, Cheryl Misak, David H. Au, Ellie Azoulay, Baruch Brody, Brenda G. Fahy, Jesse B. Hall, Jozef Kesecioglu, Alexander A. Kon, Kathleen O. Lindell and Douglas B. White, 'An Official ATS/AACN/ACCP/ESICM/SCCM Policy Statement: Responding to Requests for Potentially Inappropriate Treatments in Intensive Care Units' (2015) 191 *American Journal of Respiratory and Critical Care Medicine* 1318–30 at 1325; Leigh Hopper and Todd Ackerman, 'Inside of Me, My Son Is Still Alive', *Houston Chronicle*, 16 March 2005 (reporting that the hospital treating Sun Hudson contacted forty facilities with a newborn intensive care unit but none would accept him); Mary Ann Roser, 'Time Running Out for Baby on Life Support', *Austin Amercian-Statesman*, 8 April 2007, B01 ('Children's Hospital ... contacted 30 hospitals on behalf of Emilio [Gonzales] ... [but] none would take him.'). Commentators have observed that transfer is not an effective safeguard: See, for example, Nora O'Callaghan, 'Dying for Due Process: The Unconstitutional Medical Futility Provision of the Texas Advance Directives Act' (2008) 60 *Baylor Law Review* 527–611 at 568–69; Thaddeus Mason Pope, 'Medical Futility Statutes: No Safe Harbor to Unilaterally Refuse Life-Sustaining Treatment' (2007) 71 *Tennessee Law Review* 1–81 at 25. Notably, before the imposition of the federal Emergency Medical Treatment and Labor Act, 42 USC § 1395dd (1986) ('EMTALA'), hospitals were unwilling to accept transfers of even those patients for whom they thought treatment indicated. See, for example, Sara Rosenbaum, Lara Cartwright-Smith, Joel Hirsh and Philip S. Mehler, 'Case Studies at Denver Health: "Patient Dumping" in the Emergency Department Despite EMTALA, the Law that Banned It' (2012) 31 Health Affairs, 1749–56 at 1753.

[28] O'Callaghan, 'Dying for Due Process', 544.

[29] See, for example, Uniform Health Care Decisions Act, Cal Probate Code §§ 4735, 4740 (2000) (California); Health Care Decisions Act, Va Code § 54.1-2990 (2018) (Virginia).

find a willing and available transfer facility within ten days. *Second*, the statute affords the treating facility and its clinicians with safe harbor legal immunity from civil, criminal and disciplinary sanctions. *Third*, the treating hospital's decision is not appealable to courts or other tribunals. Its own review committee is the forum of last resort.[30]

FIVE KEY FACTORS ENABLED THE ENACTMENT OF TADA IN 1999

Equipped now with a fundamental understanding of TADA, we turn from its purpose and function, to its legislative history. In February 1997, Senator Mike Moncrief introduced TADA.[31] In April, the bill passed the Senate, and in May, it passed the House of Representatives.[32] But when the final version of the bill was sent to Governor George W. Bush, in June 1997, he vetoed it.[33]

Governor Bush's veto proclamation noted that the bill contained 'several provisions that would permit a physician to deny [treatment] to a patient who desires them'.[34] Indeed, opponents had charged that TADA would 'encourage medical professionals to participate in euthanasia ... by denying life-saving medical treatment ... to patients whose lives they independently decide are not worth living'.[35] The Governor was concerned about these 'potentially dangerous defects'.[36]

Notwithstanding all these concerns, when the legislature reconvened in 1999, Governor Bush signed an amended TADA.[37] How was the Texas Legislature able to pass such a controversial bill? Why did Governor Bush sign it?

Five key factors help explain TADA's success. *First*, a particularly broad stakeholder consensus supported the legislation. *Second*, the dispute resolution provisions were only one small part of a large and comprehensive statute. *Third*, would-be opponents were willing to compromise, because they thought the status quo presented even greater risk. *Fourth*, would-be opponents mis-estimated the capacity of

[30] Pope, 'Procedural Due Process'. Note though that the court may grant an extension to the ten-day transfer period if there is a 'reasonable expectation that a physician or health care facility that will honor the patient's directive will be found': Texas Advance Directives Act, Tex Health and Safety Code § 166.046(g) (1999) (Texas).

[31] S. 75-13, 75th Sess., at 227 (Tex. 1997).

[32] S.B. 414, 1997 Leg., 75th Sess. (Tex. 1997); S. 75-43, 75th Sess., at 832 (Tex. 1997); H. 75-84, 75th Sess., at 3861 (Tex. 1997).

[33] Elizabeth Heitman and Virginia Gremillion, 'Ethics Committees under Texas Law: Effects of the Texas Advance Directives Act' (2001) 13 *HEC Forum* 82–104 at 90.

[34] George W. Bush, 'Proclamation by the Governor of the State of Texas', Austin (20 June 1997).

[35] A. Reyna Coleman, 'House Research Organization Bill Analysis: Consolidating Statutes Governing Living Wills and Other Advance Directives', Report from the Texas House Research Organization (23 May 1997 Texas House of Representatives), www.hro.house.state.tx.us/pdf/ba75r/sbo414.pdf#navpanes=0.

[36] Bush, 'Governor Proclamation'.

[37] See S.B. 1260, 1999 Leg., 76th Sess. (Tex. 1999).

the transfer provisions to prevent hospitals from stopping treatment that patients and/ or families want. *Fifth*, this reform happened in an era when policymakers had more trust in physicians and hospitals.

Enabling Factor One: An Exceptionally Broad Stakeholder Consensus Supported TADA

Politically, TADA was an inevitable success because an exceptionally broad consensus of stakeholders supported it, including those who had earlier opposed it. To address the concerns expressed by Governor Bush in his 1997 veto message, at least twenty-four interested organisations formed the Texas Advance Directives Coalition.[38]

The Coalition's membership is remarkable. It included advisors from the legislative and executive branches. As one would expect, it included medical and health care associations.[39] Yet, the Coalition invited many other perspectives too. Most notably, it included disability,[40] right to life[41] and elder rights[42] organisations who generally opposed the right of hospitals to stop life-sustaining treatment that they judged inappropriate yet that the patient wanted.

This was a remarkable collaborative.[43] Despite this heterogeneous composition, the Coalition reached a 'watershed compromise'.[44] The Coalition reached consensus on safeguards and protections designed to resolve the 'defects' that concerned Governor Bush.[45] Experience with other 'collaborative drafting processes',

---

[38] Robert L. Fine, 'The Texas Advance Directives Act of 1999: Politics and Reality' (2001) 13 *HEC Forum* 59– 81 at 63–7; Heitman and Gremillion, 'Ethics Committees under Texas Law', 82–92; Hanoch A. Patt, 'Strange Bedfellows: The Ethics and Politics of Medical Futility in Texas', PhD dissertation, University of Texas, School of Public Health (2012); Jacqueline Christine Harvey, 'Morality and Mortality: The Role of Values in the Adoption of Laws Governing the Involuntary Removal of Life Sustaining Medical Treatment in U.S. States', PhD dissertation, University of North Texas (2012).

[39] American Cancer Society, Catholic Health Association of Texas, Texas Association for Home Care, Texas Health Care Association, Texas Healthcare Trustees, Texas Hospital Association (and eleven hospital affiliates), Texas Medical Association, Texas Medical Directors Association, Texas Nurses Association and Texas and New Mexico Hospice Association.

[40] Institute for Disability Access, ADAPT-Texas, United Cerebral Palsy of Texas and Texas Center for Disability Studies.

[41] National Right to Life Committee, Texas Alliance for Life, Texas Right to Life Committee, Texas Right to Life and Texas Alliance for Life.

[42] American Association of Retired Persons and Texas Association of Homes and Services for the Aging.

[43] See 'Report of Counsel on Health Service Organizations Texas Medical Association' from the Texas Medical Association (2006 Texas Medical Association House of Delegates), www.texmed .org/Template.aspx?id=4858 (noting some of the organisations involved in the Texas Advance Care Directives Coalition and a recommending that TMA continue to work with the Coalition to develop consensus).

[44] Emily Ramshaw, 'Bills Challenge Care Limits for Terminal Patients', *Dallas Morning News*, 15 February 2007.

[45] See Ibid. (noting that the 'watershed compromise' created the 'ten-day transfer rule').

particularly in the environmental area, shows that when stakeholders can form a consensus, they can often translate that consensus into legislation.[46] After all, it is relatively easy for elected representatives to vote for bills that have no opposition.

Enabling Factor Two: TADA's Dispute Resolution Provisions Were Only a Small Part of a Much Broader Bill

Broad stakeholder consensus made it easy for Texas lawmakers to vote for TADA. But how was the diverse Coalition itself able to reach agreement? One key factor is that the controversial dispute resolution provisions are only a very small part of TADA. They comprise just four of TADA's seventy-one sections.[47] This is just 700 of TADA's 15,000 words. In short, more than 95 per cent of the bill that became TADA addresses matters other than medical treatment conflicts.

This small footprint had three key advantages. *First*, the dispute resolution provisions avoided scrutiny, because they were somewhat 'hidden' within a much larger bill.[48] TADA was an omnibus bill, because it bundled distinct yet similar proposals together into a single bill. While all sections were on the same broad end-of-life decision-making topic, TADA also addressed much-needed and overdue reform on advance directives, out-of-hospital do-not-resuscitate orders, and medical powers of attorney. This meant TADA was so large and complicated that many lawmakers probably did not even know what was in the bill before they voted on it.

Second, even to the extent that stakeholders or lawmakers discovered the dispute resolution provisions, Coalition members and legislators could not focus on them. They had to divide their time and attention across multiple issues.

Third, TADA permitted 'logrolling', the process whereby people trade votes or support on different matters to produce a prearranged outcome.[49] The controversial

---

[46] Clifford L. Rechtschaffen, 'The Lead Poisoning Challenge: An Approach for California and Other States' (1997) 21 *Harvard Environmental Law Review* 387–455; Janelle Knox-Hayes, 'Negotiating Climate Legislation: Policy Path Dependence and Coalition Stabilization' (2012) 6 *Regulation and Governance* 545–67.

[47] Texas Advance Directives Act, Tex Health and Safety Code §§ 166.045, 166.046, 166.052, 166.053 (1999) (Texas).

[48] Peter S. Wattson, *Omnibus Bills and Garbage Bills* (Minnesota: Senate Counsel, 2005) (calling these 'woodchucks' – inserting controversial measures into an omnibus bill to hide them). Importantly, while hidden during the enactment process, once passed, they were not hidden to Texas hospitals. The existence and availability of this dispute resolution process are well-known to hospital ICU clinicians, ethics committees, and risk managers.

[49] Anthony J. McGann, 'Logrolling and Coalitions', in Roger D. Congleton, Bernard Grofman and Stefan Voigt (eds.), *The Oxford Handbook of Public Choice*, 2 vols. (New York, NY: Oxford University Press, 2019), vol. I;Elizabeth Garrett, 'Rethinking the Structures of Decisionmaking in the Federal Budget Process' (1998) 35 *Harvard Journal on Legislation* 387–445. This has been a popular topic for analysis in economic models of politics since the 1960s. James M. Buchanan and Gordon Tullock, *The Calculus of Consent* (Ann Arbor, Michigan: University of Michigan Press, 1962).

dispute resolution provisions were intertwined with other, universally supported provisions.[50] While only a minority of Texas legislators may have supported distinct provisions of the broader TADA bill like the dispute resolution provisions, when considered as a package, TADA had majority (or even universal) support. After all, the remaining TADA provisions were relatively uncontroversial, because they focused on honouring and respecting patient wishes. In short, lawmakers were able to more easily pass TADA's dispute resolutions, by wrapping them into a bill that (on balance) everybody wanted.[51]

Enabling Factor Three: Would-Be Opponents Were Willing to Compromise Because the Status Quo Presented Even Greater Risk

TADA includes a 'reasonable effort to transfer' requirement. If the treating facility's review committee agrees with the referring physician and the surrogate does not agree with that decision, then 'the physician shall make a reasonable effort to transfer the patient to a physician who is willing to comply with the directive'.[52] The rationale is a recognition of variability in medical practice.[53] The current treating facility may be unwilling to provide the treatment requested by the surrogate. Yet, another facility might be willing to provide that same treatment.

This ability to transfer was particularly important to Texas Right to Life, a nonprofit, pro-life advocacy organisation. Formed in the 1960s, the Christian organisation had long focused its efforts on abortion, embryos and protecting the rights of 'defenseless human beings, born and unborn'.[54] While this agenda originally centred on issues at the beginning of life, it has expanded to include issues at the end of life. Accordingly, Texas Right to Life was an active participant on the twenty-four-member Texas Advance Directives Coalition. Texas Right to Life was at the table between 1997 and 1999 during the drafting of TADA. Moreover, the other Coalition members knew that Texas Right to Life's agreement was crucial, because it 'plays an influential role in Texas politics'.[55]

Originally, Texas Right to Life demanded that the treating facility continue to treat until it transferred the patient to a new facility. A 'treat 'til transfer' requirement would guarantee that hospitals could never stop treatment over family objections.

---

[50] Glen S. Krutz, 'Tactical Maneuvering on Omnibus Bills in Congress' (2001) 54 *American Journal of Political Science* 210–23.

[51] *City of Philadelphia* v. *Commonwealth*, 838 A 2d 566 (Pa. 2003).

[52] Texas Advance Directives Act, Tex Health & Safety Code § 166.046(d) (1999) (Texas).

[53] Dominic J. Wilkinson and Robert D. Truog, 'The Luck of the Draw: Physician-Related Variability in End-of-Life Decision-Making in Intensive Care' (2013) 39 *Intensive Care Medicine* 1128–32.

[54] Texas Right to Life, 'Who We Are', Texas Right to Life Committee, 2020, www.texasrighttolife.com/who-we-are/.

[55] Calvin C. Jillson, *Texas Politics: Governing the Lone Star State*, 3rd ed. (New York, NY: Routledge, 2001), 82.

Texas Right to Life later insisted on a six-month transfer period. Yet, ultimately, they agreed 'with great reluctance'[56] to a transfer period of just ten days. Why was Texas Right to Life willing to make such a significant compromise?

Texas Right to Life could have stuck to its original position and refused to negotiate on the transfer period. Yet, the health care organisations were demanding 'no grace period whatsoever'.[57] Had Texas Right to Life been intransigent, that likely would have precluded consensus within the Advance Directives Coalition. Without Coalition consensus, either the legislature may not have passed TADA or Governor Bush may have vetoed it just as he did in 1997. Either of these outcomes would have been unacceptable to Texas Right to Life.

Governor Bush had granted Texas Right to Life a significant favour in 1997. Bush stood up to large and powerful medical associations. It was unclear whether he would do that again in 1999. While Governor Bush was sympathetic to the right to life concerns, he did not have unlimited political capital. He could not continue giving Texas Right to Life everything it wanted. Instead, the governor expected Texas Right to Life to negotiate in good faith.

Further, without TADA, the status quo would prevail. That was abhorrent to Texas Right to Life, because the organisation determined that the status quo posed an even greater risk to patient rights. Six years earlier, in 1993, representatives from most of the major hospitals in Houston, Texas formed the Houston Citywide Taskforce on Medical Futility.[58] They developed a nine-step procedure for resolving futility disputes that was similar to TADA but included only a *three-day* transfer period.

Texas Right to Life may have estimated that, not only in Houston but also across Texas, some (or many) less risk-averse facilities might use the Houston process even though it lacked the explicit statutory support offered by TADA.[59] The risk of hospitals using a process with a shorter notice period than proposed in TADA became even more real in 1999, when the American Medical Association published a policy statement based on the Houston guidelines.[60]

---

[56] Elizabeth Graham, 'Euthanasia: President Bush and Texas Law', Texas Right to Life, 25 April 2005, www.texasrighttolife.com/euthanasia-president-bush-and-texas-law/.

[57] Ibid.

[58] Amir Halevy and Baruch Brody, 'A Multi-Institutional Collaborative Policy on Medical Futility' (1996) 276 *JAMA* 571–4; Amir Halevy and Baruch A. Brody, 'The Houston Process-Based Approach to Medical Futility' (1998) 14 *Bioethics Forum* 10–17; Amir Halevy and Amy McGuire, 'The History, Successes and Controversies of the Texas "Futility" Policy' (2006) 43 *Houston Lawyer*, www.thehoustonlawyer.com/aa_may06/page38.htm; Heitman and Gremillion, 'Ethics Committees Under Texas Law', 86–90.

[59] Graham, 'Euthanasia'; Heitman and Gremillion, 'Ethics Committees under Texas Law'. A new federal lawsuit alleges that a Fort Worth hospital unilaterally withdrew life support from patients with less notice than required under TADA: *De Paz Gonzalez v. Duane*, No. 4:20-CV-00072-A (ND Tex. 2020); No. 20-10615 (5th Cir. 31 March 2021) (oral argument).

[60] Council on Ethical and Judicial Affairs, American Medical Association, 'Medical Futility in End-of-Life Care: Report of the Council on Ethical and Judicial Affairs' (1999) 281 *JAMA* 937–41. Even without explicit legal authorisation, following a common policy seemed to make

In short, Texas Right to Life disliked the fact that TADA authorises clinicians and hospitals to unilaterally withdraw or withhold life-sustaining treatment after only ten days. But they saw that as the lesser of two evils. Some hospitals were already asserting a right to stop treatment without consent with even less notice and oversight. Consequently, TADA appeared to be a superior option. It appeared to constrain hospital discretion more than it unfettered it.

Enabling Factor Four: Would-Be Opponents Thought that the Transfer Mechanism Would Work and that Hospitals Would Never Stop Desired Treatment

One of the most remarkable things about TADA is that right to life organisations supported it even though those same organisations would soon become TADA's most vehement opponents and attackers. Why would Texas Right to Life support the enactment of TADA in 1999, yet begin working to dismantle it just six years later? One answer is that Texas Right to Life originally overestimated the effectiveness of TADA's transfer provision.[61]

Importantly, in those cases in which the surrogate is requesting treatment 'that the attending physician has decided, and the review process has affirmed is inappropriate treatment, the patient shall be given available [treatment] pending transfer'.[62] Texas Right to Life figured that ten days would be sufficient to find a transfer.[63]

Moreover, there was a safety valve. TADA permits a judicial extension of the ten days if there is a 'reasonable expectation that a physician or health care facility that will honor the patient's directive will be found if the time extension is granted'.[64]

In short, Texas Right to Life figured that while patients may have to switch facilities, hospitals would not deprive them of desired life-sustaining treatment. With ten days plus a possible extension, Texas Right to Life was confident that the patient's surrogates would always find another facility willing to provide the disputed treatment.

However, this is not how the transfer provision worked in practice. Only after Texas hospitals began using TADA did Texas Right to Life discover that the original ten days was often inadequate. High-profile cases were reported in the mid-2000s,

---

conduct more ethically and legally defensible than individual facilities proceeding on their own.

[61] Right to life organisations may have also thought that the ethics committee oversight would have been more robust. But just as these organisations overestimated the effectiveness of the transfer mechanism, they overestimated the effectiveness of ethics committees. Most lack the independence and neutrality to limit physician and hospital authority.

[62] Texas Advance Directives Act, Tex Health & Safety Code § 166.046(e) (1999) (Texas).

[63] Ten days is sufficient for some transfers, especially those that step down from a hospital to a nursing facility. Ten days is less likely sufficient for lateral transfers (for example from hospital to hospital) or step up transfers (where an increased level of care is sought).

[64] Texas Advance Directives Act, Tex Health & Safety Code § 166.046(g) (1999) (Texas).

showing that it is very difficult to find another facility willing to accept a patient who was the subject of the TADA process. One hospital's recent press release is emblematic:

> [We] reached out to more than 20, well-respected healthcare facilities and pediatric cardiac specialists who have the specialized training to continue [patient's] care. [E]ach medical team declined to accept her as a patient and agreed that [patient's] condition, sadly, shows no signs of improvement and there are no treatment options available to help her get better.[65]

In short, few hospitals are willing to accept the transfer of a patient after another hospital's review committee has already determined that continuing treatment is inappropriate.[66] Moreover, even if a transfer were possible, it might not be possible within the permitted time frame.[67]

Enabling Factor Five: Lawmakers Used to Trust Physicians and Hospitals to Adjudicate Treatment Disputes

Texas lawmakers enacted TADA during the 1990s when courts and legislatures were comfortable giving health care institutions significant power to make treatment decisions on behalf of their patients. For example, the US Supreme Court upheld a prison's internal institutional review process that forced an inmate to take psychiatric medication against his will.[68] Similarly, a California appellate court upheld a process by which an 'interdisciplinary team' at a long-term care facility could make treatment decisions on behalf of an incapacitated resident without an available surrogate.[69]

More than two decades later, courts and legislatures give less deference to physician and hospital decision-making.[70] There is substantially more evidence exposing clinician and hospital biases and conflicts of interest. For example, in 2019, a California court invalidated the same interdisciplinary team approach that

---

[65] Cook Children's, 'Cook Children's Statement on Patient Tinslee Lewis', Cook Children's Health Care System, 4 December 2019, https://cookchildrens.org/SiteCollectionDocuments/about/release/Cook-Childrens Tinslee-Statement-and-Condition-Update.pdf.

[66] Pope, 'Procedural Due Process'.

[67] In later years, bills supported by Texas Right to Life sought to remedy this by extending the transfer period or by requiring that the treating hospital continue to treat until it transferred the patient: Ibid., appendix.

[68] *Washington v. Harper*, 494 US 210 (1990).

[69] *Rains v. Belshe*, 32 Cal. App. 4th 157 (1995).

[70] Robert J. Blendon, John M. Benson and Joachim O. Hero, 'Public Trust in Physicians: U.S. Medicine in International Perspective' (2014) 371 *New England Journal of Medicine* 1570–2. There is a related backlash to private arbitration of treatment disputes: Kelly Bagby and Samantha Souza, 'Ending Unfair Arbitration: Fighting against the Enforcement of Arbitration Agreements in Long-Term Care Contracts' (2013) 29 *Journal of Contemporary Health Law and Policy* 183–200.

the courts had approved in the 1990s.[71] More broadly, there is substantially more legislative management of matters that previously were left to physician judgement within the treatment relationship.[72] Consequently, in the 2020s, it is less likely that lawmakers in Texas or elsewhere could enact a statute that delegates so much power and deference to physicians and hospitals. It is unlikely lawmakers could enact a statute like TADA today.

LAWMAKERS HAVE PARTIALLY DISMANTLED TADA SINCE 2015

For those interested in end-of-life law reform, it is not enough to get their desired bills enacted. They must also protect the law from repeal. Recall these four notable examples regarding medical aid in dying ('MAiD'). First, Australia's Northern Territory was the first jurisdiction in the world to have operational MAiD (law passed in 1995).[73] But the law was nullified just two years later, after just nine months in operation.[74] Second, there were numerous attempts (between 1994 and 1997) to judicially invalidate the Oregon Death with Dignity Act.[75] Third, there have been numerous attempts to legislatively override the judicial authorisation of MAiD in Montana.[76] Fourth, there are ongoing attempts to judicially invalidate MAiD laws in California and New Jersey.[77]

When lawmakers enacted TADA in 1999, it had the broad support of hospital, medical, pro-life and civil liberty groups. The legislation passed as the result of a consensus among a wide spectrum of stakeholders.[78] Yet, within just a few years of enactment, that consensus had crumbled. Strong disagreements developed over how health care providers were implementing TADA's dispute resolution provisions.[79] TADA has proven very controversial and has been the subject of significant legislative activity.

[71] *California Advocates for Nursing Home Reform v. Smith*, No. A147987 (Cal. App. 22 July 2019).
[72] Steven E. Weinberger, Hal C. Lawrence, Douglas E. Henley, Errol R. Alden and David B. Hoyt, 'Legislative Interference with the Patient–Physician Relationship' (2012) 367 *New England Journal of Medicine* 1557–9.
[73] Rights of the Terminally Ill Act 1995 (NT) (Australia); Natasha Cica, 'Euthanasia – The Australian Law in an International Context', Research Paper 4 (1996–7 Parliament of Australia).
[74] Euthanasia Laws Act 1997 (Cth) (Australia).
[75] *Gonzales v. Oregon*, 546 US 243 (2006); *Lee v. State*, 869 F. Supp. 1491 (D. Or. 1994).
[76] Montana authorised MAiD through a court decision: *Baxter v. State*, 224 P 3d 1211 (Mont. 2009). But the legislature has considered bills to override the court decision and criminalise MAiD: see, for example, H.B. 284, 2019 Leg., 66th Sess. (Mont. 2019); S.B. 290, 2021 Leg., 67th Sess. (Mont. 2021).
[77] *Ahn v. Hestrin*, No. RIC 1607135 (Riverside County Sup. Ct, Cal. 2016) (Order); *Petro v. Grewal*, No. MER-C-53-19 (NJ Sup. Ct, 1 April 2020) (order).
[78] See above, 'Enabling Factor One: An Exceptionally Broad Stakeholder Consensus Supported TADA'.
[79] Painter, 'Developments in Texas Advance Directives', 20.

Pushed largely by disability and right-to-life advocates, the Texas legislature has considered numerous bills directed at amending TADA's dispute resolution provisions. The Texas Legislature meets every other year.[80] Legislators introduced more than thirty TADA-related bills in the last ten legislative sessions (2003, 2005, 2007, 2009, 2011, 2013, 2015, 2017, 2019, and 2021).[81] These bills have been of three main types: (i) those directed at strengthening due process protections, (ii) those directed at completely eliminating the ability of clinicians to stop life-sustaining treatment without consent, and (iii) those directed at narrowing the scope of the statute.

Since 2015, lawmakers have enacted two bills of this third (narrowing) type. In two recent legislative sessions, they successively circumscribed TADA both (i) to limit the ability of hospitals to unilaterally refuse artificial nutrition and hydration and (ii) to limit the ability of hospitals to write unilateral 'do not resuscitate' (DNR) orders. Furthermore, opponents are mounting attacks on TADA not only in the legislature but also in the courts. In 2020, a Texas appellate court issued a 150-page opinion challenging TADA's very constitutionality.

2015: TADA No Longer Applies to Artificial Nutrition and Hydration

In March 2015, Representative Springer introduced H.B. 3074.[82] This legislation exempts 'artificially administered nutrition and hydration' ('AANH') from the scope of life-sustaining treatment subject to TADA's dispute resolution procedures. It is not surprising that the first cut into TADA was AANH. For decades, many states have imposed constraints on the ability of patients and surrogates to refuse AANH. It remains the most tightly regulated type of life-sustaining treatment.[83]

Clinicians may continue using TADA to stop life-sustaining medications, mechanical breathing machines, and kidney dialysis treatment. Yet, clinicians may use TADA to stop AANH only if providing it would: (i) hasten the patient's death; (ii) seriously exacerbate other major medical problems not outweighed by the benefit of the provision of the treatment; (iii) result in substantial irremediable physical pain, suffering or discomfort not outweighed by the benefit of the provision of the treatment; (iv) be medically ineffective; or (v) be contrary to the patient's or

---

[80] Kate Galbraith, 'Texas Stands against Tide in Retaining Biennial Legislature', *New York Times*, 30 December 2010, A30.

[81] Pope, 'Procedural Due Process' (collecting bills through 2017); H.B. 995, 2019 Leg., 85th Sess. (Tex. 2019); H.B. 3158, 2019 Leg., 86th Sess. (Tex. 2019); H.B. 3369, 2019 Leg., 86th Sess. (Tex. 2019); H.B. 3597, 2019 Leg., 86th Sess. (Tex. 2019); H.B. 3743, 2019 Leg., 86th Sess. (Tex. 2019); S.B. 2089, 2019 Leg., 86th Sess. (Tex. 2019); S.B. 2129, 2019 Leg., 86th Sess. (Tex. 2019); S.B. 2355, 2019 Leg., 86th Sess. (Tex. 2019).

[82] H.B. 3074, 2015 Leg., 84th Sess. (Tex. 2015).

[83] Alan Meisel, Kathy L. Cerminara and Thaddeus Mason Pope, *Right to Die: The Law of End-of-Life Decisionmaking*, 3rd ed. (New York, NY: Aspen Publishers, 2021), ch. 6. See also Chapter 10 for how artificial nutrition and hydration has been uniquely regulated in England and Wales.

surrogate's clearly documented desires. These are narrow conditions that rarely obtain in the real world of medical futility disputes.

2017: TADA No Longer Applies to Many DNR Orders

Following the path taken in 2015, in a special 2017 session, the Texas Legislature removed yet another medical procedure from the scope of hospital authority under TADA.[84] Effective in April 2018, the new law forbids facility-based clinicians from writing DNR orders without patient or surrogate consent except under very narrow circumstances.[85]

Under TADA, clinicians could write a DNR order notwithstanding patient or surrogate objections. In contrast, under the new statute, the only circumstance under which clinicians may write a DNR without consent is when death is imminent and a DNR order is medically appropriate. Even then, clinicians may not write a DNR order, if that would be contrary to the patient's prior directive. Therefore, clinicians could not write a DNR order for a patient who left prior instructions that she would want CPR.[86]

2019–2021: Texas Courts Weigh TADA's Constitutionality

While most opponents of TADA have attacked it in the state legislature, some have challenged TADA in the courts. There have been several constitutional challenges during TADA's first twenty years.[87] But the courts in those cases never ruled on the merits. In contrast, two cases have very recently addressed the issue of TADA's constitutionality.[88]

Christopher Dunn v. Houston Methodist Hospital.[89] The first of these cases reached the Supreme Court of Texas. In December 2015, Houston Methodist

[84] S.B. 11, 2017 Leg., 85th Sess. (Tex. 2017) (signed 6 August 2017), effective 1 April 2018, codified as: Texas Advance Directives Act, Tex Health and Safety Code §§ 166.201–166.209 (1999) (Texas).

[85] Ibid. § 166.203; Dept. of State Health Services, Hospital Licensing, 43(37) Tex. Reg. 5952–56 (14 September 2018). While still relatively uncommon, a growing number of US jurisdictions have been enacting similar laws: see Meisel, Cerminara and Pope, Right to Die, ch. 13.

[86] Courtenay Bruce, Trevor Bibler, Andrew Childress and Savitri Fedson, 'Legislating How Critical Care Physicians Discuss and Implement Do-Not-Resuscitate Orders' (2018) 44 *Journal of Critical Care* 459–61.

[87] See, for example, *Aguocha-Ohakweh v. Harris County Hospital District*, No. 4:16-CV-903 (SD Tex. 11 April 2017) (order); *Gonzales v. Seton Family Hospitals*, No. 1:07-CV-00267 (WD Tex. 4 April 2007) (Complaint); *Davis v. Memorial Hermann*, No. 2009-07079 (Harris County District Court, Tex. 4 February 2009) (petition).

[88] In May 2020, a new case challenging TADA's constitutionality was filed in Federal Court: *Ohakweh v. Harris Health System*, No. 4:20-cv-01651 (SD Tex. 12 May 2020).

[89] *Dunn v. Methodist Hospital*, No. 2015-69681 (Harris County District Court, Tex. 20 November 2015) (temporary restraining order).

Hospital used TADA with patient Christopher Dunn. In a subsequent lawsuit, Dunn raised a variety of issues about the constitutionality of TADA, including infringement of his right to procedural and substantive due process. He argued that TADA infringed on his due process rights under the 14th Amendment of the US Constitution and Article I, Section 19, of the Texas Constitution, because:

(1) TADA fails to provide an adequate venue to be heard regarding a critical medical decision.
(2) TADA fails to produce sufficient evidentiary safeguards against medical providers, leaving them free to make life-determining medical decisions with unregulated discretion.
(3) TADA fails to provide a reasonable amount of time for a patient to be transferred.

In essence, Dunn alleged that TADA is unfair to patients because it provides no opportunity for patients to be heard in life-altering medical decisions. Dunn also argued that his right to substantive due process was violated because TADA deprived him of a substantive privacy right to make his own medical decisions.[90]

The Harris County Court denied Dunn's claims and dismissed the lawsuit for two reasons.[91] First, because Dunn had already died, the case was moot. Second, the court determined that it lacked subject matter jurisdiction, explaining: 'It would be a big mistake to throw out a statute in place for nearly 20 years that seems to be working pretty well … If you think the law doesn't provide sufficient protection for patients, go to the Legislature to remedy it.'[92] The Court of Appeals affirmed the dismissal, explaining that the case was moot, because Dunn had already died.[93] The Texas Supreme Court affirmed on the same ground.[94]

Tinslee Lewis v. Cook Children's Hospital.[95] Nevertheless, just as the Dunn case was ending, another case was just beginning. Tinslee Lewis arrived at Cook Children's Hospital in Fort Worth shortly after her birth in February 2019. Because Tinslee was born with Ebstein's anomaly, a rare congenital heart condition, she has remained at

[90] For a comprehensive list of these judgements see Thaddeus Mason Pope, 'Medical Futility and Non-Beneficial Treatment Cases', http://thaddeuspope.com/medicalfutility/futilitycases.html. Several prior lawsuits alleged that TADA is unconstitutional, because it authorises hospitals to deprive patients of their life without the procedural due process protections required by the US Constitution. For various reasons, no court ever reached a decision on the merits in any of those lawsuits.
[91] *Kelly v. Methodist Hospital*, No. 2015-69681 (Harris County, 189th Judicial District, Tex. 13 October 2017).
[92] Todd Ackerman, 'Judge Lets One-of-a-Kind "Futile Care" Law Stand', Houston Chronicle, 22 September 2017.
[93] *Kelly v. Houston Methodist Hospital*, No. 01-17-00866-CV (Tex. App. 26 March 2019).
[94] *Kelly v. Houston Methodist Hospital*, No. 19-0390 (Tex. 4 October 2019).
[95] *T.L. v. Cook Children's Medical Center*, 607 S.W.3d 9 (Tex. App. 24 July 2020), rev. denied, No. 20-0644 (Tex. 16 October 2020), cert. denied, 141 S. Ct. 1069 (11 January 2021), on remand, No. 048-112330-19 (Tarrant County Dist. Ct. Tex.).

Cook, critically ill, for her entire life. During that time, she has received aggressive interventions including multiple complex surgeries and extracorporeal membrane oxygenation (ECMO) which replaces the function of the heart and lungs. But by July–August 2019, Tinslee's condition deteriorated even further. So, in early September 2019, Cook clinicians began talking to Tinslee's family about instituting a DNR order and withdrawing non-palliative support.[96]

Unable to reach consensus, Cook used the TADA dispute resolution process. On 30 October 2019, its ethics committee agreed with Tinslee's treating clinicians that life-sustaining treatment was inappropriate. The hospital planned to withdraw treatment on 10 November 2019. But Tinslee's family obtained a temporary restraining order that was eventually extended until 2 January 2020.[97] While the restraining order was originally designed to permit the family additional time to find a transfer facility, the family used the court proceeding to challenge TADA's constitutionality.

On 12 December 2019, the parties presented evidence and argument regarding TADA's constitutionality to a Fort Worth trial court.[98] In January 2020, that court rejected the family's challenge. But the Texas Court of Appeals reversed that decision, sending the case back to the district court for trial in late 2021 or early 2022.[99]

FACTORS ENABLING JUDICIAL AND LEGISLATIVE ATTACKS ON TADA

Over the past four years, TADA has been repeatedly and increasingly attacked in both the legislature and the courts. Therefore, it is important to examine why TADA attracts these attacks. Two factors are particularly noteworthy. First, TADA violates constitutional procedural due process requirements. Second, TADA lacks a mechanism for systematic data collection.

Factor One: TADA Violates Constitutional Procedural Due Process Requirements

I have argued the merits of TADA's constitutionality at length.[100] It fails to comply with fundamental notions of fairness and procedural due process, because the

---

[96] Cook Children's, 'Press Releases', Cook Children's Health Care System, 2020, https://cookchildrens.org/about/public-relations/Pages/Press-Releases.aspx.

[97] Kaley Johnson, '"Is Tinslee's Case Hopeless?" Debate Over Baby on Life Support Continues at Hearing', *Fort Worth Star-Telegram*, 12 December 2019.

[98] *T.B.L. v. Cook Children's Medical Center*, No. 323-112330-19 (Tarrant County, 323rd District Court, Tex., Tex. 20 November 2019).

[99] *T.L. v. Cook Children's Medical Center*, 607 S.W.3d 9 (Tex. App. 24 July 2020), rev. denied, No. 20-0644 (Tex. 16 October 2020), cert. denied, 141 S. Ct. 1069 (11 January 2021), on remand, No. 048-112330-19 (Tarrant County Dist. Ct. Tex.).

[100] See, for example, Thaddeus Mason Pope, 'Texas Advance Directives Act: Nearly a Model Dispute Resolution Mechanism for Intractable Medical Futility Conflicts' (2016) 16 *QUT Law*

ultimate decision-maker is not neutral and independent. It is the hospital's own review committee. Furthermore, this committee operates without transparency or judicial review.

I am not alone. Other law professors have made similar arguments.[101] Even the Attorney General of Texas, someone with the official responsibility of defending the state's laws, has filed multiple briefs challenging TADA's constitutionality.[102] Yet, this is not the place to delve into the substance of the constitutional arguments. The point, here, is that TADA's widely recognised constitutional defects have drawn legislative and judicial attacks.[103]

In every legislative session since 2003, legislators have introduced and debated multiple bills to amend or repeal TADA. Most of those bills focused on procedural due process, for example on the amount of notice that families receive before the ethics committee meeting or before the hospital's withdrawal of support. While these bills were not framed in terms of constitutional law, they were motivated by and defended on grounds of fundamental fairness.

The legislature is not the only front on which TADA has been attacked. At least four separate lawsuits have challenged TADA's constitutionality. Like the legislative bills, these lawsuits focus on TADA's lack of procedural due process and fundamental fairness, including the short notice period, the lack of a neutral decision-maker, the want of standards for the composition or operation of the committee and the absence of judicial review.

While TADA's constitutional defects may have attracted legislative and judicial attacks, it is unclear whether these defects were avoidable. As discussed above, TADA resulted from substantial compromise among a large and diverse group of stakeholders. That messy process of give and take, of blending and adjusting, meant that the bill was not expertly researched and edited to comport with constitutional mandates.[104] Yet, that compromise and consensus building process was essential to get the bill passed.

Review 22–53; Pope, 'Procedural Due Process'; Thaddeus Mason Pope, 'The Texas Advance Directives Act'.

[101] See, for example, O'Callaghan, 'Dying for Due Process'.

[102] *T.B.L. v. Cook Children's Medical Center*, No. 323-112330-19 (Tarrant County, 323rd District Court, Tex. 20 November 2019) (amicus curiae brief); *Kelly v. Houston Methodist*, No. 2015-69681 (Harris County, 189th District Court, Tex. 24 October 2016) (amicus curiae brief).

[103] To be fair, TADA is not unique in this respect. Many controversial end-of-life legislative reforms are attacked in the courts. For example, soon after California and New Jersey enacted MAiD statutes, opponents obtained court orders temporarily enjoining the laws: *Ahn v. Hestrin*, No. RIC 1607135 (Riverside County Sup. Ct, Cal. 2016); *Petro v. Grewal*, No. MER-C-53-19 (NJ Sup. Ct, 1 April 2020).

[104] Mark J. Oleszek and Walter J. Oleszek, 'Legislative Sausage Making: Health Care Reform in the 111th Congress', in Jacob R. Straus (ed.), *Party and Procedure in the United States Congress* (Lanham, MD: Rowman and Littlefield Publishers, 2012), 253–86; James F. Manning, 'The Nondelegation Doctrine as a Canon of Avoidance' (2000) *Supreme Court Review* 223–77.

Factor Two: TADA Lacks a Systematic Data Collection and Reporting Mechanism

The second reason that TADA has been especially vulnerable to attack is that it never included any reporting requirements.[105] Consequently, no thorough and systematic data exist on how Texas hospitals have been using TADA over the past twenty years. This dearth of evidence makes it difficult to rebut or dispel allegations of abuse.

Nobody knows how many times TADA has been used. Nobody knows the age, race or diagnosis of the subject patients. Nobody knows their reasons for demanding non-recommended treatment. Nobody knows the hospitals' reasons for judging those treatment requests to be inappropriate. Admittedly, there are some data from privately conducted studies.[106] But these were small scale relative to the size of Texas (nearly thirty million citizens and over 400 hospitals).

It is more difficult to rebut charges of discrimination or bias when one has little or no data on how hospitals are using the law. Moreover, the lack of transparency itself makes TADA suspect.[107] The cases that get covered in the press get sensationalised, because all the information about the case comes from the patient's family. Because of patient confidentiality rules, hospitals are unable to defend themselves and tell their side of the story.[108] Nor are they able to rely upon aggregate data about how TADA typically works, because there are no such aggregate data.

TADA's lack of data collection contrasts sharply with another innovative end-of-life law. Every one of the ten US jurisdictions that has enacted a statute authorising MAiD has included a detailed reporting requirement.[109] Everyone can see how many patients obtained a prescription and how many patients ingested the drugs. Everyone can see key demographic data about these individuals, including their insurance status, age, race, diagnosis and education level.

---

[105] Several bills have tried to add such a requirement. See, for example, S.B. 303, 2013 Leg., 83rd Sess. (Tex. 2013); H.R. Journal, 2011 Leg., 82d Sess. (Tex. 2011), at 5136.

[106] Pope, 'Procedural Due Process'.

[107] Jenny De Fine Licht, Daniel Naurin, Peter Esaiasson and Mikael Gilljam, 'When Does Transparency Generate Legitimacy? Experimenting on a Context-Bound Relationship' (2014) 27 *Governance* 111–34.

[108] See, for example, Baylor Health Care System, 'Tirhas Habtegiris Case: Media Statement', February 2006, http://thaddeuspope.com/images/FN173_Habtegiris_-_Baylor_Press_Release_Feb._2006_.pdf.

[109] Death with Dignity Act, Or Rev Stat § 127.865 (1994) (Oregon); End of Life Option Act, Cal Health and Safety Code § 443.19 (2015) (California); End-of-Life Options Act, Colo Rev Stat § 25-48-111 (2016) (Colorado); Death with Dignity Act of 2016, DC Code §§ 7–661, 661.07 (2017) (District of Columbia); Our Care, Our Choice Act 2018, Haw Rev Stat Ann §§ 327L1–25 (2018) (Hawaii); An Act to Enact the Maine Death with Dignity Act, 22 Me Rev Stat Ann § 2140 (2019) (Maine); Medical Aid in Dying for the Terminally Ill Act, NJ Stat Ann §§ 26:16-1–20 (2019) (New Jersey); Elizabeth Whitefield End-of-Life Options Act, H.B. 47, 55th Legis. (2021) (New Mexico); Patient Choice and Control at End of Life Act, 18 Vt Stat Ann § 5293 (2013) (Vermont); Death with Dignity Act, Wash Rev Code § 70.245.150 (2008) (Washington).

Admittedly, the MAiD data collected and reported by the several states are incomplete and variable.[110] But some data are better than no data, which is what we have for TADA. Indeed, the MAiD data have enabled three important results. First, they have enabled states to resist legal and political attacks.[111] Second, MAiD data have enabled other states to enact nearly identical legislation by rebutting attacks with evidence-based track records.[112] Third, data have been used to evaluate the operation and justifiability of existing MAiD laws.[113]

CONCLUSION

TADA takes a unique approach to end-of-life medical treatment conflicts. Few other jurisdictions authorise hospitals to act as the unreviewable adjudicators of life-and-death disputes with the families of their own patients. Law reformers looking to enact similar innovations might learn several things from two decades of experience with TADA.

First, controversial provisions are more likely to pass if they are part of a larger, broader bill. This makes them less visible and consequently less likely to be attacked. This is particularly the case when the rest of the bill addresses needed and less controversial reforms. Nevertheless, this strategy has risks and drawbacks, and can work against coherent end-of-life reform. For example, in 2017, Nevada legislators were considering amendments to the Uniform Determination of Death Act to clarify the authoritative medical criteria for diagnosing death on neurological criteria.[114] Because the amendments were urgently needed, right-to-life advocates inserted a clause – inconsistent with the rest of the law – requiring continued organ-sustaining treatment for pregnant women even when determined to be dead.[115]

[110] National Academies of Sciences, Engineering, and Medicine, Health and Medicine Division and Board on Health and Sciences Policy, in Rebecca A. English, Catharyn T. Liverman, Caroline M. Cilio and Joe Alper (rapporteurs), *Physician-Assisted Death: Scanning the Landscape: Proceedings of a Workshop* (Washington, DC: National Academies Press, 2018), 126–8; Jean T. Abbott, Jacqueline J. Glover and Matthew K. Wynia, 'Accepting Professional Accountability: A Call for Uniform National Data Collection on Medical Aid-in-Dying', *Health Affairs Blog*, 20 November 2017; Thaddeus Mason Pope, 'Medical Aid in Dying: Key Variations among U.S. State Laws' (2020) 14 *Journal of Health & Life Sciences Law* 25–59.
[111] H.B. 284, 2019 Leg., 66th Sess. (Mont. 2019).
[112] Katrina Hedberg and Craig New, 'Oregon's Death with Dignity Act: 20 Years of Experience to Inform the Debate' (2017) 167 *Annals of Internal Medicine* 579–83. This point is also made in Chapter 7 in the context of the various factors which led to MAiD law reform in the United States.
[113] *Truchon v. Attorney General* [2019] QCCS 3792 (11 September 2019). The role of social science evidence in the *Truchon* case is discussed further in Chapter 2. See also Chapter 4 in relation to the use of data in the ongoing evaluation of the Dutch assisted dying law.
[114] Thaddeus Mason Pope, 'Brain Death Forsaken: Growing Conflict and New Legal Challenges' (2017) 37 *Journal of Legal Medicine* 265–324.
[115] Uniform Determination of Death Act, Nev Rev Stat § 451.008 (2017) (Nevada).

Second, build a broad stakeholder consensus before entering the formal legislative process. The Texas Advance Directives Coalition engaged in an iterative, deliberative process. The members of the Coalition debated the tough issues and reached difficult compromises. Consequently, much of the hard 'work' was completed outside the formal legislative process, paving the way for the bill's smoother passage through the legislature.

Third, stakeholders are prepared to come to 'the table' willing to compromise when confronted with the prospect of a very undesirable outcome if they cannot reach a better negotiated agreement. Texas Right to Life felt pressured to accept the ten-day waiting period, because many Texas hospitals were planning to adopt TADA-like policies and procedures with an even shorter waiting period. Health care providers would prefer the explicit permission and immunity afforded by a statute. But they can often alternatively design and implement their own practices because medicine is largely a self-regulated profession.

Fourth, once the law is in effect, collect and report data on the law's operation. If the law is working well, the government can use these data to rebut attacks and other jurisdictions can use these data to enact similar laws. However, if the law is producing unintended impacts, including outcomes that are inconsistent with human rights or constitutional norms, the data can inform evidence-based reform.

POSTSCRIPT

Legislative and judicial attacks on TADA continue as this book goes to press.

By May 2021, multiple bills were introduced and heard in both the House and Senate of the Texas Legislature. Some of these bills are directed at improving TADA's fairness and procedural due process protections.[116] Others are directed at eliminating the 'ten day countdown' and at prohibiting hospitals from unilaterally withdrawing treatment when transfers cannot be found.[117]

Meanwhile, the Tinslee Lewis case on TADA's constitutionality is heading to trial in the Tarrant County District Court sometime between July 2021 and January 2022. Whether the court rules for the family or for the hospital, the judgment is likely to be appealed. Since the Texas Court of Appeals already issued a 150-page opinion at the preliminary injunction stage, that court is unlikely to reach a different result after final judgment. Consequently, the likely non-prevailing hospital will probably seek further appellate review by the Texas Supreme Court and the U.S. Supreme Court as it did at the preliminary injunction stage. Those appeals may not be exhausted until 2023.

---

[116] H.B. 3099, 2021 Leg., 87th Sess. (Tex. 2021); S.B. 1381, 2021 Leg., 87th Sess. (Tex. 2021); S.B. 1944, 2021 Leg., 87th Sess. (Tex. 2021).
[117] H.B. 2609, 2021 Leg., 87th Sess. (Tex. 2021); S.B. 917, 2021 Leg., 87th Sess. (Tex. 2021).

10

Challenging Mandatory Court Hearings for People in Vegetative and Minimally Conscious States

How to Change the Law

Celia Kitzinger and Jenny Kitzinger

INTRODUCTION

On 30 July 2018, a landmark decision was handed down by the UK Supreme Court. In *An NHS Trust v. Y* ('*Re Y*'),[1] the Court ruled that it is not mandatory to seek judicial approval for decisions to withdraw feeding tubes from patients in vegetative states ('VS')[2] or minimally conscious states ('MCS'). The courts are still available, of course, where the patient's best interests are in dispute (e.g. between family and clinicians) or where the decision is 'finely balanced'.

We welcomed this decision. Our research at the Coma and Disorders of Consciousness Research Centre ('CDOC Research Centre') over the previous ten years had shown how mandatory court hearings work against these patients' best interests – in particular by creating a situation in which patients are treated by default (sometimes for decades) without any consideration of whether or not ongoing clinically assisted nutrition and hydration ('CANH') is in their best interests.[3] We also found that, ironically, an unintended consequence of the

---

[1] *An NHS Trust v. Y* [2018] UKSC 46 ('*Re Y*').

[2] We are aware that there has been growing discomfort internationally with referring to people as being in a 'vegetative' state and that this term has increasingly been replaced by others such as 'unresponsive wakefulness syndrome' (the term preferred by the European Task Force on Disorders of Consciousness). In the UK, however, the Royal College of Physicians decided to retain the term 'vegetative' as a diagnostic category: 'Prolonged Disorders of Consciousness Following Sudden Onset Brain Injury: National Clinical Guidelines', Report from a Working Party 2020 of the Royal College of Physicians (2020 RCP) ('National Guidelines'). The Guidelines note that although some families dislike it, others find the term helpful as a way of making clear that the patient is not aware and not suffering: see '1.2.1 Terminology' at 23–4.

[3] Our full list of publications on this topic is available here: Comas and Disorders of Consciousness Research Centre, 'Articles/Chapters', 2020, Cardiff University, https://cdoc.org.uk/publications/academic-articles/. See for example Jenny Kitzinger and Celia Kitzinger, 'Why Futile and Unwanted Treatment Continues for Some Patients in Permanent Vegetative States (And What to Do about It): Case Study, Context and Policy

apparent requirement for court applications was that various forms of life-sustaining treatment were being withdrawn very early (e.g. in intensive care) for some patients, perhaps earlier than the patient might have otherwise chosen for themselves, precisely to avoid missing the 'window of opportunity' for death without judicial scrutiny.[4] There are many obstacles to proper best interests decision-making about CANH for this patient group, but mandatory judicial scrutiny before treatment can be withdrawn was one key contributing factor which has now been removed.

This chapter highlights the significance of the Supreme Court judgement, tells the story of the movement for law reform that cumulated in that judgement, and explores the role played by different evidence and arguments, case law, professional bodies, and key networks in creating that change. In particular, we explain how we, as academics, advocates and activists, contributed to the collective effort that achieved this reform.

Our involvement in efforts to change the law over almost a decade was messy and protracted. We had no idea what would work and what wouldn't. In this chapter, we discuss some of the wide range of strategies we adopted (or simply found ourselves using). These included academic articles and executive summaries of them; advocacy for families and personal involvement in cases coming before the courts; live-tweeting court hearings; delivering training to judges; taking part in working parties and guideline development groups; and providing evidence to select committees and consultations. It also included developing multi-media learning resources[5]; appearing in the media; and working with artists to find creative ways of communicating with broader audiences.[6]

Legal reform was the outcome of collective and committed engagement from many people including individual families seeking justice for their relatives and a network of dedicated professionals (some of whom had personal experience too), meeting at conferences, seminars, workshops and court hearings – and sometimes at patients' bedsides. This engagement coalesced over time into a multi-disciplinary team of experts committed to exposing and exploring the problem of mandatory court applications and challenging its chilling effect on best interests decision-making. By 2017, a series of research publications, legal developments and medical ethics discussions had converged to challenge the purported requirement for court authorisation of CANH-withdrawal from this patient group, and this network of professionals (working alongside and in intersecting ways with patients' families) had

Recommendations' (2017) 23 *International Journal of Mental Health and Capacity Law* 129–43.

[4] Jenny Kitzinger and Celia Kitzinger, 'The "Window of Opportunity" for Death after Severe Brain Injury: Family Experiences' (2012) 35 *Sociology of Health and Illness* 1095–112.

[5] See, for example, healthtalk, 'Family Experiences of Vegetative and Minimally Conscious States: Overview', 2019, University of Oxford, https://healthtalk.org/family-experiences-vegetative-and-minimally-conscious-states/overview (ESRC grant ES/K00560X/1).

[6] More information about our impact activities is available on our website: https://cdoc.org.uk/. For artist collaborations see https://cdoc.org.uk/impact/artist-collaborations/.

collaborated for some years to explore various avenues for reform. This chapter is necessarily our own account of the process of legal change, and reflects our own role in it. Others would have different stories to tell from their own different locations.

In this chapter, we first briefly outline the diagnostic terminology relating to the VS and the *permanent* VS ('PVS') and related conditions. Second, we describe the Supreme Court judgement and its implications for patients, families and practitioners. Third, we present the legal situation prior to the Supreme Court decision, and then, fourth, we explore the specific legal arguments that made the Supreme Court decision possible. Fifth, we describe our own contributions as academic social scientists working with colleagues in law, medicine and beyond to create legal reform – especially in relation to the Court of Protection Practice Direction routinely cited to justify previous practice. Finally, we (briefly) discuss the difference the Supreme Court decision has made to decision-making about CANH in cases we have subsequently been involved in. We conclude by revisiting the events which started us out on this journey ourselves and reflect on what our experience shows about the strategies academics can use – in conjunction with advocacy and activism underpinned both by research and by personal experience – to inform and influence legal reform.

DIAGNOSTIC TERMINOLOGY

The term VS was invented by Jennett and Plum (neurologists from Glasgow and New York, respectively) in 1972.[7] They wrote about 'a syndrome in search of a name', observing that 'new methods of treatment may, by prolonging the lives of patients with conditions which were formerly fatal, result in situations never previously encountered'.[8] The patients with severe brain damage they were encountering had, with the help of modern medical technologies, recovered from 'sleep-like coma in that they have periods of wakefulness when their eyes are open and move' but who were characterised by 'absence of function in the cerebral cortex as judged behaviourally'. Their article describe patients whose eyes are often open, who may 'blink to menace'; they may move away from 'noxious stimuli'; they sometimes show a 'grasp reflex'; they can exhibit 'grimacing', 'chewing and teeth-grinding', 'grunting or groaning' and 'limb flexion'.[9] This description remains a recognisable characterisation of people in VS today. These patients are not 'brain dead' (by any definition internationally, then or now), nor are they 'locked in' (described by Jennett and Plum as 'entirely awake, responsive and sentient' but 'tetraplegic and mute'[10]). The name these researchers chose to describe this new syndrome was

---

[7] Bryan Jennett and Fred Plum, 'Persistent Vegetative State after Brain Damage: A Syndrome in Search of a Name' (1972) 299 *The Lancet* 734–7.
[8] Ibid. at 734.
[9] Ibid. at 734, 735.
[10] Ibid.

'vegetative' – justified by reference to dictionary definitions of the term as 'an organic body capable of growth and development but devoid of sensation and thought'.[11] They suggest the term 'persistent vegetative state' (rather than *permanent* VS) to characterise the condition of someone who remains in this state for some (unspecified but lengthy) duration because 'exactly how long such a state must persist before it can be confidently declared permanent will have to be determined by careful prospective studies'.[12] Even back then, the authors expressed concern that 'the indefinite survival of patients in this state presents a problem with humanitarian and socio-economic implications which society as a whole will have to consider'.[13]

Terminology and diagnostic criteria have developed significantly over the last nearly fifty years, as reflected in the UK's 2020 *Prolonged Disorders of Consciousness Following Sudden Onset Brain Injury: National Clinical Guidelines* ('National Guidelines'),[14] produced (with our input as members of the Guidelines Development Group) by the Royal College of Physicians. The National Guidelines concern what are now referred to as 'disorders of consciousness' which include 'coma' (the 'sleep-like coma' referred to by Jennett and Plum – a usually short-term acute state of unconsciousness immediately following brain injury), and the 'prolonged' disorders of consciousness (i.e. those that persist for more than four weeks). These prolonged disorders of consciousness are the VS, and the MCS formally invented in 2002[15] to describe patients who do not quite meet the diagnostic criteria for coma or the VS. Whereas VS patients display no behavioural evidence of themselves or their environment, MCS patients show inconsistent but clearly discernible evidence of responses 'above the level of spontaneous or reflexive behaviour, which indicate some degree of interaction with their surroundings'.[16] These responses might include following simple commands (e.g. 'lift your right hand'), touching or holding objects in a way that accommodates the size and shape of the object, and episodes of crying or smiling in response to appropriate cues.[17] A person is said to have 'emerged' from the MCS if these sorts of responses become reliable and consistent.[18] The longer a person remains in a prolonged disorder of

---

[11] Ibid. at 734, 736.

[12] Ibid. at 736.

[13] Ibid. at 734, 737.

[14] Royal College of Physicians, 'National Guidelines'.

[15] J. T. Giacino, S. Ashwal, N. Childs, R. Cranford, B. Jennett, D. I. Katz, J. P. Kelly, J. H. Rosenberg, J. Whyte, R. D. Zafonte and N. D. Zasler, 'The Minimally Conscious State: Definition and Diagnostic Criteria' (2002) 58 *Neurology* 349–53.

[16] Royal College of Physicians, 'National Guidelines', 25 at Table 1.2: 'Definitions of Disorders of Consciousness'.

[17] Ibid., 30 at Box 1.2: 'Behaviours Compatible with MCS' in Royal College of Physicians.

[18] Ibid., pt. 1.6.

consciousness, the less likely they are ever to regain full consciousness. Definitions of when a state becomes 'permanent' have varied historically and cross-nationally.[19]

The distinction between VS and MCS (and when they should or should not be considered 'permanent') has increasingly been recognised as potentially problematic.[20] These diagnoses can be challenging to make in practice and may not necessarily be relevant to decision-making about life-sustaining treatment (e.g. when a person would not want to be given treatments to keep them alive whether they were in a VS or an MCS, given their prognosis). The judicial focus on establishing conclusively that a person is in a PVS before authorisation of withdrawal of life-sustaining treatment has been substantially replaced (in England and Wales) with a consideration of whether the person, with their current and likely future impairments post brain-injury, would want to continue to receive life-sustaining treatments.[21] The National Guidelines emphasise the importance of determining what is in the person's best interests regarding treatment at each point from intensive care, through high dependency, rehabilitation and the care home. In particular, '[b]est interests discussions should not be delayed until the condition is diagnosed as

---

[19] The 1994 US Guidelines defined the state of 'permanent VS' (twelve months after traumatic brain injury and three months after non-traumatic brain injury) as the point after which recovery of consciousness was deemed to be highly improbable: Stephen Ashwal, Ronald Cranford, James L. Bernat, Gastone Celesia, David Coulter, Howard Eisenberg, Edwin Myer, Fred Plum, Marion Walker, Clark Watts and Teresa Rogstad, comprising the Multi-Society Task Force on PVS, 'Medical Aspects of the Persistent Vegetative State (First of Two Parts)' (1994) 330 *New England Journal of Medicine* 1499–508 at 1501–2. The 2018 Guidelines have replaced 'permanent' with the word 'chronic' to reflect the fact that a small minority of patients continue to make progress into further consciousness after these time points: Joseph T. Giacino, Douglas I. Katz, Nicholas D. Schiff, John Whyte, Eric J. Ashman, Stephen Ashwal, Richard Barbano, Flora M. Hammond, Steven Laureys, Geoffrey S. F. Ling, Risa Nakase-Richardson, Ronald T. Seel, Stuart Yablon, Thomas S. D. Getchius, Gary S. Gronseth and Melissa J. Armstrong, 'Practice Guideline Update: Disorders of Consciousness', Report from the Guideline Development, Dissemination, and Implementation Subcommittee of the American Academy of Neurology, the American Congress of Rehabilitation Medicine and the National Institute on Disability, Independent Living, and Rehabilitation Research (2018 AAN, ACRM and NIDILRR) at 59–61. The 2013 UK Guidelines adopted a more cautious period of six months for diagnosis of a VS in non-traumatic brain injury as 'permanent' and advised that MCS may be considered 'permanent' between three and five years post-injury: 'Prolonged Disorders of Consciousness: National Clinical Guidelines', Report from a Working Party 2013 of the Royal College of Physicians (2013 RCP) at 9–11. The 2020 UK National Guidelines adopt a three-stage classification of both VS and MCS into 'continuing' (more than four weeks), 'chronic' (three months following non-traumatic injury or one year following traumatic injury for VS patients; nine months following non-traumatic injury or eighteen months following traumatic injury for MCS patients) and 'permanent' (once a patient has been in chronic VS or MCS for a least six months in the absence of any discernible trajectory of change): Royal College of Physicians, 'National Guidelines', 37.

[20] Sarah Nettleton, Jenny Kitzinger and Celia Kitzinger, 'A Diagnostic Illusory? The Case of Distinguishing "Vegetative" and "Minimally Conscious" States' (2014) 116 *Social Science and Medicine* 134–41.

[21] This principle of best interests decision-making was firmly established in the case of *Briggs* v. *Briggs and Others* [2016] EWCOP 53.

"chronic" or "permanent" but should take place whenever a treatment decision is made'.[22] This perspective is increasingly reflected and promoted by clinicians in rehabilitation and beyond.[23] Diagnosis takes a back seat to, and becomes the servant of, the person's best interests – rather than driving treatment decisions.

In the Supreme Court case of *Re Y*[24] that we describe in the next section, the judgement written by Lady Black, and agreed with by other judges, refers in its conclusion to the umbrella category, 'prolonged disorders of consciousness':[25]

> I do not consider that it has been established that the common law or the E[uropean] C[onvention on] H[uman] R[ights], in combination or separately, give rise to the mandatory requirement, for which the Official Solicitor contends, to involve the court to decide upon the best interests of every patient with a prolonged disorder of consciousness before CANH can be withdrawn.

In this chapter, we mostly use the terms VS (or PVS when that is the relevant diagnosis) and MCS rather than 'prolonged disorders of consciousness'. We do so because those are overwhelmingly the terms that were used in the meetings we took part in, the discussion documents that were circulated and the debates that were aired by the family members who talked with us and by the legal and medical professionals throughout this period. For example, in the next section we describe the person at the centre of the Supreme Court hearing, Mr Y, as in a VS (and not a PVS) because at the time the initial Court application was made, less than six months had elapsed since his brain injury and so a PVS diagnosis was not possible under the then-current National Guidelines – and the case was brought to court despite the fact that the apparent requirement for Court applications referred only to those in a PVS.

THE SUPREME COURT JUDGEMENT IN *RE Y*

Until the Supreme Court judgement in *Re Y*[26] it was conventional wisdom for lawyers in England and Wales that CANH could not lawfully be withdrawn from patients in VS or MCS without authorisation from the courts – *even when families and clinical teams were in complete agreement that continuing life-sustaining treatment was not in the patient's best interests*. Neither families nor doctors appeared to have the authority to make the decision to stop this form of medical treatment – unless or until someone decided to bring a case to the court, and had the

---

[22] Royal College of Physicians, 'National Guidelines', 37.
[23] Derick T. Wade, 'How Many Patients in a Prolonged Disorder of Consciousness Might Need a Best Interests Meeting about Starting or Continuing Gastrostomy Feeding?' (2018) 32 *Clinical Rehabilitation* 1551–64.
[24] *An NHS Trust v. Y* [2018] UKSC 46.
[25] Ibid. at [126].
[26] *An NHS Trust v. Y* [2018] UKSC 46.

knowledge, commitment and financial resources to do so. Believing that only the courts could make the decision to withdraw CANH many clinicians abdicated decision-making responsibility. Families would often not raise questions of treatment withdrawal because they felt they would be 'on trial', caught up in expensive and protracted legal action and associated publicity about 'right to die' and 'euthanasia'.[27]

Our research was cited in formal written submissions to the Supreme Court, and an extract was read aloud in the hearing by Counsel for the Official Solicitor (the Official Solicitor is the civil servant who acts as litigation friend for adults who lack capacity).[28] Our research draws attention to the impact of mandatory judicial scrutiny not only on the cases that *did* reach court (adding months of delay to an already protracted process), but also on the vast majority of cases in which no application was made to the court and treatment continued by default whether or not that is what the patient might have wanted.

The Supreme Court decision was very important because it removed a significant barrier for clinicians trying to make best interests decisions about their patients and brought the treatment of this particular patient group into line with best interests decision-making processes for other patients. It is common ground that good medical practice for other patient groups includes withdrawing (or withholding) CANH, either because a capacitous patient refuses it or, if the patient lacks capacity to make this decision, as the outcome of a best interests decision that takes into account the potential harms and benefits of such interventions and what the patient themselves would have wanted.[29]

We were personally involved in the landmark case of *Re Y*[30] because the clinical team responsible for Mr Y asked us to provide support for the family (Mr Y's wife and two adult children) at the point at which a court case started to be considered. Following a cardiac arrest, Mr Y, a fit and active man in his fifties, had been resuscitated, and survived with extensive brain damage caused by a lack of oxygen. He required CANH to keep him alive. He was diagnosed as being in a VS with no prospect of improvement by both his own specialist clinician and by an independent expert. His wife and their two children believed that Mr Y would not wish to be kept

---

[27] Celia Kitzinger and Jenny Kitzinger, 'Court Applications for Withdrawal of Artificial Nutrition and Hydration from Patients in a Permanent Vegetative State: Family Experience' (2016) 42 *Journal of Medical Ethics* 11–17.

[28] More information about the Official Solicitor is available here: Official Solicitor and Public Trustee, 'What Official Solicitor and Public Trustee Does', UK Government, 2020, www.gov .uk/government/organisations/official-solicitor-and-public-trustee. There has been some concern about the way in which this role has been performed; see Alex Ruck Keene, 'Litigation Friend or Foe?, Mental Capacity Law and Policy', 13 April 2016, www .mentalcapacitylawandpolicy.org.uk/litigation-friend-or-foe/.

[29] See Chapter 11 for a detailed discussion of the best interests test in England and Wales, including the role of the patient's wishes in this test.

[30] *An NHS Trust v. Y* [2018] UKSC 46.

alive under these circumstances. The clinical team and the family agreed that it was not in Mr Y's best interests for CANH to be continued.

In such circumstances, the conventional wisdom of the time was that cases should be referred to a hearing at the Court of Protection at which the judge would be asked to authorise CANH-withdrawal. The Court of Protection, established under the Mental Capacity Act 2005 (England and Wales), makes decisions on behalf of adults who lack the mental capacity to make such decisions for themselves (including people with dementia, intellectual impairments, mental illnesses and so on). We have attended many such cases specifically for consideration of CANH-withdrawal from people in VS and MCS[31] (and, more recently, for consideration of a wide range of different decisions such as where they should live, whether they should have surgeries, or if they should be prescribed contraception[32]). But this case was different. Rather than applying to the Court of Protection and asking for a declaration that continued CANH was not in Mr Y's best interests, so that doctors could lawfully withdraw it, the relevant National Health Service ('NHS') Trust responsible for treating Mr Y applied instead to the Queen's Bench Division of the High Court asking for a declaration that it was not mandatory to seek the Court's approval for withdrawal of CANH from patients like Mr Y (in VS or MCS) when the clinical team and the patient's family are agreed that it is not in the patient's best interests to continue to receive that treatment.

This application was a timely and strategic intervention to challenge the conventional wisdom that all such withdrawals require court approval. There was nothing unique about Mr Y's circumstances in particular: any patient in a VS or MCS could have been a candidate for a similar case, so long as family and clinicians were in agreement that continuing CANH was not in the patient's best interests. The Trust's decision to make an application to the court to declare that an application was not mandated (rather than making an application to withdraw treatment) arose in the context of a long history of increasing concern among a network of professionals about the negative effects of mandatory judicial scrutiny. As we will describe, that concern had already had some impact on the courts. The application on behalf of Mr Y was the next step in the journey towards dismantling a legal practice with unintended consequences that harmed patients and families.

The judge in the High Court at first instance approved the declaration, stating her view that:[33]

---

[31] See Celia Kitzinger and Jenny Kitzinger, 'Supporting Families Involved in Court Cases about Life-Sustaining Treatment: Working as Academics, Advocates and Activists' (2019) 33 *Bioethics* 896–907.

[32] Celia Kitzinger, 'When Remote Justice Works', Transparency Project, 4 May 2020, www.transparencyproject.org.uk/when-remote-justice-works/; Celia Kitzinger, 'How to Observe Remote Hearings in the Court of Protection', Transparency Project, 7 June 2020, www.transparencyproject.org.uk/how-to-observe-remote-hearings-in-the-court-of-protection/.

[33] *NHS Trust* v. *Y and Anor* [2017] EWHC 2866 at [52].

where the clinicians have followed the MCA [Mental Capacity Act] and good medical practice, there is no dispute with the family of the person who lacks capacity or others interested in his welfare, and no other doubts or concerns have been identified, there is no requirement to bring the matter before the court.

An appeal was brought by the Official Solicitor. To avoid delay and because this was a matter of strong public interest, the appeal leapfrogged the Court of Appeal and went straight to the Supreme Court, which confirmed the earlier decision:[34]

> If the provisions of the MCA 2005 [Mental Capacity Act] are followed and the relevant guidance observed, and if there is agreement upon what is in the best interests of the patient, the patient may be treated in accordance with that agreement without application to the court.

This groundbreaking judgement did not emerge 'out of the blue', nor was it a natural outcome of some kind of 'legal evolution' or 'social progress'. It is the result of determined effort from committed professionals and families who mounted sustained challenges to mandatory court applications over many years. We turn now to the origins of the belief that court applications are mandatory for CANH-withdrawal from this patient group, before moving on to document some of the criticisms of and challenges to it.

'THE LAW' PRIOR TO THE SUPREME COURT DECISION

In English law, decisions about continuing, withholding or withdrawing life-prolonging medical treatment from adults who lack the capacity to make those decisions for themselves are normally made by treating clinicians. In the absence of a valid and applicable Advance Decision to Refuse Treatment (sometimes known as a 'living will'[35]), this decision is made by the clinical team in the person's 'best interests' (not 'substituted judgement', where the decision made should reflect what the person themselves would have wanted if they could decide).[36] 'Next of kin' do not have decision-making rights – although they should be consulted about what the person would have wanted. Unless there is disagreement between family and clinicians (and sometimes despite disagreement), clinicians can lawfully act upon their decisions without involving the courts. Withdrawal of CANH from patients in a VS or MCS was an apparent exception to this general rule.

The origin of the purported requirement for judicial scrutiny before CANH could be withdrawn or withheld from patients in PVS or MCS cases lies in the case of

[34] *An NHS Trust v. Y* [2018] UKSC 46 at [126].

[35] Note, however, that only 4 per cent of the UK population has an Advance Decision to Refuse Treatment: 'YouGov Survey: Compassion in Dying Results', Report from YouGov (2013 YouGov).

[36] Mental Capacity Act 2005 (UK), s. 4.

Airedale NHS Trust v. *Bland* (*'Bland'*)[37] – the first CANH-withdrawal case considered by the House of Lords (now the Supreme Court[38]). One of the judges in House of Lords, Lord Keith, agreed with the Court of Appeal's suggestion that future PVS cases should be referred to the court as an interim measure – until a sufficient body of expertise had been acquired:[39]

> The decision whether or not the continued treatment and care of a PVS patient confers any benefit on him is essentially one for the practitioners in charge of his case. The question is whether any decision that it does not and that the treatment and care should therefore be discontinued should as a matter of routine be brought before the Family Division for endorsement or the reverse. The view taken by the President of the Family Division and the Court of Appeal was that it should, at least for the time being and until a body of experience and practice has been built up which might obviate the need for application in every case. As Sir Thomas Bingham M.R. said, this would be in the interests of the protection of patients, the protection of doctors, the reassurance of the patients' families and the reassurance of the public. I respectfully agree that these three considerations render desirable the practice of application.

The requirement for judicial scrutiny for PVS (and MCS) patients was subsequently laid out in the Court of Protection Practice Direction 9E, entitled 'Applications Relating to Serious Medical Treatment'.[40] This Practice Direction was initially issued in 2007 and was reissued in virtually identical form in 2015. Of significance was that the scope of this Direction had expanded beyond PVS patients considered in *Bland*[41] to now include patients in MCS:[42]

---

[37] *Airedale NHS Trust* v. *Bland* [1993] AC 789.

[38] For readers unfamiliar with the role of the UK Supreme Court a very helpful discussion (including a comparison with the United States Supreme Court) is available here: Colin McIntyre, Joseph Farmer and Michael Deacon, 'Supreme Courts: The US and UK Compared', Law Society of Scotland, 2015, www.lawscot.org.uk/members/journal/issues/vol-60-issue-02/supreme-courts-the-us-and-uk-compared/.

[39] *Airedale NHS Trust* v. *Bland* [1993] AC 789 at 859 (Lord Keith).

[40] Court of Protection, Practice Direction 9E: Applications Relating to Serious Medical Treatment (1 July 2015), supplementing Part 9 of the Court of Protection Rules 2017 (England and Wales). Practice Directions, and amendments to them, supplement the Court of Protection Rules and are made by the President of the Court of Protection under the powers delegated to him or her by the Lord Chief Justice under section 52(3) of the *Mental Capacity Act* 2005 (England and Wales) and Schedule 2, Part 1, paragraph 2(2) of the Constitutional Reform Act 2005 (England and Wales) and are approved by the Minister of State for Justice and Civil Liberties, by the authority of the Lord Chancellor: Courts and Tribunals Judiciary, 'Court of Protection: Practice Directions', Judicial Office, 19 December 2017, www.judiciary.gov.uk/publications/court-of-protection-practice-directions/.

[41] *Airedale NHS Trust* v. *Bland* [1993] AC 789.

[42] Court of Protection, Practice Direction 9E: Applications Relating to Serious Medical Treatment (1 July 2015), para. 5(a). We understand that MCS was added – without consultation or discussion – to the Practice Direction in its revised version in 2015. According to the Official Solicitor: 'The reason for the addition of the cases of those in the MCS was that it is not at all clear why those who are or may be in the PVS should have greater protection than those in the

Cases involving any of the following decisions should be regarded as serious medical treatment for the purpose of the Rules and this practice direction, and should be brought to the court:

  (a) decisions about the proposed withholding or withdrawal of artificial nutrition and hydration from a person in a permanent vegetative state or a minimally conscious state; ...

A version of this requirement also appeared in section 6.18 of the *Mental Capacity Act 2005 Code of Practice*:[43]

  The Court of Protection must be asked to make decisions relating to:
  - the proposed withholding or withdrawal of artificial nutrition and hydration ('ANH') from a patient in a permanent vegetative state ('PVS') .

It was also included in the 2013 version *National Clinical Guidelines on Prolonged Disorders of Consciousness*, on the advice of the lawyers involved in the Working Party that developed the Guidelines:[44]

  In English and Welsh law, a decision to withdraw CANH in patients with PDOC [prolonged disorders of consciousness] cannot be made by clinicians alone but must be referred to the Court of Protection, for a judge to make the decision.

Finally, the key textbook, *Principles of Medical Law* includes a chapter by Sir James Munby (then President of the Family Division of the High Court) which likewise explicitly states:

  Withdrawal of artificial nutrition and hydration from a patient in a permanent vegetative state requires the prior sanction of the court.[45]

The language employed in these documents (that CANH-withdrawal from these patients 'should', 'must' or 'requires' a court application) makes it unsurprising that

---

MCS': Alistair Pitblado, Official Solicitor, Letter to the Court of Protection Rules Committee (15 July 2017).

[43] 'Mental Capacity Act 2005: Code of Practice', Code of Practice from the Department of Constitutional Affairs, issued by Lord Falconer, Secretary of State for Constitutional Affairs and Lord Chancellor (2007 UK Government). The Code has status in law insofar as 'if a court or tribunal believes that anyone making decisions for someone who lacks capacity has not acted in the best interests of the person they care for, the court can use the person's failure to comply with the Code as evidence': 5. We note that the Code refers only to PVS patients (and not MCS patients) as those from whom CANH-withdrawal requires an application to the court (presumably because it was written before the revision to the Court of Protection, Practice Direction 9E: Applications Relating to Serious Medical Treatment in 2007).

[44] Royal College of Physicians, 'Prolonged Disorders of Consciousness: National Clinical Guidelines', 88, recommendation 5.7. This background is explained in the 2020 National Guidelines: Royal College of Physicians, 'National Guidelines', 97–9.

[45] James Munby, 'Consent to Treatment: Patients Lacking Capacity and Children', in Andrew Grubb, Judith Laing and Jean McHale (eds.), *Principles of Medical Law*, 3rd ed. (Oxford: Oxford University Press, 2010), para. 10.222 (exactly the same statement is made in the 2004 edition at para. 4.220).

lawyers employed by NHS Trusts and Clinical Commissioning Groups[46] routinely advised their clients not to withdraw feeding tubes from VS or MCS patients without court approval.

The legal situation existing prior to the Supreme Court decision in 2018 raised a number of medico-legal and ethical concerns in relation to which we (or others) might want to create legal change – and many of these concerns remain after the Supreme Court decision. These include for example: how is 'sanctity of life' weighted in such cases; is CANH correctly described as 'medical treatment' or is it rather 'basic care'; can the distinction between 'acts' and 'omissions' be maintained in cases of CANH-withdrawal; can decisions that inevitably lead to someone's death ever be in that person's 'best interests'; is 'best interests' (rather than 'substituted judgement') the appropriate criterion to use in deciding such cases; (how) is a PVS patient actually any more 'alive' than a 'brain dead' patient; and (as Lord Browne-Wilkinson said in *Bland*[47]) 'how can it be lawful to allow a patient to die slowly, though painlessly, over a period of weeks from lack of food but unlawful to produce his immediate death by a lethal injection, thereby saving his family from yet another ordeal to add to the tragedy that has already struck them?' These are issues which have been widely discussed elsewhere but they are not the focus of the discussion in this chapter which concentrates more narrowly on our own agenda for legal reform.

LEGAL ARGUMENTS DEVELOPED TO CHALLENGE THIS 'LAW'

Law reform sometimes has relatively straightforward goals: creating new legislation based on presumed consent for organ donation, changing the statutory time limit for abortion, or introducing exceptions to legislation that criminalises 'assisting a suicide' to permit medically assisting dying. In such cases there is a clearly demarcated procedure for statutory reform via the parliamentary process.

The case study reported here is less straightforward because its aim was not to create a new statute or to alter an existing one. The legal framework that (allegedly) mandated a court application before a feeding tube could lawfully be withdrawn from a patient in a PVS or MCS was derived from common law (*Bland*[48]) and entered medico-legal consciousness largely via Court of Protection Practice Direction 9E[49] which purported to reflect the law. In legal terms, the questions that needed to be answered to create the legal reform that we were recommending

---

[46] For information about Clinical Commissioning Groups and how they work, see: United Kingdom National Health Service, 'Clinical Commissioning Groups (CCGs)', NHS, 2020, www.england.nhs.uk/ccgs/.
[47] *Airedale NHS Trust v. Bland* [1993] AC 789 at 885.
[48] *Airedale NHS Trust v. Bland* [1993] AC 789.
[49] Court of Protection, Practice Direction 9E: Applications Relating to Serious Medical Treatment (1 July 2015).

were: (1) is there in fact a legal requirement to bring these cases to the courts (as opposed to a requirement of good practice) and (2) if it *is* a legal requirement, should it remain so? As it turned out, the first question was (eventually) answered in the negative.

A key player in developing a legal analysis of the claim that the law required applications to court for PVS and MCS patients prior to treatment withdrawal was barrister Alex Ruck Keene[50] (also our colleague on the CDOC Practice Direction 9E Working Party ('CDOC PD9E Working Party'), see below). He pointed out that there is nothing in the Mental Capacity Act 2005 (England and Wales) that 'imposes any form of statutory duty on medical professionals either to provide specific forms of treatment or to bring applications in relation to medical treatment to the Court of Protection'. The Code of Practice, he said, is essentially 'guidance' (not law) and '[i]t is unfortunate, to put it mildly, that the material provisions of the Code are both distinctly ambiguous and arguably incorrect as a matter of law'. Finally, he drew attention to the status of Practice Direction 9E,[51] arguing that such Directions 'can only relate to the practice and procedure of the Court of Protection *when applications are made to it*' and cannot stipulate that certain applications must be made. This latter argument was the one that eventually prevailed – but it took some time to reach a point where this was accepted by the judiciary.

Practice Directions are intended to assist in interpreting the law: there are forty-five of them accompanying the Court of Protection Rules and many deal with fairly mundane matters such as the need to paginate court bundles (Practice Direction 13B[52]) or the fee for examiners of the court (Practice Direction 14C[53]). Practice Direction 9E specified that decisions about withdrawal of feeding tubes from VS and MCS patients should be brought to the court.[54]

Practice Directions (and the Court of Protection Rules they supplement) are regularly revised and updated, and a new round of updating was initiated by the ad hoc Court of Protection Rules Committee in 2015, offering us the opportunity to input into the process. When we did so, however, the status of the Practice Direction itself began to unravel as it became increasingly clear that – in the words of the Vice President of the Court of Protection: 'the existing PD 9E should not have included provisions as to what cases should be brought to court' because

[50] Alexander Ruck Keene, 'Procedure, Practice and Legal Requirements: A Commentary on "Why I Wrote My Advance Decision"' (2017) 43 *Journal of Medical Ethics* 435–8.
[51] Court of Protection, Practice Direction 9E: Applications Relating to Serious Medical Treatment (1 July 2015).
[52] Court of Protection, Practice Direction 13B: Court Bundles (1 July 2015).
[53] Court of Protection, Practice Direction 14C: Fees for Examiners of the Court (1 December 2017).
[54] Court of Protection, Practice Direction 9E: Applications Relating to Serious Medical Treatment (1 July 2015), para. 5(a).

'a practice direction cannot properly dictate when an application should be brought'.[55] Consequently, Practice Direction 9E was subsequently deleted but without changing 'the law' – since whether or not applications to the Court were required by law was newly understood to be (and always to have been) independent of a Practice Direction which had no legal power to pronounce on the subject.

Removing and not replacing Practice Direction 9E did not 'change the law': the law remained whatever it was before the Practice Direction undertook (erroneously) to pronounce on it. This left many questions. For example, did the recommendation in *Bland*[56] in 1993 still stand – or had the conditions been met such that 'a body of experience and practice has been built up which might obviate the need for application in every case'? Did the subsequent implementation of the Mental Capacity Act 2005 (England and Wales) and its case law (notably *Aintree*,[57] *Burke*[58] and *Briggs*[59]) substantially alter or develop the law in this area – in particular by clarifying that all medical treatments given to patients who lack capacity must be demonstrably in patients' best interests, and by increasingly ensuring that patients' own (prior) values, wishes, feelings and beliefs are central to best interests decision-making. Lawyers expressed radically different understandings about what in fact the law did require, and the Court of Protection Rules Committee requested guidance from the relevant professional bodies on what would constitute good medical practice in this area.

Not surprisingly, given this scenario, despite the deletion of Practice Direction 9E[60] – which had been a key target for our legal reform endeavours – NHS lawyers and medical defence unions continued to advise that all cases of withdrawal of CANH from VS and MCS patients should be referred to the Courts. During 2017 and 2018 a number of uncontested cases reached the Court of Protection. The most significant of these was *M v. A Hospital*[61] because, in addition to seeking the court's agreement that it would be lawful to withdraw CANH, counsel for the patient (Victoria Butler-Cole, another of our colleagues on the CDOC PD9E Working Party, see below) filed a submission arguing that there was no obligation in law or good practice for a declaration or decision of the Court of Protection to be obtained in the circumstances of this case. The submission from the Official Solicitor, by contrast, 'trenchantly asserts that an application to court should be

---

[55] Justice Charles, Vice President of the Court of Protection, Chairman of the Court of Protection Rules Committee, Letter to the CDOC PD9E Working Party (28 July 2017).

[56] *Airedale NHS Trust v. Bland* [1993] AC 789.

[57] *Aintree University Hospitals NHS Foundation Trust (Respondent) v. James (Appellant)* [2013] UKSC 67.

[58] *R (Burke) v. General Medical Council (Official Solicitor and Others Intervening)* [2005] EWCA Civ 1003.

[59] *Briggs v. Briggs and Others* [2016] EWCOP 48.

[60] Court of Protection, Practice Direction 9E: Applications Relating to Serious Medical Treatment (1 July 2015).

[61] *M v. A Hospital* [2017] EWCOP 19.

made in every case of proposed withdrawal of CANH, unless there is a valid advance directive' and this 'led to an equally robust response from Ms Butler-Cole'.[62] The judge (Jackson J) considered that 'it was not necessary as a matter of law for this case to have been brought to court'[63] and, crucially, that there was no obligation under Article 2 of the European Convention on Human Rights[64] for the state to mandate court oversight as a matter of law. Jackson J concluded:[65]

> In my judgment, therefore, a decision to withdraw CANH, taken in accordance with the prevailing professional guidance . . . will be lawful . . . The court is always available where there is disagreement, or where it is felt for some other reason that an application should be made, but this will only arise in rare cases.

The Official Solicitor argued that this opinion was *obiter* (because the application to withdraw treatment for this particular patient had already been determined) and that it therefore did not provide legal protection for clinicians. Subsequent discussions from lawyers about the precise status of the judge's position, for example, claiming it as a judicial dicta standing 'somewhere between a ratio decidendi and an obiter dictum'[66] did little to reassure clinicians, or the Trust lawyers who continued to advise applications to court before withdrawing CANH from VS or MCS patients. It seemed that only a Supreme Court decision would settle the matter.[67]

DEVELOPING AND DEPLOYING RESEARCH SHOWING THE NEED FOR LEGAL REFORM

In this section, we address the importance for law reform of going further than simply generating the evidence base and pursuing traditional dissemination routes. We highlight the role of deploying research findings through advocacy (including

---

[62] *M v. A Hospital* [2017] EWCOP 19 at [30].

[63] Ibid. at [5].

[64] Convention for the Protection of Human Rights and Fundamental Freedoms, Rome, 4 November 1950, in force 3 September 1953, 213 UNTS 221.

[65] *M v. A Hospital* [2017] EWCOP 19 at [37]. This judgement was preceded by an earlier *obiter* observation (apparently unprompted) in the Court of Appeal in *Director of Legal Aid Casework and Others* v. *Briggs* [2017] EWCA Civ 1169 at [108] (King LJ):

> [I]f the medical treatment proposed is not in dispute, then, regardless of whether it involves the withdrawal of treatment from a person who is minimally conscious or in a persistent vegetative state, it is a decision as to what treatment is in P's best interests and can be taken by the treating doctors who then have immunity pursuant to section 5 MCA [Mental Capacity Act].

[66] 39 Essex Chambers, 'M v A Hospital: Summary', 39 Essex Chambers, 20 September 2017, www.39essex .com/cop_cases/m-v-hospital/, quoting *Brunner* v. *Greenslade* [1971] Ch 993 at 1002 (Megarry J).

[67] As noted below, we did consider asking parliament to address this issue but determined that this reform path was very unlikely to succeed.

developing multi-media resources, doing mass media work and rolling out targeted training) and also, in this case, initiating a specific working party on the core issue.

Generating the Evidence Base

As academic social scientists, our own research has focused predominantly on the experience of families of VS and MCS patients and providing longitudinal insight into the patient's journey through different parts of the medico-legal system. Our findings complement the work of many clinical and legal experts working on medical decision-making and mental capacity. Similar issues to those we highlighted were evident in the excellent analyses of those working specifically on prolonged disorders of consciousness (e.g. Wade, Turner-Stokes, Ruck Keene)[68] as well as in broader issues relating to death and dying (e.g. Marsh, Gwande, Mannix)[69] – and of course the moving autobiographical accounts of families themselves (e.g. Spinney, Rentzenbrink).[70]

In the multi-disciplinary context of the CDOC Research Centre (which we co-direct), our research combined with that of legal, philosophical, economic, literary and medical scholars to argue that, if in fact there was a legal requirement mandating judicial scrutiny of CANH-withdrawal from PVS and MCS patients, such a requirement was detrimental and should be abolished. We found:

- **Unjustified legal anomaly:** The requirement for judicial approval before certain treatments can be withdrawn from patients in a PVS is a legal anomaly in domestic law and out of kilter with international law.[71]
- **Significant economic cost:** The cost to the NHS of requiring a court hearing before a feeding tube can be withdrawn (or withheld) from a

---

[68] D. T. Wade, 'How Often Is the Diagnosis of the Permanent Vegetative State Incorrect?: A Review of the Evidence' (2018) 25 *European Journal of Neurology* 619–25; Lynne Turner-Stokes, 'A Matter of Life and Death: Controversy at the Interface between Clinical and Legal Decision-Making in Prolonged Disorders of Consciousness' (2017) 43 *Journal of Medical Ethics* 469–75. See also Alex Ruck Keene's 'Mental Capacity Law and Policy' Blog here: www.mentalcapacitylawandpolicy.org.uk/about-the-author/.

[69] Henry Marsh, *Do No Harm: Stories of Life, Death and Brain Surgery* (London: Weidenfeld and Nicolson, 2014); Atul Gwande, *Being Mortal: Illness, Medicine and What Matters in the End* (London: Profile Books, 2014); Kathryn Mannix, *With the End in Mind: Dying, Death and Wisdom in an Age of Denial* (London: Harper Collins, 2017).

[70] Lu Spinney, *Beyond the High Blue Air* (London: Atlantic Books, 2016); Cathy Rentzenbrink, *The Last Act of Love* (London: Picador, 2015).

[71] Simon Halliday, Adam Formby and Richard Cookson, 'An Assessment of the Court's Role in the Withdrawal of Clinically Assisted Nutrition and Hydration from Patients in the Permanent Vegetative State' (2015) 23 *Medical Law Review* 556–87; Celia Kitzinger and Jenny Kitzinger, 'Family Perspectives on Proper Medical Treatment', in Sara Fovargue and Alexandra Mullock (eds.), *The Legitimacy of Medical Treatment: What Role for the Medical Exception?* (New York, NY: Routledge, 2015).

PVS patient in straightforward cases where clinicians and family agree that this is in the patient's best interests is on average about £122,000 per case. This displaces alternative NHS services and causes a loss of nine quality-adjusted life years from other patients.[72]

- **Deterring CANH-withdrawal counter to patient's best interests:** The requirement for court applications before treatment withdrawal from PVS and MCS patients leads to long-term and invasive treatment that is not in the patient's best interests. There are between 4,000 and 16,000 PVS patients in England and Wales, and about three times that many patients in MCS.[73] Very few applications for treatment withdrawal have reached the courts: a leading barrister reports that his search of legal databases BAILLI and Westlaw found only around ten cases where permission has been sought to withdraw CANH from a person in a PVS or MCS in the nine years between October 2007 and October 2016;[74] the Royal College of Physicians[75] estimates forty cases between 1993 and 2013. Our own estimate – derived from extrapolation from the number of interviews we have carried out with family members of PVS and MCS patients who have been the subject of court hearings that have not been publicly reported – is that there have been maybe 150 such cases in the twenty-seven years since *Bland*.[76] Since no court in England and Wales has, to our knowledge, ever found a feeding tube to be in the best interests of a PVS patient, this means that many PVS patients are receiving treatment that is not in their best interests and often this continues over years or decades (for one family we worked with, for example, the patient had been in PVS for almost thirty-four years, since an injury pre-dating *Bland*[77]). Our interviews with family members of people in PVS and MCS found this is in part due to the legal process acting as a deterrent to both clinicians and families.[78] Families and

---

[72] Adam Formby, Richard Cookson and Simon Halliday, 'Cost Analysis of the Legal Declaratory Relief Requirement for Withdrawing Clinically Assisted Nutrition and Hydration (CANH) from Patients in the Permanent Vegetative State (PVS) in England and Wales', Research Paper 108 from the Centre for Health Economics (2015 University of York) at 12.

[73] Zoë Fritz and Sarah Bunn, 'Vegetative and Minimally Conscious States', Post Note No. 489 from the Parliamentary Office of Science and Technology (March 2015 Houses of Parliament, UK).

[74] Alex Ruck Keene, 'Advance Decisions to Refuse Life-Sustaining Treatment and the Court of Protection', Mental Capacity Law and Policy, 31 October 2016, www .mentalcapacitylawandpolicy.org.uk/advance-decisions-to-refuse-life-sustaining-treatment-and-the-court-of-protection/.

[75] Royal College of Physicians, 'National Guidelines', 63.

[76] *Airedale NHS Trust v. Bland* [1993] AC 789.

[77] Ibid.

[78] Kitzinger and Kitzinger, 'Court Applications for Withdrawal of Artificial Nutrition and Hydration'.

clinicians hope that the patient will die in some other way without requiring a court application: we heard many stories about infections left untreated to allow death – leading families to witness the repeated 'near deaths' of their relative, and some deaths (e.g. from lung infections and gangrene) that seem less well controlled and more traumatic (at least for families) than death after CANH-withdrawal.

- **Delaying CANH-withdrawal counter to patients' best interests – after a best interests decision has been made by clinicians and before it is approved by the court.** There are systemic failures within both the medical and legal systems which result in long delays once applications are initiated.[79] These include delays in actually submitting applications to the court due to lack of knowledge or understanding of how the system is supposed to work; disputes about who should fund the application; failures of communication within the multi-disciplinary team as to who is responsible for what; delays caused while medical records – sometimes going back years and dispersed across different hospitals, rehabilitation centres and care homes – are sought out; long waits for the independent expert approved by the court to carry out additional examinations in what doctors often describe as an attempt to 'dot the "i"s and cross the "t"s'; and often, delays in judges' capacity to hear the case which is rarely considered 'urgent'.
- **Prompting potentially premature withdrawal of life-sustaining treatment:** Awareness of some of these problems for patients in prolonged disorders of consciousness could mean that clinicians (or families) felt pressure to stop life-sustaining treatment before the patient entered a 'persistent' or 'permanent' state.[80] For some, this could mean patients were potentially deprived of an opportunity of meaningful (to them) recovery.

Advocacy for Reform

On the basis of our research findings, our efforts to change the (purported) requirement for court applications included the following advocacy strategies.

Traditional Academic Dissemination
The evidence base developed through our research was disseminated through the traditional academic forums of publications and conference presentations. We

[79] Jenny Kitzinger and Celia Kitzinger, 'Causes and Consequences of Delays in Treatment-Withdrawal from PVS Patients: A Case Study of *Cumbria NHS Clinical Commissioning Group v. Miss S and Others* [2016] EWCOP 32' (2016) 43 *Journal of Medical Ethics* 459–68; Kitzinger and Kitzinger, 'Court Applications for Withdrawal of Artificial Nutrition and Hydration'.
[80] Kitzinger and Kitzinger, 'The "Window of Opportunity" for Death after Severe Brain Injury'.

published in peer-reviewed journals an overview of family experience of instigating and supporting withdrawal applications,[81] an analysis of costs[82] and a case study where it took three years for the case to reach and progress through the court to an eventual declaration that CANH-withdrawal was in the patient's best interests (even though the whole family and clinicians had agreed at the outset of the process that treatment was not in the patient's best interests).[83] Another case study showed how the purported requirement for a court application contributed to a patient being kept alive – contrary to what his family believe he would have wanted – for more than two decades.[84] In these publications we made clear statements about the harm caused by the apparent requirement to make court applications before withdrawing CANH from these patients. We also produced an executive summary of our findings,[85] printed copies of which we used as a resource to support conference talks and meetings of our CDOC PD9E Working Party (see below).

Broader Dissemination outside Academia

In addition to the above academic outlets, we pursued wider dissemination via:

- The CDOC Research Centre's website, blogs and social media – in particular our twitter feed[86] from which, among other things, we have live-tweeted court cases.[87]
- Mass media contributions, including appearing on national news and current affairs programmes in connection with our case studies. For example, in 2016 Jenny appeared alongside the family, in extensive media coverage across a range of programmes during which the patient's mother and brother spoke out against the injustice done to the patient, and the pain they had themselves endured due to long delays. We highlighted the context of the individual family, our broader research findings and the need for legal reform. In September 2017, we contributed to news coverage (again in relation to a particular court case)

---

[81] Kitzinger and Kitzinger, 'Court Applications for Withdrawal of Artificial Nutrition and Hydration'.

[82] Formby, Cookson and Halliday, Research Paper 108 from the Centre for Health Economics.

[83] Kitzinger and Kitzinger, 'Causes and Consequences of Delays in Treatment-Withdrawal from PVS Patients'.

[84] Kitzinger and Kitzinger, 'Why Futile and Unwanted Treatment Continues for Some PVS Patients'.

[85] Celia Kitzinger, 'Serious Medical Treatment and the Law Concerning Patients in a Permanent Vegetative State', Executive Summary from the Coma and Disorders of Consciousness Research Centre (2015 Cardiff University), http://cdoc.org.uk/publications/summaries-and-com mentary/.

[86] The Coma and Disorders of Consciousness Research Centre's website is: https://cdoc.org.uk. The Centre's Twitter handle is: @CDOCuk.

[87] Jenny Kitzinger and Celia Kitzinger, 'How (And Why) to Tweet from the "Secret" and "Shadowy" Court of Protection', Transparency Project, 3 July 2017, www.transparencyproject .org.uk/how-and-why-to-tweet-from-the-secret-and-shadowy-court-of-protection/.

highlighting our research about the effects of a perceived need to go to court for decisions about withdrawing CANH from PVS and MCS patients even after families and clinical teams agreed it was not in the patient's best interests. Contributions included appearances on Radio 4's 'The Today Programme' and the BBC lunchtime news, as well as a series of other outlets (e.g. BBC Radio Wales and the LBC radio) and talking to print journalists (e.g. the New Scientist).

- The creation of a multi-media resource 'healthtalk'[88] based on clips from our research interviews. This has become widely used for supporting families and educating professionals (and we have since developed e-learning courses specifically for professionals; see cdoctraining.org.uk).
- Targeted engagement with key professional audiences – for example, distributing executive summaries, and by presenting our work at practitioner events (e.g. the Court of Protection Practitioners' Association). By invitation, we provided Continuing Professional Development for a range of professionals including conducting training days at care homes. We also contributed by invitation to an annual training seminar for twenty-four High Court judges (January 2017) and were asked to submit our slides – in which we presented the evidence and argument for ending the alleged requirement for court approval as a follow-up resource.[89]

Creation of Targeted Events for Dissemination

Throughout our work we built networks between academics from different disciplinary backgrounds and with medical and legal practitioners. This started with a Wellcome Trust Seminar we organised in 2010 at the very beginning of our work in this area, and has subsequently continued via collaborations with practitioners in creating our healthtalk module (discussed above), co-researching concerns raised by Independent Mental Capacity Advocates about their role[90] and with allied health professionals.[91] We also work with lawyers and clinicians when we support families through the court process. To focus on the particular issue of the law in relation to

[88] healthtalk, 'Family Experiences of Vegetative and Minimally Conscious States, University of Oxford, 2019, https://healthtalk.org/family-experiences-vegetative-and-minimally-conscious-states/overview (ESRC grant ES/K00560X/1).

[89] These slides are available here: Celia Kitzinger and Jenny Kitzinger, 'Delays in Treatment Withdrawal from Adults in Vegetative and Minimally Conscious States', Coma and Disorders of Consciousness Research Centre, 2017, http://cdoc.org.uk/high-court-seminar/.

[90] Doris A. Chatfield, Sue Lee, Jakki Cowley, Celia Kitzinger, Jenny Kitzinger and David K. Menon, 'Is There a Broader Role for Independent Mental Capacity Advocates in Critical Care?' (2017) 23 *Nursing in Critical Care* 82–7.

[91] Julie Latchem, Jenny Kitzinger and Celia Kitzinger, 'Physiotherapy for Vegetative and Minimally Conscious State Patients: Family Perceptions and Experiences' (2015) 38 *Disability and Rehabilitation* 22–9.

CANH-withdrawal we drew on our existing contacts to organise two conferences specifically on this issue – both attended by senior clinicians, barristers and a High Court judge. The first focused on the national situation (held in York, May 2014); the second explored the situation internationally with representative experts from different European countries and from the United States (held in Oxford, April 2017).[92]

The CDOC Practice Direction 9E Working Party

Our work in this area created an environment in which the requirement for court applications was intensively discussed by a wide variety of stakeholders, including families, advocates, allied health professionals, independent mental capacity advocates, solicitors, barristers and judges. We began to see opinions shift, with increasing recognition of the harm caused by the requirement for a court application, and with a developing interest from some practising lawyers (e.g. Alex Ruck Keene) in the extent to which Practice Direction 9E[93] in fact accurately reflected case law and statute. We see it as evidence of our impact in the field that the Court of Protection Rules Committee undertook to extend their review to include (as they had not initially proposed to) a review of Practice Direction 9E.[94]

The CDOC PD9E Working Party was created in 2015, and chaired by Celia, and expenses for meetings were supported by Economic and Social Research Council Impact Acceleration Account funding. It was composed of a group of senior lawyers with experience in the Court of Protection (including Alex Ruck Keene and Victoria Butler Cole, mentioned earlier) and senior clinicians with expertise in VS and MCS, including Lynne Turner Stokes, Chair of the Royal College of Physicians' Working Party on Prolonged Disorders of Consciousness, and Veronica English, as a representative from the British Medical Association. We were joined by one of the UK's most senior and respected neurorehabilitation specialists, Derick Wade, other academics (e.g. medical lawyer and ethicist Penney Lewis), allied health professionals (e.g. physiotherapist and former care-home manager Julie Latchem) and an Independent Mental Capacity Advocate (Jakki Cowley). The CDOC PD9E Working Party drew on our published research findings in conjunction with professionals' medico-legal and advocacy expertise to consider what changes were needed in relation to Practice Direction 9E.[95] The CDOC PD9E Working Party submitted a report to the Court of Protection Rules

---

[92] Information about the other events on this topic that we have organised and contributed to are available here: Coma and Disorders of Consciousness Research Centre, 'News 2010–12', Cardiff University, 2012, http://cdoc.org.uk/news-2/.

[93] Court of Protection, Practice Direction 9E: Applications Relating to Serious Medical Treatment (1 July 2015).

[94] Ibid.

[95] Ibid.

Committee recommending that court applications should not be required for 'straightforward' cases where family and clinicians are in agreement that continued life-prolonging treatment is not in the patient's best interests. We also recommended 'streamlining' the application process to avoid delays between the best interests decision to withdraw CANH and the eventual court decision. We obtained the formal support of the British Medical Association for our recommendations:[96]

> The BMA strongly supports the proposal for a streamlined process for seeking court approval in cases where all relevant parties agree that continuing to provide clinically assisted nutrition and hydration to a patient in a permanent vegetative state is not in the patient's best interests. As research by the CDOC Research Centre shows, it is in the interests of patients and their families that any unnecessary delays are avoided: providing a clear process for preparing and submitting such applications will help to achieve this. In the longer term, once this process is established and with appropriate safeguards, we hope that further consideration will be given to whether these uncontested cases should continue to require court approval.

The Court of Protection Rules Committee worked slowly and its processes were somewhat impenetrable to those outside of it (and sometimes, it seems, to its own members). The CDOC PD9E Working Party saw a number of draft versions of a reworked Practice Direction 9E.[97] The first version did not require automatic court applications for withdrawal of life-prolonging treatment from PVS patients – indeed it stated that if an application was made to the court then the justification for doing so should be spelt out. It also included a 'checklist' for court applications, derived in large part from the report we had sent to the Rules Committee. This draft was later abandoned and a very different draft was circulated – which explicitly declined to specify the circumstances under which an application should or should not be made to the court (and dealt only with the procedures for managing applications once they had been made). The shift from the first to the second version seems to have been prompted by the argument (advanced especially by barrister Alex Ruck Keene and subsequently – we understand – agreed by the Rules Committee as a whole) that instructions about which cases should come before the court are beyond the remit of what a Practice Direction can legitimately do. The second draft (at least the second draft circulated to our group) of Practice Direction 9E[98] was in turn abandoned after a public meeting of the Rules Committee attended by eight members of the CDOC PD9E Working Party. At that meeting we expressed considerable concern about how this (second) draft would be interpreted in practice – potentially not only as meaning that PVS and MCS cases should continue to be referred to the court but as actually

[96] Dr John Chisholm, Chair of the BMA's Medical Ethics Committee, Letter to CDOC PD9E Working Party (19 October 2015) (provided for submission to the Court of Protection Rules Committee).

[97] Court of Protection, Practice Direction 9E: Applications Relating to Serious Medical Treatment (1 July 2015).

[98] Ibid.

broadening the requirement for court applications in respect of serious medical treatments.[99] Several of us also conveyed our concern (and the evidence for it) that far from 'protecting' patients and their families (a claimed benefit of court applications), the requirement for judicial scrutiny actually caused harm.[100]

Representatives from the office of the Official Solicitor[101] – and the comments provided by the Official Solicitor himself in a letter submitted to the Court of Protection Rules Committee – were equally forthright in the position that all PVS and MCS cases *should* come before the court as a matter of good practice. As summarised by the meeting's Chair, Mr Justice Charles: 'The underlying issues raise important legal, medical and ethical issues upon which competing views are strongly held and promoted by individuals and groups.'[102]

The outcome of that meeting was reflected in the decision of the Court of Protection Rules Committee to abandon Practice Direction 9E altogether:

I shall recommend and so instruct work to be done to remove and not replace PD 9E and to remove and not replace references in the Rules and PDs (including PD 12A) to serious medical treatment cases.[103]

Practice Direction 9E[104] was finally abolished but 'the law' concerning court applications for PVS and MCS patients remained as it always was. But there were now strongly discrepant views on what in fact 'the law' did say on this matter, as discussed above.

The Official Solicitor was of the view (relying on *Bland*[105]) that the law required that such applications be made at least as a matter of 'good practice' and stated that

99 Lynne Turner Stokes, Derick Wade, Raanan Gillon, Celia Kitzinger and Veronica English, Letters to the Court of Protection Rules Committee. All of these parties attended the meeting and submitted letters to this effect.

100 The claim that court applications 'protect' patients (and families and the public) was initially advanced in *Airedale NHS Trust v. Bland* [1993] AC 789 and was restated in the Official Solicitor's letter to the Court of Protection Rules Committee: Alistair Pitblado, Official Solicitor, Letter to the Court of Protection Rules Committee (15 July 2017). Both Derick Wade and Celia Kitzinger challenged this claim.

101 The Official Solicitor is a government appointed lawyer who acts as litigation friend for those without legal capacity: Official Solicitor and Public Trustee, 'What Official Solicitor and Public Trustee Does'. There had been some concern about the way in which this role was being performed; see Ruck Keene, 'Litigation Friend or Foe?'.

102 Justice Charles, Chairman of the Court of Protection Rules Committee, Meeting Notes (28 July 2017) (circulated to all present at the meeting). Those notes also record: 'a representative of the Official Solicitor expressly warned that the written comments from non-members of the committee came from people with vested interests'. Non-members of the Court of Protection Rules Committee present were – with only one or two exceptions – members of the CDOC PD9E Working Party.

103 Justice Charles, Chairman of the Court of Protection Rules Committee, Meeting Notes (28 July 2017) (circulated to all present at the meeting).

104 Court of Protection, Practice Direction 9E: Applications Relating to Serious Medical Treatment (1 July 2015).

105 *Airedale NHS Trust v. Bland* [1993] AC 789.

'surely clinicians do not want to act otherwise than in accordance with good practice and in accordance with their duty of care'.[106] Equally clearly, some barristers believed that court applications could not be a legal requirement pointing for example to the fact that a court declaration that withdrawal is lawful cannot make lawful that which, absent a declaration, would be unlawful. As stated in *Principles of Medical Law*:

> There is therefore never any legal necessity to obtain a declaration before proceeding either to treat or to stop the treatment of an adult who lacks capacity (though the courts have indicated that, in certain circumstances, good practice requires that a declaration should be sought).[107]

If, in fact then, an application was not 'legally required' but was considered (by the courts) to be a matter of 'good practice', the obvious difficulty was that some very senior clinicians in this field did not consider it 'good practice' to continue to give treatment to patients that is not in their best interests while waiting for judicial approval. Moreover, a judge cannot instruct doctors to give medical treatment counter to their professional clinical judgement.[108] This argument was incorporated – by Victoria Butler Cole, a member of the CDOC PD9E Working Party – into an application to withdraw CANH from a PVS patient. The judge was invited to declare that the case did not need to be brought before the court (and did so declare, as discussed earlier *M v. A Hospital*[109]). Recognising that these dicta were viewed as *obiter* in some quarters (most importantly, by the Official Solicitor), it was apparent that a Supreme Court hearing was the next step.

The British Medical Association, which had for more than a decade expressed the view that clinicians (not judges) should be the decision-makers concerning CANH for patients in VS and MCS[110] appointed a 'core group' of experts to advise it on the development of Guidance for decision-making about CANH for adults who lack the capacity to consent.[111] Three people from the CDOC PD9E Working Party were among the eleven core group members (Celia Kitzinger, Alex Ruck Keene and Lynne Turner-Stokes), with another six forming part of the wider professional

---

[106] Alistair Pitblado, Official Solicitor, Letter to the Court of Protection Rules Committee (15 July 2017).

[107] Munby, 'Consent to Treatment', para. 10.125.

[108] *Burke, R (on the application of) v. General Medical Council and Others* [2005] EWCA Civ 1003.

[109] *M v. A Hospital* [2017] EWCOP 19.

[110] See British Medical Association, *Withholding and Withdrawing Life-Prolonging Medical Treatment: Guidance for Decision-Making*, 3rd ed. (London: Blackwell Publishing, 2007). See also the 1st and 2nd editions.

[111] 'Clinically Assisted Nutrition and Hydration (CANH) and Adults Who Lack the Capacity to Consent: Guidance for Decision-Making in England and Wales', Guidance from the Royal College of Physicians and British Medical Association (2018 RCP and BMA), www.bma.org .uk/advice-and-support/ethics/adults-who-lack-capacity/clinically-assisted-nutrition-and-hydration.

consultative group (Yogi Amin, Victoria Butler Cole, Jakki Cowley, Jenny Kitzinger, Julie Latchem and Derick Wade). Draft Guidance was provided to the Supreme Court in advance of their decision in *Re Y*[112] and a final version was published, jointly with the Royal College of Physicians and endorsed by the General Medical Council, after the decision was handed down by the Court. Based on the new legal and regulatory position, it provides comprehensive guidance to clinicians about decision-making concerning CANH for adults who lack the capacity to consent, starting from the position that clinicians can and should take responsibility (in the vast majority of situations) for making and implementing these decisions without the involvement of the courts.

AFTER THE SUPREME COURT DECISION

Outcomes of the Decision

The landmark Supreme Court decision in *Re Y*[113] at the end of July 2018 was widely reported in the media. We were called on by journalists to comment on the judgement and appeared on the main evening news bulletins for the BBC and Channel 4.[114] Since then, and in part due to the publicity the decision received, we have seen a rapid increase in the number of clinicians and families approaching us for help with reviewing whether or not CANH is in a patient's best interests. Most of these decisions have not necessitated involvement of the courts because, following a review of the evidence (including the patient's prognosis, and values, beliefs, wishes and feelings) families and clinicians agreed that continuing CANH was not what the person would want, and definitely not in the patient's best interests. Some of these cases were 'waiting in the wings', as lawyers held back on making court applications pending the outcome of the Supreme Court hearing that might make them redundant: once the way forward was clear, they proceeded without delay. Others were cases that were initiated as a direct result of media publicity about the Supreme Court decision as families became aware, sometimes for the first time, of the lawful possibility of withdrawing CANH from their relative, or felt free, at last, to raise the question of withdrawal with clinicians without the daunting prospect of a court application. The significance of the judgement, then, resonated not just in the medico-legal world but also impacted, via media reports, on the families whose loved ones were at the centre of these cases.

Some practitioners report there has been a fundamental shift in culture in some units, where senior clinicians are now much more willing to consider withdrawal

---

[112] *An NHS Trust v. Y* [2018] UKSC 46.
[113] Ibid.
[114] See, for example, Jenny Kitzinger, Interview with BBC News, 1 August 2018, www.youtube .com/watch?time_continue=7&v=LzwTcEgFmpA.

(though other clinicians seem impervious to the change). In the best interests reviews that we are seeing, it seems to us that these are conducted in a robust way – and some are taking place in an efficient and timely fashion. Problems remain however, and we are now reviewing case studies to explore the significance of the Supreme Court decision for on-the-ground practice.[115] We find that there are still delays in best interests decision-making, difficulties with organising and coordinating services, evasion of decision-making responsibility and undeclared conscientious objection. Extensive training and culture changes are needed in some places (and we are now working on this with delivering e-learning[116]). Overall, however, the ending of the perceived requirement for court approval has resulted in a more transparent, more efficient and more person-centered approach to best interests decision-making for these patients.

Our Reflections on Our Role(s)

We have focused in this chapter on our role as scholars and as activists for other families, but we were first catapulted into engaging with the need for legal reform through our own family experience. Our sister, Polly Kitzinger, was in a car crash in 2009 and left with devastating brain injuries, originally in a VS and then MCS. It was clear early on that her injuries were incompatible with any kind of future she would have valued for herself. The best possible scenario, if she were to regain consciousness, was that she might be able to be wheeled into a garden and enjoy the sun and make some limited choices, but her doctors believed she would never regain the mental capacity to make any serious decisions about her own life. That was not a future Polly would have found acceptable for herself.

We advocated for Polly's right not to have life-sustaining interventions imposed on her – but were overruled by doctors who insisted that treatments must continue for a year from the date of injury until it was determined whether or not she would regain some level of consciousness. After that, they said, a court case would be required before withdrawal of CANH could be considered. This seemed to us not only a fundamental violation of her human rights (Polly had always been very outspoken on what she would want in this sort of situation) but also incompatible with the Mental Capacity Act 2005 (England and Wales). Doctors were, at the very least, abdicating their responsibility to act in Polly's best interests and/or were abusing

---

[115] Jenny Kitzinger and Celia Kitzinger, 'Out of Court: Decisions about CANH for Patients in Permanent Vegetative States after Re Y', *International Journal of Mental Health and Capacity Law* (under submission).

[116] The training resources produced by the CDOC Research Centre are available here: Coma and Disorders of Consciousness Research Centre, 'Welcome to Our Training Resources', Cardiff University, 2020, https://cdoctraining.org.uk.

their power to impose their values and beliefs upon her.[117] Lawyers were, at least at first, unwilling to represent us (because it was 'too early') and then advised us against pursuing Polly's case (because – as Polly regained some minimal consciousness – it was 'too late'). We were distraught and outraged on Polly's behalf. It was this experience that set us off on the journey of trying to discover how other clinicians practised, what happened to other families and patients and the role of the law in all this.

After a few years, Polly did eventually regain full consciousness, albeit with profound brain damage. Her feeding tube was removed and she is now spoon-fed. The legal reform documented in this chapter cannot change the fate to which she has been condemned by the system at the time, and by how the individual doctors who treated her chose to implement it. However, it is clear that the legal reform ushered in by the Supreme Court can, and does, make a difference to some patients (and their families) who find themselves in similar situations now.

Without the barriers and delay introduced by mandatory court applications, clinicians can, and should, implement best interests decision-making in a timely fashion. That includes making decisions about whether or not CANH continues to be in the patient's best interests at regular interviews (at least once a year according to the Guidance[118] we helped to co-author). In the decade or so since doctors delivered to Polly life-sustaining medical treatments that she would have refused if she could, case law has repeatedly affirmed and developed the principle that great weight should be attached to patients' past and present wishes in any decisions made about them.[119] The Supreme Court judgement in *Re Y*[120] means that patients with the most profound brain injuries are no longer singled out and treated differently from other patients. Individualised person-centred care is now clearly supposed to take priority over diagnostic determinism. There is no longer any requirement built into the system for best interests decision-making to be obstructed by lengthy bureaucratic delays for court applications. Polly has been part of making that happen and what was done to her (and to our whole family) meant that giving up on the struggle to contribute to that change was never an option for us.

When we started our efforts at reforming law and clinical practice, we were both full professors in (different) universities involved in (separate) social science research projects that included health-related issues. Within a year, we had begun to work together to combine our skills and expertise to research other families' experience of having a relative with catastrophic brain injuries. We knew that research on its own

---

[117] We wrote about our family experience here: Celia Kitzinger and Jenny Kitzinger, '"M", Polly, and the Right to Die', Hastings Bioethics Forum, 12 October 2011, www.thehastingscenter.org/m-polly-and-the-right-to-die/.

[118] 'Clinically Assisted Nutrition and Hydration (CANH) and Adults Who Lack the Capacity to Consent', Guidance from the Royal College of Physicians and British Medical Association.

[119] See Chapter 11 for a discussion of role of the patient's wishes in assessing best interests.

[120] *An NHS Trust v. Y* [2018] UKSC 46.

would never be sufficient to create the changes we were seeking – but we also knew that without research into the effects of current law and practice on patients and their families, we would not have a full picture of what was happening or what the barriers might be to changing that. We were also vulnerable – especially in the first few years – to being dismissed as 'just angry family members', projecting our grief and distress at our sister's injury onto the medico-legal professions. Our family experience was both the impetus for seeking legal reform, but also an impediment to being taken seriously since it was assumed that we (unlike other professionals!) had vested interests that would bias our inquiries. We were committed from the outset to contributing high-quality research evidence to the ongoing discussions about law reform, and also to ensuring that our evidence was made available to key people in the right places at the right times such that it might in turn have a chance of influencing practice. At the same time, our status as 'family members' enabled us to collaborate – in ways researchers without family experience would have found harder – with families of VS and MCS patients, to ensure that their message was heard and to support them in speaking directly to the media. Two family members in particular stand out as having 'gone public' about the way their loved one was treated and campaigned against the delays and obstacles to treatment withdrawal: Lindsey Briggs, wife of the police officer, Paul Briggs, and Jean Simpson, mother of Jodie. Both have spoken out about what happened in an effort to protect others.[121]

Strategies for Reform

Legal reform depended heavily upon collaborations with family members and with relevant professionals, including co-publication with practitioners[122] and not just in designing the research itself but also through multiple dissemination and engage-ment strategies. Sometimes our initiatives fell on stony ground; sometimes (unex-pectedly) they flourished, and we never seemed to know in advance which way it would go. For every route we found through the maze, we encountered many dead ends. The failures and obstacles were part of the route to success. Early on, for example, we considered the possibility of asking parliament to legislate on whether or not decisions to withdraw CANH from these patients needed to be heard before the courts. Celia obtained a two-week secondment to the UK Parliament (funded by

---

[121] See Lindsey Briggs' interview: 'I Begged to Let My Husband Die', This Morning, 20 August 2017, www.youtube.com/watch?v=cr75QNHVDqw. See also Jean Simpson's statements: Sanchia Berg, 'Permanent Vegetative State: A Family's Agony', BBC News, 23 September 2016, www.bbc.co.uk/news/magazine-37444379.

[122] See, for example, Derick T. Wade and Celia Kitzinger, 'Making Healthcare Decisions in a Person's Best Interests When They Lack Capacity: Clinical Guidance Based on a Review of Evidence' (2019) *Clinical Rehabilitation* 1571–85; Lynne Turner-Stokes, Jenny Kitzinger, Helen Gill-Thwaites, Diane E. Playford, Derick Wade, Judith Allanson and John Pickard, 'FMRI for Vegetative and Minimally Conscious States' (2012) 345 *British Medical Journal*, DOI: http://dx.doi.org/10.1136/bmj.e8045.

an Economic and Social Research Council Impact Acceleration Account grant) to explore this, and discovered this was very unlikely to occur as there was widespread difficulty in differentiating the concerns relating to Practice Direction 9E[123] from those of the Assisted Dying Bill which was also being discussed in Parliament at the time. On the other hand, an inward secondment for Jakki Cowley,[124] an Independent Mental Capacity Advocate, to work with us was invaluable, as her intense and skilled focus on supporting families and advocating for patient's voices to be heard relieved us of continuing at the forefront of that role, releasing our time for other dimensions of advocacy and activism. Involving Jakki was a planned strategy that stemmed from an application for 'Impact Acceleration' funding from the UK's Economic and Social Research Council. Many other 'successes' were based on more spontaneous and low-cost endeavours and the success felt serendipit-ous – such as the impact of live-tweeting a treatment-withdrawal court case in the Royal Courts of Justice (the first ever live-tweeted hearing). The 'success' of this enterprise was not only extensive engagement across a wide network of health care professionals, ethicists and lawyers, it also led to us being invited to teach senior judges (at their annual training seminar, mentioned earlier) because the judge who happened to be organising it noticed our tweets (and links to our research). Indeed, given this was the first time a live case had been tweeted from the Court of Protection like this, such scrutiny and attention was perhaps inevitable – although the subsequent invitation came as a surprise.

Our novel interventions sometimes yielded unanticipated benefits, and although at various times we wrote down our targets and strategies for creating legal reform, we often found ourselves going down different routes and seizing opportunities as they presented themselves. As members of committees and working parties (notably those of the British Medical Association and the Royal College of Physicians), we certainly presented our research to inform the committee and the guidance it produced, but equally we learnt from those on these (and other) committees what further research was needed to address issues of concern, and would redirect our research endeavours accordingly. There was (and remains) way too much to accom-plish and we are constantly reviewing and revising our priorities. We discovered that 'job sharing' is a very effective way of working for us – we respond to many invitations with the offer that one or other of us will contribute, attend or present, leaving us with flexibility to move commitments between us closer to the time. For many purposes we are (and are viewed as) interchangeable, but we have also developed specialisms: Jenny in working with the media and with artists to create different ways of communicating with professionals and publics, and currently in

---

[123] Court of Protection, Practice Direction 9E: Applications Relating to Serious Medical Treatment (1 July 2015).

[124] Jakki Cowley worked with us two days a week over six months, and she describes some of the work she did with us in her book: Jakki Cowley, *Life, Death and the Journeys in Between: Stories of an Advocate* (Online: Lulu, 2020).

developing e-learning for health care professionals; Celia in working on end-of-life decision-making more broadly, and currently in directly interrogating law-in-action by observing and reporting on court hearings. Legal reform has meant persistence over time and the willingness to keep going despite dead ends and obstacles. It has meant not accepting 'no' as an answer, maintaining a meticulous and dogged attention to detail and being prepared to challenge professionals in other disciplines about their own area of expertise. We learned not to simply accept lawyers' statements about what the law was (lawyers sometimes get the law wrong!), and we've almost certainly been present in more court hearings about CANH-withdrawal from patients in VS or MCS than most lawyers and definitely more than any judge. Above all, it has meant building networks of expertise and exchange not just with lawyers and doctors, but also with advocates and with a range of health care professionals delivering care on the front line to get a holistic picture of how issues play out over time in the diverse settings the patient moves through (e.g. intensive care, rehabilitation units and long-term care placements).

In collaboration with other dedicated professionals, we have collectively and individually had a huge impact in analysing the issues at stake (within and outside the court room) and creating a momentum for reform. In our experience, it relied crucially upon bringing together a multi-disciplinary group of people to discuss issues across traditional divides and boundaries and to begin thereby to build an informed 'culture' of commitment to change.

In a generous tribute to our work, Victoria Butler Cole QC, a practising barrister involved in much of the case law that contributed to building the momentum for change, comments that she has 'seen firsthand how the work of the Kitzingers has had an impact'. It has, she says, 'directly contributed to the dramatic and positive evolution of the law and practice over the last seven years.' She sees our publications and associated engagement work as 'a brilliant example of the way that academic activity can be integrated into the development of the law, and how the experiences of people affected by legal requirements and practices can be properly heard'. We were chastened to read her considered view that:

> I am in no doubt that, without their input, the removal of the longstanding requirement to obtain court authorisation before withdrawal of life-sustaining treatment from these patients could take place, would not have happened. And by that, I mean not that it would have happened but at a later time or in a different way, but that it simply would not have happened at all.[125]

It is a privilege and an honour to have been able to create legal change through our research and advocacy. We hope the detailed description of our work in this chapter can help other scholars to do the same.

---

[125] Victoria Butler Cole QC, Letter to 'whom it may concern' (21 July 2020).

11

Withholding and Withdrawing Life-Prolonging Treatment and the Relevance of Patients' Wishes

Reforming the Mental Capacity Act 2005

Emily Jackson

INTRODUCTION

This chapter is concerned with a particular type of life and death decision: namely the decision to withhold or withdraw life-prolonging treatment from a patient who now lacks the capacity to make this decision for themselves. In England and Wales, these decisions have for many years been governed by a 'best interests' test. Until very recently, the withdrawal of clinically assisted nutrition and hydration ('CANH') from a patient in a prolonged disorder of consciousness required a court order,[1] but whether it is a court deciding that it would be lawful to withdraw CANH, or a doctor deciding not to attempt cardio-pulmonary resuscitation ('CPR'), the sole criterion is whether the treatment in question is in this patient's best interests.

Over the past three decades, there has been a remarkable shift in the meaning of 'best interests', from the doctor's paternalistic and supposedly objective judgement about what is 'best' for the patient, to the view that the patient's own wishes – past or present – should usually be decisive. Initially, the English courts had carved out a 'best interests' test for this sort of substitute decision-making at common law, which over time had placed more emphasis upon what the patient would have wanted. When the law relating to adults who lack capacity was codified by the Mental Capacity Act 2005 (England and Wales) ('Mental Capacity Act'), the legislation offered a statutory checklist of factors relevant to the best interests assessment, including 'the person's past and present wishes and feelings' and 'the beliefs and values that would be likely to influence his decision if he had capacity'.[2] Since 2013,[3] the courts have gone further still, and, in some circumstances, appear to treat the patient's wishes as the decisive or trumping factor.

---

[1] The requirement for a court order was removed by the UK Supreme Court in *An NHS Trust v. Y* [2018] UKSC 46 ('*Re Y*'). See Chapter 10 for the evolution of this requirement.

[2] Mental Capacity Act 2005 (England and Wales), ss. 4(6)(a)–(b).

[3] *Aintree University Hospitals Foundation Trust v. James* [2013] UKSC 67.

At the moment, there is therefore an interesting gap between what the statute says and the way in which it has been interpreted by the courts. Doctors seeking guidance on how much weight to place on the patient's own wishes when making a best interests decision will receive different advice depending upon whether they read the legislation, or refer to guidance issued by the National Institute for Health and Care Excellence ('NICE'), or consult the law reports. Three years ago, the Law Commission had recommended an amendment to the statute which would have brought it more into line with its current judicial interpretation, but the government decided not to take this forward.

In this chapter, I will suggest that a discrepancy between what the legislation requires, on the one hand, and NICE advice and court judgments, on the other hand, is unnecessarily confusing for health care professionals, and for patients and their families. If there is, or if there should be, a rebuttable presumption in favour of making the patient's wishes decisive, it would be preferable for the statute to state this clearly and unequivocally. At the very least, the new version of the Mental Capacity Act's Code of Practice should, when published, offer clearer guidance to clinicians, patients and families.

FROM *BOLAM* TO A PRESUMPTION OF PRIMACY

The best interests test for the treatment of adults who lack capacity in English law originated in *Re F (Mental Patient: Sterilisation)*.[4] Finding a 'startling' absence of 'English authority on the question whether as a matter of common law (and if so in what circumstances) medical treatment can lawfully be given to a person who is disabled by mental incapacity from consenting to it',[5] the House of Lords invoked the doctrine of necessity in order to authorise the sterilisation operation which was judged to be in F's best interests. According to Lord Bridge, it was 'axiomatic that treatment which is necessary to preserve the life, health or well being of the patient may lawfully be given without consent'.[6] If 'necessity' only covered treatment provided in order to preserve someone's life, he reasoned that 'many of those unfortunate enough to be deprived of the capacity to make or communicate rational decisions by accident, illness or unsoundness of mind might be deprived of treatment which it would be entirely beneficial for them to receive'.[7]

By the time this common law principle was codified in section 1(5) of the Mental Capacity Act,[8] the meaning of 'best interests' had developed. In 1989, there had been no mention of the patient's views, values or beliefs. Instead, when deciding what

---

[4]   *Re F (Mental Patient: Sterilisation)* [1990] 2 AC 1.
[5]   Ibid. at 71.
[6]   Ibid. at 52 (Lord Bridge).
[7]   Ibid.
[8]   S. 1(5) states that: 'an act done, or decision made, under this Act for or on behalf of a person who lacks capacity must be done, or made, in his best interests'.

medical treatment was in a patient's best interests, the test was what _other doctors_ would consider to be in his or her best interests: that is, the 'reasonable doctor' test for whether a doctor had breached his or her duty of care in negligence was applied to the question of what treatment would be in an incapacitated patient's best interests.[9] Sixteen years later, this objective and paternalistic approach to determining what is in a patient's best interests had been supplemented by the recognition that the patient might have a view about their treatment, or relevant values and beliefs, which ought to be taken into account.[10] By 2005, it was widely acknowledged that determining what is in a patient's 'best interests' was no longer a purely objective exercise, but as the Law Commission report which preceded the Mental Capacity Act had put it, contained a 'strong element of substituted judgment'.[11]

Supplementing the section 1(5) requirement to take decisions in the patient's best interests, section 4 of Mental Capacity Act sets out a non-exhaustive checklist of factors that decision-makers must consider when deciding what is in a person's best interests. This covers factors such as whether it is likely that the person will at some time have capacity in relation to the matter in question, and requires the decision-maker to take into account the wishes, values and beliefs of the person who lacks capacity (described in the statute as P). P's wishes and beliefs are not given any particular priority, however. This was deliberate. The then government's view was that 'prioritisation of the factors would unnecessarily fetter their operation in the many and varied circumstances in which they might fall to be applied'.[12]

In practice, until the judgment of the UK Supreme Court in _Aintree University Hospitals Foundation Trust_ v. _James_,[13] the courts tended to consider 'the extent to which P's wishes and feelings, if given effect to, can properly be accommodated within the court's overall assessment of what is in her best interests'.[14] This meant that where the patient's life was potentially at stake, their wishes might be trumped by concern for the preservation of life. In _Re M (Adult Patient) (Minimally Conscious State: Withdrawal of Treatment)_,[15] for example, Baker J explained that '[t]he first principle is the right to life . . . It carries very great weight in any balancing

---

[9] _Re F (Mental Patient: Sterilisation)_ [1990] 2 AC 1 at 68 (Lord Brandon). The 'reasonable doctor' test was developed in _Bolam_ v. _Friern Hospital Management Committee_ [1957] 1 WLR 582, and is known as the _Bolam Test_.

[10] See, for example, the comments of Lord Hoffmann in the Court of Appeal in _Airedale NHS Trust_ v. _Bland_ [1993] AC 789.

[11] 'Report on Mental Incapacity Law Com No 231', Report from the Law Commission (1995 UK Government) at para. 3.25.

[12] 'Government Response to the Scrutiny Committee's Report on the Draft Mental Incapacity Bill', Cm 6121, Report from the Department of Constitutional Affairs (2004 UK Government).

[13] _Aintree University Hospitals Foundation Trust_ v. _James_ [2013] UKSC 67.

[14] _Re M (Statutory Will)_ [2009] EWHC 2525 (Fam) at [35] (Munby J), quoted, for example, in _A London Local Authority_ v. _JH_ [2011] EWCOP 2420 and _An NHS Trust_ v. _DE_ [2013] EWHC 2562 (Fam).

[15] _Re M (Adult Patient) (Minimally Conscious State: Withdrawal of Treatment)_ [2011] EWHC 2443.

exercise'.[16] It was impossible to be certain how M felt about her life in a minimally conscious state. There were clear statements from her partner and family about what they thought M would have wanted, but Baker J held that 'the court must be particularly cautious about attaching significant weight to statements she made before her collapse'.[17] Instead, Baker J concluded that 'the importance of preserving life is the decisive factor in this case'.[18]

Then in *Aintree University Hospitals Foundation Trust* v. *James*,[19] Lady Hale, with whom the other Justices agreed, did not describe the patient's perspective as simply one material factor, to be 'accommodated' within the doctor's objective 'best interests' assessment. Instead, she said that 'the purpose of the best interests test is to consider matters from the patient's point of view'.[20] Lady Hale was careful to stress that that does not necessarily mean that the patient's view must prevail, because, just like patients with capacity, 'we cannot always have what we want'.[21] But, if it is 'possible to ascertain the patient's wishes and feelings, his beliefs and values or the things which were important to him, it is those which should be taken into account because they are a component in making the choice which is right for him as an individual human being'.[22]

In the cases that have followed *Aintree*, P's wishes have been taken very seriously indeed, even when they have been in conflict with an 'objective' view of what might be clinically best for P, and even when P's life is at stake. In multiple cases, the courts have been clear that it may be in P's best interests for their life to come to an end in a way that is consistent with their core values and beliefs.[23]

For example, ten months after Mr Briggs had sustained serious brain injuries in a road traffic accident, and despite the view of his treating team that he should be transferred to a rehabilitation unit, in *Briggs* v. *Briggs*,[24] Charles J was clear that 'if the decision that P would have made, and so their wishes on such an intensely personal issue can be ascertained with sufficient certainty it should generally prevail over the very strong presumption in favour of preserving life'.[25] Charles J was of the view that Baker J's warning in *Re M* that the court should be 'particularly cautious

[16] Ibid. at [222].
[17] Ibid. at [228].
[18] Ibid. at [249]. See also *A Local Authority* v. *E* [2012] EWHC 1639, a case involving a thirty-two-year-old woman with severe anorexia, in which Peter Jackson J was faced with the need to strike a balance 'between the weight objectively to be given to life on one hand and to personal independence on the other' (at [5]). In this case, the preservation of E's life took priority over her wish to refuse artificial feeding (at [137]).
[19] *Aintree University Hospitals Foundation Trust* v. *James* [2013] UKSC 67.
[20] Ibid. at [45].
[21] Ibid.
[22] Ibid.
[23] *Wye Valley NHS Trust* v. *B* [2015] EWCOP 60. For further discussion, see Lucy Series, 'The Place of Wishes and Feelings in Best Interests Decisions: *Wye Valley NHS Trust* v. *Mr B*' (2016) 79 *Modern Law Review* 1101–15.
[24] *Briggs* v. *Briggs* [2016] EWCOP 53.
[25] Ibid. at [62].

about attaching significant weight' to M's previously expressed wishes 'runs counter to the holistic approach that the Supreme Court confirms is to be taken to enabling P to do what he would have wanted if of full capacity'.[26] Instead, Charles J took seriously the views of members of Mr Briggs's family that he 'would regard his present situation as horrible and one that he would not wish to continue'.[27] As a result, he concluded that, if Mr Briggs had had capacity, he would 'not have consented to further CANH treatment', and therefore 'his best interests are best promoted by the court not giving that consent on his behalf'.[28]

In *RAO* v. *ROO*,[29] Williams J accepted that while 'the weight to be attributed to P's wishes and feelings will differ',[30] and that 'a host of matters must all go into the balance',[31] he had to consider in particular, 'the values and beliefs of ROO as well as any views she expressed when she had capacity that shed light on the likely choice she would make if she were able to and what she would have considered relevant or important'.[32] Importantly, he then explained that 'Where those views can be ascertained with sufficient certainty they should carry great weight *and usually should be followed*; as they would be for a person with capacity who did express such views' (my emphasis).[33] To say that P's views 'usually should be followed' is to say that there needs to be a reason to go against P's views, which is, in effect, to say that there is a presumption in favour of following them. Because Williams J found that ROO would not want to be given artificial nutrition, he '*therefore* [did] not consider it to be in ROO's best interests' (my emphasis).[34]

Of course, not all patients want to refuse life-prolonging treatment. In *University Hospitals Birmingham NHS Foundation Trust* v. *HB*,[35] for example, Keehan J found that HB's daughter FB was 'accurately reflecting the views that her mother conveyed to her', namely that 'were she to become ill again, that she would want all possible steps to be taken to keep her alive'.[36] As a result, while in the future CPR might not be in HB's best interests, 'that stage has not been reached yet', and Keehan J found that it would be in HB's best interests to administer CPR, in order to give her 'a very, very small chance of life'.[37]

In *Royal Bournemouth and Christchurch Hospitals NHS Foundation Trust* v. *TG*,[38] Cohen J was asked to decide whether TG, who was in a 'vegetative' state,

---

[26] Ibid. at [80].
[27] Ibid. at [111].
[28] Ibid. at [129].
[29] *RAO* v. *ROO* [2018] EWCOP 33.
[30] Ibid. at [32].
[31] Ibid. at [35].
[32] Ibid.
[33] Ibid.
[34] Ibid. at [74].
[35] *University Hospitals Birmingham NHS Foundation Trust* v. *HB* [2018] EWCOP 39.
[36] Ibid. at [26].
[37] Ibid. at [36].
[38] *Royal Bournemouth and Christchurch Hospitals NHS Foundation Trust* v. *TG* [2019] EWCOP 21.

should continue to be intubated. He paid tribute to the drafting of statements filed on behalf of the family, setting out what mattered most to TG. First, 'family was central to her', and if her presence was a comfort to others, TG would want to be there 'whatever the cost to her'. Secondly, her religious beliefs led her to believe that life had 'intrinsic value' and it was for God alone to take it away.[39] While recognising that his decision would place 'a huge burden on the treating team', Cohen J decided 'against their advice' that it was in TG's best interests that intubation should continue.[40]

It is clear that when a patient's wish is a manifestation of their deeply held beliefs – as will usually be the case when the question is whether their life is worth living – this should count for more than an out-of-character or fluctuating whim. In recent cases, judges in the Court of Protection have sought to understand what has mattered most to the patient over the course of their life, be it 'respectability, security and a good face to the world'[41]; 'fierce independence'[42]; 'privacy, personal autonomy and dignity'[43]; or a religious belief that 'someone else should not play an assisting role in shortening life merely because of the subjective quality of that life'.[44] As Johnston et al. explain, 'the way a person has lived their life – what we could describe as their narrative up to and beyond the point of incapacity – seems increasingly to have legal relevance in the determination of current best interests'.[45] Johnston et al. further point out that tools are being developed which enable busy health care professionals to access this sort of 'narrative' information about the values and beliefs that have mattered most to their patients.[46]

Fistein et al. have suggested that it might be possible to divide people's attitudes towards life-limiting conditions into roughly three groups.[47] A first group – especially in the early stages of a disease – will prioritise living in the moment, and prefer not to

---

[39] Ibid. at [24].
[40] Ibid. at [30].
[41] *M v. N* [2015] EWCOP 76 at [58].
[42] *Wye Valley NHS Trust v. B* [2015] EWCOP 60 at [43].
[43] *Sheffield Teaching Hospitals v. TH* [2014] EWCOP 4 at [53]. See also *United Lincolnshire Hospitals NHS Trust v. N* [2014] EWCOP 16 at [29].
[44] *St George's NHS Foundation Trust v. P* [2015] EWCOP 42 at [38].
[45] Carolyn Johnston, Natalie Banner and Angela Fenwick, 'Patient Narrative: An "On-Switch" for Evaluating Best Interests' (2016) 38 *Journal of Social Welfare and Family Law* 249–62.
[46] See, for example, the 'Life Story Toolkit' produced by Dementia UK available at: www .dementiauk.org/for-healthcare-professionals/free-resources/life-story-work/. See also Irene J. Higginson, Jonathan Koffman, Philip Hopkins, Wendy Prentice, Rachel Burman, Sara Leonard, Caroline Rumble, Jo Noble, Odette Dampier, William Bernal, Sue Hall, Myfanwy Morgan and Cathy Shipman, 'Development and Evaluation of the Feasibility and Effects on Staff, Patients, and Families of a New Tool, the Psychosocial Assessment and Communication Evaluation (PACE), to Improve Communication and Palliative Care in Intensive Care and During Clinical Uncertainty' (2013) 11 *BMC Medicine* 213.
[47] Elizabeth Fistein, Gemma Clarke, Anthony Holland and Stephen Barclay, '"This Condition Isn't Going to Get Any Better So I Can't See Why We're Prolonging It": Risks and Benefits of Using Empirical Research to Inform Normative Decisions Concerning End-of-Life Care' (2018) 22 *Journal of Disability and Religion* 283–97.

think too much about what lies ahead. A second group prioritises planning ahead, and trying to exercise control over what happens to them in the future. The third group prioritises prolonging life at all costs, and is often willing to trust doctors to do whatever it takes to keep them alive. As the end of life becomes closer, the division may be into the two latter groups, those who want to plan and exercise choice and control, and those who simply want their doctors to keep them alive. So while individuals' decision-making is to some extent infinitely variable, at the same time, it seems likely that, as Wade and Kitzinger suggest, 'most people will have a general disposition towards a certain style for making decisions and rely on a certain small set of important values or attitudes'.[48] When a judge is faced with the question of whether P's life-prolonging treatment should be withdrawn, the starting point is invariably an attempt to find out, and if possible abide by, P's 'important values'.

This involves drawing a crucial distinction between wishes that reflect a person's core values, and preferences which might instead be the result of delusions, phobias or addictions. As Callaghan and Ryan put it, not 'all statements about "what I want"' are, in fact, 'meaningful acts of "will"'.[49] To respect the wishes of someone suffering from psychosis or delirium might amount to abandoning them when they need help and support. Even if it is usually in someone's best interests to have their preferences respected, this will not universally be the case for patients who lack capacity. If a patient who lacks capacity wants to refuse a simple life-saving procedure because a voice in their head has told them that the doctor is the devil, a doctor who respected that refusal without question would not be acting in their patient's best interests.

In *Cambridge University Hospitals NHS Foundation Trust v. BF*,[50] MacDonald J decided that a total abdominal hysterectomy was in the best interests of a woman suffering from severe paranoid schizophrenia, who had been diagnosed with Stage IIIB ovarian cancer. Her wishes were contradictory: when she had capacity, she had agreed to the treatment and signed a consent form, but subsequently she said that she did not want to have the operation because 'bad voices' and 'bad machines' were controlling her mind. Without the operation, she might be likely to die within six months. The risk of harm was significant, and the grounds for her refusal were the result of 'intrusive auditory hallucinations telling her not to have the surgery'.[51] MacDonald J was therefore convinced that BF would be likely to 'prioritise potentially life-saving treatment and the chance of continued life over the opportunity to bear children in the circumstances where, left untreated, her ovarian cancer will likely result in her death'.[52]

---

[48] Derick T. Wade and Celia Kitzinger, 'Making Healthcare Decisions in a Person's Best Interests When They Lack Capacity: Clinical Guidance Based on a Review of Evidence' (2019) 33 *Clinical Rehabilitation* 1571–81.

[49] Sascha Mira Callaghan and Christopher Ryan, 'Is There a Future for Involuntary Treatment in Rights-Based Mental Health Law?' (2014) 21 *Psychiatry, Psychology and Law* 747–66.

[50] *Cambridge University Hospitals NHS Foundation Trust v. BF* [2016] EWCOP 26.

[51] Ibid. at [53].

[52] Ibid. at [65].

In contrast, where the patient's wishes could be said to reflect their core beliefs, the judiciary has been increasingly willing to give effect to them. The same cannot necessarily be said of health care professionals, however, who in practice make the majority of best interests decisions under the Mental Capacity Act. In its post-legislative scrutiny of the Mental Capacity Act, the House of Lords Select Committee explained that 'especially in medical settings, the concept of best interests as defined by the Act was not well understood'.[53] In particular, it had received evidence that: 'Best interests decision-making is often not undertaken in the way set out in the Act: the wishes, thoughts and feelings of P are not routinely prioritised. Instead, clinical judgements or resource-led decision-making predominate'.[54]

Three years later, the Law Commission had found little improvement. Family members 'reported that best interests decisions by health and social care profession-als were often made without reference to their loved one's wishes and feelings, and that professionals often "pick and choose" which factors on the check-list to priori-tise to suit their own preferred outcomes'.[55] According to the Law Commission's consultees, 'the concept of best interests was often interpreted in a medical and paternalistic sense'.[56] In addition, even if the judiciary normally prioritises the patient's wishes and preferences, Lucy Series has pointed out that this has not universally been the case.[57]

Given that the Act itself does not direct decision-makers to give any priority to P's wishes and beliefs, one possible solution might be to formalise best practice in the Court of Protection by setting out two rebuttable presumptions on the face of the statute. First, if it would not result in any significant harm to P, there should be a presumption that their wish to refuse an unwanted medical intervention should be respected. Secondly, even if there is a risk of significant harm to P from respecting their wishes, their refusal of unwanted medical intervention should be respected, provided that it is (or was) grounded in their core values and beliefs, that is, in views that are, or were, of profound importance to P.

It is well established in English law that 'a patient cannot demand that a doctor administer a treatment which the doctor considers is adverse to the patient's clinical needs',[58] so, just as with patients who have capacity, it is only refusals of medical treatment that could be decisive in this scheme. For all patients, capacitous or not,

---

[53] '*Mental Capacity Act 2005: Post-Legislative Scrutiny*', HL Paper 139, Report of Session 2013–14 from the Select Committee on the Mental Capacity Act 2005 (2014 UK Parliament, House of Lords) at para. 92.
[54] Ibid. at para. 104.
[55] 'Mental Capacity and Deprivation of Liberty', Law Com No. 372, Report from the Law Commission (2017 UK Parliament, House of Commons) at para. 14.7.
[56] Ibid.
[57] Series, 'The Place of Wishes and Feelings in Best Interests Decisions'. See, for example *RB v. Brighton and Hove City Council* [2014] EWCA Civ 561.
[58] *R (on the application of Burke) v. General Medical Council* [2005] EWCA Civ 1003 at [55].

their desire to receive a particular treatment is relevant to the doctor's decision to provide it, but the doctor cannot be compelled to act contrary to their clinical judgement.[59] In practice, this means that it will not always be possible to respect a patient's desire for their life to be preserved at all costs, and difficult cases will arise in which a patient's preference for life-prolonging treatment cannot be respected, either because no clinician is willing to provide the treatment that the patient wants (I return to this point below), or because the NHS has decided that the treatment is insufficiently cost-effective to justify its provision.

Refusals of unwanted medical treatment are, however, importantly different from requests for particular treatments, which might be rejected on resource grounds, or because the procedure is not clinically appropriate.[60] As David Feldman explains:

> Being subjected to treatment, especially invasive treatment, without one's consent is calculated to threaten one's sense of one's own worth and the feeling of being valued by others. How valuable can a person be, one might ask, if others are prepared to do things to him which remove from him any control over his own destiny? What could be less compatible with one's dignity than being treated as a person to whom such a thing might be done lawfully and properly?[61]

PRESUMPTIONS VERSUS JUDICIAL DISCRETION

While it could be argued that in recent court decisions the judiciary is applying a presumption that patient's core beliefs should trump other considerations, the judiciary itself has tended to resist further specification of the best interests test, on the grounds that these cases are fact-specific,[62] and 'infinitely variable'.[63] For example, in *M* v. *N*,[64] in setting out the respect to be afforded to P's wishes under the Mental Capacity Act, Hayden J explained that:

> Respecting individual autonomy does not always require P's wishes to be afforded predominant weight. Sometimes it will be right to do so, sometimes it will not. The factors that fall to be considered in this intensely complex process are infinitely variable e.g. the nature of the contemplated treatment, how intrusive such treatment might be and crucially what the outcome of that treatment may be for the

---

[59] Ibid.
[60] Ibid. at [31]: 'The proposition that the patient has a paramount right to refuse treatment is amply demonstrated by the authorities ... The corollary does not, however, follow, at least as a general proposition. Autonomy and the right of self-determination do not entitle the patient to insist on receiving a particular medical treatment regardless of the nature of the treatment.'
[61] David Feldman, 'Human Dignity as a Legal Value: Part II' (2000) *Public Law* 61–76. See also David Feldman, 'The Developing Scope of Article 8 of the European Convention on Human Rights' (1997) 3 *European Human Rights Law Review* 265–74.
[62] See, for example, *Re M (Statutory Will)* [2009] EWHC 2525 (Fam) at [35].
[63] *Portsmouth NHS Trust v. Wyatt* [2004] EWHC 2247 (Fam) at [23].
[64] *M v. N* [2015] EWCOP 76.

individual patient. Into that complex matrix the appropriate weight to be given to P's wishes will vary.[65]

Similarly, in *Wye Valley NHS Trust* v. *B*,[66] Peter Jackson J said that: 'there is no theoretical limit to the weight or lack of weight that should be given to the person's wishes and feelings, beliefs and values. In some cases, the conclusion will be that little weight or no weight can be given; in others, very significant weight will be due'.[67]

Even if the weight given to P's wishes will inevitably vary, at the same time it might be helpful, especially for clinicians, patients and relatives, if an attempt was made to set out the circumstances in which P's wishes normally might be expected to be either disregarded or followed. Indeed, in *M* v. *N*,[68] Hayden J appeared to suggest that there should be just such a presumption, where the wishes of an incapacitated adult are 'important', and communicated with 'cogency and authenticity':

> the presumption of life, predicated on what is often referred to as the 'sanctity of life' or the 'intrinsic value of life', can be rebutted (pursuant to statute) on the basis of a competent adult's cogently expressed wish. It follows, to my mind, by parity of analysis, that the importance of the wishes and feelings of an incapacitated adult, communicated to the court via family or friends but with similar cogency and authenticity, are to be afforded no less significance than those of the capacitous.[69]

In this case, with the help of her family, Hayden J had painted a vivid picture of Mrs N's personality and priorities, through which it had become evident that '[f]ew ... were less well placed to withstand the ravages and vicissitudes of this degenerative disease than Mrs N'.[70] Hayden J was therefore:

> left with little doubt that Mrs. N would have been appalled to contemplate the early pain, increasing dependency and remorseless degeneration that has now characterised her life for so long. I have no difficulty in accepting the family's view that she would not wish to continue as she is.[71]

Of course these cases are fact-specific, so a decision to withdraw CANH from Mrs N does not tell us whether CANH would be withdrawn from a different patient in the future. Similarly, a presumption in favour of following P's wishes would not tie a judge's hands to a particular outcome; it would simply offer a starting point for their decision. As we saw earlier, there is evidence that the best interests test has been

[65] Ibid. at [28].
[66] *Wye Valley NHS Trust* v. *B* [2015] EWCOP 60.
[67] Ibid. at [10].
[68] *M* v. *N* [2015] EWCOP 76.
[69] Ibid. at [32].
[70] Ibid. at [57].
[71] Ibid. at [60].

poorly understood by clinicians.[72] If the best interests test continues to be misapplied by those who are most frequently responsible for taking medical decisions for adults who lack capacity,[73] giving some further structure to decision-making under the statute may lead to better decisions, and greater consistency.[74]

The flexibility of the section 4 checklist has undoubtedly enabled the judiciary to apply it sensitively and empathetically, in order to produce patient-centred decisions about what medical treatment is in P's best interests. But with the advantages of flexibility come the potential disadvantages of inconsistency, such as the likelihood that different decision-makers will come to different decisions on the same facts.[75] If respect for the patient's wishes matters, it is unsatisfactory for too much to turn on who happens to be making the best interests assessment on any particular day.

I am certainly not advocating the removal of discretion, and rebuttable presumptions leave open the possibility of cases for which they are a poor fit. Nevertheless, it might be predicted that there is likely to be some resistance, not least from judges, to the constraints of statutory presumptions. In practice, it might be more straightforward to include them in the Code of Practice, and to describe them instead as 'starting points'. In both cases, however, specific and defensible justification for departing from the presumption, or starting point, should be required. Busy and non-legally trained health care professionals are unlikely to consult the law reports regularly, and need clearer prospective guidance than the Act and the Code of Practice currently provides that:

- if there is evidence – either contemporaneous or based upon their previous values – that an incapacitated patient would not wish to undergo further medical treatment, there should be a presumption in favour of complying with their preference; and

---

[72] Select Committee on the Mental Capacity Act 2005, 'Mental Capacity Act 2005: Post-Legislative Scrutiny'; Law Commission, 'Mental Capacity and Deprivation of Liberty', para. 14.7. See also Paul Willner, Jennifer Bridle, Vaughn Price, Simon Dymond and Glenda Lewis, 'What Do NHS Staff Learn from Training on the Mental Capacity Act (2005)?' (2013) 18 *Legal and Criminological Psychology* 83–101.

[73] As Emma Cave has explained: 'The MCA's concessions to a relational approach focus on enablement and the relevance of the person's past and present views when making a decision in their best interests, but they are poorly implemented. The legislation is not currently living up to its promises to protect and promote even this limited conception of relational autonomy': Emma Cave, 'Determining Capacity to Make Medical Treatment Decisions: Problems Implementing the Mental Capacity Act 2005' (2015) 36 *Statute Law Review* 86–106.

[74] Better training may also be necessary, see Kathryn Hinsliff-Smith, Ruth Feakes, Gillian Whitworth, Jane Seymour, Nima Moghaddam, Tom Dening and Karen Cox, 'What Do We Know about the Application of the Mental Capacity Act (2005) in Healthcare Practice Regarding Decision-Making for Frail and Older People? A Systematic Literature Review' (2017) 25 *Health and Social Care in the Community* 295–308.

[75] Helen J. Taylor, 'What Are "Best Interests"? A Critical Evaluation of "Best Interests" Decision-Making in Clinical Practice' (2016) 24 *Medical Law Review* 176–205.

- that presumption could, however, be rebutted if respecting their wishes would expose them to a risk of serious harm, *and* their preference for no treatment is not grounded in values or beliefs that are, or were of profound importance to them.

LAW REFORM

It could be argued that by giving priority to the patient's wishes, the judiciary has simply been bringing the Mental Capacity Act's substitute decision-making regime more closely into line with Article 12(4) of the United Nations Convention on the Rights of Persons with Disabilities[76] ('CRPD'), which requires that 'measures relating to the exercise of legal capacity respect the rights, will and preferences of the person'. The Oxford English Dictionary's definition of 'respect' is to 'treat or regard with deference, esteem, or honour', which implies more than merely taking P's views into account, which is all that is required by section 4 of the Mental Capacity Act. By giving no particular priority to P's 'will and preferences', and treating them as simply one relevant factor, section 4 is not compliant with Article 12(4) of the UN CRPD. However, it could also be argued that just prioritising the patient's wishes would not go far enough, and that the CRPD instead requires that the patient's wishes are always respected.

In 2017, the Law Commission published recommendations for reforming the Mental Capacity Act. These were principally directed towards amending the much-criticised Deprivation of Liberty Safeguards (which had introduced a formal process to authorise what had previously been the *de facto* detention of compliant patients who had been admitted to psychiatric wards 'voluntarily', but who would have been 'sectioned' if they tried to leave). In addition, having found that the best interests test was poorly understood by health care professionals, the Law Commission took the opportunity to make some recommendations about reform of the section 4 checklist. It proposed that the Act should be amended to ensure that decision-makers must 'ascertain', rather than merely 'consider', P's wishes,[77] and that they 'must give particular weight to any wishes or feelings ascertained'.[78] Its draft bill also placed additional requirements on decision-makers 'to explain their decisions not to follow [P's] wishes and feelings'.[79]

Some of the Law Commission's respondents had recommended the introduction of a 'rebuttable presumption that [P's] wishes and feelings should be followed (with departure only occurring if there were "compelling reasons" or "serious adverse

---

[76] General Assembly Resolution 61/106, 24 January 2007.
[77] Law Commission, 'Mental Capacity and Deprivation of Liberty', para. 14.16.
[78] Ibid. at para. 14.17.
[79] Ibid. at para. 14.19.

consequences")'.[80] While it was 'attracted by the idea of a rebuttable presumption', the Law Commission concluded that this could not be achieved by a simple amendment to the section 4 checklist of factors that should be taken into account by best interests decision-makers. Instead, it would require a qualification to one of the founding principles of the Act, set out in section 1(5), that any act done for P must be done in their best interests.[81] This option had not been consulted upon and, according to the Law Commission, 'would be far beyond our remit'.[82]

The Mental Capacity Amendment Bill did not contain any amendments to section 4, or indeed to section 1.[83] The government's Impact Assessment simply stated that 'the Law Commission also proposed making some wider amendments to the Mental Capacity Act which we have decided not to legislate for at this point, as we think there are other effective levers to deliver improvement in these areas'.[84]

It is not clear whether the publication in 2018 of a NICE guideline on decision-making and mental capacity was one of those 'other effective levers'. The NICE guideline is specifically addressed to service providers, commissioners (i.e. those responsible for deciding which services the NHS should fund) and health care practitioners, and it states that 'carers and practitioners must, wherever possible, find out the person's wishes and feelings in order to ensure any best interests decision made reflects those wishes and feelings unless it is not possible/appropriate to do so'.[85] In addition, if the best interests decision 'does not accord with the person's wishes and feelings, the reasons for this should be clearly documented and an explanation given'. Documentation 'should also make clear what steps have been taken to ascertain the person's wishes and feelings and where it has not been possible to do this, the reasons for this should be explained'.[86]

This looks rather like a presumption in favour of respecting the person's wishes, unless to do so would be impossible and/or inappropriate. Unfortunately, however, the NICE guideline does not offer any further guidance on the circumstances in which it would be 'impossible' or 'inappropriate' to respect P's wishes. It is also important to acknowledge that the NICE guideline is inconsistent with the wording of section 4(6) of the Mental Capacity Act, according to which the patient's wishes are merely one relevant factor, with no particular priority. Instead of clarifying the

---

[80] Ibid. at para. 14.8. See also Alex Ruck Keene and Cressida Auckland, 'More Presumptions Please? Wishes, Feelings and Best Interests Decision-Making' (2015) 5 *Elder Law Journal* 293–301.

[81] Law Commission, 'Mental Capacity and Deprivation of Liberty', para. 14.14.

[82] Ibid.

[83] Mental Capacity (Amendment) Act 2019 (England and Wales).

[84] 'Mental Capacity Amendment Bill Impact Assessment', Report from the Department of Health and Social Care (2018 UK Government).

[85] 'Decision-Making and Mental Capacity', Guideline from the National Institute for Health and Care Excellence (2018 NICE) at para. 1.5.13.

[86] Ibid.

weight to be given to P's wishes, the creation of a gap between the statutory wording and NICE guidance may add to health care professionals' confusion.

The NICE guideline's emphasis upon the importance of P's views is nevertheless in line with the now extensive body of post-*Aintree* case law. But if section 4 of the Mental Capacity Act should now be interpreted *as if it said* that there is a presumption in favour of following P's wishes, it would be clearer and more helpful to those who must apply the best interests test in practice if this was set out unambiguously on the face of the statute.

CONCLUSION AND UNRESOLVED QUESTIONS

This chapter has made the fairly modest claim that because the judiciary's current interpretation of the Mental Capacity Act's best interests test (according to which P's wishes are, in certain circumstances, decisive) is preferable to the wording of the statute (where P's wishes are simply one relevant factor), the statute should be amended in order to ensure that health care professionals can no longer be in any doubt about the importance of respecting P's wishes.

It is worth noting, however, that if the 'best interests' test had continued to be part of the common law, a presumption in favour of following the patient's wishes and feelings could have been introduced through the normal process of judicial development. Once the law is codified, a widening gap between the clear language in the statute itself, and its application by the courts, becomes confusing for those who are bound by it. When drafting new legislative proposals, it is therefore important always to consider how they might be 'future proofed'. With the benefit of hindsight, it might have been easier to strengthen the protection of the interests of patients who lack capacity if the checklist of relevant factors, and their priority, had been set out instead in a Code of Practice.

Finally, while there would be merit in resolving the discrepancy highlighted here between what the statute says and what it ought to say, it is worth acknowledging that there are other important issues which would remain unresolved, even if the wording of sections 1 and 4 of the Mental Capacity Act was brought into line with its judicial interpretation.

First, as we saw earlier, in addition to respecting patients' contemporaneous or previous wish not to receive life-prolonging treatment, there have also been cases in which a patient's desire to receive life-prolonging treatment has been respected by the courts. On the one hand, if someone believes very strongly in the value of life, no matter how compromised, and wants to have their life preserved by whatever means possible, that belief is likely to be as important to them as the desire in another person not to be kept alive, once life has lost meaning to them. On the other hand, there is an important difference between a request for life-prolonging treatment and a refusal. Adults with capacity have the right to refuse unwanted treatment, but they do not have the right to be provided with whatever medical treatment they desire. On the contrary, for resource reasons, and also because doctors cannot be forced to treat patients contrary to their clinical judgement, a request for treatment can only ever be relevant but not decisive.

This means that in a case like *Royal Bournemouth and Christchurch Hospitals NHS Foundation Trust v. TG*,[87] the court's decision that intubation should continue when doctors believed it was not in TG's best interests could only ever be advisory. If intubating TG would be likely to cause such significant harm to her that it would be a breach of a health care professional's duty of care, then the fact that TG wanted to be intubated would not be sufficient to ensure that her wishes are followed. If the treatment TG's family were certain she would wish to continue to receive was instead an expensive new cancer drug, which NICE had decided was insufficiently cost-effective to justify NHS provision,[88] TG's preference to preserve life at all costs would be trumped by resource considerations. In practice, then, it is important to acknowledge that doctors possess a *de facto* right to veto patients' positive preferences for life-prolonging treatment. Respect for a patient's core beliefs where this involves access to life-prolonging treatment, rather than its refusal, is determinative only insofar as their decision is one which is both affordable and with which at least some doctors agree.

Secondly, if a patient is capable of expressing their views, or if they have made a valid and applicable advance decision, there may be no doubt about what the patient wanted. More commonly, in the absence of a contemporaneous refusal or a binding advance decision, courts now go to considerable lengths to find out from the patient's family and carers what mattered to P. It is now common for judgments to contain rich and detailed portraits of P's life before he or she lost capacity, such as Hayden J's descriptions of first Mrs P and second Mrs Rushton:

> What emerges from the family's evidence is that Mrs P was headstrong, frequently combative, effervescing with ideas and projects ... A Methodist and tea-totaller, she discovered, in her 40s, the pleasures of the grape which she came to with the zeal of the convert. She drank rather too much and rather too frequently. Her partner, Z, told me how he missed sitting up with Mrs P late into the night, drinking whilst he, largely unsuccessfully (he told me), tried to change her opinions on the political issues of the day ... Though Mrs P regularly spoke in public and could be gregarious she was immensely private about her own health. She never, for example, took her medication in front of people. One of her sisters told me how she would always take her medication discretely in the bedroom. She would not talk about her health issues and she would brook no criticism of her smoking habits.[89]

---

[87] *Royal Bournemouth and Christchurch Hospitals NHS Foundation Trust v. TG* [2019] EWCOP 21.

[88] In addition to issuing good practice guidelines, NICE is also responsible for carrying out technology appraisals of medicines in order to decide whether they are sufficiently cost-effective to justify NHS funding.

[89] *Salford Royal NHS Foundation Trust v. P* [2017] EWCOP 23 at [30], [31], [33].

Mrs Rushton was full of life. She enjoyed bird watching, she enjoyed classical music, she was a member of a sewing group and joined in many activities that were associated with her local community and church. She strikes me as one of life's organisers. Indeed, I am told that she managed the catering at one of her children's weddings, for 120 guests. When her husband died she struggled on as best she could, keeping as busy as possible. Although there were times, at family gatherings surrounded by her sons and grandchildren, when the sunshine came back into her life, the reality appears to have been as her son, Hugh, told me so eloquently, that after her husband's death, *'the sweetness went out of her life'* (emphasis in original).[90]

Of course, there will be cases where the patient does not have anyone to speak for them, or where the judge decides that the family's evidence is unreliable,[91] but in the vast majority of cases, the patient's family is responsible for communicating the patient's wishes. In almost all cases, the evidence provided by family members is compelling, and often also extremely moving. But it is important to acknowledge that there may be times when there is a gap between what the patient would have wanted and what their family think they wanted.

In practice, the recent UK Supreme Court decision in *An NHS Trust v. Y ('Re Y')*,[92] may make it harder for judges to identify those rare cases where there is a discrepancy between the patient's wishes and their family's evidence of their wishes.[93] Following *Re Y*,[94] cases involving the withdrawal of CANH only need to go to court if the decision is 'finely balanced', or if there is a dispute between the family and the medical team as to what the patient would have wanted, and hence what is in their best interests. If the family and the medical team agree, and the decision is not 'finely balanced', then, provided that the proper guidance is followed,[95] the decision to withdraw CANH can be taken in the same way as other best interests decisions. While the need to go to court was distressing for relatives and caused delay, potentially meaning that patients were subjected to invasive treatment that was not in their best interests for many years, some commentators have expressed the concern that, by removing the role of the Official Solicitor and the court from decisions to withhold or withdraw CANH, there is no 'independent and neutral person' whose role is to 'provide the patient with a voice in the decision-making'.[96]

---

[90] *NHS Cumbria CCG v. Rushton* [2018] EWCOP 41 at [6]–[7].
[91] *Abertawe Bro Morgannwg University Local Health Board v. RY* [2017] EWCOP 2.
[92] *Re Y* [2018] UKSC 46. See Chapter 10 for further consideration of this requirement.
[93] *Re Y* [2018] UKSC 46.
[94] Ibid. See Chapter 10 for further consideration of this requirement.
[95] 'Clinically-Assisted Nutrition and Hydration and Adults Who Lack the Capacity to Consent: Guidance for Decision-Making in England and Wales', Guidance from the Royal College of Physicians and British Medical Association (2018 RCP and BMA).
[96] Elizabeth Wicks, 'An NHS *Trust and Others* v *Y and Another* [2018] UKSC 46: Reducing the Role of the Courts in Treatment Withdrawal' (2019) 27 *Medical Law Review* 330–8.

Charles Foster, for example, has argued that *Re Y* 'amplifies the clinicians' voices' and 'risks drowning out other, non-professional voices ..., making doctors the sole de facto decision-makers, so transforming the value judgement or value-laden determination demanded by statute into a matter of factual professional declaration'.[97] This, in my view, overstates the problem, given the emphasis the Royal College of Physicians and the British Medical Association's guidance places on gathering as much evidence as possible about the patient's previously expressed wishes,[98] and given that, almost all of the time, the best people to represent the patient's core beliefs when they can no longer articulate them are those close to them. But health care professionals need to be alive to the risk that 'families and carers will be too intimidated or too ignorant to contribute to the discussion and will be led passively to acquiesce'.[99] Families, particularly those who find health care professionals intimidating, may therefore need support in order to be able properly to represent the patient's views, and to challenge health care professionals' judgement about what is in the patient's best interests. There is also inevitably a small risk that families may unwittingly (or wittingly) misrepresent the patient's wishes. As a result, cases should be taken before the Court of Protection not only where there is a dispute, but where there is any room for doubt about whether P in fact wanted what their family say they wanted.[100]

Lastly, it could be argued that the emphasis placed upon a patient's wishes and beliefs regarding life-prolonging treatment is part of a wider concern with what makes a good death. There is now a weight of evidence that what we want for ourselves and for others at the end of life – that is, what makes a death 'good' – is for the person who died to have been able to exercise some control and choice over the dying process.[101] A death which is compatible with someone's core beliefs and preferences is better for them, and for the people they leave behind, than one in which their preferences were ignored.

But while the courts have interpreted the Mental Capacity Act flexibly in order to ensure that patients who lack capacity can nevertheless die in ways which reflect their wishes and values, this emphasis upon respecting patients' wishes may serve to widen the gulf between patients who do and who do not require medical treatment to keep them alive. If a patient needs dialysis or CANH, their right of refusal, and in

[97] Charles Foster, 'The Rebirth of Medical Paternalism: An NHS Trust v Y' (2019) 45 *Journal of Medical Ethics* 3–7.
[98] RCP and BMA, 'Clinically-Assisted Nutrition and Hydration and Adults Who Lack the Capacity to Consent'.
[99] Ibid.
[100] For example in *A Clinical Commissioning Group* v. *P* [2019] EWCOP 18, there was no dispute between the treating team and P's family, but the decision was brought before the court because of 'certain contrary views expressed by the dedicated staff who now care for P and the neutral position taken by her treating clinicians': at [61] (MacDonald J).
[101] Simon Read and Sara MacBride-Stewart, 'The "Good Death" and Reduced Capacity: A Literature Review' (2018) 23 *Mortality* 381–95.

practice, their right to ensure that their life is brought to an end consistently with their core beliefs, may now continue to exist after they lose capacity. For patients who do not need life-prolonging treatment, but who no less fervently wish their lives to be brought to an end, the strength of their wish is irrelevant.

In England and Wales, the wishes of patients, like Tony Nicklinson,[102] Noel Conway,[103] Paul Lamb[104] and Paul Newby,[105] who have sought to challenge the 'blanket ban' on assisted suicide in the courts, were at least as clear and unequivocal as the wishes of the patients discussed in this chapter. Their wishes could also be said to be part of their core beliefs about what makes life worth living. But their need for positive assistance to bring their lives to an end means that those beliefs must be ignored, regardless of how unbearable life has become for them. Of course, positively bringing a patient's life to an end is importantly different from respecting a refusal of unwanted medical treatment, but it is worth acknowledging that English law's current concern to ensure that some people's lives come to an end in a way which is compatible with their core beliefs has its limits, and that not everyone would accept that the line is drawn in the right place.[106]

---

[102] *R (Nicklinson and Another)* v. *Ministry of Justice* [2015] AC 657.

[103] *R (Conway)* v. *Secretary of State for Justice* [2020] QB 1.

[104] Paul Lamb, 'I Want to Die with Dignity – And I Will Fight for the Right at the High Court', *The Guardian*, 5 July 2019.

[105] BBC News, 'Assisted Dying: Terminally Ill Man Challenges Law in High Court', BBC, 20 October 2019.

[106] See Chapters 2–8 for reform (or reform attempts) in various jurisdictions throughout the world.

12

International Perspectives on Reforming End-of-Life Law

Ben P. White, Lindy Willmott, Jocelyn Downie, Penney Lewis, Celia Kitzinger, Jenny Kitzinger, Kenneth Chambaere, Thaddeus Mason Pope, Luc Deliens, Mona Gupta, Emily Jackson, Agnes van der Heide, Eliana Close, Katrine Del Villar and Jodhi Rutherford[*]

INTRODUCTION

This book has shed light on how and why reform of law that regulates the end of life occurs. Law reform in any area can be challenging, but this is particularly so in relation to such a sensitive and complex field. The book drew together ten case studies from six jurisdictions (the United Kingdom, the United States, Canada, Australia, Belgium and the Netherlands) considering different aspects of end-of-life law reform. Some case studies were framed as practical 'how to' guides, providing direct lessons about how to achieve law reform. This perspective is novel because very little has been written articulating a 'roadmap' for reform in this area. Downie and Scallion's analysis of how medical assistance in dying became part of Canadian law federally and the lessons for law reformers is one case study that does this. Another is the Kitzingers' account of how their research and advocacy led to removal of a supposed requirement to obtain court approval before withdrawing artificial nutrition and hydration from certain patients.

Other case studies took a more conceptual approach to their analysis of law reform. For example, Orentlicher's analysis of end-of-life law reform in the United States argues that moves to allow assisted dying are consistent with already existing values in the end-of-life field. Taking a different tack, Lewis charts how a law reform proposal for prior judicial approval for assisted dying can simultaneously attract support from both opponents and proponents of law reform, and yet fail to meet key regulatory goals.

Many of the case studies in this book are about law reform in relation to assisted dying. And we note at this point that this chapter will use this generic terminology of

[*] The authors acknowledge that within the authorial team there is a diversity of views about what constitutes optimal end-of-life law. This includes differences in opinion about the various assisted dying models in operation internationally (and about assisted dying generally). The authors would like to acknowledge the helpful research assistance of Emily Bartels.

assisted dying (as explained in Chapter 1) unless the context requires otherwise.[1] This focus on assisted dying is not surprising given the current hive of activity on this distinct issue in many parts of the globe. But there are also three case studies outside that field which consider the regulation of withholding and withdrawing life-sustaining treatment: the Kitzingers' examination of the requirement for court approval to withdraw artificial nutrition and hydration in certain cases; Pope's analysis of the passing and subsequent challenges to the Texas Advance Directives Act (resolving medical treatment disputes that arise at the end of life); and Jackson's discussion of how the best interests test for medical decision-making evolved over time. This wider perspective is important because the issues that arise for assisted dying will be relevant for law reform of other areas of end-of-life law and vice versa. Nevertheless, given the focus on assisted dying in this book, much of the discussion below will necessarily focus on reform in the context of that issue.

The purpose of this final chapter is to draw together the themes that emerge from an analysis of these ten case studies. Although it is true, as noted in the opening chapter, that 'all politics is local',[2] there are patterns that emerge about end-of-life law reform that transcend jurisdictional boundaries and the particular case study being considered. This chapter employs the comparative law method[3] to explore these themes, as we can better understand our own individual law reform process by seeing it through different eyes. A global/comparative perspective enables us to realise that what may seem local and parochial is part of a wider movement of law reform internationally. In doing so, we aim to shed light on how and why law reform occurs in the end-of-life field, and by doing so to contribute to reflections about law reform more generally.

CONCEPTUALISING LAW REFORM

Before considering reform in the context of end-of-life law, it is important to acknowledge two conceptual points about law reform. The first is that, as noted in the book's opening chapter, the term 'reform' implies that the change proposed or occurring is a positive advancement in law.[4] But the case studies, and the wider

---

[1] As outlined in Chapter 1, assisted dying is referred to using a variety of terms which differ by jurisdiction and ideological outlook (e.g. 'voluntary assisted dying', 'medical aid in dying' and 'euthanasia'). While authors have tended to use local terminology in their chapters, for the purposes of this comparative chapter, we will use the generic term 'assisted dying', as defined in Chapter 1, unless context requires otherwise.

[2] This was a famous saying of the former Speaker of the United States House of Representatives, Tip O'Neill: Andrew Heywood, *Politics*, 2nd ed. (New York, NY: Palgrave Macmillan, 2002), 157.

[3] Mark Van Hoecke, 'Methodology of Comparative Legal Research' (2015) December *Law and Method* 1–35.

[4] William H. Hurlburt, *Law Reform Commissions in the United Kingdom, Australia and Canada* (Edmonton: Juriliber, 1986), ch. 1.

literature on end-of-life law and bioethics, show that legal changes in this area are contested.[5] What one considers to be progress, others consider bad lawmaking. This is particularly evident in relation to assisted dying laws. It will be clear from this chapter and the case studies as a whole, that most, if not all, of the authors regard many of the reforms in this book as positive developments. Indeed, many actively advocated for change in the reform process described. Further, the academic work of many contributing authors also supports the reforms outlined in this book. We acknowledge therefore that law reform as a concept discussed in this book is not a value-neutral one.

The second conceptual point relates to the agent (or agents) *undertaking* law reform. In other words, who initiates law reform, who manages the reform process, and who is responsible for making decisions about matters such as whether or not to reform and if so, what change to law should occur? Traditionally, responsibility for law, and therefore law reform, has been seen as residing with the State, because ultimately law can be changed only by the State acting through parliament or the judiciary. If seen through this top-down lens, law reform is a State-led process in which non-State groups and individuals participate. Victoria's wide and inclusive reform process led by the Government, which ultimately resulted in the passing of its assisted dying laws, provides an excellent case study of this.

However, even accepting such a State-oriented reference point (and some do not),[6] non-State actors such as interest groups, organisations and individuals often play a critical role in law reform. While decisions about whether or not to change the law and what changes to make ultimately rest with the State, others can initiate and lead reform processes. In other words, while law reform can occur top-down, it may also be driven bottom-up.

Some of the case studies in this book provide examples of this. The Kitzingers' case study describes how they, as academics but also family members, initiated and drove a reform process aiming to change the supposed need for mandatory court supervision of some medical decisions in relation to patients with cognitive impairments. Similarly, the case of *Carter v. Canada (Attorney General)* ('*Carter*')[7] in Canada depended on individual litigants (supported by legal counsel and advocacy organisations) to initiate a challenge to the validity of the law as it then was, ultimately

---

[5]   See for example Emily Jackson and John Keown, *Debating Euthanasia* (Oxford: Hart Publishing, 2011).

[6]   Regulation theorists are increasingly arguing that regulation (of which law is a part) is becoming decentred, with non-State actors being pivotal in regulating or guiding behaviour in society: see, for example, Julia Black, 'Decentring Regulation: Understanding the Role of Regulation and Self-Regulation in a "Post-Regulatory" World' (2001) 45 *Current Legal Problems* 103–46 at 103–4; Julia Black, 'Critical Reflections on Regulation' (2002) 27 *Australian Journal of Legal Philosophy* 1–35 at 1–2. This is perhaps truer when talking about regulation other than law (e.g. policy or guidelines) given that law, narrowly construed, generally remains the province of the State.

[7]   *Carter v. Canada (Attorney General)* [2015] 1 SCR 331.

resulting in a change to that law. Bottom-up reforms cannot occur without the State, at least when they require legal reform. As noted, the State controls formal changes to law. But they do remind us that there can be many agents of change in law reform.

LAW REFORM CAN OCCUR THROUGH DIFFERENT REGULATORY PATHS

The two main paths for end-of-life law reform, as noted above, are legislative change or judicial change through the courts.[8] In terms of legislative reform, this may occur by passing a new piece of legislation or amending existing legislation. Most commonly, this occurs through parliament as illustrated, for example, in the cases of the Belgian, Victorian, Texan and Québec legislation. In some jurisdictions, new legislation could also come into force via a citizen or voter referendum, as occurred in Oregon in relation to its assisted dying laws and some of the other US states that followed those reforms, such as Washington and Colorado. It is also possible to have a combination of both. Although not one of the case studies in this book, in 2019, the New Zealand Parliament passed assisted dying legislation, which became law only because it was then approved by the public at a referendum during the country's election at the end of 2020.[9]

End-of-life law can also change through judicial decision. One of the case studies which provides an example of this is *Carter*[10] where the Canadian Supreme Court held that the blanket criminal law prohibition on assisting a person to die violated the Canadian Charter of Rights and Freedoms.[11] The Supreme Court's ruling meant that the federal parliament could not prohibit assisted dying when the conditions set out in the decision were met, for example, the person had a grievous and irremediable medical condition. This then prompted the federal parliament to develop a legislative framework for assisted dying.[12]

[8] For a wider discussion of the various paths to law reform for assisted dying, see Jocelyn Downie, 'Permitting Voluntary Euthanasia and Assisted Suicide: Law Reform Pathways for Common Law Jurisdictions' (2016) 16 *QUT Law Review* 84–112. Another path has been proposed in some US states. Because the practice of medicine is largely self-regulated, some have argued for reform through evolution in the standard of care: Kathryn Tucker, 'Aid in Dying: An End-of-Life Option Governed by Best Practices' (2012) 8 *Journal of Health and Biomedical Law* 9–26.
[9] End of Life Choice Act 2019 (NZ), s. 2; Electoral Commission of New Zealand, '2020 General Election and Referendums: Referendums Results', https://electionresults.govt.nz/electionre sults_2020/referendums-results.html.
[10] *Carter v. Canada (Attorney General)* [2015] 1 SCR 331.
[11] Canada Act 1982 (UK), c. 11, sch. B, pt. 1, ss. 7, 15 ('Canadian Charter of Rights and Freedoms').
[12] Montana's case, *Baxter v. State*, 224 P 3d 1211 (Mont. 2009), is another example of assisted dying becoming lawful through judicial decision, although of note is that this case did not prompt a legislative response as in Canada. A further example of judicial initiation of reform is in Colombia where a decision of its Constitutional Court (Sentence C-239 (1997), Ref. Expedient D-1490 (Constitutional Court of the Republic of Colombia, 20 May 1997)) eventually prompted further regulation to permit access to assisted dying: see Penney Lewis, 'Legal Change on Assisted Dying', in S. Westwood (ed.), *Regulating the Ending of Life: Death Rights* (London: Routledge, 2021) (in press).

In contrast to cases such as *Carter*,[13] which adjudicate on statutes, changes to the common law through judicial decisions tend to be more incremental. This is illustrated in Jackson's chapter describing the evolution of the best interests test in England and Wales, following codification of factors relevant to a best interests assessment in the Mental Capacity Act 2005 (England and Wales).

Although not law, how actors behave at the end of life is also affected by policy and/or guidelines, which can be alternative paths to reform.[14] One of the case studies described challenges to the practice direction of the Court of Protection in England and Wales which stated that court approval was required for certain decisions to withdraw artificial nutrition and hydration. The culmination of that advocacy was a UK Supreme Court decision, *Re Y*[15] that concluded approval was not required as a matter of course. The abolition of the practice direction through a Court decision, brought about at least in part by advocacy, represents a significant example of law reform.

Another example, although not considered in this book, is the development of prosecutorial guidelines[16] which set out the factors that the Director of Public Prosecutions in England and Wales should take into account when deciding whether a person will be prosecuted for assisting another's suicide. Although they have not changed the law that governs assisted suicide, they have brought greater clarity and transparency to the question of whether a person is likely to face prosecution for assisting a suicide.

As is clear from the above discussion, the paths to law reform overlap. For example, judicial cases have prompted the enactment of legislation (*Carter*[17]), the production of guidelines (*R (Purdy) v. Director of Public Prosecutions*),[18] or the

---

[13] *Carter v. Canada (Attorney General)* [2015] 1 SCR 331.
[14] This can give rise to questions about what counts as law, but scholars are increasingly looking beyond the primary sources of law to include other normative forces in wider regulatory analyses about what shapes behaviour. See, for example, Black, 'Decentring Regulation', 103–4; Black, 'Critical Reflections on Regulation', 1–2.
[15] *An NHS Trust v. Y* [2018] UKSC 46.
[16] Director of Public Prosecutions, 'Suicide: Policy for Prosecutors in Respect of Cases of Encouraging or Assisting Suicide', Crown Prosecution Service, October 2014, www.cps.gov.uk/legal-guidance/suicide-policy-prosecutors-respect-cases-encouraging-or-assisting-suicide. These guidelines were created after the House of Lords ruled that the Director of Public Prosecutions must create offence-specific prosecutorial guidelines for assisted suicide: *R (Purdy) v. Director of Public Prosecutions* [2010] 1 AC 345. Critiques of these guidelines include: Ben White and Jocelyn Downie, 'Prosecutorial Guidelines for Voluntary Euthanasia and Assisted Suicide: Autonomy, Public Confidence and High Quality Decision-Making' (2012) 36 *Melbourne University Law Review* 656–705; Jocelyn Downie and Ben White, 'Prosecutorial Discretion in Assisted Dying in Canada: A Proposal for Charging Guidelines' (2012) 6 *McGill Journal of Law and Health* 113–72. See also Penney Lewis, 'Informal Legal Change on Assisted Suicide: The Policy for Prosecutors' (2011) 31(1) *Legal Studies* 119–34.
[17] *Carter v. Canada (Attorney General)* [2015] 1 SCR 331.
[18] *R (Purdy) v. Director of Public Prosecutions* [2010] 1 AC 345.

abolition of a court's practice directions (*Re Y*).[19] In addition, guidelines and policies can shape how both cases and legislation are interpreted and operationalised.[20] The interaction between these sources of law (and 'soft' law of policies and guidelines[21]) suggests that law reform efforts are not focused only on a single legal instrument. This discussion also suggests that law reform is not a finite/discrete exercise with a definite end point. Although the law, once reformed, may stay that way, it also may change again as one reform may be overturned, qualified or explained by other developments that follow (more on this below).

The existence of different paths to law reform invites reflection about the relative strengths and weaknesses of legislation, case law and policy or guidelines in bringing about effective change. For example, there can be limitations in relying solely on case law to reform end-of-life law, particularly in relation to assisted dying. Unless a judicial decision prompts legislative or other regulatory reform, or a substantial body of case law emerges, it may be difficult to craft a comprehensive regulatory system through a handful of court judgements, which inevitably focus on the individual case before the court. If it is accepted that it is appropriate to have a detailed process for oversight and reporting of assisted dying, legislation provides a more appropriate vehicle to do that.[22]

Downie and Scallion, in contrasting the federal Canadian law with the Québec experience, also conclude in favour of reform initiated by the legislature rather than through the courts. They argue that the Québec legislative journey provided an opportunity for significant consultation and reflection in developing the law rather than having reform forced upon a parliament which then has to react, possibly within a tight time frame. When reform is initiated by a parliament, it has greater autonomy in designing its preferred legal framework, rather than having its parameters determined by the courts.[23] However, parliaments may judge that the public will be more accepting of change if they wait until they are required to act by the courts.

---

[19] *An NHS Trust v. Y* [2018] UKSC 46. Other overlap can be seen in this case, as formal guidance documents from leading medical bodies were explicitly acknowledged by the Supreme Court as part of the relevant regulatory framework considered in its deliberations: at [77], [107].

[20] See, for example, Canadian Association of MAID Assessors and Providers, 'The Clinical Interpretation of "Reasonably Foreseeable"', January 2019, https://camapcanada.ca/wp-content/uploads/2019/01/cpg1-1.pdf.

[21] 'Soft law' refers to quasi-laws, such as rules, policies or guidelines, which are not enforceable in a legal sense, but influence both the interpretation of primary and delegated legislation and public behaviour. See, for example, Greg Weeks, *Soft Law and Public Authorities: Remedies and Reform* (Oxford: Hart Publishing, 2016), 13–17.

[22] Of course, not everyone accepts that such a process is appropriate: Tucker, 'Aid in Dying', 9–26.

[23] See also Lewis, 'Legal Change on Assisted Dying'.

LAW REFORM IS MORE LIKELY TO SUCCEED WITH 'GOOD PROCESS'

Many of the case studies highlighted the importance of a good process in securing law reform, particularly those that occurred through legislation. There are a range of features that are generally agreed upon as being part of a 'good process' when making law or public policy. They include: an extended period of time for consideration; engagement with available evidence about current practice and the need for reform; open public and professional dialogue about reform; and clear communication with the community about the nature of the proposed reform.[24]

Some of these are discussed further below in other sections but it is widely agreed that at the heart of a good law reform process is broad and inclusive consultation.[25] As Willmott and White note in relation to the Victorian assisted dying reforms, two key purposes of consultation are optimal design of the law and building support for the law by involving key stakeholders in the process.[26] Consistent with reforms in areas outside of end-of-life law,[27] wide consultation has been significant for successful reform in the case studies considered. As noted already, the extended Victorian assisted dying reform process was rated positively[28] and this was an integral factor which facilitated the eventual passage of the legislation. Consensus-building processes were also regarded as being pivotal in the Texas reforms and in Québec.[29]

---

[24] These (and other) elements are outlined in the 'Wiltshire Test: Ten Criteria for a Public Policy Business Case': Matthew Lesh, 'Evidence Based Policy Research Project' (2018 Institute of Public Affairs) 5–6; John H. Howard, 'Public Policy Drift: Why Governments Must Replace "Policy on the Run" and "Policy by Fiat" with a "Business Case" Approach to Regain Public Confidence' (2012 Institute of Public Administration Australia) vii–viii. For other discussions of 'good process' in making law or public policy see Michael Hallsworth and Jill Rutter, 'Making Policy Better: Improving Whitehall's Core Business' (2011 Institute for Government) 14; Andrew Wyatt, 'Policy Cycle Models: Are We Throwing the Baby Out with the Bath Water?', in Gemma Carey, Kathy Landvogt and Jo Barraket (eds.), *Creating and Implementing Public Policy: Cross-Sectoral Debates* (New York, NY: Routledge, 2016), 41–57.

[25] See, for example, Peter M. North, 'Law Reform: Processes and Problems' (1985) 101 *Law Quarterly Review* 338–58. See also the extended discussions of the importance of consultation for law reform in a range of settings in Brian Opeskin and David Weisbrot (eds.), *The Promise of Law Reform* (Leichhardt: The Federation Press, 2005).

[26] See also Peter M. North, 'Law Reform: The Consultation Process' (1982) 6 *Trent Law Journal* 19–31.

[27] See, for example, successful law reform efforts following extensive consultation in areas of Australian succession law and anti-discrimination law in Sarah Moulds, 'Community Engagement in the Age of Modern Law Reform: Perspectives from Adelaide' (2017) 38 *Adelaide Law Review* 441–62; and criminal law in Eurydice Aroney and Penny Crofts, 'How Sex Worker Activism Influenced the Decriminalisation of Sex Work in NSW, Australia' (2019) 8 *International Journal of Crime, Justice and Social Democracy* 50–67.

[28] Lesh, 'Evidence Based Policy Research Project'.

[29] Also of note, in Jersey, is a more recent innovation in participation in law reform processes for assisted dying through the proposed use of citizen juries: Government of Jersey, 'Jersey Assisted Dying Citizens' Jury', www.gov.je/Caring/AssistedDying/Pages/CitizensJuryOnAssistedDying .aspx.

The opposite was noted in relation to the Canadian federal law case study: a failure to consult with experts contributed to the drafting of the legislation being problematic, and a resulting negative response from many.

Hillyard and Dombrink's study of the Oregon assisted dying law reform process also identified the significance of engaging with stakeholders across a range of fields and the value of building a broad coalition of diverse stakeholders in support of the law.[30] But it is not just in the top-down legislative setting that good process is important. The Kitzingers' case study also involved building a coalition of supporters interested in challenging the requirement for court approval. They included health and legal practitioners and academics, as well as families of patients subject to this requirement. Recognising that reform can also be generated from the bottom-up, the principles of wide and inclusive consultation with all key stakeholders apply here as well.

Who to consult and involve in the law reform process is critical. One key group noted in some of the case studies was the medical profession. Doctors are integrally involved in providing end-of-life care, and medical associations and groups also wield considerable lobbying power in policy-making.[31] The technical knowledge and expertise of the medical profession empowers it both to support change or block it. The role and participation of medical organisations in end-of-life law reform has differed depending on their attitude or involvement in different countries, and the social and political roles of its organisations. (Indeed, this diversity in medical opinion on assisted dying exists among doctors as *individuals*, with palliative care specialists – at least in some countries – expressing opposition to reform at a higher rate than other specialties, whose views have tended to be more mixed.[32])

At one end of the spectrum, the medical profession has traditionally been seen as a major barrier to assisted dying reform, often by framing assisted dying as incompatible with professional medical ethics. For example, this has been the case in the United Kingdom and Australia, where the major medical associations have generally opposed reform.[33] At the other end of the spectrum, assisted dying reform in Québec

[30] Daniel Hillyard and John Dombrink, *Dying Right: The Death with Dignity Movement* (New York, NY: Routledge, 2001).

[31] Jenny M. Lewis, *Health Policy and Politics: Networks, Ideas and Power* (East Hawthorn, Vic: IP Communications, 2005); Jenny M. Lewis, 'Being Around and Knowing the Players: Networks of Influence in Health Policy' (2006) 62 *Social Science and Medicine* 2125–36.

[32] C. Seale, 'Legalisation of Euthanasia or Physician-Assisted Suicide: Survey of Doctors' Attitudes' (2009) 23 *Palliative Medicine* 205–12; Linda Sheahan, 'Exploring the Interface between "Physician-Assisted Death" and Palliative Care: Cross-Sectional Data from Australasian Palliative Care Specialists' (2016) 46 *Internal Medicine Journal* 443–51.

[33] BMA, 'The BMA's Position on Physician-Assisted Dying: The BMA's Policy Position on Voluntary Assisted Dying and How It Has Been Reached', *British Medical Association*, 28 February 2020, www.bma.org.uk/advice-and-support/ethics/end-of-life/the-bmas-position-on-physician-assisted-dying; AMA, 'Euthanasia and Physician Assisted Suicide', Position Statement from the Australian Medical Association (2016 AMA), https://ama.com.au/system/tdf/documents/AMA%20Position%20Statement%20on%20Euthanasia%20and%20Physician%20Assisted%20Suicide%202016.pdf?file=1&type=node&id=45402. See also Jodhi Rutherford,

emerged from and was driven by the medical regulator, le Collège des Médecins du Québec. In that province, the conceptualisation of assisted dying in certain circumstances as being an act of care located this issue within the medical domain and, therefore, it was seen to be the responsibility of the professional regulator to address it. The importance of some support for reform within the medical profession is also seen in the case study examining the extension of the Belgium assisted dying law to minors. Hillyard and Dombrink also consider that careful engagement with the medical profession about the Oregon assisted dying law led to the neutrality of key medical groups who had traditionally opposed changing the law.[34]

A related theme is the use of experts[35] in law reform. The case studies from Victoria (which took an approach that Western Australia largely followed[36]), Québec, Belgium and the Netherlands all reported the engagement of experts in law reform processes in various ways such as the establishment of expert panels to advise governments or formal hearings with experts to share their knowledge. Expert participation is likely to have dual functions: it helps improve proposed decision-making about what sort of law to enact, but also lends credibility to the reform process and its resulting law. The Ministerial Advisory Panel established in Victoria to develop the legislative framework is a good example of this, particularly given it comprised respected leaders in diverse fields.

Experts can also be pivotal in reform through judicial cases. The *Carter*[37] litigation drew heavily on experts providing social science evidence that assisted dying

---

'The Role of the Medical Profession in Victorian Assisted Dying Law Reform' (2018) 26 *Journal of Law and Medicine* 246–64. Ball also notes that some consider the American Medical Association as the strongest secular opponent to assisted dying reform in that country: Howard Ball, *At Liberty to Die: The Battle for Death with Dignity in America* (New York, NY: New York University Press, 2012).

[34] Hillyard and Dombrink, *Dying Right*. See also Ball's discussion of the role of medical groups in the historical analysis of law reform in the US: Ball, *At Liberty to Die*.

[35] We note though that while law reform processes have typically engaged doctors and academics as experts, who is considered an 'expert' is contested and changing. For example, patients and their carers or family members have been recognised as experts regarding their own care: Ian Kramer, 'Patients as Experts' (2005) 12 *Nursing Management* 14–15; Kerstin Blomqvist, Eva Theander, Inger Mowide and Veronica Larsson, 'What Happens When You Involve Patients as Experts?: A Participatory Action Research Project at a Renal Failure Unit' (2010) 17 *Nursing Enquiry* 317–23. Family members have also been found to be active participants in assisted dying decision-making: Bernadette Roest, Margo Trappenburg and Carlo Leget, 'The Involvement of Family in the Dutch Practice of Euthanasia and Physician Assisted Suicide: A Systematic Mixed Studies Review' (2019) 20 *BMC Medical Ethics* 1–21; Marianne C. Snijdewind, Donald G. van Tol, Bregje D. Onwuteaka-Philipsen and Dick L. Willems, 'Complexities in Euthanasia or Physician-Assisted Suicide as Perceived by Dutch Physicians and Patients' Relatives' (2014) 48 *Journal of Pain and Symptom Management* 1125–34.

[36] *Final Report from the Ministerial Expert Panel on Voluntary Assisted Dying* (2019 Government of Western Australia, Department of Health).

[37] *Carter v. Canada (Attorney General)* [2012] BCSC 886, affirmed by *Carter v. Canada (Attorney General)* [2015] 1 SCR 331.

systems can be implemented safely (this is discussed further below).[38] Experts can also have an important role to play *after* a relevant law has been passed. The ongoing evaluation of the assisted dying law described in the Netherlands case study is an example of how experts' assessment of a law's operation can determine whether changes in law and practice are required. Another example of expert review following legislative enactment is the work of the Council of Canadian Academies Expert Panel on Medical Assistance in Dying. The Expert Panel reported on issues flagged in the federal legislation for further review: access by mature minors, advance requests and access solely for mental illness.[39]

A law reform process can generate credibility in other ways. A key finding from the Victorian case study was the significance of the government, rather than a single member of parliament in their individual capacity, leading the assisted dying reform process. Assisted dying is generally treated as a conscience issue, so each member of a parliament is allowed to vote according to their conscience rather than according to party lines.[40] For example, conscience voting occurred in the Belgian law extension to minors, in Québec, and in Victoria (and indeed in all Australian parliamentary votes on this topic[41]). But even with the choice that a conscience vote provides for individual parliamentarians, it is significant if the carriage of the reform, including advocacy in support of (or at least explaining the justification for) change, has rested with the government rather than an individual. This obviously has implications for the likelihood of success if only because of the differential level of resourcing available for government-led reform. However, the fact that a government is leading reform, rather than an individual parliamentarian, also lends

---

[38] Jocelyn Downie, 'Social Science and Humanities Evidence in Charter Litigation: Lessons from *Carter v Canada* (Attorney General)' (2018) 22 *The International Journal of Evidence and Proof* 305–13. Downie and Scallion's chapter in this book also notes that this evidence was critical in the subsequent case of *Truchon v. Attorney General of Canada* [2019] QCCS 3792 (CanLII), challenging Canada's federal legislation.

[39] 'The State of Knowledge on Medical Assistance in Dying for Mature Minors', Report from the Expert Panel on Medical Assistance in Dying (2018 Council of Canadian Academies); 'The State of Knowledge on Advance Requests for Medical Assistance in Dying', Report from the Expert Panel on Medical Assistance in Dying (2018 Council of Canadian Academies); 'The State of Knowledge on Medical Assistance in Dying Where a Mental Disorder Is the Sole Underlying Medical Condition', Report from the Expert Panel on Medical Assistance in Dying (2018 Council of Canadian Academies).

[40] Note, however, that despite a conscience vote being offered, this may not always result in a free vote as informal party pressure can be brought to bear: Lindy Willmott and Ben White, 'Private Thoughts of Public Representatives: Assisted Death, Voluntary Euthanasia and Politicians' (2003) 11 *Journal of Law and Medicine* 77–92; Lindy Willmott, Ben White, Christopher Stackpoole, Kelly Purser and Andrew McGee, '(Failed) Voluntary Euthanasia Law Reform in Australia: Two Decades of Trends, Models and Politics' (2016) 39 *University of New South Wales Law Journal* 1–46 at 13–14; Alison Plumb, 'The Future of Euthanasia Politics in the Australian State Parliaments' (2014) 29 *Australasian Parliamentary Review* 67–86.

[41] Willmott et al., '(Failed) Voluntary Euthanasia Law Reform in Australia', 13.

credibility to the process. This shifts assisted dying from a fringe reform effort to the mainstream and one to be taken seriously.

LAW REFORM OFTEN REQUIRES COMPROMISE

Law reform, regardless of the topic, often requires compromise.[42] The analogy sometimes given is choosing between half a loaf of bread (an imperfect reform that is the subject of compromise) or starving (insisting on what might be an optimal model which fails to become law). Reform in the end-of-life field is no exception, and indeed there may be a greater imperative for compromise given the strong and vested interests as reflected in the historical difficulties in passing assisted dying legislation. How much to compromise, or indeed whether to compromise at all, is a challenging question and case studies in this book illustrate the sorts of compromises that might be needed to effect change.

In Belgium, for example, to secure agreement to expand the assisted dying laws to include access to minors, more restrictive eligibility criteria and additional safeguards for this cohort were included. Indeed, the issue of access for minors was the subject of compromise in the original 2002 law, and was excluded at that time to secure the necessary political support for law reform. Similarly, the Texas Advance Directives Act only passed because of negotiation and compromise amongst key groups which led to a new agreed model.

Legislative compromise is often the result of the necessity to generate sufficient political support for a law to pass. Both of the examples given above involved the formation of unusual coalitions. In Belgium, the coalition was between both government and non-government parties. For the Texas reforms, the Texas Advance Directives Coalition brought together a diverse group of organisations that might ordinarily be expected to have very different views such as medical and health care associations and disability, right to life and elder rights organisations. The process of reaching consensus required explicit compromise about the precise terms of the law.

One (unsurprising) outcome of compromise is the likelihood of settling on a narrow or conservative legal model. It is easier to gain the necessary political and public support for law reform that is modest and incremental. This was the case in Oregon where an assisted dying model was advanced that permitted only physician-assisted dying (i.e. writing a prescription for medication which the patient themselves must take rather than a physician administering that medication).[43] Similarly, the Victorian Premier, Daniel Andrews, proclaimed the Victorian assisted dying

---

[42] See, for example, North, 'Law Reform: Processes and Problems', 338–58; Laura Barnett, 'The Process of Law Reform: Conditions for Success' (2011) 39 *Federal Law Review* 161–93.
[43] Hillyard and Dombrink, *Dying Right.*

legislation to be the most conservative model in the world.[44] The proposed requirement for prior judicial approval for assisted dying in the United Kingdom further
illustrates the conservative results of compromise. In discussing the 'consensus' that
appears to have emerged, Lewis observes that even proponents of assisted dying have
accepted this arguably impractical requirement in the interests of gathering sufficient political support. A final example may also be the decision of the Canadian
government to pass its federal assisted dying law, but identify for further review the
issues of access for mature minors, access solely for mental illness and advance
requests for assisted dying.

A second outcome of compromise is that it can lead to a failure to achieve desired
regulatory goals. Lewis's analysis of the proposal for prior judicial review before
assisted dying can be accessed demonstrates a failure to meet suggested regulatory
goals. For example, the time taken for such a process may have the practical effect of
precluding access for a person who typically seeks assisted dying, namely a cancer
patient with a limited time to live. This disconnect between the law and its
regulatory goals can occur because the decision to accept a particular compromise
is a tactical, rather than a principled one. A recent analysis of the Victorian assisted
dying law has also concluded that in some respects it has failed to align with its own
publicly identified regulatory goals.[45] The recent experience in Canada also reflects
a failure to achieve the required regulatory outcome. There were discrepancies
between the principles that had to guide law reform (here, constitutional rights that
the Supreme Court found had been breached by the Canadian criminal law which
prohibited all forms of assisted dying) and the actual law passed by the Canadian
parliament in response to the *Carter*[46] decision.[47]

LAW REFORM IS INCREASINGLY DEPENDENT ON EVIDENCE

One noteworthy trend, which perhaps features more prominently in law reform in
the end-of-life area than in other legal contexts, is the use of evidence. Historically,
lawmaking has not engaged with evidence in the same way as in other fields.[48]

---

[44] Premier Daniel Andrews, 'Voluntary Assisted Dying Model Established Ahead of Vote in
Parliament', Office of the Premier of Victoria, 25 July 2017.

[45] Ben P. White, Katrine Del Villar, Eliana Close and Lindy Willmott, 'Does the Voluntary
Assisted Dying Act 2017 (Vic) Reflect Its Stated Policy Goals?' (2020) 43 *University of New
South Wales Law Journal* 417–51. US states are also considering whether their traditional
safeguards are too burdensome and are unduly restricting access: see, for example, H.B. 2419,
2020 Leg., 66th Sess. (Wash. 2020) (studying barriers to the use of the Washington Death with
Dignity Act: Death with Dignity Act, Wash Rev Code § 70.245 (2008) (Washington)).

[46] *Carter v. Canada (Attorney General)* [2015] 1 SCR 331.

[47] The legislation was found to have breached the Canadian Charter of Rights and Freedoms (the
very same rights that were at the heart of *Carter v. Canada (Attorney General)* [2015] 1 SCR 331)
in *Truchon v. Attorney General of Canada* [2019] QCCS 3792 (CanLII)).

[48] Jeffrey J. Rachlinski, 'Evidence-Based Law' (2011) 96 *Cornell Law Review* 901–24.

Ben P. White et al.

Ben P. White et al.

While evidence-based medicine,[49] evidence-based health policy[50] and evidence-based business[51] have all become established approaches in those fields, evidence-based approaches are yet to fully gain traction in the discipline of law. But this is changing and there are increasing calls for evidence-based lawmaking,[52] including in relation to end-of-life law and particularly assisted dying, which lends itself to fact-based arguments.[53]

This trend towards greater use of evidence in lawmaking is evident in many of the case studies considered in this book. Social science evidence about how assisted dying regimes operated in countries where it is lawful was the subject of extensive consideration by the trial judges in the *Carter* and *Truchon v. Attorney General of Canada* (*'Truchon'*) decisions.[54] This research was tendered to the court and some of the experts who produced this research were called to give evidence and subject to cross-examination.[55] The trial judge in *Carter* explicitly based some of her findings on the evidence that it was possible to design a safe and effective assisted dying system.[56] These findings were not disturbed on appeal. This same evidence was also considered and relied upon by the parliamentary committees in the Victorian (and later Western Australian) reform processes. Evidence about the Oregon regime was also regarded as influential in supporting reform in subsequent US states. For example, when deliberating about assisted dying reform in Washington, Ball notes the significance of considering a decade of experience under Oregon's laws.[57] Finally, empirical evidence about the incidence of assisted dying in a country *before* it is lawful has also been influential in law reform. Evidence that assisted dying was already happening in Belgium prior to the 2002

---

[49] David L. Sackett, William M. C. Rosenberg, J. A. Muir Gray, R. Brian Haynes and W. Scott Richardson, 'Evidence Based Medicine: What It Is and What It Isn't' (1996) 312 *BMJ* 71–2.

[50] Katherine Baicker and Amitabh Chandra, 'Evidence-Based Health Policy' (2017) 377 *New England Journal of Medicine* 2413–15.

[51] Vishwanath V. Baba and Farimah Hakem Zadeh, 'Toward a Theory of Evidence Based Decision Making' (2012) 50 *Management Decision* 832–67.

[52] See, for example, Rachlinski, 'Evidence-Based Law'; Scott Burris, Laura Hitchcock, Jennifer Ibrahim, Matthew Penn and Tara Ramanathan, 'Policy Surveillance: A Vital Public Health Practice Comes of Age' (2016) 41 *Journal of Health Politics, Policy and Law* 1151–73.

[53] Ben P. White and Lindy Willmott, 'Evidence-Based Law-Making on Voluntary Assisted Dying' (2020) 44(4) *Australian Health Review* 544–546.

[54] *Carter v. Canada (Attorney General)* [2015] 1 SCR 331; *Truchon v. Attorney General of Canada* [2019] QCCS 3792 (CanLII); Downie, 'Social Science and Humanities Evidence in Charter Litigation', 305–13.

[55] See, for example, the complete list of experts called by the plaintiffs, the Attorney General (Canada) and the Attorney General (British Columbia): *Carter v. Canada (Attorney General)* [2012] BCSC 886 at [160]. Note also that this is a further example of experts being used as an important part of the reform process, as noted above.

[56] *Carter v. Canada (Attorney General)* [2012] BCSC 886, affirmed by *Carter v. Canada (Attorney General)* [2015] 1 SCR 331 at [3], [8].

[57] Ball, *At Liberty to Die*.

law[58] was a key factor for reform, with some arguing that regulation of this practice was needed.

One key outcome of the use of evidence in law reform debates is what has been referred to as a 'shrinking battlefield'.[59] Because there is evidence that assisted dying regimes can operate safely and effectively, arguments against reform which make claims about risks to the vulnerable should now be hard to sustain. This reduced ground to marshall arguments against assisted dying has shaped the nature of assisted dying debates and made reform more likely. This evidence can also change the views of some who, after engaging with the evidence, reduce their opposition to assisted dying reform, or indeed may be willing to support it.

It is not just in relation to assisted dying that evidence has been influential in bringing about reform. The Kitzingers' case study about withdrawing artificial nutrition and hydration reports on the systematic research undertaken by them and others to document the economic and personal costs of applying for court approval to withdraw treatment. This evidence was translated into easy to digest forms to assist with its wide dissemination to policy-makers and key stakeholders, ultimately supporting the case for change. This evidence was also placed before the UK Supreme Court in *Re Y*,[60] and informed professional guidance issued by the British Medical Association and the Royal College of Physicians. On the other hand, a perceived *lack* of evidence about the operation of the Texas Advance Directives Act (e.g. it is unknown the number and demographic characteristics of patients who have had the dispute resolution process invoked) was identified as contributing to the persistent challenges that have been mounted against it.

AN ENVIRONMENT CONDUCIVE TO LAW REFORM

Many of the case studies of successful reform also include discussions of failed attempts to change the law about assisted dying. Many of those reform efforts have been long-standing. In Australia, after earlier success with the Northern Territory legislation, there were approximately forty Bills aiming to change the law in Australia before the Victorian, and now Western Australian and Tasmanian, law changed.[61]

[58] Luc Deliens, Freddy Mortier, Johan Bilsen, Marc Cosyns, Robert Vander Stichele, Johan Vanoverloop and Koen Ingels, 'End-of-Life Decisions in Medical Practice in Flanders, Belgium: A Nationwide Survey' (2000) 356 *The Lancet* 1806–11.

[59] Ben White and Lindy Willmott, 'Future of Assisted Dying Reform in Australia' (2018) 42 *Australian Health Review* 616–20.

[60] *An NHS Trust v. Y* [2018] UKSC 46.

[61] Willmott et al., '(Failed) Voluntary Euthanasia Law Reform in Australia', 1–46; White and Willmott, 'Future of Assisted Dying Reform in Australia', 616–20. For a comprehensive analysis of the arguments raised by politicians in debates on these Bills, see Andrew McGee, Kelly Purser, Christopher Stackpoole, Ben White, Lindy Willmott and Juliet Davis, 'Informing the Euthanasia Debate: Perceptions of Australian Politicians' (2018) 41 *University of New South Wales Law Journal* 1368–417.

Lewis notes ten failed attempts at reform in the UK Parliament to date, and almost twenty years elapsed after the *Rodriguez* v. *British Columbia (Attorney General)*[62] case before the Canadian law was again challenged in *Carter*.[63] In Belgium, there had been ongoing discussion, even since the debates at the time the initial law passed in 2002, about whether assisted dying should extend to minors.

So, what factors contribute to an environment conducive to law reform? It has already been observed that a good process that includes engagement with experts and key stakeholders is more likely to lead to reform. But there can be other wider factors that may contribute to a favourable reform 'environment' such as the emergence of influential individuals or groups, legal changes outside the end-of-life law field, shifts in community sentiment and when the political parties represented in parliaments favour reform.

An important component in a reform environment is the leadership of one or more individuals in advancing the debate. There is a long history of the advocacy of individuals or a small group in bringing about social change and law reform more generally and that also appears to be true in the end-of-life field. The Victorian assisted dying case study names a number of key individuals whose leadership roles in politics, public advocacy and policy-making were influential in the assisted dying law passing.[64] In a different way, Gloria Taylor and Kay Carter's family as plaintiffs in the Canadian Charter of Rights and Freedoms challenges were pivotal to the law changing there. The same could be said for Jean Truchon and Nicole Gladu in the subsequent litigation in Québec. The Kitzingers themselves could also be included in this category as academic advocates and family members arguing for change. In some instances, the participation of a key group rather than an individual has been decisive in law reform efforts. The Québec assisted dying reform provides a good illustration of a key group, here its medical regulator, playing an important role in framing the eventual debate about reforming the law.

Another example, this time from the United States, was twenty-nine-year-old Brittany Maynard who moved to Oregon to access assisted dying for a brain cancer and whose advocacy is widely regarded as critical for the passage of assisted dying legislation in California. A key feature of Maynard's advocacy from a law reform perspective was the successful harnessing of the media.[65] In the weeks before her death, Maynard and her husband, Dan Diaz, partnered with the advocacy group

---

[62] *Rodriguez v. British Columbia (Attorney General)* [1993] 3 SCR 519.

[63] *Carter v. Canada (Attorney General)* [2015] 1 SCR 331.

[64] These key figures included: former Chief Minister of the Northern Territory, Marshall Perron; Premier of Victoria, Daniel Andrews; former Minister for Health, Jill Hennessy MP; media personality, Andrew Denton; neurosurgeon and former federal President of the Australian Medical Association, Professor Brian Owler; and retired urologist and activist, Dr Rodney Syme.

[65] Kimberly Lauffer and Sean Baker, 'U.S. Media Coverage of Brittany Maynard's Choice to Die: How Ideology and Framing Converged' (2019) 12 *Atlantic Journal of Communication* 1–14.

Compassion and Choices, to publicise her story.[66] The video interview they created immediately garnered considerable public and media attention globally.[67] She recorded a second video which was tendered as evidence to the California legislature ahead of the Senate committee vote on the State's assisted dying law.[68] These examples of individual or organisational advocacy are linked to the conceptual point made at the outset of this chapter that reform can occur both from the top-down and from the bottom-up. However, regardless of where a reform process sits within this spectrum, it is clear that key individuals and organisations can have decisive roles as instigators and/or drivers of reform.

An environment for law reform may also develop because of a change in a different, although related, legal context. For example, the *Carter*[69] challenge was made possible because of changes in Charter jurisprudence. These occurred in non-assisted dying contexts, but were capable of being applied to the blanket criminal law prohibition against assisted dying. That new legal environment was pivotal to the success of the *Carter*[70] challenge.

Other changes may be more incremental, so that the window for reform is not flung open at once but slowly pushed further and further ajar. The gradual accumulation of empirical evidence that assisted dying regimes can operate safely (mentioned above) is one such example. Perhaps another is the gradual shift of community sentiment in support of reform, as occurred in Oregon. Clark examined the right to die movement in the United States and why the use of citizen-initiated ballot measures had been an effective vehicle of law reform (she considers the initial failure to pass laws in Washington and California, followed by success in Oregon[71]).

---

[66] 'Brittany Maynard', Compassion and Choices, 2020, https://compassionandchoices.org/stories/brittany-maynard. See also Barbara Coombs Lee and David Grube, 'Medical Aid in Dying: The Cornerstone of Patient-Centered Care' (2017) 41 *Generations: Journal of the American Society on Aging* 39–41.

[67] At the time of her death, Maynard's video was reported to have over nine million views on YouTube: BBC, 'Right-to-Die Advocate Brittany Maynard Ends Life', *BBC News*, 3 November 2014, www.bbc.com/news/world-us-canada-29876277. An exclusive story of Maynard's death on the *People* magazine website had the largest audience any Time Inc. brand publication had ever had for a single story, according to internal figures: Michael Sebastian, 'Brittany Maynard Story Leads to Record Digital Traffic for People', *Ad Age*, 6 November 2014, https://adage.com/article/media/brittany-maynard-story-sets-digital-traffic-record-people/295738.

[68] Eliana Dockterman, 'Watch Brittany Maynard's Video in Support of Right-to-Die Legislation', *Time*, 25 March 2015, https://time.com/3759208/brittany-maynard-right-to-die-video-california/.

[69] *Carter v. Canada (Attorney General)* [2015] 1 SCR 331.

[70] Ibid.

[71] Nina Clark, *The Politics of Physician Assisted Suicide* (New York, NY: Routledge, 1997). See also Thaddeus M. Pope, 'Legal History of Medical Aid in Dying: Physician Assisted Death in U.S. Courts and Legislatures' (2018) 48 *New Mexico Law Review* 267–301. Early assisted dying reform in Washington, California and Oregon involved a citizen-initiated ballot process in which a petition signed by registered voters could lead to a public vote on proposed legislation if sufficient support was achieved. In California, a 1988 attempt failed to achieve sufficient support to place legislation authorising both self-administration and practitioner administration assisted dying on the ballot. Further attempts restricted to legislation permitting

She concludes that a failure of the traditional policy machinery of government to engage substantively with the issue combined with a sense that 'time had come' for assisted dying meant that these initiatives were a logical outlet for this desire for change.[72]

A final, and perhaps obvious, example is the political environment in which end-of-life reform is considered. For example, the composition of a parliament will have a significant impact on the likelihood of a law being passed and the content of any such law. Particularly critical here is the political philosophy of the governing party or parties. Historically, socially progressive parties are more likely to undertake and support reform than conservative or religiously aligned parties.[73] Of course, reform may be required of governments, regardless of their political philosophy, to comply with constitutionally entrenched human rights, as occurred in Canada. But generally speaking, changes are more likely to occur with progressive governments, as recently occurred in Victoria. This was also the case in the Netherlands where the assisted dying legislation was enacted while the coalition government was comprised of liberals and social democrats and did not include the Christian Democratic Party.[74]

The foregoing discussion reveals some themes that transcend individual case studies. However, the factors that will ultimately lead to reform in any one jurisdiction at any particular time are idiosyncratic. The impact of particular individuals, the position and involvement of key groups and the composition of parliaments will vary in each jurisdiction. To this extent, as mentioned earlier, all politics is local. The triggers for change and how the window for reform arises will vary significantly from place to place. That said, being attentive to external factors which can make an

---

self-administration in Washington, in 1991, and California, in 1992, failed at the ballot stage. Oregon enacted its assisted dying legislation successfully using the ballot process in 1994 after remodelling its campaign and inclusions based on the previous failed attempts. Washington also passed legislation modelled on the Oregon Act through a successful ballot initiative in 2008. Colorado passed nearly identical legislation through a ballot initiative in 2016.

[72] Clark, *The Politics of Physician Assisted Suicide*. It is significant to note that those early pre-1994 ballot initiatives were for both self-administration and practititioner administration assisted dying. All subsequent bills in the United States have been limited to legislation permitting only self-administration: Pope, 'Legal History of Medical Aid in Dying', 267–301.

[73] Although not always. For example, the Northern Territory assisted dying legislation was passed when a conservative government was in power: Willmott et al., '(Failed) Voluntary Euthanasia Law Reform in Australia', 13.

[74] John Griffiths, Heleen Weyers and Maurice Adams, *Euthanasia and Law in Europe: With Special Reference to the Netherlands and Belgium* (Portland, OR: Hart Publishing, 2008), 29–50; Heleen Weyers, 'Euthanasia: The Process of Legal Change in the Netherlands: The Making of the "Requirements of Careful Practice"', in A. Klijn, F. Mortier, M. Trappenburg and M. Otlowski (eds.), *Regulating Physician-Negotiated Death* (The Hague: Elsevier, 2001), 11–27; Francis Pakes, 'Under Siege: The Global Fate of Euthanasia and Assisted-Suicide Legislation' (2005) 13 *European Journal of Crime and Justice* 119–35; Francis Pakes, 'Tolerance and Pragmatism in the Netherlands: Euthanasia, Coffeeshops and Prostitution in the "Purple Years", 1994–2002' (2003) 5 *International Journal of Police Science and Management* 217–28.

environment ripe for reform may be strategic for those seeking to bring about change, or they may even wish to take steps to try and create such an environment.

The other global observation about environment is that reform generally only occurs after persistent agitation for change. Reform on any topic rarely happens quickly and this seems particularly so in the end-of-life field. All of the case studies described, in various ways, were the result of a long process which finally culminated in reform.

CRITICAL EVALUATION OF LAW REFORM AND PROPOSED LAW REFORM IS IMPORTANT

The case studies show that critical evaluation of proposed laws and indeed laws which have been enacted is important. The reason for evaluating proposed reforms is self-evident. The utility of a law and its likelihood of achieving proposed policy goals are important to consider when deciding whether or not the law, as proposed, should pass. Lewis's evaluation of prior judicial approval for assisted dying is a good example of this. As mentioned above, the quality of a law and its alignment with regulatory goals can sometimes be a casualty of compromise.[75] Given the difficulty of passing a law, and the difficulty of changing even a flawed law, careful evaluation of proposals is critical. We consider this should occur both in relation to the proposed law's stated policy goals[76] but also in relation to the proposal's alignment with wider values or ethical principles.[77]

But it is not just evaluation *prior* to a law coming into force that is important. The Netherlands has made a key contribution to assisted dying law reform internationally through the ongoing and rigorous government-funded evaluation of the operation of its law, providing a crucial evidence base for other jurisdictions to assess.[78] These reviews are undertaken by independent academics and their outcomes are publicly available. This transparency has not only supported law reform in other jurisdictions, but has also facilitated frank discussions about the efficacy of the Dutch law within

---

[75] White et al., 'Does the Voluntary Assisted Dying Act 2017 (Vic) Reflect Its Stated Policy Goals?', 417–51.

[76] Ibid.

[77] For an example of an articulation of the values that should guide assisted dying reform, see Lindy Willmott and Ben White, 'Assisted Dying in Australia: A Values-Based Model for Reform', in K. A. Petersen and I. R. Freckelton (eds.), *Tensions and Traumas in Health Law* (Sydney, NSW: The Federation Press, 2017), 479–510. For an example of this approach in relation to unilateral medical decisions about withholding and withdrawing potentially life-sustaining treatment, see Jocelyn Downie, Lindy Willmott and Ben White, 'Cutting the Gordian Knot of Futility: A Case for Law Reform on Unilateral Withholding and Withdrawal of Potentially Life-Sustaining Treatment' (2014) 26 *New Zealand Universities Law Review* 24–59; Jocelyn Downie, Lindy Willmott and Ben White, 'Next Up: A Proposal for Values-Based Law Reform on Unilateral Withholding and Withdrawal of Potentially Life-Sustaining Treatment' (2017) 54 *Alberta Law Review* 803–29.

[78] Bregje Onwuteaka-Philipsen, Lindy Willmott and Ben P White, 'Regulating Voluntary Assisted Dying in Australia: Some Insights from the Netherlands' (2019) 211 *Medical Journal of Australia* 438–39.e1.

that jurisdiction. The Dutch case study in this book reports on the most recent (third) evaluation and its implications for the existing law. It reviews the law and its operation against the law's identified policy goals, providing opportunities for reflection on possible changes to the law and its application in practice. The evaluation also includes a study of public opinion to determine the degree and nature of support for the law. Given the debates about the operation of all assisted dying laws, including whether they should be narrowed or widened, that will continue after their enactment, a systematic method of evaluation should be encouraged. As already noted, the failure to do this in relation to the Texas Advance Directives Act has made it vulnerable to challenge for failing to operate fairly and effectively.

LAW REFORM EFFORTS ARE ONGOING

It is apparent from the book as a whole and this chapter in particular that law reform at the end of life is an ongoing exercise. This is especially evident in relation to law regulating assisted dying. Even if such a law is passed, there are likely to be calls from all sides for ongoing consideration of that law. For some individuals or groups, the law will not go far enough and they may advocate widening the law or considering categories of cases not currently covered. Other groups or individuals may continue their efforts to either narrow the law or repeal it entirely.

There have been sustained efforts to repeal or amend many of the end-of-life laws discussed in this book (and beyond). The enactment of a law might serve as a catalyst for efforts to change or repeal the law by judicial, legislative and/or policy means.[79] The Texas Advance Directives Act case study is an excellent case in point. The law passed after significant compromise, but since then there have been attempts (some successful) to narrow the scope of its application (e.g. to exclude artificial nutrition and hydration) as well as attempts to overturn the entire law on the ground that it is unconstitutional. The Belgian law extending assisted dying to minors was also the subject of an unsuccessful constitutional challenge,[80] as was the Oregon assisted dying law (challenged in numerous cases[81]). Another example is the Northern Territory assisted dying law, which was also unsuccessfully challenged on constitutional grounds,[82] but was ultimately overturned by the federal Australian government after only a brief period of operation.

This book has included two of the very few major changes internationally to the scope of assisted dying laws. The first is the Belgian extension of their law to include

---

[79] Ball, *At Liberty to Die*. One of Ball's key contributions to law reform literature is to document the battles that continue after assisted dying laws are passed.
[80] Judgement 153/2015, Constitutional Court of Belgium (29 October 2015) (English translation).
[81] See, for example, Ball, *At Liberty to Die*. Assisted dying laws in California, New Jersey, Oregon, and Vermont were subjected to judicial challenges. Assisted dying laws in Montana and Washington, DC were subject to legislative challenges.
[82] *Wake and Gondarra v. Northern Territory and Asche* (1996) 5 NTLR 170.

access for minors in limited circumstances. Although controversial internationally at the time of passing, this case study has shown that this change was the product of debate and consideration over an extended period of time, that the law was subject to parliamentary and other scrutiny, and in practice has represented a very modest change of law with only four minors having used the law since its passing in 2014. The second is the *Truchon*[83] case, which struck down the Québec requirement that a patient be 'at the end of life' and the federal requirement that 'natural death has become reasonably foreseeable' on the grounds that they violated the Canadian Charter of Rights and Freedoms. In this instance, it could be argued that rather than extending the scope of law in Canada, this case simply reflects the position that was required by Canada's constitutional law.

The Dutch system of official and regular evaluations of their assisted dying law reflects government recognition that review of the law and its operation should be ongoing. As noted above, that evaluation includes whether the existing law is working as intended, as well as the views of the general public about the current scope of the law and whether it should be extended to other groups of people who do not currently have access to assisted dying.

One lesson for those interested in law reform – particularly in a field that is as important and emotionally charged as end-of-life law – is that it is an open-ended process, rather than a one-off event. Even if a law is enacted, we should expect ongoing discussion about its operation, its scope and whether it should be retained, amended or repealed. Reform is a journey and not a destination, and those active in the field need to adopt a long-term approach and be prepared for these ongoing debates. The Dutch approach also counsels a willingness to evaluate end-of-life law and to be open to reforms that such evaluation may signal.

DESIGN OF LAW IS CHALLENGING

Before turning to the future of law reform in this area, a final point to note is the challenge of designing law to govern end-of-life decision-making. We have mentioned that sometimes the design of a law can be complicated by a decision to compromise. This can result in inconsistency within the law, a failure to align with regulatory objectives and suboptimal lawmaking generally.

But even where compromise does not occur, designing law to govern the complex interface between law and medicine in the setting of end-of-life decision-making is difficult, at both a policy and a practical level.[84] One example in the assisted dying context is whether to adopt a model that permits or requires administration of the

---

[83] *Truchon v. Attorney General of Canada* [2019] QCCS 3792 (CanLII).
[84] Ben White, Lindy Willmott and Eliana Close, 'Victoria's Voluntary Assisted Dying Law: Clinical Implementation as the Next Challenge' (2019) 210 *Medical Journal of Australia* 207–9.e1.

assisted dying medication by a doctor (or health professional), one that requires the person to take that medication themselves, or one that permits both, in some or all circumstances. These are matters about which people and policy-makers can have different views, depending on the values or principles they prioritise as most important.

Even if higher-level principles can be agreed upon, expressing them in concrete legislative form can be challenging. Long-standing regulatory challenges when designing law include the problems of rule indeterminacy and interpretation.[85] Orentlicher commented that the US model of assisted dying reflects a preference for 'bright-line' policy choices, which is manifested, for example, in the inclusion of a six-month anticipated time period until death in their laws. This can be contrasted with the more open-ended and subjective approaches to assessing time to death that have been used in Canada, such as natural death being reasonably foreseeable (federal) or a patient being at the end of life (Québec). Putting aside recent changes to the Canadian law, the point here is that both bright-line and more subjective approaches bring challenges. The US model is arguably arbitrary in selecting a specified time frame,[86] whereas the Canadian and Québec approaches proved difficult to interpret and apply consistently. There is not scope here to critique these various approaches, but it is sufficient to observe the inherent challenges in drafting a law which is certain but does not unjustly exclude access to assisted dying for some people.

Another challenge is that it cannot always be predicted how a law will work in practice. The consensus that supported the Texas reforms was based in part on assumptions that did not eventuate, namely that hospital transfers would be readily available for patients. The Canadian federal law failed to anticipate situations such as people voluntarily stopping eating and/or drinking to become eligible for assisted dying, or ceasing pain medication to maintain decision-making capacity in order to provide informed consent immediately prior to receiving assistance in dying. There are also examples of these unforeseen consequences outside the case studies. One from the Victorian law is the much-discussed prohibition on health professionals

---

[85] Karen Yeung, 'Regulating Assisted Dying' (2012) 23 *King's Law Journal* 163–79.

[86] In the Australian context, charges of arbitrariness in terms of criteria about expected time until death have been made in Willmott and White, 'Assisted Dying in Australia', 503–4 and White et al., 'Does the Voluntary Assisted Dying Act 2017 (Vic) Reflect Its Stated Policy Goals?', 417–51. Prognostication about time until death is notoriously difficult: Joanne Lynn, Frank E. Harrel Jr., Felicia Cohn, Mary Beth Harrell, Neal Dawson and Albert W. Wu, 'Defining the "Terminally Ill": Insights from SUPPORT' (1996) 35 *Duquesne Law Review* 311–36; Eric Chevlen, 'The Limits of Prognostication' (1996) 35 *Duquesne Law Review* 337–54; James Downar, Russell Goldman, Ruxandra Pinto, Marina Englesakis and Neill K. J. Adhikari, 'The "Surprise Question" for Predicting Death in Seriously Ill Patients: A Systematic Review and Meta-Analysis' (2017) 189 *Canadian Medical Association Journal* E484–93; Paul Glare, Christian Sinclair, Michael Downing, Patrick Stone, Marco Maltoni and Antonio Vigano, 'Predicting Survival in Patients with Advanced Disease' (2008) 44 *European Journal of Cancer* 1146–56 at 1147.

raising the topic of assisted dying with their patients.[87] Although designed to ensure the patient's decision was voluntary and not a result of influence from health professionals, in practice it has led to confusion about what health professionals can and cannot say (as well as the wider question of whether this prohibition is consistent with the assisted dying law's policy goals.)[88] As has been suggested above, for example in contrasting the Québec legislation with the federal Canadian law reform, a good consultation process may assist with addressing some of these challenges. However, it is not always possible to foresee the various possible issues that can arise with a law once implemented.

LIMITS OF A CASE STUDY APPROACH: WHAT IS MISSING?

This chapter has undertaken a comparative law analysis of ten case studies of reform in six countries. The breadth of this analysis has helped provide new insights about law reform that would otherwise not emerge. Although ten case studies is regarded as a large sample in comparative law terms, such an approach necessarily has some limitations. One is that not all cases of end-of-life law reform can be examined.[89] Another is that the majority of the case studies focus on assisted dying. While this reflects important recent trends in assisted dying reform internationally, this has implications for the applicability of the analysis to end-of-life law reform more broadly.

The case studies also generally consider reforms or proposed reforms that are relatively recent, including new developments rather than original law reforms in jurisdictions that legalised assisted dying some time ago, such as Belgium and the Netherlands. There is literature considering reform from earlier eras,[90] and that has informed the present analysis. But that experience is now dated and occurred in a different environment, for example, before there was a body of reliable social

---

[87] *Voluntary Assisted Dying Act 2017* (Vic), s. 8. See also: Lindy Willmott, Ben White, Danielle Ko, James Downar and Luc Deliens, 'Restricting Conversations about Voluntary Assisted Dying: Implications for Clinical Practice' (2020) 10 *BMJ Supportive and Palliative Care* 105–110; Carolyn Johnston and James Cameron, 'Discussing Voluntary Assisted Dying' (2018) 26 *Journal of Law and Medicine* 454–63; Bryanna Moore, Courtney Hempton and Evie Kendal, 'Victoria's Voluntary Assisted Dying Act: Navigating the Section 8 Gag Clause' (2020) 212 *Medical Journal of Australia* 67–8.e1; White et al., 'Does the Voluntary Assisted Dying Act 2017 (Vic) Reflect Its Stated Policy Goals?', 417–51.

[88] Willmott et al., 'Restricting Conversations about Voluntary Assisted Dying', 105–10; Johnston and Cameron, 'Discussing Voluntary Assisted Dying', 454–63; Moore, Hempton and Kendal, 'Victoria's Voluntary Assisted Dying Act', 67–8.e1; White et al., 'Does the Voluntary Assisted Dying Act 2017 (Vic) Reflect Its Stated Policy Goals?', 417–51.

[89] For example, a case study about reform of the law governing palliative care was not selected by any of the contributing authors for inclusion in this book. Further, the need to select a feasible number of case studies also meant that not all significant cases of end-of-life law reform could be included.

[90] See, for example, Ball, *At Liberty to Die*; Clark, *The Politics of Physician Assisted Suicide*; Hillyard and Dombrink, *Dying Right*; Pope, 'Legal History of Medical Aid in Dying', 267–301.

science evidence about how assisted dying regimes can function in practice. Accordingly, the case studies in this collection represent a deliberate choice to provide an analysis of modern efforts to undertake end-of-life law reform.

A final limitation is that the case studies in this book predominantly consider instances when reform did occur. This prevents an effective comparison between case studies of successful reform and those where reform was unsuccessful, although some insight into this comes from jurisdictions where the law changed after a history of many failed attempts. This focus on cases of successful reform may also prioritise particular perspectives because, by definition, reform that is successful means that barriers and opponents to change were not sufficient to prevent the law from changing. As a result, the focus of these case studies was more often on the reasons why the law changed – that is, the facilitators of reform and the individuals or groups who were influential in fostering change – rather than on the reasons why reform was challenging. This is perhaps particularly so for those case studies examining why reform had happened after many failed attempts; the 'how to guides' necessarily focus more on the facilitators of reform than the barriers to it.

One implication of this is that the case studies include only modest discussion of opposition from certain groups. For example, some literature about assisted dying law reform identifies churches, particularly the Catholic Church, and other religious organisations as having long-standing opposition to assisted dying.[91] Yet these groups received limited consideration in the preceding chapters.[92] The opposition of medical associations and bodies in some jurisdictions to assisted dying reform was also given modest attention. As noted, the limited engagement in this book with these potentially opposing groups may be due to the book's focus on successful cases of law reform. But it may also reflect the declining influence on the formation of

---

[91] Taylor E. Purvis, 'Debating Death: Religion, Politics, and the Oregon Death with Dignity Act' (2012) 85 *Yale Journal of Biology and Medicine* 271–84; Ball, *At Liberty to Die*; Steven Kettell, 'How, When, and Why Do Religious Actors Use Public Reason? The Case of Assisted Dying in Britain' (2019) 12 *Politics and Religion* 385–408; Eli D. Stutsman, 'Political Strategy and Legal Change', in Timothy E. Quill and Margaret P. Battin (eds.), *Physician-Assisted Dying: The Case for Palliative Care and Patient Choice* (Baltimore: Johns Hopkins University Press, 2004), 259.

[92] For example, Raus, Deliens and Chambaere note the opposition of churches, particularly the Belgian Catholic Church, to the extension of assisted dying to minors. Van der Heide, Legemaate, Delden and Onwuteaka-Philipsen note that the absence of the Christian Democratic political party from the coalition government was a key factor in the passage of assisted dying legislation in the Netherlands. Willmott and White note that leaders of religious and faith-based organisations actively provided evidence to the Parliamentary Inquiry that preceded assisted dying legislation in Victoria. Lewis notes that groups calling for prospective judicial approval of assisted dying legislation in Canada and the United Kingdom include those opposed to reform on religious grounds. Orentlicher also notes that the Catholic Church has been vocal in ethical debate surrounding assisted dying and the withdrawal of life-sustaining treatment. Pope acknowledges that the Texas Advance Directives Act was enacted in part due to the support of a broad coalition of stakeholders, including the Christian group, Texas Right to Life, while the loss of this consensus resulted in attempts to dismantle the legislation.

public policy of these and other groups who oppose assisted dying reform.[93] This is an empirical question not resolved in this book but is one which warrants future research.

FUTURE OF END-OF-LIFE LAW REFORM

Reforming end-of-life law is a challenging exercise. In the opening chapter, we identified five features that made reform in this area even more difficult than law reform generally. Law reform at the end of life involves issues of obvious gravity and significance that concern every individual in society; it requires deliberation on complex ethical issues and engages sincerely held values about which reasonable people can differ; there is a large and complex body of empirical evidence to grapple with and interpret; it requires legal mastery to draft new end-of-life laws or coherently amend existing complex laws; and finally, aligning oneself with a particular position on assisted dying can be politically dangerous.

These ten case studies across six jurisdictions provide global lessons about how law reform can occur, despite these challenges. One clear theme that emerged is that law reform in this field is hard. However, a review of the current landscape reveals an environment that is increasingly more conducive to reform. Internationally, at least in relation to assisted dying, there is a growing momentum for change.[94] First, there has been a slow but steady trend towards enacting assisted dying laws internationally, which itself can create an environment for further reform.[95] This has been supported by the body of social science evidence and its use in debates, creating a 'shrinking battlefield' which can limit opponents' arguments that previously had traction.[96] This evidence can also change the minds of individuals and organisations who may have opposed assisted dying.

Societal attitudes and values that support reform also appear to be evolving. Patient autonomy, including in relation to end-of-life choices, is increasingly becoming an important social norm that is driving changes to the law. Orentlicher has argued that these values already underpinned existing laws about withholding and withdrawing life-sustaining treatment in the United States, and are now being reflected in the passage of limited assisted dying laws in a growing number of states. While individual rights have historically been a feature of the US legal system, this trend is emerging more generally in the Western countries included in this book. For example, in the Netherlands and Belgium, where arguably the assisted dying law initially developed primarily as a compassionate

---

[93] See, for example, the discussion of the declining influence of the Catholic Church on public policy in Purvis, 'Debating Death', 271–84; Kettell, 'How, When, and Why Do Religious Actors Use Public Reason?', 385–408.

[94] White and Willmott, 'Future of Assisted Dying Reform in Australia', 616–20.

[95] Ibid.

[96] Ibid.

response to suffering, there appears to be growing recognition of patient autonomy as an important justification for their laws.[97] We also see greater recognition of patient views, albeit in a more modest way, in Jackson's analysis of how the best interests test has evolved in England and Wales.

As a result, we anticipate that assisted dying law reform, and other end-of-life law reform, is likely to continue. The rate of change to date has been slow but these factors are likely to align to bring about ongoing change in the law, and perhaps at a faster rate than in the past. The future reform attempts that will be successful are likely to be those that have some or all of the features outlined earlier in this chapter.

The subtitle of this book, 'Politics, Persuasion and Persistence', captures the essence of many of the issues considered in this chapter. Reform is most likely to succeed if careful attention is paid to the politics of reform. This, of course, encompasses the political or parliamentary process, which is often a critical component in reform. But the politics of reform also should involve a robust law reform process that includes broad and inclusive consultation involving experts, key stakeholders and the wider community.

Persuasion is linked to the politics of reform but also refers to the types of arguments that should be mounted. A key component is the importance of evidence. Persuading lawmakers about the importance of reliable evidence and explaining what it means in a particular context has been significant in effecting legal change, and will continue to be so. Persuasion should also focus on arguments at a principled level. Proposing reforms that are internally sound, consistent and align with the identified regulatory goals is important and essential to effective advocacy.

Finally, persistence is an essential part of law reform. All of the case studies of reform resulted from long-standing efforts over an extended period of time. Sometimes this required waiting for the right reform environment to emerge, and at other times it was possible to advocate to create that environment. In all cases, however, there were no overnight successes.

We conclude by briefly noting the implications that this review has for law reform generally. When thinking about reform in the end-of-life field, we have naturally drawn on wider law reform debates and scholarship. As noted in the opening chapter, we acknowledge that this book sits within a long-standing tradition of discussion about how and why law reform occurs. The factors that support reform

---

[97] Pauline S. C. Kouwenhoven, Ghislaine J. M. W. van Thiel, Agnes van der Heide, Judith A. C. Rietjens and Johannes J. M. van Delden, 'Developments in Euthanasia Practice in the Netherlands: Balancing Professional Responsibility and the Patient's Autonomy' (2019) 25 *European Journal of General Practice* 44–8; H. A. M. J. ten Have, 'Euthanasia: Moral Paradoxes' (2001) 15 *Palliative Medicine* 505–11; Joachim Cohen, Isabelle Marcoux, Johan Bilsen, Patrick Deboosere, Gerrit van der Wal and Luc Deliens, 'Trends in Acceptance of Euthanasia Among the General Public in 12 European Countries (1981–1999)' (2006) 16 *European Journal of Public Health* 663–9.

to occur in other socially progressive settings such as same-sex marriage,[98] abortion,[99] non-therapeutic sterilisation[100] or access to IVF[101] are also relevant here.

Indeed, many of the contributors to this book have been involved in law reform processes on a range of topics and in a range of roles, including as a parliamentarian, law reform commissioners, experts before courts and parliaments, litigants in public interest cases and members of pro bono legal teams advancing those cases. In the same way that this book benefitted from insights from the wider law reform field, we hope too that reform in the end-of-life area may help shed light on and advance thinking about law reform generally. End-of-life law reform may therefore be seen as a case study of how change can occur. The authors hope that the findings of this book may be useful for law reformers striving in other controversial fields to change the law.

---

[98] See, for example, Celia Kitzinger and Susan Wilkinson, 'Social Advocacy for Equal Marriage: The Politics of "Rights" and the Psychology of "Mental Health"' (2004) 4 *Analyses of Social Issues and Public Policy* 173–94; Rosemary Auchmuty, 'Same-Sex Marriage Revived: Feminist Critique and Legal Strategy' (2004) 14 *Feminism and Psychology* 101–26; Jamie Gardiner, 'Same-Sex Marriage: A Worldwide Trend?' (2010) 28 *Law in Context* 92–107.

[99] See, for example, Jenny Morgan, 'Abortion Law Reform: The Importance of Democratic Change' (2012) 35 *University of New South Wales Law Journal* 142–74; Mary Ziegler, 'The Framing of a Right to Choose: *Roe v. Wade* and the Changing Debate on Abortion Law' (2009) 27 *Law and History Review* 281–330; Joanna N. Erdman, 'The Politics of Global Abortion Rights' (2016) 22 *The Brown Journal of World Affairs* 39–57; Emily Jackson, 'Abortion', in *Regulating Reproduction Law, Technology and Autonomy* (Oxford: Hart Publishing, 2001), ch. 3, 71–111.

[100] See, for example, Penney Lewis, 'Legal Change on Contraceptive Sterilisation' (2011) 32 *Journal of Legal History* 295–317; Emily Jackson, 'Birth Control', in *Regulating Reproduction Law, Technology and Autonomy* (Oxford: Hart Publishing, 2001), ch. 2, 11–69.

[101] Emily Jackson, 'Reproductive Technologies', in *Regulating Reproduction Law, Technology and Autonomy* (Oxford: Hart Publishing, 2001), ch. 5, 161–259; Anna Smajdor, 'The Changing Face of IVF Regulation' (2008) 3 *Expert Review of Obstetrics and Gynecology* 433–6; Kirsty Horsey, 'Revisiting the Regulation of Human Fertilisation and Embryology', in Kirsty Horsey (ed.), *Revisiting the Regulation of Human Fertilisation and Embryology* (New York, NY: Routledge, 2015), 1–11.

Index

advance care planning *See* advance directive

advance consent *See* advance directive

advance directive 2, 7, 14, 23, 28–30, 34–6, 45, 48, 69, 71, 73–4, 77, 82, 108, 119, 162, 177, 181–3, 188, 195, 197, 210, 216, 246, 259, 261

  assisted dying, eligibility for 34, 162, 176–7, 259, 261

advance request *See* advance directive

aid in dying *See* assisted dying

artificial nutrition and hydration *See* clinically assisted nutrition and hydration

assisted dying

  advocacy against 12–14, 30, 41–2, 50, 56, 58–61, 65, 74, 79, 92, 103–5, 107, 109, 121, 123–4, 127, 143, 163, 186, 250, 257, 268, 272–3

  advocacy for 12, 14, 30, 41, 43, 53, 56, 58–61, 65–6, 77, 79, 84, 87, 89, 92, 101, 107, 109–11, 121–3, 125, 127, 143, 158, 250, 259, 261, 264–6, 268, 273

  conscientious objection 173

  eligibility criteria 1, 23–8, 32, 34–7, 44–51, 54, 57, 60, 62, 66, 68–9, 82, 93, 96–7, 99, 108–9, 116, 118–20, 123–6, 128–31, 139, 141, 145–6, 148, 153–4, 158, 160–1, 167–8, 172, 174–6, 253, 260–1, 269–70

  ethical arguments

    appropriate care 172, 175

    collective responsibility 173–4

    counter-transference, risk of 32, 79

    palliative care, importance of 44, 92, 107, 156, 158, 164

    patient dignity 12, 49, 60–1, 65, 71, 75, 79, 115, 172, 175

    patient right to autonomy 12, 58, 65, 76, 79, 91, 95, 108, 114, 130–1, 134, 139, 141–2, 151, 164, 175–6, 273

preventing traumatic death 27, 92, 101, 107, 110, 135, 147

sanctity of life 12, 95

slippery slope 19, 56

suffering, relief from 10, 28, 49, 61, 65, 68, 71, 76–7, 82, 92, 96, 107, 114, 130, 134–5, 139, 142, 147–9, 154–5, 160–3, 172–4, 249, 274

unnatural death 156

vulnerable individuals, abuse of 19–20, 32, 51, 56, 61, 79, 92–4, 96, 105, 108–9, 114, 120, 122, 124, 126–7, 130–4, 139–42, 149, 154, 156, 158, 160–1, 164, 176, 263

individuals tired of life 72–3, 75–8, 82, 140–1

individuals with mental illness as a sole underlying condition 29–30, 32, 36, 45, 66, 72–3, 77–9, 99, 108, 117, 140–1, 154, 176, 259, 261

judicial approval 15, 113, 119–24, 126–7, 129, 131, 133, 135–7, 139, 141, 143, 250, 261, 267

minors 15, 23, 29–30, 36, 41–2, 47–51, 53–4, 57–62, 69, 73, 77, 82, 117, 162, 175, 258–61, 268, 272

procedural safeguards 20, 24, 27–9, 31, 34–7, 44–6, 50, 54–8, 62, 64, 66–75, 77, 80–2, 93, 95, 97–101, 107–9, 114–22, 124–7, 129–31, 133, 136, 139, 141, 143, 145–7, 154, 158, 161–3, 167–8, 175, 199–200, 260–1, 269–71

terminology 5, 8–9, 40–1, 43, 65, 70, 77–8, 82, 146, 251

therapeutic act, as a 173–5, 177, 258

assisted suicide *See* assisted dying

Australia

  Australian Capital Territory

    parliament 85, 88

    constitutional law 85, 268

Australia (cont.)
  criminal law 85, 89–90, 92, 107, 111, 135
  federal government 4, 85, 268
  health law 2, 13, 111
  law reform
    legislative path 1, 3–4, 6, 13, 15, 84–8, 90–7,
      99–103, 105–7, 109–11, 131, 142, 253, 256,
      259, 262–3
    process 4, 13, 15, 84–98, 100–7, 109–12, 143,
      252, 256, 258–9, 262–3
  New South Wales
    parliament 88, 131
  Northern Territory
    assisted dying legislation 4, 69, 84–5, 87, 142,
      193, 263, 266, 268
    government 85
  politics 13, 84, 86–90, 93–4, 97, 100–3, 105, 107,
    109–10, 112, 143, 259, 261, 264, 266
  Queensland
    parliament 88, 111
  South Australia
    parliament 88
  Tasmania
    assisted dying legislation 1, 4, 6, 87, 88, 112, 263
    parliament 88
  Victoria
    assisted dying legislation 1, 4, 6, 15, 27, 84–7,
      93, 97–100, 107, 109, 111–12, 115, 118, 143,
      252–3, 256, 261, 263–4, 270
    government 84–5, 89, 93–5, 97, 99–103, 107,
      109–10
    parliament 85, 88–9, 91, 96–8, 100–1, 103–5,
      109–10, 135, 143
  Western Australia
    assisted dying legislation 1, 4, 6, 27, 84, 86–7,
      111, 115, 263
    parliament 88
autonomy
  bioethical principle 12, 58, 65, 76, 95, 108, 114,
    130–1, 134, 139, 141–2, 151–2, 164, 175–6,
    237, 240, 242, 273

Belgium
  assisted dying legislation 5, 40–9, 51, 53, 57, 59,
    61, 97, 114, 116–17, 128–9, 141, 174, 253,
    258, 260, 271, 273
    minors 15, 41–2, 47–53, 55–8, 60–2, 259–60,
      264, 268–9
  constitutional law 56–7, 268
  criminal law 5, 46–7, 60, 137
  health law 44, 47, 50, 58–9
  law reform
    legislative path 15, 40–2, 44, 47–8, 51–5, 61,
      253, 259, 269

    process 15, 40–1, 43–4, 51–5, 58, 60–2, 258–60,
      262, 264, 269
  parliament 40, 53–5, 57–9, 61–2
  politics 43, 52–5, 58, 61–2, 260

Canada
  assisted dying legislation 1, 6, 15, 17–18, 21, 23–31,
    34–7, 97, 113, 115–16, 120, 123, 161, 163,
    167–8, 175–7, 250, 255, 261, 269–71
  constitutional law 18–19, 22, 25–6, 36–7, 119–20,
    122–3, 138, 142, 166–7, 253, 261, 264–6, 269
  Council of Canadian Academies 30, 38, 39, 80,
    143, 259
  criminal law 1, 6, 17–18, 22, 31, 37, 120, 122–3, 135,
    166–7, 171, 175, 253, 261
  federal government 21–7, 29–31, 34–6, 122,
    166–7, 253, 261
  health law 18, 165–6
  law reform
    judicial path 1, 4, 6, 17, 19–23, 25–6, 31, 37,
      119–20, 122–3, 138, 167, 252–4, 261–2,
      264–5, 269
    legislative path 1, 6, 15, 17–18, 22–3, 26, 28–31,
      34–6, 120–3, 253–5, 257, 261
    process 15, 17–19, 21–6, 29–31, 33–4, 36–7, 113,
      120, 122–3, 143, 166, 177, 255, 257, 259,
      262, 264–5
  parliament 6, 17, 25–6, 29–31, 33–4, 36, 120, 123,
    253, 261
  politics 18, 21–2, 25–6, 31, 123, 167, 266
  provincial government 18, 22, 166–7
  Québec *See* Québec
cancer
  assisted dying, eligibility for 53, 71–2, 78, 128–9,
    132–4, 138–9, 155, 158, 261, 264
capacity
  advance directives 74, 162, 176
  assisted dying, eligibility for 28, 35–7, 45, 47–8,
    50–1, 54, 57–8, 60–2, 69, 71, 73–4, 79, 98,
    108, 118, 125–6, 130–2, 137, 141, 145–7, 152,
    157, 161, 174, 270
  consent to treatment 7, 24, 121, 125–6, 150, 162,
    208, 215, 217, 233, 238–9, 245
  consent to withholding or withdrawing life-
    sustaining treatment 7, 125, 131, 208–10,
    225, 232
  decision-making capacity 7, 28, 35, 69, 108, 125,
    131–2, 141, 146–7, 152, 157, 161–2, 182, 192,
    209, 225–7, 232–9, 241–3, 270
  guardianship 7–8, 13, 94, 152, 162, 182, 208, 233,
    236, 242
  mental capacity legislation 2, 7, 10, 12, 121, 125,
    209–10, 212, 214–16, 227, 232–4, 239,
    242–5, 248, 254

minors 47–8, 50–1, 54, 57–8, 60–2, 69, 73, 146, 152, 162, 182
clinically assisted nutrition and hydration 3, 7, 15, 194, 202–4, 207–8, 212–13, 215–17, 219–20, 223, 225–6, 228–9, 231–2, 236, 241, 247–8, 250, 254, 263, 268
cognitive disorders *See* mental illness
Colombia
   assisted dying legislation 6, 115, 118–19, 253
   constitutional law 115, 142, 253
   law reform
      judicial path 6, 115, 253
      legislative path 6, 253
comparative law method 251, 271–3
competence *See* capacity
consent
   medical treatment 7–8, 47, 58, 156, 160, 162, 181–3, 191–2, 194–5, 213, 225, 233, 235–6, 238, 240–1, 245–6, 270
   substitute decision-making 182–3, 195, 236
criminal law
   abortion 55, 122, 150, 189, 213, 275
   assisting suicide 2, 5, 8–9, 17–18, 22, 31, 37, 63, 65–8, 72–3, 75, 89, 92, 107, 111, 120, 124, 135–7, 139, 166–7, 171, 213, 253–4, 261, 265
   manslaughter 5
   medical exceptions or defences 8, 60, 63, 65, 67–8, 71–2, 76, 82, 85, 114, 123, 142–3, 186, 213, 216
   murder 5, 8, 63–4, 67, 70, 74–5, 156

death
   death certificate study 76–7, 80
   determination of 4, 200
   reasonably foreseeable 2, 23–9, 34–6, 46, 96, 117, 123, 141, 148, 168, 176, 269–70
disability 14, 24, 29, 32, 34–5, 45, 99, 117, 132, 139, 168, 176, 187, 194, 233
   advocacy groups 187, 193, 260
   dementia 7, 34–5, 45, 53, 72–4, 77–8, 82, 140–1, 209
      assisted dying, eligibility for 140–1
   discrimination 131, 151, 243
   intellectual and developmental disorders 34
doctrine of double effect 8, 70–2, 78

euthanasia *See* assisted dying

futile treatment *See* withholding and withdrawing life-sustaining treatment

Germany
   constitutional law 2, 6
   criminal law 2, 6

law reform
   judicial path 2
guardianship and substitute decision-making
   adults 2, 7–8, 10, 12, 94, 147, 149, 162, 182–3, 189, 192, 195, 225, 232–6, 241
   best interests test 16, 152, 162, 202–3, 206, 208–10, 212–13, 215, 218, 220–1, 223, 226–8, 232–48, 251, 254, 274
   doctrine of necessity 233
   minors 7, 42, 50, 147, 152, 181–3, 197
   non-beneficial treatment 203, 206, 209, 225

human rights 2, 10, 12, 56, 97, 114, 124–6, 142, 150, 201, 207, 216, 227, 243, 266

law reform
   citizen-initiated ballot 265
   complex legislation 12–13, 269
   consensus-building 36, 55, 104, 106, 112, 121–2, 186–90, 193, 198, 201, 256, 260–1, 267–70
   consultation 17, 21–3, 25–6, 31, 34, 36–7, 54, 84, 90–2, 94–5, 103–5, 116–17, 121–2, 129, 143, 166, 174, 176–7, 190, 203, 211, 255–8, 269, 271, 274
   debate 1, 13, 26, 43, 54, 58, 60, 62–4, 66, 73, 82, 97, 100–1, 103, 105, 111, 121–3, 127, 130, 142, 175–7, 207, 263–4, 268–9, 273–4
   evidence-based law-making 12, 16, 18–21, 23, 25, 30–3, 36–7, 43, 52, 59, 64–5, 67, 70, 76, 81–2, 90–3, 95, 102, 106, 109–10, 113, 127, 142–3, 160, 172, 174, 197–201, 203, 216–17, 222, 229–30, 256, 258–9, 261–3, 265, 267, 269, 273–4
   global themes 1, 5, 10, 14–16, 250–1, 255, 266–8, 271, 273–4
   good process 256–9, 264, 267, 269, 271, 274
   judicial path 1–2, 4, 6, 10, 12, 15, 17–20, 22, 25, 31, 36–7, 65–6, 113–15, 119–20, 122–4, 126, 138, 142–3, 145, 149, 157, 159–60, 164, 167, 177, 193–8, 202–4, 207–9, 213–16, 225–6, 228, 233, 245, 247, 249, 252–5, 258, 261–5, 269
      litigation strategy 17–20, 31
   law reform commission 11, 88, 112, 233–4, 239, 243, 275
   legal challenges and repeal of legislation 2, 4, 15, 17, 23–6, 56–7, 84–5, 142, 159, 181, 191, 193–8, 200–1, 251, 255, 263, 268–9
   legislative path 1–4, 6, 10, 12–13, 15, 17–18, 21–3, 26, 28–31, 34–7, 40–2, 44, 47–8, 51–5, 61, 63, 68–9, 76, 84–8, 90–7, 99–103, 105–7, 109–11, 113, 115, 120–4, 126–7, 130–1, 142–3, 145, 157, 159, 164–6, 174, 176–7,

180, 188, 192–8, 200–1, 213, 229, 233, 242, 244–5, 252–62, 264, 268–9, 273
conscience vote 55, 86, 101, 174, 259
legislative drafting 26, 28–9, 31, 35, 37, 105, 174, 186, 188–9, 200, 245, 257, 270, 273
parliamentary inquiries and committees 12, 23, 26, 30, 34, 85, 87–96, 101–7, 109–11, 122, 135, 143, 166, 174, 258, 262, 265, 272
referendum 4, 85, 106, 145, 157, 159, 253
regulatory goals 128–31, 134, 142–3, 153, 162, 213, 242, 245, 250, 261, 267–70, 274
media 75, 89, 101–2, 104, 106, 110–11, 159, 166, 170–1, 203, 220–1, 226, 229–30, 264
policy-making 10–13, 23, 25, 27, 52–3, 64–5, 67–8, 86, 90, 103–5, 109, 151–2, 159, 170–1, 174, 176–7, 181, 187, 190, 192, 201, 239, 244, 252, 254–7, 263–4, 266–9, 271, 273
prosecutorial guidelines 254
staged reform 17, 29–30, 36–7
stakeholders 1, 12–14, 21–5, 27, 30–1, 34, 36, 44, 52, 54, 64–6, 71, 73–4, 77, 82, 84, 87, 89–90, 92, 95–6, 101–6, 109–12, 114, 122–3, 158, 160, 167, 169–71, 174–7, 186–90, 192–3, 198, 201, 203–4, 207–10, 213–15, 217–18, 220–5, 227–31, 233, 239, 241, 245, 252, 256–7, 260, 263–6, 268–9, 272–5
advocacy groups 12–14, 30, 34, 87, 89–91, 93, 95, 101–2, 104–5, 110–12, 122, 158, 187, 189–91, 193, 200, 203–4, 207–8, 210, 213–14, 217, 219–22, 226–31, 252, 254, 257, 259, 264–6, 268, 272–5
Brittany Maynard 158, 264–5
experts 20–3, 25–6, 30, 32–4, 43, 54, 59, 61–2, 64–5, 67, 70, 73, 79, 81–2, 88–92, 94, 106, 110, 172, 225, 229, 231, 257–9, 262, 274–5
medical associations 13, 23, 52, 59, 61, 63, 66, 68, 91, 94, 101, 106, 122, 166, 169–71, 177, 187, 190, 192–3, 201, 215, 222–3, 225, 230, 248, 255, 257, 263, 272
medical regulator 23, 122, 165–7, 169–77, 258, 264
life-sustaining treatment *See* withholding and withdrawing life-sustaining treatment
Luxembourg
assisted dying legislation 6, 115–16, 119, 128–9
criminal law 6, 137

medical aid in dying *See* assisted dying
medical assistance in dying *See* assisted dying

medical treatment
medical treatment legislation 2, 10, 13, 47, 59, 180–1
non-beneficial treatment 7–8, 15, 148, 150, 182, 184–5, 189, 191, 195, 197, 199, 202, 207, 209, 211, 218, 223, 225–6, 238, 240, 246–7
mental capacity *See* capacity
mental disability *See* mental illness
mental disorders *See* mental illness
mental illness 29–30, 32, 34–6, 45–6, 73, 77–9, 98–9, 108, 131, 139–41, 147, 154, 158, 162, 209, 238, 259, 261
anxiety 34
depression 66, 118, 131–4, 156, 161
eating disorder 34, 235

Netherlands
assisted dying legislation 5, 15, 40–1, 51, 60–1, 63–4, 67–72, 74–6, 80–2, 97, 114,
116–17, 128–9, 136, 148–9, 266, 269, 271, 273
minors 41, 51, 60–1, 69
criminal law 5, 63, 65–9, 71–6, 80–2, 136
government 65, 67–8, 70, 74, 76
health law 63, 70, 72
law reform
judicial path 65–6
legislative path 15, 63, 68–9, 76
process 15, 63–4, 66–8, 70–2, 81–2, 258–9, 267, 269
parliament 67, 76, 82
politics 63–5, 68, 76, 82, 266
Regional Euthanasia Review Committees 67–9, 71–4, 76, 78–82, 116, 136, 139, 141
neurological disease
assisted dying, eligibility for 137–8
New Zealand 8, 106, 138, 267
assisted dying legislation 1, 253
criminal law 135
law reform
judicial path 138
legislative path 1, 106
parliament 106, 253
politics 106

palliative care 3–4, 8–10, 14, 20, 30, 44, 70, 78, 90–1, 94, 96, 106–7, 119, 134, 156, 158, 164, 171–3, 197, 257, 271
continuous deep sedation 3, 9, 78
palliative medication 8–9, 28, 35, 60, 70, 72, 78
palliative sedation *See* palliative care
physician-assisted dying *See* assisted dying

physician-assisted suicide *See* assisted dying
preserving life
  bioethical principle 150, 152, 186, 213, 234–5, 241,
    245
prolonged disorder of consciousness 3, 7, 157, 182,
    202–12, 214–15, 217–18, 221, 223, 229, 232,
    236
  coma 7, 204–5
  diagnostic criteria 205–7
  minimally conscious state 202, 205–7, 209–18,
    221–5, 227, 229, 231
  permanent vegetative state 45, 48, 204, 206–7,
    210–14, 217–18, 221, 223–5
  post-coma unresponsiveness 7
  sleep-like coma 205
  terminology 204–7
  United Kingdom National Clinical Guidelines
    202, 205–7, 212
  vegetative state 202, 204–10, 213–16, 222, 225, 227,
    229, 231, 236
  withdrawing life-sustaining treatment 202–3,
    207–29, 231–2, 247–8, 250, 252, 254–5,
    257, 263
    mandatory court hearings 202–3, 207–29,
      231–2, 247–8, 250, 252, 254–5, 257, 263
psychiatric illness *See* mental illness

Québec
  assisted dying legislation 2, 15, 18, 21, 25, 31, 36–7,
    115–16, 123, 166–7, 174–7, 253, 255, 264,
    269–71
  Collège des Médecins du Québec 39, 165–7,
    169–77, 179
  criminal law 171, 175
  government 21–2, 31, 166, 174–5
  health law 169–70, 173
  law reform
    judicial path 123, 264
    legislative path 21, 31, 123, 142, 166, 174, 177,
      255, 259
    process 15, 18, 21–3, 31, 166–7, 169, 171, 174–7,
      253, 255–6, 258–9, 264
  parliament 21, 166, 174, 255
  politics 167

religion
  advocacy groups 121, 148, 187, 189–91, 193, 200,
    260, 272
  Catholic Church 13, 56, 65, 90, 148, 272
  life-sustaining treatment, refusal of 147, 152–4
  sanctity of life 12, 152–3, 187, 189–91, 193, 200,
    213, 235, 237, 241, 245, 260
right to life *See* religion:sanctity of life
right to self-determination *See* autonomy

Switzerland
  criminal law 6

terminal sedation *See* palliative care

United Kingdom
  criminal law 124, 126, 135, 143, 254
  health law 2, 15, 121
  law reform
    judicial path 2, 15, 113, 124, 126, 143, 202–4,
      207–9, 213–16, 225–6, 228, 233, 245, 247,
      249, 254, 263
    legislative path 15, 113, 121, 123–4, 126–7, 130,
      142, 213, 229, 233, 242, 244–5, 254, 264
    process 11, 15, 123–4, 128, 203–4, 210, 213–14,
      217, 223–5, 229–30, 254, 264
  parliament 113, 123–4, 127, 130, 142, 216, 229,
    264
  politics 12–13, 123, 261
United States
  California
    assisted dying legislation 6, 97, 115, 145, 159,
      193, 264, 266
  Colorado
    assisted dying legislation 6, 97, 115, 145, 159,
      253
  constitutional law 114, 153, 157, 159–60, 164,
    180–1, 194–5, 197–8, 201, 268
    procedural due process 196–8, 201
  criminal law 135, 137, 143, 156, 186
  District of Columbia
    assisted dying legislation 6, 115, 145, 159
  federal government 159
  Hawaii
    assisted dying legislation 6, 115, 118, 133, 145,
      158–9
  Kentucky
    health law 3
  law reform
    bright-line rules 10, 149, 151–5, 160–1,
      164, 270
    judicial path 6, 15, 138, 145, 149, 157, 160, 164,
      193, 195–8, 253
    legislative path 1, 3, 6, 115, 145, 157, 159, 164,
      180, 186, 188, 192–8, 200–1, 253, 264
    process 10, 15, 143, 146, 157–60, 163–4, 186–93,
      198, 200–1, 250, 253, 256, 258, 260, 262,
      264–6, 268, 270, 273
  Maine
    assisted dying legislation 1, 6, 115, 145, 159
  Montana
    assisted dying law 6, 145, 193, 253
  Nevada
    health law 200

United States (cont.)
  New Jersey
    assisted dying legislation 1, 6, 115, 145, 159, 193
    health law 3, 150, 157
  New Mexico
    assisted dying legislation 164, 199
  Ohio
    health law 3
  Oregon
    assisted dying legislation 6, 27, 97, 114, 117,
       128, 131, 134, 145–7, 157–60, 163, 193, 253,
       257–8, 260, 266, 268
    politics 260
  politics 10, 13, 152, 159, 186–7, 189–90, 200
  Texas
    health law 180–6, 188–201, 251, 260, 263, 268,
       270
       dispute resolution 15, 180–6, 188–94,
          196–201, 251, 268, 270
       guardianship and advance directives 181–2,
          188–9, 191, 195, 201
    law reform
       process 181, 187–90, 192–4, 198, 200–1, 253,
          256, 260, 268, 270
       parliament 186, 194, 198, 201
       politics 186–7, 189–91, 198, 260
  Vermont
    assisted dying legislation 6, 97, 115, 143, 145,
       158–9
    politics 143
  Washington
    assisted dying legislation 6, 97, 115, 145, 159,
       253, 266
unresponsive wakefulness syndrome *See* prolonged
    disorder of consciousness

voluntariness
    assisted dying, eligibility for 125–6, 130–2,
       161, 271
voluntary assisted dying *See* assisted dying
voluntary euthanasia *See* assisted dying
voluntary stopping eating and drinking 9, 28,
    270

withholding and withdrawing life-sustaining
       treatment
    advocacy for change to law and practice 203–4,
       207–9, 213–15, 218–22, 228–31
    clinically assisted nutrition and hydration 3, 7, 9,
       15, 149, 173, 194, 202–4, 207, 212–13,
       215–17, 219–20, 225, 227–9, 231–2, 236,
       241, 247, 249–50, 254, 263, 268
    concerns about withholding or withdrawing
       treatment 13, 149, 156, 187, 191, 194, 197,
       199, 272
    ethical issues 161, 187, 191–2, 197, 199–200, 213,
       218–19, 224, 227–8, 238, 240, 245,
       273
    lawful withholding or withdrawing of treatment
       2, 4, 6–9, 15, 70, 78, 146–7, 150–1, 153,
       155–6, 162, 182, 185, 191, 194, 197, 200,
       203, 206–7, 219, 231–2, 238, 251,
       273
    minors 146
    non-beneficial treatment 148–9, 182–5, 189, 191,
       197, 199, 202, 209, 211–12, 218–19, 223,
       226–7, 238, 240, 246–7
    patient rights 7, 20, 47, 50, 59, 125, 146–7, 150–5,
       157, 160–2, 183, 240, 245–6
    preventative care, refusal of 29, 59, 147,
       152–3

Lightning Source UK Ltd.
Milton Keynes UK
UKHW022133310522
403817UK00003B/38